The
Shoulders
We Stand
On

The Shoulders We Stand On

[A HISTORY OF BILINGUAL EDUCATION IN NEW MEXICO]

Edited by
Rebecca
Blum Martinez
and
Mary Jean
Habermann
López

UNIVERSITY OF NEW MEXICO PRESS
ALBUQUERQUE

ISBN 978-0-8263-6017-5 (cloth)
ISBN 978-0-8263-6019-9 (e-book)

Library of Congress Control Number: 2020945642

COVER ILLUSTRATIONS

Early 1900s classroom | wwing | istockphoto.com

Map of New Mexico and Arizona, 1891 | by Appleton, D. & Co.,
David Rumsey Historical Map Collection

DESIGNED BY Mindy Basinger Hill
COMPOSED IN Adobe Caslon Pro

WE DEDICATE THIS BOOK to the many devoted and courageous educators, policy makers, leaders, parents, and students who committed themselves to the protection and maintenance of their languages and cultures in New Mexico. We hope their example will inspire present and future generations.

Contents

REBECCA BLUM MARTÍNEZ

AND MARY JEAN HABERMANN LÓPEZ

Introduction

"But what of those of our citizens that were here on this land second only to
the Indian? . . . Unlike the Anglo American, the Spanish-speaking American
had to give way, as did the American Indian. He lost lands which he had held
for centuries. He lost his footing in his community. He became the governed in
his village. His language, which had been the tongue of commerce, became the
mark of the 'foreigner.' Suddenly, this was no longer his land or home."
JOSEPH MONTOYA [1969[1]]

This book had its genesis several centuries ago. The long struggle of the Indigenous people and the Nuevomexicanos who came after them to maintain their
languages, their cultures, and their lifeways began in 1598, with the Spanish
conquest of New Mexico. In their search for riches in the legendary seven cities
of Cibola and their quest for control of the territory, the Spaniards committed
acts of devastating physical and spiritual violence, killing and enslaving untold
numbers of Indigenous people. Those who survived were impoverished—materially, by having to relinquish their harvests and cotton cloth to the Spanish
conquerors through the brutal encomienda system; and spiritually, by having
to take on new beliefs and being severely punished for continuing their own
spiritual practices. Despite these great hardships, the Pueblo people persisted
in their own spiritual practices, adopting many of the trappings of the Spanish
religion while continuing to speak their own languages. Over time, these adaptations became enmeshed with Indigenous cultures, blending aspects of Spanish
culture into the existing Pueblo cultures.

The descendants of the Spanish conquistadores established themselves in small
villages close to their churches and learned to farm in these lands from the Pueblo
people. They continued speaking their language, Spanish, and practicing their

religion, and they learned to love the land that they had come to call home. Their interactions with their Pueblo neighbors was often contentious, but over the years of living in close proximity, relations improved. Because these Nuevomexicanos were so far from the Spanish centers of power in Mexico, communication and interaction with their southern brethren was inconsistent. When Mexico won its independence from Spain, communication with the south became even more difficult because of the turmoil within the new country. During this period and on into the territorial period, Nuevomexicanos took leadership roles in governing themselves. The experience in self-governance and the isolation from both Mexico and the US provided Nuevomexicanos the space and time to further develop an independent identity that included their language and culture. This identity would prove crucial in the elaboration of the state constitution and the inclusion of protections for the Spanish language and the education of a bilingual citizenry.

Thus, when Anglo Americans began to make incursions into the territory, they found a small group of elite Spanish-speaking leaders and many poor Spanish-speaking working farmers. Pueblo villages had continued their own self-governing practices, adding the veneer of governors and other leaders who would protect Pueblo cultures from forces outside the community (for a deeper discussion of these historical periods, see Gonzales-Berry and Maciel 2000; Meléndez 1997; Nieto-Phillips 2004; Sando 1992).

The events described in this book are, in a very real sense, the consequence of the history of the state. As coeditors, we wanted to ensure that the efforts of the pioneers in bilingual education were understood and known to those interested in or working in bilingual education. For the most part, those pioneers are never mentioned in the books and articles that describe the bilingual education reform movements in the United States. Great attention is paid to Texas and California, where much was accomplished that would impact the rest of the country. This movement is often depicted as beginning in the early 1960s. However, the story of New Mexico's efforts to maintain the languages and cultures of the state begins with the resistance of the Pueblo people, and later, of the Diné and Spanish-speaking Nuevomexicanos. The struggle for linguistic and cultural survival is an old one in New Mexico, as the first four chapters in this book describe.

This volume is a collection of essays and scholarly review articles covering different aspects of bilingual education for both Indigenous people and those who are Spanish-speaking. We focus on the early 1960s through the 1980s, as these twenty years encompass both the early attempts to enact bilingual education and the years when there was great activity in the field.

The essays include personal recollections from the authors, as they themselves were involved in different aspects of this movement. Their firsthand experiences provide insights into the personal impetus to this work and the challenges they faced, which reflect many of the experiences of bilingual educators both in the state and nationally. Their experiences also provide detailed descriptions of how the foundations of bilingual education were developed and established and of the relationships between state efforts and those at the national level.

Documentation for much of the information in this book was difficult to locate, and much work went into searching for articles, documents, hearings, original legislation, and correspondence that would help to tell the stories. Without the support of Gabriel Meléndez, the Center for Regional Studies as well as the College of Education we would not have had the resources to document much of this book. We are indebted to the assistance of Mishelle Jurado, who spent many months searching, scanning, and uploading many of the public documents that we would need. Coeditor Mary Jean Habermann López, former director of bilingual education at what was then the New Mexico State Department of Education had the prescience to copy many of the letters, documents, and correspondence that was housed in her office during her tenure there. These documents were invaluable in piecing together much of what went on in the sixties and seventies in bilingual education. This book would not be possible without those documents. Mía Sosa-Provencio and Rebecca Sánchez were fortunate to learn of an oral history that had been conducted by Elizabeth Gallagher, a professor emerita of Eastern New Mexico University. Indeed, one of the challenges we faced was the fact that so much of this history relied on an oral tradition and was not available in written form. Another wonderful source were the interviews we were able to have with those who worked in this educational reform. Many of our coauthors participated with us in this work; it is for this reason that each of us has written a short personal reflection at the beginning of our chapters.

Although there are connections between and among many of the chapters, we have organized the book into three major sections. Part One, "Indigenous New Mexico," provides readers with some of the history of the first New Mexicans and their long and continuous struggle to maintain their languages and cultures. Their physical and constant presence on the land provides the underpinnings from which to advocate for their cultural and linguistic rights as the natural expression of their birthright. The oral tradition is highlighted in all three chapters of this section, as the knowledge, worldviews, and core values of each

Indigenous culture were passed from one generation to the other through oral means. Young Indigenous children were socialized through oral practices; mentorship, observation, and participation were the teaching and learning systems in the communities. Songs, prayers, and oratory were a natural part of learning. All this was accomplished through the languages they spoke. Language, then, is at the very heart of New Mexico Indigenous life.

This section begins with a chapter written by Regis Pecos, former governor of the Pueblo de Cochiti and special assistant to the majority floor leader of the New Mexico House of Representatives. Pecos provides us with a glimpse into the oral traditions of his community, calling upon the wisdom and beauty of this culture and also upon the forewarnings of the elders. Adapting the oratory style of his people, he writes in English and interweaves the history of the Pueblo people and their interactions with both Spanish and American colonial powers. In chapter 2, Vincent Werito presents a history of the Diné people's interactions with the Americans and the resulting linguistic and educational policies meant to destroy their language and culture. The Diné project of self-determination in education is explained through interviews with two pioneers, Anita Pfeiffer and Wayne Holm, both founders of exemplary Diné bilingual schools. In chapter 3, Christine Sims discusses the uniqueness of the Pueblos themselves—their languages, the purposes for their bilingual programs, and the difficulties in establishing language programs. Her chapter helps explain why tribes have exercised sovereign control over their language programs and the certification of native language proficiency, despite the continuing ignorance of state policy makers.

Part Two, "Experimentation, Policy, and Legislation," focuses on the Spanish-speaking Nuevomexicanos, those Spanish-speaking people who can trace their presence in New Mexico for several hundred years. Like the Indigenous people, Nuevomexicanos also have experienced a deep rootedness of place, a sense of belonging, and a profound respect for the cultures they have inherited (Gonzales-Berry and Maciel 2000). Nuevomexicanos have been using Spanish within the fabric of their society for over three hundred years. Though the border moved with the coming of the Americanos, the people did not. In chapter 4, Felipe Gonzales chronicles the struggle in New Mexico for bilingual education as the New Mexico territory took steps to become a state and the missteps after statehood that resulted in an all-English instructional approach that continued for many years while the struggle to make a public place for the Spanish language continued.

As with the Indigenous New Mexicans, for Nuevomexicanos, much of their learning was also based on orality. Former lieutenant governor Roberto Mondragón, author of the nation's first bilingual education bill, has dedicated his life to preserving the folklore of his people, documenting *cuentos*, *dichos*, *adivinanzas*, and *canciones* (stories, sayings, riddles, and songs) that speak to the worldview and wisdom of the Nuevomexicano culture. Catholic hymnals and devotionals, which provided Nuevomexicanos with written texts during the territorial period, promoted both religious education and literacy. During this period, Spanish language newspapers were also available to support gains in literacy (see Meléndez 1997). In the rural villages, often in one-room schoolhouses, Nuevomexicanas were responsible for initiating children into the written forms of their language.

In chapter 5, May Jean Habermann López describes the first real experiment in Spanish language and literacy instruction in Pecos, New Mexico, which would have profound implications for New Mexico education and education nationally. Because the success of this project was documented, it provided the needed evidence that teaching children to read and write in their home language first was a viable and successful practice. This was the evidence that was presented at the Tucson symposium, which, together with other successful bilingual programs, was the impetus for the 1968 national Bilingual Education Act.

In chapter 6, Rebecca Blum Martínez documents the initial policies and legislation that followed the Pecos project. Given the success of the Pecos project and the growing interest expressed at the Tucson symposium by national leaders, including Senator Montoya, the New Mexico State Board of Education issued a policy on bilingual education in 1967. The efforts of Representative Roberto Mondragón and other legislators resulted in New Mexico's passing the first bilingual education law in the United States in 1969, a fitting response to a long historical contest. The decision by Attorney General David Norvell, based on the prescience of the authors of the New Mexico Constitution, underscored the justification for much of what has developed in bilingual education in the state. Each of the players who were responsible for early legislation and policies that supported bilingual education were in a very real sense the descendants of the Nuevomexicanos who had endeavored for so long to find a public and respected space for their language.

The experiences of the Spanish-speaking people in the south—some of whom were Nuevomexicano, others of whom were the children of more recent immigrants from Mexico—were very different from the experiences of Spanish-speaking people in the north. For those in the south, the influence of

Texas and the proximity of the border made for a more oppressive system, in which Spanish-speaking families and children were segregated from their Anglo counterparts. Mía Sosa-Provencio and Rebecca Sánchez provide a description of the bleak conditions in Portales, New Mexico, and the heroic efforts of the Serna family and their allies in bringing to fruition a groundbreaking lawsuit against the school district for discrimination and a lack of equal opportunity. This lawsuit, *Serna v. Portales*, occurred at the same time that *Lau v. Nichols*, which guaranteed English learners equal access to the curriculum through instruction in the native language and English as a second language (ESL), was making its way through the United States Supreme Court.[2]

The *Serna* case focused on Spanish-speaking children and their right to a bilingual and bicultural education. The resulting decision specified that a bilingual, bicultural program had to be instituted. Although the *Lau* case had enormous ramifications for English learners in the nation, in New Mexico, a precedent had been set for bilingual education.

In the final chapter in this section, Rebecca Blum Martínez and Mary Jean Habermann López focus on New Mexico's national influence during the 1960s and 1970s, which can be attributed in great part to the influence of US Senator Joseph Montoya. Like many of his fellow Nuevomexicanos, Montoya was steeped in the languages and traditions of his people. Raised in the small hamlet of Peña Blanca, where he was supported and taught by his parents, grandparents, uncles, aunts, godparents, and others, Montoya spent his early life in a way similar to that of former lieutenant governor Roberto Mondragón, who stated, "The values of honesty and hard work taught to me by my grandfather, when I labored in the fields as a young boy, have stayed with me all my life" (1970).

Enjoying the support of extended family and community and knowing that he belonged to a particular place, Montoya was provided the strength and courage to fight for his language and culture and for those of his neighbors, the Cochiti people. His concern for children, the future leaders of their communities, made him an advocate, from the time he was a state senator, for the inclusion of the children's heritage in the school curriculum. He persisted in this advocacy at the national level when he was elected to the US Senate. His role in the creation and revision of the Bilingual Education Act and his mentorship and advocacy for the languages and cultures of New Mexico paved the way for the New Mexican experience to inform national policy. Much of the early discussion about bilingual education in the United States was about immigrant students. It took New Mexican voices to remind policy makers that there were Indigenous and Spanish-speaking people present long before English speakers who were also worthy of concern and consideration when developing educational policy.

Part Three, "Innovations, Preparation, and Leaders," is concerned with the practice of bilingual education in schools and in the preparation of bilingual teachers in special institutes and universities. Beverly Argus-Calvo, Mary Jean Habermann López, and Rebecca Blum Martínez describe the early innovations in Las Cruces in 1967 (the first dual-language immersion program in the state and possibly in the nation) and in West Las Vegas, at the Armijo School, which demonstrated that children could be successful in both languages when they were first taught in their home language. These programs also demonstrated the elements necessary to provide a sound bilingual education program. Those elements—fluent bilingual and biliterate teachers with historical and cultural knowledge, Spanish language materials that reflected the linguistic and cultural experiences of the children, and policies that would ensure a quality program— are each discussed in this section.

Supporting sound instruction in two languages was a tremendous challenge for New Mexico's practicing Spanish bilingual teachers because few had received university preparation in the language. Chapter 9 describes innovative teacher preparation programs offered by pioneers Miguel Encinias and Cecilio Orozco at the University of Albuquerque and New Mexico Highlands University, respectively, to meet this need.

In chapter 10, Thomasina Hannum and Loretta Salazar describe the evolution of the bilingual education endorsement process for teachers and the need to prepare them in the Spanish language, valuing both the vernacular and standard Spanish. Because of New Mexico's isolation from Mexican institutions, where more robust literacy was available, a vernacular with archaic forms and loans from English developed that became the language of everyday Nuevomexicanos. For many Nuevomexicanos, this vernacular was the source of their pride, and learning to read and write a more literate language was a new and often foreign experience. It took many years and much contention before all bilingual educators embraced both varieties.

The need for materials that would support the objectives of a bilingual education nationally and locally are described by Julia Rosa López-Emslie in chapter 11. In the early days of this movement, there was a growing realization that the materials had to reflect the particular Spanish variety and the cultural experiences of bilingual students. Curricular materials from Spain and Mexico often were as foreign to Nuevomexicano children as English language materials. The efforts of the Spanish Curriculum Development Center and those of Dolores Gonzales were especially important in providing materials that spoke to the experiences of New Mexican students.

The work of the State Bilingual Advisory Committee (SBAC) in partnership with the New Mexico State Department of Education laid the policy groundwork that was needed to ensure quality teachers (with bilingual education certification requirements), quality programs (with program and staffing requirements), and bilingual student progress (with identification and assessment procedures). May Jean Habermann López describes the activities of the SBAC across the years and how this committee has provided the state with invaluable, sound educational advice, and how many of New Mexico's leaders, both Indigenous and Spanish-speaking, have volunteered their time and expertise for the benefit of the children.

The concluding chapter is divided into two sections. In the first, María Luisa González and Beverly Argus-Calvo describe six of the many early Spanish-English pioneers who advocated for bilingualism and bilingual education in New Mexico. These individuals clearly knew the personal, academic, and linguistic value of additive bilingual programs, as well as the importance of English language development. Learning through two languages "to understand and participate in the cultures of their environment," the goal of New Mexico bilingual education for all, was what Senator Matías Chacón, sponsor of the New Mexico Bilingual Multicultural Education Act of 1973, had intended.[3]

In the second section of the last chapter, Rebecca Blum Martínez highlights those Indigenous innovators who envisioned groundbreaking models for the education of Indigenous children. Their work, advocacy, and persistence derive from the continuous struggle for Native American self-determination and are a testament to the strength of their intellectual, spiritual, and cultural traditions.

Many of the initiatives described in this volume were in response to the profound psychological damage done to speakers of Spanish and Indigenous languages through years of full-all-English instruction and repression of their languages. Children were ashamed of who they were, and the schools made sure that parents knew that English was the only path to success. Bilingual education pioneers responded to this situation with courage, knowledge, and a deep and abiding love for their languages, cultures, and people of New Mexico.

Some of our coauthors met and worked with the pioneers described in this book. Some are pioneers themselves who have dedicated their lives to ensuring that the languages and cultures of their people are maintained, honored, and included as a part of children's socialization and schooling.

As coeditors and coauthors, we stand on the shoulders of those described in this book. Our work has been made possible by those visionary and courageous forerunners who have inspired us to continue their efforts. It is our hope that those who read it are inspired to do the same for future generations.

NOTES

1. S.740 Hearings before the Subcommittee on Executive Reorganization of the Committee on Government Operations, United States Senate, 91st Cong (1969) p. 8. Testimony of Joseph Montoya.

2. Lau v. Nichols, 414 US 563, 94 S.Ct. 786, 39 L.Ed.2d 1 (1974).

3. New Mexico Statutes, 22.23.2 Definitions, NMSA, 1978. This definition was changed in 2004 with the reauthorization of the Bilingual Multicultural Education Act.

REFERENCES

Gonzales-Berry, Erlinda, and David Maciel, eds. 2000. *The Contested Homeland: A Chicano History of New Mexico*. Albuquerque: University of New Mexico Press.

Meléndez, A. Gabriel. 1997. *So All Is Not Lost: The Poetics of Print in Nuevomexicano Communities, 1834–1958*. Albuquerque: University of New Mexico Press.

Nieto-Phillips, John M. 2004. *The Language of Blood: The Making of Spanish-American Identity in New Mexico, 1880s–1930s*. Albuquerque: University of New Mexico Press.

Sando, Joe. 1992. *Pueblo Nations*. Santa Fe: Clear Light.

[PART ONE] Indigenous New Mexico
The Critical Role of Language in a Way of Life

This first section of our book features the first nations of New Mexico: Indig-enous voices and experiences from the days of precontact through the present. Regis Pecos, writing in English but endeavoring to give readers a sense of the oral tradition of his community of Cochiti Pueblo, evidences the singular role of language for him and his people. His chapter traces the historical trajectory of his community from the time of emergence, through migration, to first contact with the Spanish and their ruthless oppression of Indigenous beliefs and way of life. Pueblo adaptation to the new rulers included the acceptance of Catholicism and external governing structures that served to protect their most cherished principles and values. The coming of the Americans (Anglos, in New Mexico parlance) brought further dangers as the Americans sought to destroy Pueblo agrarian practices, a communal way of life, and internal organizational structures through relocation, reorganization, and criminal acts of religious intolerance.

These same laws and policies were forced upon the Diné (Navajo), as described by Vincent Werito in chapter 2. The Diné, who were originally nomadic, adopted sheep herding from the Spanish and moved their herds when better and greener pastures were needed. When the invading Anglos came into their territories, the Diné fought to protect their lands. Ultimately, they were forced to concede to the US Army and were force-marched to Bosque Redondo, where many people died. Later, other measures were imposed, such as the Sheep Reduction Act, that left many Diné with no real means of sustenance. Despite these experiences, the Diné maintained their language and way of life. Federal educational policies and laws such as the establishment of boarding schools and forced attendance by Diné children (and Indigenous peoples across the United States) became a cruelly effective weapon to destroy Indigenous cultures.

The introduction to Christine Sims's chapter provides an example of the grievous abuse that Indigenous children suffered in schools. Like the Diné, Pueblo children were subjected to harsh punishments for using their languages in school, and the first bilingual programs in public schools for both Diné and Pueblo children were aimed at assisting children to learn English. However, in contrast to the Diné, the many Pueblo nations that strove to maintain their beliefs and cultural practices had firm restrictions on a written form of their languages and how those languages could be used outside of their communities. As Sims describes, this assured a distinct purpose, conception, and framework for Pueblo bilingual programs, materials development, and teacher preparation.

As described in all three chapters, the Indigenous people of New Mexico have continuously resisted attempts by others to destroy their languages and cultures and have struggled heroically to maintain their languages, which hold the keys to their values, beliefs, and lifeways. Unfortunately, the constant attacks on their languages, particularly in schools, has affected the vitality of many Indigenous languages. Pecos, Werito, and Sims underscore the importance of Indigenous self-determination in addressing this serious situation.

[1] The Gift of Language from One Pueblo Perspective

Language is the means of transferring knowledge from one generation to the next by word of mouth. The sacred gift of language is the most precious gift that one can pass on to others to sustain a way of life gifted to us by our Creator. It is the spirit that guides us into the inner most realms of Pueblo worldview and is the means that provides the gift of becoming an intimate part of all relations to fulfill our purpose.

REGIS PECOS [Cochiti Pueblo, Leadership Institute]

Language is the gift to us from our creator. It is the means through which we find understanding and meaning of our place and purpose in this world. It is the means that allows us to be meaningful participants in a Pueblo way of life. Language has a spirit, and it must be nurtured to fulfill its purpose, to thrive in its existence, to flourish in its role, to be vibrant in its contribution, bringing other living spirits to life into a world of coexistence and interdependence. Language is the vehicle for prayers to be communicated for the conscious connections to all things. Language allows us to hear the words of life's celebration. And language is the means by which we are able to participate in the most intimate way in ceremony, the communion of the physical and the spiritual, the transcendence to and from the depth of the dualities of existence, physically and spiritually, the life here experienced through birth, and the life beyond experienced through death unknown to us but connected to us spiritually. Language embodies the gifts of expression and is essential for the knowledge and understanding of our being as gifted to us, to continue from one generation to the next, by word of mouth, from one person to the other. This is the heart of oral tradition. It is the breadth of our existence as gifted to us by our Creator.

This transference of knowledge by word of mouth from one generation to the next since time immemorial is a purposeful process for the gift of a way of life to continue. It is how our defined purpose is fulfilled. It is the measure of our deepest love for who we are and where we come from. The expression of this deep love is epitomized by our gifting to the next generation all of what we inherited from the previous generation through language. The old people say that when language dies, it will be the end of that deep understanding and of knowing to be shared in its purest and deepest spiritual form. Our purpose and way of life will end. Knowledge of our ways will continue, but the spirit of our being, our connections, cannot live without our original language. For language is the means that sustains our connections of here and the beyond, the physical and the spiritual. The two realms will be separated by the inability to communicate in the ways gifted to us. It will, as the old people say, be the beginning of a new existence absent the spirit. It will be the death of our spiritual connections and a life of hollow existence. It will be a time when we will have eyes to see but be blind, ears to hear but be deaf, when our hearts will beat but without the soul to feel the spirit of love and compassion. It will be a life of survival, absent a life of spiritual living. Our ancestors' voices will call out for us, and we will be unable to respond. It will be the beginning of our disconnection and the end of life as we have known it to be, since the time of our emergence. The old people say that what was gifted to us can never be taken away. But there may be a time when it is given away when our pathways are no longer visible and the spirit of our mother tongue perishes by our own making.

PROPHETIC TRUTH—A CHALLENGE
TO MEASURE OUR LOVE OF A PRECIOUS GIFT

What was foretold was that along our journey, there would be many challenges to our existence, to our way of life. Each generation would face challenges as protectors, as guardians, as stewards of the gifts of our creator intimately tied together by language. The deepest expression of our love to a way of life gifted to us the old people say, is the degree to which we as a people contribute to the maintenance and vibrancy of the spirit of our mother tongue. For how can we not gift to those we love the means with which to be connected to all things alive in this world, to be connected to all life that continues in the spiritual world? When we lose language, they say, it will be because we no longer believe that it is worthy of its existence. We may find this possibility to be a harsh warning, but it speaks to our own responsibility—a powerful lesson. It was foretold what might happen when we deviate from the Original Instructions. It is, they say, the truth. After all, how can we contribute to the death of our very essence and existence?

THE GIFT OF COMMUNICATING A SENSE
OF PURPOSE, MEANING, AND UNDERSTANDING

In the beginning, at the time of emergence, our creator gifted to us the Original Instructions and entrusted to us all that would be required for our sustenance along our journey, spiritually and physically. With those gifts came instructions of how to be, how to live, how to care, how to love, how to respect, and how to nurture the spirits of these gifts so that they would provide all that would be necessary to keep purpose and perspective along the journey that continues today. This journey demands that we be fully cognizant of the spirit of language and our responsibility as speakers of the language to its sustenance. The Original Instructions teach us that each gift is dependent on all the others. When one element dies, eventually all will see the same fate. For all things are connected.

Language is central to the maintenance of Indigenous customs and laws. Indigenous jurisprudence cannot survive without language. The creator gifted to us our customs and laws for the maintenance of balance and harmony among the people. At the heart of the process is our ability to sustain balance among all our relations. This is only possible through language. In all proceedings, language is the means by which conflicts are resolved and people are brought back into good standing for the health and wellbeing of the individual and the community. The application of core values in conflict resolution cannot be fully appreciated in a language not our own. Without our beloved language, we cannot understand the depth of the principles of forgiveness as an essential part of restorative justice for the maintenance of the whole. The governance of the people cannot survive without our language. The spirit of governance is brought to life with the breadth of the spirit of language. When our language ceases to exist, so will our understanding, in the deepest sense of the meaning of balance.

THE CHOSEN PATH WOULD BE ONE OF SACRIFICE
AND IN RETURN, THE RECOGNITION OF WHAT IT
MEANS TO BE ALIVE

It was foretold at the time of our emergence that our path as chosen and pre-scribed for us was to ensure the wellbeing of others, of all life. It would be a path of great difficulty, a path that would require much sacrifice to fulfill our purpose.

But, in exchange for our sacrifice, the creator gifted to us all the prayerful elements—the immense beauty of prayers, songs, and ceremony—that allow us to realize, to know, and to understand the meaning of love, respect, and compassion and to feel the beauty of these spirits within us. These gifts allow us to share and gift to others these cherished spirits that will guide them in their part of the journey. It is how we are intricately bound together. It is the fulfillment of our mutual responsibility to one another.

THE FIRST CHALLENGE AND THE COST OF DEVIATING FROM THE PRESCRIBED PATH

The first challenge our people faced, was the deviation from our core values along our migration and journey. Those from an earlier time along our journey lost their way by deviating from the Original Instructions. The hardship and sacrifice became too much to bear, and some expressed resentment for such harshness. It was a representation of the loss of faith. To those unable to bear the sacrifices were given other languages, and the result was the inability to communicate. This caused separation resulting in the parting of ways and the pursuit of separate journeys. Those who chose to deviate and separate perished. In time, the creator provided the means for redemption and added pardon to our essential core values. The lessons were learned, and the Creator provided the means to find our way back to the prescribed pathways to find our way to our destination to the center points, where we exist to this day. It is a lesson to be mindful of.

DEATH, COMPROMISE, OR ADAPTION

It was also foretold that along our journey, others from other directions would cross our path. So it was the Conquistadors entered, like thunder and lightning, and with great force threatened all of the gifts of our creator, our very existence. As protectors, as guardians, our forefathers rose and sacrificed their lives to protect our way of life. They rose in the ultimate expression of love through resistance and the ultimate sacrifice, epitomized by death. Through their resistance and sacrifice, our forefathers reclaimed their rightful place and adapted to protect and preserve all the gifts of the creator, defining our inheritance. An essential part of preserving and protecting the gifts was to embrace the spirit of reconciliation and the necessary adaptations as another lesson.

In the aftermath of their sacrifice was the continued challenge of protecting and preserving our way of life. The resilience and wisdom with which they responded, the breadth of their effort on our behalf was the Ingenious adaptation that protected the essence of what was gifted to us, what defined our way of life—the covenants and tenants of our greater purpose.

In their adaptation, they embraced Catholicism so that the Pueblo way of life could continue. From this union was born a unique blending into one existence and purpose. In yet another extraordinary response, the Pueblo people of that time, unwilling to compromise their gifted spirit of governance, embraced an overlay of a secular Spanish form of governance to preserve their own Indigenous systems and institutions. Out of this union was born a unique theocratic governance framework. This birth of the blending of church and state continues to this day. There was in that experience a genuine reconciliation so that all that was gifted at the time of emergence would continue. The outcome from this experience and adaptation was the extraordinary gift that continues to this day. It is epitomized by each prayerful celebration as we see and experience from one season to the next an adherence to the Pueblo ceremonial calendar. The language, the words, are deeply embodied in the heart of each ceremony, transforming it into blessings to guide our lives.

EXTERMINATION, DISRUPTION, IMPOSITION, ASSIMILATION-RESISTANCE

Historians have proclaimed that no other people within what is now the United States of America has been subjected to more policies and laws purposefully conceived to exterminate their people and lifeways than Indigenous peoples. Policies were conceived and laws enacted to remove and disconnect us from our places of belonging, the places that define our purpose in this world, the places that define who we are. Policies and laws were established to prohibit the speaking of our languages, and our people were persecuted for fulfilling the covenants of a way of life in a country founded upon the free exercise of religion (Indian Religious Crimes Code). Laws were enacted to force the reorganization of our Indigenous governance systems (Indian Reorganization Act). Efforts were made to redefine our governance and our jurisprudence systems and institutions. There were efforts to redefine and substitute our Indigenous laws and customs. There were efforts to diminish them with imposed judicial systems and institutions of the dominant society. Attempts to dismantle the cornerstones and the pillars of our societies governing our people and relationships with all life were forceful and persistent, and they continue to this day.

In the name of a democratic form of government, they imposed systems to replicate their own systems and institutions. They compartmentalized a governance framework creating an executive branch, a legislative branch, a judicial branch, and an electoral system to elect leaders. It would begin a process of marginalizing the traditional governance system. At the core of Indigenous governance systems were leaders with a command of language and the deep cultural understanding that language facilitates.

The electoral system would shift those cultural core values that had traditionally been at the heart of individuals rising into leadership positions. In the new imposed system and paradigm, knowledge of Indigenous ways became secondary. In fact, over time, it became a liability. In the imposed political process, individuals who were valued for their cultural ways and knowledge were defined as "traditionalists." They were considered backward and as standing in the way of progress. Those embracing the imposed systems, institutions, and values would in time distance themselves—consciously or unconsciously—from their core values to be politically viable; they would be defined as the "progressives." The electoral system and a newly defined political process would, in time, diminish the place and role and status of those holding deep cultural knowledge. Selling oneself in this imposed process of electoral politics created winners and losers. In time, the outcome of the process created factionalism and eventual dysfunction and paralysis. Over time, the more you reflected and embraced the imposed governmental framework, the more federal resources you received and the more successful you were deemed.

In the midst of these imposed changes, many Pueblos resisted and held strongly to the gifted Indigenous customs and laws and their cherished governance systems and institutions. In fact, they did not just survive, they thrived, and they remain vibrant to this day. They were guided by the lessons learned in previous times to adapt and not to compromise. Striking a balance was the heart of their wisdom and their vision. The ultimate tribute to them is that nearly a century later, those with imposed systems are now shifting to reclaim their Indigenous systems and institutions that they left behind as no longer necessary. They come to seek guidance from those who were unwilling to compromise these gifted forms of governance. Those who were once labeled backward and as standing in the way of progress are now living treasures.

EDUCATION, THE MORE HUMANE TREATMENT OF THE INDIAN, KILL LANGUAGE AND CULTURE

In the time of Great Grandpa and Grandma, white agents came one day to take the youngest children to government schools far away. They said that the great white father had created schools to learn the white man's ways. To implement its policy, it created the boarding schools to assimilate Indian people into mainstream society. The process involved removing children from their parents, families, homes, and communities and relocating them to boarding schools hundreds of miles away. There, they were prohibited from speaking their languages and practicing their culture. If one wanted to kill the language and culture, the mantra went, one only needed to remove the children from their culture and deny them their language.

Many suffered through this time. As in previous times, many found the harsh experiences too difficult to bear. Their minds and their hearts were burdened, and eventually they succumbed. They died to survive. In time, they would realize the devastation that manifested in their offspring and those that followed, yearning to find the pathway back to the center places of our existence. In surviving, they died. Some were harsh in their treatment of those among us who once abandoned our way of life. Some, mindful of the stories of lessons learned in previous times, embraced and pardoned those who were forced to wander away from the prescribed pathway, welcoming them home. Others, the old people say, continue to wander. In time, they will become unaware of who they are and where they belong. Without language, they say, upon their death their spirits will wander without finding their way back home. It will be the ultimate disconnection.

FROM SEGREGATION IN BOARDING SCHOOLS TO FORCED INTEGRATION INTO PUBLIC SCHOOLS, THE BEGINNING OF SELF-HATRED AND PSYCHOLOGICAL GENOCIDE

After a time of much suffering, the generations that followed were forced into public schools. They were subjected to long daily bus rides to schools far away from home. The legacy of forced integration and the lack of English fluency resulted in the beginning of a process of self-hatred. As people of those generations recall, we were made fun of because we were not fluent in the white man's language. We were made fun of and we were discriminated against. Many of that generation have shared the painful decision that when they had children, they would not teach them our language and have them suffer as they themselves did. They were made to feel ashamed and embarrassed. They were made to hate themselves. A whole generation grew up in this time. The precious gift of our creator was now transformed into a liability. Many were torn apart.

And then the nation that took our lands, prohibited us from speaking our language, made it a crime to practice our way of life, forced us to replicate their form of government, and dismissed our laws and customs as irrelevant came to ask our people to fight distant wars against people we had never seen. Many went off to war, and our people and our way of life suffered. The legacy of this time in many of our communities was that the transfer of essential cultural knowledge from one generation to the next generation was interrupted.

Upon their return, our people suffered much from what they had seen and experienced. Many would never be the same. Their families would suffer along with them. Others, seeing as was prophesized another world and the attraction of another way of life, would make a conscious choice that there was a better way of life. Their language and culture were no longer useful, and they abandoned the gifts of the creator. The time away left many voids, as the holders of our cultural knowledge and ways of our people since time immemorial had no one to pass the knowledge on to for future generations. In only a couple of generations, the threat of the extinction of the gifts given to us by the creator had become manifest.

HEAD START, BUT A HEAD START TO WHERE?

In time, a new war would be declared, a different kind of war with a different kind of casualty. In retrospect, it would be just as devastating as the death experienced by soldiers.

Ironically, this new declaration of war would be extended to our homelands. This war would be declared on poverty, the result of years of neglect. This war would bring unprecedented resources, amounts never before seen or experienced. One such classic opportunity was the introduction of the Head Start program into tribal communities.

The elders resisted this introduction of another language so early in the lives of our youngest children. They feared that in time, the new language would become dominant. The traumatic experience of the first onslaught to kill our mother tongue with boarding schools and the stealing of the youngest children had hurt badly. The second wave was when their children were forced into integration, whose trauma manifested in hatred of self and original home. The elders were wary of the potential consequences of repeating what they had experienced firsthand, of subjecting yet another generation of children to yet another wave of cultural and spiritual attack. This time they sensed that the movement would come from within.

In the end, Head Start programs were fully embraced. Tribal councils endorsed the implementation, and community members raced to fully implement the promise of the "great equalizer." What we failed to ask was, "Where is Head Start a head start to?" At what expense—and with what compromise—would such an embrace come if not of our fragile languages, which survived for so long against policies and actions conceived to kill our mother tongue. How was this different from previous times when children were removed from their families, their communities, and taken hundreds of miles away from home and forbidden to speak their languages? And our forefathers vehemently opposed, and rightfully so these strategies. Now our people, our own leaders, were implementing these programs in our own schools and in our own communities. No one is to blame. We failed to draw from the lessons learned from the past. "Be mindful of our past experiences, or we may become our own worst enemy," the old people would say. Did they foresee what would happen?

It was through no fault of anyone's. It was the beginning of reimaging and reinventing programs of assimilation. The unintended consequences were profound, painfully reflected in grandparents who were now forced to use their broken English in their attempt to communicate with their grandchildren, and in great grandchildren who no longer spoke the language. This was the beginning of our unconscious contributions to a language shift.

It would take nearly fifty years and multiple generations before the Health and Human Services Administration would recognize their contribution to the gradual death of Indigenous languages and shift their policies to encourage tribes to incorporate Indigenous languages into Head Start programs. The new policy encouraged tribes to design and implement language immersion programs. By this time, it was part of a conscious effort to save our languages.

After years contributing to the death of Indigenous languages, Congress would shift its position with the enactment of the Native Languages Act. New Mexico language advocates were central in this triumphant reversal. Esther Martinez of Ohkay Owingeh, Chris Sims of Acoma, and Carlos Pecos of Cochiti were the pioneers to develop the first language maintenance programs.

THE ULTIMATE IRONY IN THIS TIME OF SELF-DETERMINATION

The cumulative effect of the onslaught of policies and laws purposefully conceived to kill our mother tongue is culminating in this era of self-determination, the greatest challenge along our journey. We are now at a point where we have never been. We are struggling to acknowledge the reality of our circumstances. We are in a state of denial that our most precious gift to us by our creator is in its weakest and most fragile state. When we have overcome our denial, we celebrate the resilience and perseverance that we are committed to do whatever is necessary so that our languages will survive.

However, it was also prophesized that if we are not mindful of our past experiences, we could become our own worst enemy. In our communities, we are beginning to see what our forefathers foretold. It was prophesized long ago that when we began to use language as a means to measure our self-worth and the self-worth of others, we would contribute to our own demise. We would become out of balance with our core values. The imbalance of our core values, they say, would impact our decision-making. They said, language has a spirit that will not accept being reduced to a tool that values one over another. If we move unconsciously into that realm, they said, it will be the beginning of our demise. Language will be used to divide us. We will unknowingly become selfish with language. And in our selfishness, we will suffocate the spirit of our language. It will be the beginning of our deterioration from within. It comes from the use of language as a commodity and not a living spirit. It would be the beginning of a hollow existence. In that realm, other aspects of life will take priority, and the maintenance of language, the gift from our creator, will become secondary. In time, they say, all life will become spiritless. Without language, culture will be diminished. Other aspects of life will become more important. As that gap widens, in time it will become too overwhelming and it will become easy to die and not survive. The sacrifice would be too great. Individualism will overcome the vibrancy of communalism. The spirit of "I" will overcome the spirit of "we."

If this continues, will we be the blameworthy ones, the ones who, in this time of self-determination, contributed to the ultimate death of our languages?

HOW REPLICATION OF PROGRAMS PLAY
AN UNCONSCIOUS PART

In this time of unprecedented opportunities for our people, we can become the victims of our own demise by unconsciously replicating programs designed for others without a conscious examination of their impacts. Head Start, a program intended to provide early opportunities for learning and for becoming proficient in English for transition, is a classic example. What we failed to ask was, What would become of our languages? What would be the cost of an earlier acquisition of English? And how was this different from the harsh policies in the early days of boarding school, when speaking our native languages was prohibited as part of the assimilation policy? It was, as research shows, the beginnings of a quiet paradigm shift. It was the beginning of what we now know as a language shift. With the full implementation, embraced by tribal leaders, directed by our own people, and taught by our own, English learning and acquisition became the celebration, a hidden form of "English Only."

Everywhere, English slowly became the language of communication. Grandmas and grandpas in their broken English became an unconscious part of that shift. Today, the grandchildren cannot communicate with Grandpa and Grandma in their language. The rare opportunity to see and hear children speak in their mother tongue to Grandma and Grandpa is a deeply emotional experience. It reflects an innermost reality—the fear that this has become an increasingly isolated experience. Is it a feeling of acceptance of this reality? Or should it be as a speaker, the impetus to fulfill one's sacred trust, to do one's part to contribute to its survival?

OUR NATION'S GOVERNMENT, ONCE THE MOST OPPRESSIVE IN THEIR INTENT TO KILL NATIVE LANGUAGES, NOW REVERSES ITS POLICIES, ENACTS THE NATIVE AMERICAN LANGUAGES ACT ARTICULATING THAT GOVERNMENT MUST "PROTECT AND PRESERVE NATIVE LANGUAGES"

The road we have travelled has been a difficult one. But in the beginning, it was foretold that our prescribed way of life would be one of great sacrifice. However, on that road of great sacrifice, we were taught, would be great rewards. We would be blessed to recognize and experience the gifts of understanding our place and purpose in this world. The loss of our languages, as was foretold, would be the end of our journey of purposeful living. There is no question that we will live on. The more important question is how. In that question of how is embedded the Original Instructions of how to live and how to be. Language survival or its death will lead us back to the beginning to reflect upon our journey in this physical world, to measure our resilience, our perseverance, our love of all that the creator gifted to us. If language survives, we would have fulfilled our ultimate sacred trust to sustain a way of life. If we should fail, it would be the death of a profoundly beautiful gift that, when it perishes, is the loss of a spiritual existence. The death of our spiritual existence will be the death of guardians and stewards. Without these essential caretakers, it will be the beginning of our self-destruction. Life without spirit is a life of hollow existence.

If language ceases to exist at some point in our lifetime, will we have the means to reenter the realm of our spiritual connections and relations? Or will that be the ultimate sacrifice that our spirits will forever wander? Language is the key here in the physical world, and language is the key to reenter the spiritual realm. Will we forever be locked out of our reentry to the place of our beginning? Without language, can we reenter where we came from, our ultimate home, to be welcomed home by all our relatives? Or will the disconnection from our language in this physical world translate into the total disconnection from those who have gone before us from all future generations born into this world. The old people say, that is the ultimate death of our way of life. While they call out to us and we can still hear them, we must respond that others who follow might continue to hear their voices, and in time hear our voices. They say, no one but ourselves can take away what the creator gifted to us. What will future generations inherit from us? And what will your contribution be?

SUGGESTED READINGS FOR ADDITIONAL INFORMATION

Sando, Joe. 1982. *The Pueblo Indians*. San Francisco: Indian Historian Press.
———. 1988. *Pueblo Nations: Eight Centuries of Pueblo Indian History*. Santa Fe: Clear Light.
Sando, Joe, and Hermann Agoyo, eds. 2005. *Po'pay: Leader of the First American Revolution*. Santa Fe: Clear Light.
Suina, Joseph. 2014. "And Then I Went to School." In *Rethinking Multicultural Education: Teaching for Racial and Cultural Justice*, edited by Wayne Au, 155–61. Milwaukee: Rethinking Schools.

VINCENT WERITO

[2] From English-Only Boarding School Policies to Total Navajo Immersion Methodologies *A Sociocultural Historical Perspective of Navajo Bilingual Education*

In this chapter, I trace the evolution and history of Navajo (Diné) bilingual education from a sociocultural historical perspective to describe the way in which Navajo bilingual education evolved from an English-only approach within the contexts of schooling to more recent community-based efforts aimed at Indigenous self-determination. To accomplish this, I draw upon a review of literature and interviews with two early pioneers of Navajo bilingual education, Anita Pfeiffer and Wayne Holm. While many other individuals could be considered pioneers in Navajo bilingual education, I chose to feature Pfeiffer and Holm in this chapter because of their groundbreaking work with the Rough Rock and Rock Point Navajo communities, respectively.[1]

A lengthier historical overview of Navajo bilingual education is well beyond the scope of this chapter, so I provide only a sociocultural and historical context about the status of the Navajo language over time to highlight the significance of two critical contemporary issues in Navajo bilingual education: Navajo language shift and the efforts of Navajo educators and communities to reverse it.[2] As such, I discuss how early attempts at Navajo bilingual education have evolved from an English as a second language (ESL) approach, which resulted in Navajo language shift, to a more recent focus on total-immersion methodologies in Navajo bilingual programs aimed at reversing language shift. Finally, I discuss why more community-based initiatives, offered within the broader context of decolonialization efforts, are needed to create new generations of speakers and to revitalize and reclaim Indigenous languages and Indigenous knowledge.

First, I address key questions relative to the history of Navajo bilingual education: How and why were bilingual programs first established? What was the overall purpose of bilingual education for Navajo children? How did those who were involved in bilingual education feel about what was occurring? What bilingual program models were being implemented in schools and communities, and how was that implementation accomplished? Next, I share my perspectives about the current status of Navajo language, underscoring the critical role that parents, teachers, and other community members as speakers serve in the transmission of Navajo language and culture. I will also discuss future prospects for Navajo bilingual education by rearticulating the question, What is the purpose of the language today and in the future for our children? Finally, I highlight the notion of advocacy and equity in language education that honors Diné core values of acknowledging relationships and asserting responsibility for revitalizing and sustaining the Diné language for present and future generations.

A SOCIOCULTURAL AND HISTORICAL PERSPECTIVE OF NAVAJO BILINGUAL EDUCATION

From the mid-1800s to the early 1900s, white Americans moved west in search of land and gold. With this westward movement came increased interactions and tensions between Indigenous people and white settler-colonialists (Dunbar-Ortiz 2014). In response to the white settlers' demands for protection against Indian tribes, the US government engaged in a long campaign of genocidal warfare against resistant Indian tribes (Dunbar-Ortiz 2014), as well as less overtly violent—but no less destructive—efforts to culturally assimilate Indigenous people into white society though eradication of lifeways and forced relocation to reservations (Adams 1995). During this period of removal and warfare, the Navajo, in what became known as the Navajo Long Walk, were rounded up by Kit Carson's mercenary forces and forced to walk over three hundred miles to Bosque Redondo in eastern New Mexico, where they would be incarcerated as prisoners of war in an internment camp at Fort Sumner for four years (House 2002; Roessel 1979). In 1868, under Article VI of the Treaty of 1868, the Navajo were allowed to return to their homelands with the US government's promise to provide an education for future generations of Navajo children (Brugge 1993, 1965). One passage of the treaty, similar to many other treaties between the US government and Indian tribes, read as follows:

To insure the civilization of the Indians entering into this treaty, the necessity
of education is admitted, especially of such of them as may be settled on said
agricultural parts of this reservation, and they therefore pledge themselves to
compel their children, male and female, between the ages of six and sixteen years,
to attend school; and it is hereby made the duty of the agent for said Indians
to see that this stipulation is strictly complied with; and the United States
agrees that, for every thirty children between said ages who can be induced or
compelled to attend school, a house shall be provided, and a teacher competent
to teach the elementary branches of an English education shall be furnished,
who will reside among said Indians, and faithfully discharge his or her duties as a
teacher. (Kappler 1904, 1015–20)

Beginning in the late 1880s, many Native American children (including Navajo)
were sent by their parents or were forcefully removed from their homes by Indian
agents to off-reservation boarding schools, such as the Carlisle Industrial School
in Pennsylvania (Adams 1995; Rehyher and Eder 2004), or to on-reservation
boarding schools, such as the Fort Defiance Boarding School in Arizona (Gilbert
2010; Roessel 1979). This was the beginning of the boarding school experiment
that would last for well over a century.

   In these early boarding schools, Indigenous children were stripped of their
cultural identity and often punished for speaking their native languages (Adams
1995). Unknown to the Navajo treaty signers, the US government's promise to
provide an education included long-range goals for assimilation into American
society and learning English through the white-dominant education system.
Consequently, these government efforts and views of Indian languages as "bar-
barous dialects" to "be blotted out and the English language substituted" became
the first English-only policy in these early boarding schools during the late 1800s
(Atkins, as cited in Crawford 1995, 26–27). The results of English-only policies
were that Indigenous languages were eradicated from the lives of these Indian
children and replaced with English (Adams 1995; Rehyner and Eder 2004). In
time, many of these Native children would return to their home communities or
be relocated to urban centers with very little English and no knowledge about
the world beyond boarding schools. While some of these children were able to
thrive in white society, most would barely survive in urban areas; some would
fail entirely and fall into obscurity and misery on the reservations (Adams 1995).

   The removal of Indigenous children from their homes and communities to
be forcefully assimilated into American society would contrast starkly with

the goals of bilingual education in the 1960s. In the early history of the boarding school era, Indigenous parents were rarely allowed to share their views or
consulted about how they themselves wished to educate their children (Child
1998). Because Indigenous people were perceived by the US government to be
childlike wards of the state (Deloria and Lytle 1983), almost every facet of their
lives was planned for them.

In the latter part of the 1800s and into the early 1900s, as more white traders
established trading posts in Navajo country, English became more accessible
for communication and trade (Kelly 1968; Roessel 1979). In the1920s, the use
of English had spread with the influx of white tourists, who came by railroads
into New Mexico and Navajo country to buy Indian arts and crafts. Yet some
groups, the Navajo among them, were resistant to full adoption of American
ways and use of English. Robert Young (1961) writes:

> The formal educational system of the non-Navajo world lying outside the
> Reservation area did not meet a felt need on the part of the Navajo people, living
> as they did within the perspective of Navajo culture. Within the traditional
> society, an educational process was carried on at home, designed to teach
> children the traditional techniques of agriculture and stock raising, the legends,
> the taboos and the practices of Navajo culture. . . . Ability to read and write
> an alien language and assume the ways of an alien people was not attractive to
> the Navajo people. . . . Nor was the Tribe subject to many pressures for cultural
> change requiring formal education as a prerequisite to successful adaptation until
> the decade of the 1930s. (11)

Prior to World War II, many Navajo communities lived in isolation from American society, in large part because of their past traumatic experiences with the
Long Walk, boarding schools, and livestock reduction.[3] During World War II, as
many Americans, including many Bureau of Indian Affairs (BIA) personnel, were
occupied overseas and government funds were redirected to the war effort, many
of the early community boarding schools were closed (Kelly 1968; Roessel 1979).

As early as the 1930s, a bicultural/bilingual approach to educating Navajo and
other American Indian students was being designed and implemented by the
BIA under the direction of John Collier, the commissioner of Indian affairs, and
his education directors, William Carson Ryan and Willard Beatty. The cross-
cultural education program was an outcome of the Meriam Report of 1928, which
exposed many problems of Indian administration.[4] William Carson Ryan, an

advocate of progressive education, pushed the Indian Service to emphasize the culture and language of the Indian children in their education by changing the curriculum (Szasz 1999). In addition to these efforts, Ryan also developed plans for community schools that "would serve a dual purpose—first as a day school for young children and second as a community center to strengthen local concern through involvement of the entire community" (Szasz 1999, 24). Willard Beatty, under John Collier's guidance, would later reach out to anthropologists and linguists in his efforts to develop a cross-cultural teacher training that included a focus on bilingual education. These efforts were based on Collier's views of integrating American Indians slowly into American society by recognizing the value of their culture.

Under Beatty's direction, early bilingual readers, titled *Indian Life Readers*, were developed and used by members of the Indian service bureau and other advocates to both accelerate English literacy and promote the use of Native languages (Lomawaima and McCarty 2006; Spicer 1981; Szasz 1999). Yet as Lomawaima and McCarty (2006) point out, while these readers were developed to include aspects of Native culture and language, in practice, they functioned to further instill white-American ideals of citizenship, meritocracy, and patriotism in young Indian minds. The underlying objective of these materials and early language policies was apparent: the assimilation of Indian children into the cultural norms of American society by using their language as the medium of instruction. In other words, based on Lomawaima and McCarty's (2004) theory of the safety zone paradigm, just as with the early attempts by missionaries to use the Native language for proselytizing, now educators were using Native English-language literacy to Americanize Indigenous children, an effort made even more effective by the decline in Native language use in the home during this time, which itself was a result of these boarding school policies and practices.

In 1946, in reaction to the number of Navajo students who had never been in school despite the creation of community schools under Collier and Ryan's direction, Willard Beatty, along with Hildegard Thompson, developed the Special Navajo Education Program (SNEP) (Holm 2017; Thompson 1975). At the time, it was estimated that roughly three-fourths of all Navajo children were still out of school (Roessel 1979; Thompson 1975). In many ways, these early experiments in Navajo bilingual education may have created an entire generation of Navajo students with very limited English skills because they were not provided with the support necessary to become fully bilingual. For example, after five years in SNEP, most Navajo students were sent back home with the assumption that they could now make a living in the white-American world. In most if not all cases, there was no support beyond the five years. Very few students who became competent English speakers continued into high school. In all these programs, language instruction was done primarily in English, with some Navajo, with the goal of transitioning students from their home language to English.

Prior to the development of SNEP, George Sánchez, a Hispanic professor from the University of Texas, was commissioned by the BIA to study the condition of Navajo education. To the surprise of the bureau, he proposed a plan for a reservation-centered education system that would have cost the government $90 million (Roessel 1979; Thompson 1975). Rather than fund an education program that would keep Navajo children closer to home, the Special Navajo Education Program was developed to send Navajo children ages twelve to eighteen years to eleven designated off-reservation boarding schools. Roessel states that the SNEP was the "first substantial attempt by the BIA to use Navajo as a language of instruction" (1979, 19). Similarly, Thompson (1975) writes:

> Classroom instruction was planned daily and jointly by the teacher and
> the Navajo aide, with a vocational teacher participating so that, for the full
> teaching day, all would be working toward the same goals and English language
> instruction. The teacher outlined the curriculum content for the day; the Navajo
> aide taught the content in the language, and the teacher then taught simple
> sentences based on the content. This process gave better assurance that the
> English taught would be meaningful to the pupils. After the English lesson the
> teacher aide questioned the pupils in the Navajo language to make sure they
> gained the correct meaning from the English presentation. (98)

These early Navajo BIA educators are essentially the first pioneers of Navajo bilingual education because they began experimenting with an educational approach to help Indian students learn English quickly and to maintain some aspects of their cultural knowledge.

Despite the growing dominance of English in many tribal reservations, some Indigenous language communities were still not heavily impacted by the presence of the English language in their lives. With changes in US economic and educational policies, however, it would only be a matter of time before English would become more prevalent as the outside world slowly encroached upon Navajo life. Robert Roessel writes:

> Following the end of World War II education at any price became the goal
> and the policy underlying both government and tribal programs and actions.

The Collier-Beatty period of the 1930s was all but dead. . . . Reactionary forces had gained control once again, with the feeling that the only good Indian was a white Indian. The community day school, stressed by Collier, as a means to keep education closer to home, was replaced with an emphasis toward off-reservation boarding schools. . . . For more than a decade following the end of the World War II cultural genocide was the deliberate, if not stated, objective of most schools teaching Navajo students. (1979, 16–17)

With the passage of the Navajo-Hopi Rehabilitation Act of 1950, a capitalist wage economy was soon imposed upon Navajo people.[5] As a result, in the 1950s and 1960s, there would be an increase in the number of community boarding schools, day schools, and trailer schools (Roessel 1979), a response to high numbers of Navajo children who were not attending school (Holm 2017; Thompson 1975), despite the government's efforts and promise to educate Navajo children as stipulated in the treaty of 1868.

After World War II, there was a shift in Indian education policy from the cross-cultural approach from the Collier era toward a more conservative political ideology that called for the termination of Indian tribes as sovereign entities. According to Szasz (1999), the shift in thinking was a result of congressional leaders' determination to end tribal sovereignty once and for all, thereby forego-ing the US government's obligations to honoring treaty rights. Stephen Wall writes:

After World War II, there was a serious economic recession that lasted from the end of the war into the early 1950s. At the same time, there was a huge need for housing and jobs for returning soldiers who wanted to start families. This was the time of a states' rights era in which there was a frontal attack on federal control over resources in the western United States. Jurisdiction to determine federal (and tribal) water rights was given to the states, the Indian Claims Commission was created to clear title to Indian land in the West, and there were moves to eliminate the national forests and other forms of federal control over land in the West. (2010, 12)

In 1954, the Navajo tribe passed a resolution approving the Navajo Emergency Education Program, which gave the BIA authority to use "different approaches to reduce the number of Navajo children out of school" while keeping them close to home (Roessel 1979, 27). These included trailer schools, public schools on the reservation, enlarged boarding schools, the SNEP, and border-town dormitories. These types of federal programs were essential to furthering cultural assimilation into the American economic system and expanding the spread of English into all aspects of Indian life.

To conceptualize the impact of different school language programs on Navajo students over time, Holm and Holm (1995) identified four approaches that look at how Navajo has or has not been used in all schools. They described how the "prestige of Navajo has declined" from a time "when children spoke Navajo because it seemed that 'everyone' around them spoke Navajo" (163). Consequently, these early attempts at bilingual education for Navajo may have created the conditions for a shift from Navajo to English as parents ceased speaking to their children in Navajo and when speaking English became the "natural" thing to do (Holm and Holm 1995, 163). Finally, under the continuous gaze of the BIA, which propagated a civilizing process that stressed English-only through their educational policies, a sense of American nationalism became entrenched in many Native communities through the use of English-only language policies (Crawford 1996, 1995) and ideological management (Spring 2005). In *The American School*, Spring (2005) refers to ideological management as the "effect of these political and economic forces on ideas disseminated to society," with schools playing a "central role in the distribution of particular knowledge to a society" (4).

The eighty-year push, beginning in the 1880s, to Americanize Indigenous people, immigrants, and others culminated in a national initiative to make English the official language of the nation (Lomawaima and McCarty 2006; McCarty 2003). These types of discourse, whose premise was that Indian students would swim if they applied themselves to their education and sink if they held onto their cultural values and languages, were based on deficit views about people of color and "minoritized" language groups. Consequently, these earlier attempts may have inspired similar bilingual language models such as the English submersion model aimed at transitioning immigrant non-English speaking children to English using a sink-or-swim approach, or the transitional bilingual model of early 1980s and 1990s (Brisk 2006; López 1991). It would not be until the1960s that a fully bilingual model, designed for learning academic content in both Navajo and English, would be considered.[6]

In response to this sociopolitical agenda, people of color—including Indigenous communities—especially those in urban centers, pushed back, often through community-based grassroots efforts (Dunbar-Ortiz 2016; May 1999). In the 1960s and early 1970s, with the passage of the Civil Rights and Bilingual Education Acts, bilingual education had not only become a hotbed for controversy, but had also evolved into an educational movement in American politics and society to end racial discrimination and to advocate for the rights of all citizens. As the civil rights movement gained national attention, some Indigenous communities began to reassert their rights to self-determination and political sovereignty. These initial efforts, which began in the 1950s, led to the creation of the tribally controlled school movement and the development of Indigenous bilingual education programs (May 1999; McCarty 2002).

Rough Rock Demonstration School

According to Anita Pfeiffer, starting the mid-1960s, Navajo and non-Navajo educators became involved in the early efforts to create Indigenous tribally controlled schools and contributed much to the development of Navajo bilingual education programs.[7] Originally from Kayenta, Arizona, on the Navajo reservation and familiar with both Western and traditional Navajo education, Pfeiffer herself pioneered many of these initiatives, providing groundbreaking leadership in the development of the early bilingual and bicultural Navajo education program at Rough Rock Demonstration School and later at the Division of Diné Education.

Pfeiffer recounted some details about the Rough Rock Demonstration School's early attempts at bicultural/bilingual education. According to Pfeiffer and other scholars who have written about Rough Rock (see McCarty [2002] and Johnson [1968]), starting in 1966, the efforts by DINE Inc. to start the Rough Rock Demonstration School evolved out of local grassroots efforts to create the first Indigenous community controlled school and programs.[8] According to Pfeiffer, DINE's first attempt was in the Lukachukai community, with two different programs and two administrators. But because the proposed demonstration school was to be placed within the existing school structure with different administrators and program models, the efforts eventually failed. Many school personnel and community members did not agree about what they wanted, and the school leadership did not consider the perspectives of the community. Pfeiffer recalled that none among the staff could agree about what they were supposed to be doing and that there was an overall lack of collaboration between the two entities. There was no long-term support for implementing a bicultural program because no one really knew how to design such a program. Also, since the BIA had its own rules, procedures, funding, and ideas about bilingual education, it did not work closely with the community, and many parents often did not know what was going on at their children's schools. The BIA had its own curriculum, and the demonstration school did not have the resources—faculty or curriculum—to develop a bicultural and bilingual program that promoted local control in a community-school setting as DINE had envisioned. Until that time, there had been little work done in any public or BIA school serving primarily Navajo children that truly infused Navajo language and culture into the overall curriculum. In response to these efforts for local control, however, the BIA convened educators and linguists at conferences to address the development of bilingual education programs for Navajo children (Ohannessian 1971).

The Rough Rock Demonstration School started with the entire school staff, the local school board, and the community members knowing fully what they needed to do to be successful. Pfieffer stated that from the beginning, learning Navajo culture and language, as well as the idea of local control, was emphasized at Rough Rock. She recalled how Robert Roessel told the Board of Education, "This is your school," to emphasize the notion of community and tribal control. Pfeiffer also recounted how all the members of the Navajo Board of Education at Rough Rock wanted the children in the community to learn Navajo but to learn English as well. Consistent with community consensus, the school embraced a "both/and" approach over an "either/or" approach to emphasize the equity of the languages in the school.

Coming with prior teaching experience, Anita and her husband, Cam, had made plans to move back to the Navajo reservation to be closer to family and to teach Navajo children. Anita described how they were recruited to teach at Rough Rock even as they were initially hired to teach at Chinle Unified Schools. She recalled how a gentleman from the newly formed demonstration school came specifically looking for her to teach there. As one of the few Navajo teachers during this time who were instrumental in designing the bicultural/bilingual program, she recalled how all the students spoke only Navajo. She also recalled how many teachers were all competent speakers of Navajo. She was hired to teach first grade, and having taught English before, she came with both teaching experience and many children's books. Since there were no textbooks when Anita and Cam arrived at Rough Rock, she and other teachers who could write Navajo spent their lunch periods translating children's books from English to Navajo. Later, the school would create the Navajo Curriculum Center to develop and prepare books for Navajo children on Navajo biographies, history, and mythologies using local knowledge and resources (Johnson 1968).

Classrooms at Rough Rock were set up in a way that would physically reflect its bilingual orientation: half the classroom reserved for Navajo only, half for English only. "We drew a line across the room," Pfeiffer said, so there was a clear division of the languages. The purpose of each language was served in their respective spaces. The Navajo space endeavored to mirror what Navajo had been in the larger community prior to the encroachment of English. Pfeiffer's teaching practices sought to affirm students' lived experiences. "We are all going to be teachers," Pfeiffer told the children. "You will teach me too!" Pfeiffer described how as part of the school's commitment to parent engagement, the teachers would meet with parents once a month to inform them of what they were doing when teaching their children:

> In the first year, every month there was a meeting where teachers would present to parents what they were teaching. We had to remind ourselves that this is their school. It was important for them to hear about what their children were learning. The idea behind these meetings was to inform parents what their children were learning but also to get ideas about what else they could be learning. It was an exchange of ideas. For example, they wanted a room totally devoted to weaving blankets and belts. The men wanted a corral to be built so that the children could learn how to the care of livestock and ride the horse. The men wanted to learn silver work and saddles. Since it was their school there were making suggestions about what they wanted for themselves and their children. Also in the first year, we set up a community office where hay could be hauled in for the community. Accounts were set up for the parents at the trading post . . . the community office also developed a post office where parents could receive their checks so they could decide how and what to pay on their bills at the trading posts. . . . The board members would talk about important issues like this. The teachers also wanted the participation of the parent, grandparents in the classroom even though the parents would say we don't' know about education. But they were told you know about the traditional knowledge like winter stories or even cooking traditional foods. The teachers reinforced the idea that parents are teachers. Parents were all interested and invested in their children's education.[9]

The Rough Rock Demonstration School inspired efforts in other Indigenous-controlled schools and hosted many visitors over its first few years, including tribal leaders, Indigenous educators from all over the world, and even US senators Robert and Edward Kennedy. This national attention attracted Navajo and non-Navajo alike, including educational researchers; national, state, and tribal leaders; and educators and community members from other Navajo communities like Ramah/Pine Hill, who were particularly interested in local control and a bicultural/bilingual approach to education (McCarty 2002; Pfeiffer 2017). "We always had visitors and people took ideas that appealed to them," Pfeiffer said. She also mentioned the many bilingual teachers who came out of Rough Rock, as well as others who became educational leaders taking on prominent roles in organizations such as the National Indian Education Association (Pfeiffer 2017; Szasz 1999). For example, she said that an outgrowth of Rough Rock at the national level was the creation of the National Indian Education Association through the collaborative leadership of Native leaders across the United States, including Ned Hatathli, a member of the Rough Rock board of directors, and Dillon Platero, who served as deputy director of the school. Also, Rough Rock's need for bicultural materials influenced the creation of the Curriculum Center at the school and later the development of the Native American Materials Development Institute at the University of New Mexico. The lessons learned from Rough Rock about teacher education inspired the formation of the Navajo Nation Teacher Education Consortium, which Pfeiffer led when she was the director of the Division of Diné Education during Navajo president Peterson Zah's administration. The goal of the consortium at the time was to create one thousand new teachers who would be trained and certified as Navajo bilingual teachers. The consortium worked with Diné College and other colleges and universities to deliver eighteen hours of coursework in Navajo language and culture and creating a new generation of Navajo bilingual educators.

Rock Point Community School

Before helping develop the ESL and Navajo bilingual programs at Rock Point Community Boarding School in the 1960s, Wayne Holm worked with monolingual Navajo children at a day school in Tséchilt'ah (Chilchiltah), New Mexico, in the early 1950s.[10] According to Holm, despite the US government's efforts to provide an education to all Navajo students as stipulated in the Treaty of 1868, some half of all school-age Navajo children had not yet attended school. In the fall of 1954, with only twelve hours of education course work at Northern Arizona University, Holm started teaching as part of the Navajo Emergency Education Program along with two other teachers at the school. It was at Northern Arizona University that he got to know Agnes Dodge, a Navajo teacher, who would later become his wife. Because of limited space, Holm taught out of the living room of the teaching quarters that were provided him by the school.

Before moving to Shiprock, New Mexico, to teach, Wayne attended Utah State University, where he tutored foreign nationals who inspired him to learn more about teaching ESL. It was there that he learned about Charles Fries and his work in anthropological linguistics leading to his text *Teaching and Learning English as a Second Language*. Holm refers to Fries as the grandfather of ESL because Fries was responsible for implementing the idea that people learn languages by acquiring the highly structured patterns of the language being taught. By sensing and using these patterns, an individual could begin to use them to say what he or she wanted to say. After moving to Shiprock, Holm met Elizabeth "Willi" Willink, whose modifications of the Fries-Rojas model for Navajo children made her, according to Holm, the person most responsible for ESL in Navajo education. He recalls how "Mrs. Willink petitioned the Bureau to allow her a leave of absence to pursue a doctoral degree with an emphasis on ESL."[11] Later, Holm and others requested that Willink be stationed at Rock Point to help develop a schoolwide ESL program that emphasized ESL and ESL content. In time, Willink would contract with the school board to become the ESL specialist, with Agnes Dodge as the Navajo language specialist. Later, the bureau would establish other ESL programs modeled on the Rock Point ESL program.

Holm's recounts how the community already had a functioning school committee organized as a standing committee of the local chapter dedicated to getting the school expanded. This committee functioned as a school board in making decisions about school programs, discretionary funds, and seeking to contract. In particular, he described the following events:

> We arrived in Rock Point in 1960. Rock Point was a poor community. It was
> a John Collier–era community boarding school. The community wanted to
> expand their little school to keep up with their children. Most of the committee
> members had little Anglo education and very little English language ability. But
> they held meetings and circulated petitions. During that year, they were told that
> by Thanksgiving, they would see their new expanded school. Thanksgiving came
> but there was still no school. So we started working together with the board on
> expanding the school. We worked with the committee with Agnes interpreting
> during the meetings. We renewed our efforts and eventually we were successful.
> The second and third schools were built in the mid 1960s.[12]

At first, the school committee had no legal authority. This changed in 1972, when Rock Point became a contract school, and like many things during this time period, the function and power of the board evolved as well.

According to Holm, this was a time when bilingual education was viewed as a problem and not an opportunity. In 1960, there were no serious bilingual programs in any Indigenous communities or schools. Although he observed the Cuban-American bilingual program at Coral Way in Florida in the mid-1960s and found it inspiring, it was not well suited to Navajo. "It was well beyond our means. So Rough Rock and Rock Point were pretty much on their own," he recalled.[13] At Rock Point, the bilingual program evolved out of the ESL program; the ESL program simply became the ESL portion of the more comprehensive bilingual program. Prior to this time, there was no agreed-upon method for teaching English as a second language, even though the BIA had developed a cross-cultural education approach several years earlier in the Collier era, as described earlier. "All programs at the time were transitional in nature," Holms reiterated, with Navajo being used "as a language of instruction in some areas while students received intensive English-as-a second-language" (Holm and Holm 1995, 143).

The Navajo bilingual program at Rock Point evolved over time to eventually emphasize Navajo as the primary language for students in coordination with an intensive ESL program. The school continued to expand the ESL-centered program throughout most of the 1960s. At the time, the emphasis was on identifying curriculum materials, learning activities, and methods that would help teachers teach the skills to students with limited proficiency in English. This included experimenting with reading in Navajo. The relative success of the expanded ESL program suggested that the ESL students at Rock Point might do even better if they were first taught to read in Navajo. The board hired one English-language teacher and started the first experimental coordinate bilingual classroom, similar to what was happening at Rough Rock with their bicultural classroom approach. With the availability of additional funds through a Title VII grant, the board was able to begin developing a full bicultural/bilingual education program in 1971. In 1972, the board finally contracted for the full operation of their school that allowed for the full endorsement of the schoolwide bilingual program.

The program model that emerged was called a coordinate bilingual education model, a hallmark of which was coordinated use of Navajo language teachers (NLTs), English language teachers (ELTs), specialists, and principals, with no teacher aides and no translation, with each teacher staying in the target language. Holm offered a full description of the coordinate bilingual program at Rock Point:

> The program had parallel but coordinated teachers, specialists, and principals. Coordination was important. Time-wise, the program went from two-third

Navajo at Kindergarten to half Navajo in grades 1 and 2 to one-third Navajo in grades 3 to 6. In Kindergarten, there were two NLTs and one ELT. Each had a separate instructional area. In the 1st and 2nd grades, there was one NLT and one ELT. They taught separately but worked as a team: planning separately but working cooperatively. In the 3rd grade classrooms, there was a single ELT. But students went out, in half class groups to NL specialists in: Literacy, Social Studies, and Science. Each of these specialists had his or her own room, and taught all in Navajo. Different subjects were taught in different ways: Literacy (reading and writing) was taught in Navajo in 1st grade. Later English literacy was introduced in 2nd grade. Math was taught in Navajo in Kindergarten to 2nd grade and in English from third grade on up. Social Studies was taught all in Navajo from Kindergarten to 6th grade. Science was taught in Navajo from grades 3rd to 6th.[14]

Other aspects of the program included the building of a hogan (a traditional Navajo home structure), adjacent to the classrooms, for eating and home-based activities. Teachers without degrees—both NLT and ELT—were required to work toward obtaining a degree, as some college courses were being taught onsite throughout the school year. Further, as the program expanded, efforts were made to find or develop culturally and linguistically appropriate and relevant materials such as linguistic readers or manipulative math, and instructional methods that were consistent with the school's program goals (Reyhner 1990).

This approach was very different from the SNEP model described earlier, which emphasized translations from one language to the other and thus established an implicit hierarchy that gives the dominant language, English, a higher status. In contrast, in the Rock Point bilingual model, there was awareness about making the two languages equal in status throughout the school day and even within the entire curriculum. Navajo was introduced to children as early as kindergarten, for example, and in first grade were taught to read in Navajo, with half of their instruction in their native language. Instruction in English literacy started in the second grade. In subsequent years, variations of this coordinate bilingual maintenance model would be expanded beyond the middle school grades into high school.

As early as the 1970s, research studies on Navajo bilingual education programs like the one at Rock Point had shown that learning Navajo in addition to English directly and positively influenced academic achievement for Navajo students in reservation communities (McCarty 2002; Rosier and Holm 1980). Using a quantitative approach in a longitudinal study, Rosier and Holm (1980) found that children in Navajo bilingual programs achieved better scores on tests that measure reading, writing, and math skills across the grade levels compared to those who attended English-only schools. Rosier and Holm (1980) highlighted how children in these bilingual programs faired against those in the earlier ESL-only program, finding that younger children in both types of programs did equally well in all areas, but adults who learned Navajo reading first fared better than their children who learned English reading first. More recent studies on Navajo immersion programs also suggest that there are positive correlations between language maintenance and academic achievement (Johnson and Legatz 2006).

FUTURE PROSPECTS FOR NAVAJO BILINGUAL EDUCATION

Despite its well-documented benefits, Navajo bilingual education is still a contested idea today. It is thus critical that we continue to seek to understand and to advocate for the cultural shifts and educational practices and policies that will ensure the language's survival and ongoing vitality (Holm and Holm 1995; Sposky 2002). Unless Indigenous languages are acknowledged as being equal to other languages in all aspects of a community's livelihood, recognized as still being functional and purposeful in today's contexts, and used and validated in academic contexts, they will continue to be marginalized and devalued. Also, only when Indigenous language communities reassert their Indigenous language in all settings and speakers of Indigenous languages reaffirm and rearticulate their roles as fluent speakers by using the language in all settings can it be possible to pass the language to the next generations, whether in the home, the school, or in communities (Aguilera and LeCompte 2008; Hinton 2013).

For the past eighteen years, I have worked as a K–12 teacher, a Navajo bilingual teacher, and a resource teacher supporting other Navajo language teachers in rural and urban contexts. More recently, I served as an assistant professor teaching graduate-level courses in American Indian Education and related to Navajo bilingual education. From this experience and knowledge, I am familiar with many of the challenges and possibilities of teaching Navajo within school or community settings. I am also aware of critical issues facing Navajo communities and their implications in the perpetuation of the Diné language for future generations.

In the following section, I address four critical questions relative to understanding Navajo's current statues and future prospects: What is the case for

Diné today? How effective are the current language policies and mandates for Diné? What types of policies and strategies do we need to effectively revitalize and teach our language? What are individuals, communities, and the Diné tribe as a nation doing now to mitigate the threat of language loss? Posing such questions is one way to begin addressing the critical issues and questions that arise across different communities around levels of language use and planning (Hornberger 1997).

Until the late 1960s and early 1970s, Diné was the primary spoken language in many homes on the Diné reservation, and many Diné children came to school speaking only Diné (Holm and Holm, 1995; McCarty 2002). Prior to that time, the language had not yet been severely threatened by the intrusion of a more dominant language. While the Bilingual Act of 1968 and the civil rights movement of the 1960s may have been instrumental in helping create bilingual programs in schools with large populations of English learners (Brisk 2006) and to provide appropriate language instruction to students whose first language is not English, the shift from Navajo to English had already begun. According to studies by Platero (1970) and Holm (1989), there was an increasing number of school-age (five-year-old) children coming to school who did not speak Navajo. In *A Place to be Navajo*, McCarty (2002) describes how this shift over time from Diné to English greatly impacted the Rough Rock and other surrounding communities years after the demonstration project. From her work on the Diné reservation over the last two decades, McCarty writes that "we have observed an alarming shift in children's use of and proficiency in Diné. More and more children come to school each year with only passive knowledge of the community language" (15). The obvious questions are what is happening, how did this happen, and why is it happening now? A simple response is that language shift occurs when one language is gradually replaced by another language.

According to US census data from 1980 to 2010, the number of Diné speakers between the ages of five and seventeen has dramatically decreased, from about 48 percent to less than 5 percent (United States Census Bureau 2013; cited in Crawford 1996). Also, according to past and more recent studies (Holm and Holm 1995; House 2002; Lee and McLaughlin 1999), Diné children are still coming to school not speaking Navajo, either because their parents are not speaking to them in the language or the status of the language has declined. Unfortunately, there is limited information on the most recent status of the language in terms of identifying numbers of speakers and research specific to the effectiveness of current language programs, whether in rural or urban settings. Obviously, new research data are needed that would provide more information about what is happening in Navajo communities with regard to language.

Evangeline Parsons-Yazzie (1997) notes that because Navajo children are no longer growing up with extended families with grandparents and many parents are not using the language with their children, the traditional intergenerational passing of the Diné language from grandparent to parent to child in an extended family setting has eroded, thereby leading to language shift in many Diné communities. Other researchers have linked language shift to other factors, such as non-Indigenous-speaking children being ridiculed by older speakers for their lack of language facility and external pressures from an English-dominant society and culture (House 2002; Lee 1999). Consequently, even with the recent implementation of bilingual programs, the number of young Native speakers of Indigenous languages is in steep decline.

Within each Indigenous language community engaged in language revitalization efforts, there must be clear goals for perpetuating the language, creating a new generation of speakers, and understanding how bilingual education can serve their community's needs. In this process, each community that works to revitalize its language must first understand how its language came to be threatened in the first place (an insight lacking in many Native communities), and then identify ways to reverse language shift in the home, school, and community (Fishman 2001). Diné language educators, speakers, and advocates must measure their own goals about the purpose of bilingual education against both past experiences and future aspirations for their communities and for the next generation of Diné youth (Spolsky 2002). Several key questions can guide this effort: How are Diné bilingual programs serving their purpose? In what ways should Diné bilingual programs evolve to meet the needs of today? And in what ways do current goals in Diné bilingual programs align with the long-term efforts of cultural sustainability and the larger goals of the language community with respect to their rights to language as sovereign Indigenous nations?

With the adoption of the United Nation's Declaration on the Rights of Indigenous People in 2007 and later with the signing of the document by President Obama in 2010, many Indigenous communities in the US are both reasserting their legal rights as US citizens and affirming their human rights as free and sovereign Indigenous nations (Indigenous Peoples Law and Policy Program 2012).[15] For example, the increasing efforts by Indigenous communities to come together in solidarity and resist the US gas and oil industry in the name of the No Dakota Access Pipeline movement is indicative of these struggles to uphold the sacred mandates and laws of their ancestors and to assert their human rights to land, water, and education, including their language. In particular, Articles 2, 11, and 13 of the UN declaration describe the ways by which Indigenous communities as free and equal to all other people can exercise their freedom and rights to use and transmit their languages to future generations as sovereign nations without fear of assimilation, discrimination, or manipulation (Indigenous Peoples Law and Policy Program 2012, 27–31).

Using the UN document as a tool for decolonization, before moving forward with language revitalization efforts, Diné language communities must first understand the key factors that caused some Indigenous languages to become threatened languages in the first place (Fishman 1991, 2001; Hinton 2013). Next, through the process of naming oppression (Freire 2000), Diné language communities and educators today can engage in acts of decolonization by deconstructing dominant ideological notions of what constitutes equity and equality of opportunity in language education (including bilingual education) in schools and community settings. In doing so, they will assert their human rights to language and education based on their unique Indigenous perspective about the purpose and significance of their language for future generations. Finally, they can begin to develop ideas and strategies to more effectively reverse language shift in the larger community.

FUTURE IMPLICATIONS AND RECOMMENDATIONS

In addressing critical issues of language shift, every Indigenous language group that is concerned about language loss must advocate and take responsibility for their own languages. Only when Indigenous language communities reclaim the essential purposes of using their Indigenous language in all facets of their lives—whether for communicating across generations or perpetuating community lifeways—and speakers of Indigenous languages rearticulate their roles as knowledge bearers of the language, will it be possible to pass on the language to the next generation. As highlighted in both the Rough Rock and Rock Point community school cases, everyone in the community, including schools administrators and educators, must reaffirm how their school and their community are in service to one another and find creative ways to perpetuate the local Indigenous languages and knowledge. The US government's past practices of divesting Indigenous communities of their children's education by excluding the community in that critical task must be challenged. The historical separation of school from community must be exchanged for a system that weaves both together, where school become a Diné space that in which Diné youth can be fully Navajo (McCarty 2002). In communities such as Rough Rock and Rock Point, the schools were central to the overall economic, cultural, political, and social aims of the larger community. This allowed for increased engagement and participation from everyone.

While research data on Navajo bilingual education suggests positive correlations between language maintenance and academic achievement (Johnson and Legatz 2006; Rosier and Holm 1970), we must consider several important questions: What does this relationship mean to the overall status and/or goals of a community with regard to the future of the Diné language? Why do we continue to conflate academic achievement with creating a new generation of speakers of the language? And what is being done for Diné students who are not in a bilingual education program? We must also address an even more critical question: How will younger generations learn their heritage language if they are not fully supported at home and in the larger community? Finally, there are looming questions about what has been and is being done at the federal, state, and tribal government levels. But more importantly, what is happening in the community settings and in the home contexts of Navajo families to reverse Navajo language shift?

Even though policies do exist that support Indigenous language education, such as the Navajo Nation education policy, which specifically states, "Instruction in the Diné language shall be made available for all grade levels [in] all schools serving the Diné Nation" (Division of Diné Education 2003), there appears to be little progress in creating a new generation of Navajo speakers in current Navajo bilingual programs. Despite all the government laws, mandates, and policies that now promote Indigenous language revitalization efforts and all the school-based immersion programs that have moved toward language immersion methodologies, Diné is still severely threatened. So how do we change the current situation? How do we reverse Navajo language shift?

In response to these types of questions, I offer some recommendations out of hope and humility about ways that Diné communities can engage in language and community revitalization as a decolonizing project.

First, Diné language speakers must use their language every day and in different contexts throughout the community and without shame. The saying "use it or lose it" is very relevant to our situation now. In *Reversing Language Shift*, Joshua Fishman, modeling intergenerational transmission of languages, describes eight stages of language shift based on the degree and usage of the language from the individual to societal levels. Fishman proposes that since home languages were primarily transmitted from one generation to the next through natural settings like the home and the neighborhood, families and communities are the most important actors to reversing language shift. In a later work, "Why Is It So Hard to Save a Threatened Language," he writes, "Societally based RLS (reversing language shift) cannot be accomplished if it is not accomplished at the intimate family and local community levels" (Fishman 2001, 4). Thus, to effectively reverse Navajo language shift, Navajo language communities and particularly speakers of the language must use the language again in their homes and in the larger community and stop shifting the responsibility to schools with bilingual programs.

Second, communities must find a renewed purpose for the use of Navajo in all aspects of life—community, school, and in society at large. For example, the Navajo language could be integrated more into the total learning experiences of children where it is appropriate and relevant to their lived experiences and realities. That is, the language must be used throughout the school in authentic ways for communication and not only in the classrooms to teach content or vocabulary. Much of this could be achieved by language status equalization in the home and school settings by advocating more immersion-type approaches in classrooms and even total-immersion schools that use Navajo throughout the day for communication, instruction, learning, teaching, and all the day-to-day activities of the school.

In their 1994 pseudo-retrospective article "Laanaa Nisin: Diné Education in the Year 2004," Anita Pfeiffer and Wayne Holm expressed an earnest hope about possible transformations that could be effected by restructuring Diné education if they were to get what they desired—*laanaa nisin*—in Diné language education. In the article, they describe a "Navajo renaissance" and a Diné society "on the verge of achieving relatively stable societal bilingualism where it is good to be and speak Diné (Pfeiffer and Holm 1994, 37). Obviously, much of what they wished for in this article has not happened, mainly because what they perceived would need to happen still is not happening today. They wrote:

> We have to take part in a massive but incremental change in people's
> perceptions- to where a critical mass of the people feel that it is good to be what
> one is, and that only talking that language will enable one to participate fully as
> a member of that group. Unless people feel that their language does something

for them that cannot be done as well in English, they will not persist, or use that language with their children. (37)

Obviously, serious consideration must be given to addressing the "ideological base that appears to have been seriously weakened by external forces"(Spolsky 2002, 157). That is, there must continue to be efforts to make Navajo a language of prestige and purpose in the home, school, and community, as well as to the larger society.

Often, within the efforts to revitalize Indigenous languages at the community level, little attention is paid to the role and responsibilities of parents who are proficient speakers of the language. In many Indigenous communities, the tradi-tional ways of learning language and cultural values have been lost as a result of the impact of boarding schools and with the advent of Anglo-Protestant societal values and beliefs. While the Diné language's marginalization in schools and in the dominant Euro-American society has much to do with how dominant language ideologies play out in our communities, the decline of Diné language must also be attributed to the ways in which people have internalized dominant ideologies about how the language is perceived and used. Tove Skutnabb-Kangass (1999, 1988) postulates that similar to internalized racism, internalized lingui-cism turns individuals from one language group against both themselves and against individuals from another language group. As a result, many Indigenous community members face the shame or stigma of not being able to speak their heritage language because they still wrestle with the idea of why it is even im-portant to learn the language at all. The notion of learning English for success in schools and life, which has become central to the dominant discourse in education today, has been uncritically embraced by speakers of the language. Therefore, it is imperative that Navajo parents and community members who are speakers of the language reflect and act upon their role and responsibility to perpetuate the language and validate its use. More language advocacy is needed within the home, school, and community contexts that emphasize the use of the language. For example, community forums could be planned to address these critical questions while also finding ways to address these concerns and issues. Also, families can create language policies in their homes that send a powerful message to the young children that speaking the Navajo language is crucial to its maintenance and survival. Furthermore, Diné language educators and advo-cates could consider innovative ways to help and support parents by providing them opportunities to learn and use immersion strategies in the home and or by revisiting the natural Diné approach or way of talking to children and relearning how to socialize them (Hinton 2013).

Finally, I posit that Navajo language educators continue to advocate for more total immersion methodologies in their teaching practices and in school programs. School and community leaders could reconsider language policies and work with parents to find more language spaces for using the language through implementing partial immersion programs or even creating full-immersion schools. In some cases, there are renewed efforts by parents who are advocating for adult language classes that support the efforts of school-based programs. Also, awareness grows about the need to reverse Navajo language shift, more community-based efforts, including immersion day camps, language advocacy groups, and even the use of technologies as language-learning aids, must be considered and utilized. I have seen firsthand the value of starting language groups in the home to advocate the use of the language. Some activities could include using the language around the dinner table, playing games, and using traditional games and cultural activities to use the language that could include family and close friends. In some rural Diné communities, close-knit families are making good use of family reunions or holiday breaks from school or work to engage in culture-based immersion activities that are tailored to both the family's strengths and local contexts. As such, research is needed that links tribal sovereignty and self-determination in education with recent efforts by schools and communities to help the younger generation relearn and sustain the language .

CONCLUSION

From the early 1930s to the mid-1960s, with the continued advance of English hegemony and American colonization onto Navajo lands, many Diné parents were coerced, forced, and manipulated into sending their children to Anglo schools to learn the English language (House 2002). The advent of public schools and boarding dorms in the late 1950s and the shift from an agrarian lifestyle to a capitalist wage economy continues to exert great pressure on the lifeways of Diné people. As a result, in the decades after World War II, the Diné language has undergone a dramatic shift from Navajo toward English in the home, school, and the larger community contexts (House 2002). As many young Navajo children began to learn English in schools, they risked losing their home language in the process. Further, as Navajo communities began to embrace English as essential to success in American society, they risked losing the language on a larger scale.

Consequently, a bicultural and bilingual approach to teaching Navajo children within school settings evolved, although with ambiguities and ambivalence contributing to much uncertainty about its design, goals, and purpose, especially for maintaining or sustaining the language for future generations. From a historical perspective, this uncertainty could be attributed to past assimilationist ideologies and xenophobic attitudes about foreigners and/or the many distinct cultures and language communities that are still represented in the United States today.

The present sociocultural and political contexts for Navajo bilingual education are obviously very different from those of thirty years ago because of language shift (Benally and Viri 2005; Holm and Holm 1995). Moreover, what was considered Navajo bilingual education from the 1960s to the 1980s is not the same for the current generation of Navajo children who are not speakers of their heritage language. Many students today do not speak their heritage language to carry on a conversation with each other, their parents, elders, or even teachers. Further, many older speakers of Navajo are not aware of language shift or are complacent, neither speaking to nor teaching the younger Navajo generation, even as the youth want to learn the language (Lee 1999, 2006). Finally, even the notion of what it means to revitalize the Navajo language within the larger community is one of the key issues that continues to be ignored, neither discussed in depth nor examined critically by Diné communities themselves.

To move from decolonization to transformation, Indigenous communities must find ways to counter language oppression, heal from historical trauma, and return to land-based cultural practices (Alfred 2009). For Indigenous liberation, they must also find solutions for decolonizing education in general (Battiste 2002, 2008). In my own work as a Diné language advocate and educator, I have begun working with my community to address language shift and culture loss by developing a Diné-centered community-based approach to draw upon the community's local assets and strengths to educate the next generation, with the long-term goals of cultural and ecological sustainability. In this way, the local cultural knowledge of a community could be reinfused into the language-learning activities of the homes, schools, and even the communities. More importantly, the language will become critical in the community's reaffirmation of its local cultural knowledge and identity through the processes of decolonizing and healing. To accomplish this, the community must trust in its language. If we are to survive into the next century—especially in the face of powerful neoliberal, English-only, ultra-right-wing, white-nationalist political forces that aim to reverse policies and laws that protect and honor the rights of

Indigenous communities and other communities of color in the United States and abroad—we must all trust in our language, our cultural ways of knowing, our total way of life, and ourselves.

NOTES

1. Many educators were instrumental in the development of Navajo bilingual education. Acknowledging them all would require another volume.

2. For a more detailed historical overview of Navajo bilingual education, see Szasz, *Education and the American Indian*; and Lomawaima and McCarty, *To Remain An Indian*. For more information about the Rough Rock Demonstration School, see McCarty, *A Place to Be Navajo*.

3. The Navajo livestock reduction occurred under John Collier's administration during the early 1930s. Many Navajo families lost their livelihoods when the US government reduced their livestock to address concerns of overgrazing. For more information about the Navajo livestock reduction, see Boyce, *When Navajos Had Too Many Sheep*.

4. See Lewis Meriam, *The Problem of Indian Administration; Report of a Survey Made at the request of Hubert Work, Secretary of the Interior, and Submitted to Him, February 21, 1928*, https://narf.org/nill/resources/meriam.html.

5. The US Long Range Navajo-Hopi Rehabilitation Act authorized improvements over a ten year period to help Indians achieve economic stability and adopt a constitution to manage their own affairs.

6. Wayne Holm, personal interview with author, July 5, 2017.

7. Information for this section was provided by Anita Pfeiffer in a personal interview with the author, June 21, 2017. Quotes are transcribed from that interview.

8. DINE was the non-profit organization created by Roessel and the Rough Rock Demonstration School leaders to serve as the legal entity to receive funds and operate of the school.

9. Anita Pfeiffer, interview with author, June 21, 2017.

10. Information for this section was provided by Wayne Holm in a personal interview with the author, July 5, 2017. Quotes are transcribed from that interview.

11. Holm interview.

12. Ibid.

13. Ibid.

14. Ibid.

15. UN General Assembly, Resolution 61/295, United Nations Declaration on the Rights of Indigenous Peoples, A/RES/61/295 (October 2007), http://www.refworld.org/docid/471355a82.html.

REFERENCES

Adams, David W. 1995. *Education For Extinction: American Indians and the Boarding School Experience, 1878–1928.* Lawrence: University of Kansas Press.

Aguilera, Dorothy, and Margaret LeCompte. 2008. "Restore My Language and Treat Me Justly: Indigenous Student's Rights to Their Tribal Languages." In *Affirming Students' Right to Their Own Language: Bridging Language Policies and Pedagogical Practices,* edited by J. Scott, D. Straker, and L. Katz, 68–84). New York: Routledge.

Alfred, Gerald T. 2009. "Colonialism and State Dependency." *Journal of Aboriginal Health* 5, no. 2: 42–60.

Battiste, Marie Ann. 2002. *Decolonizing Education: Nourishing the Learning Spirit.* Saskatoon, SK: Purich.

———. 2008. "The Struggle and Renaissance of Indigenous Knowledge in Eurocentric Education." In *Indigenous Knowledge and Education: Sites of Struggle, Strength, and Survivance,* edited by Malia Villegas, Sabina Neugebauer, and Kerry Venegas, xx. Cambridge, MA: Harvard Educational Review.

Benally, AnCita, and Dennis Viri. 2005. "*Dine Bizaad* at a Crossroads: Extinction or Renewal?" *Bilingual Research Journal* 29, no. 1: 85–108.

Bourdieu, Pierre. 1999. *Language and Symbolic Power.* 5th ed. Cambridge, MA: Harvard University Press.

Boyce, George. 1974. *When Navajos Had Too Many Sheep: The 1940s.* San Francisco: Indian Historian Press.

Brisk, Marie. 2006. *Bilingual Education: From Compensatory to Quality Schooling.* 2nd ed. Mahwah, NJ: Lawrence Erlbaum.

Brugge, David. M. 1965. *Long Ago in Navajoland.* Window Rock, AZ: Navajo Publications.

———. 1993. "Henry Chee Dodge: From the Long Walk to Self-Determination." In *Indian lives: Essays on nineteenth-and twentieth-century Native American leaders,* edited by L. G. Moses and R. Wilson, 91–112. Albuquerque: University of New Mexico Press.

Crawford, James. 1992. *Hold Your Tongue: Bilingualism and the Politics of English Only.* New York: Addison-Wesley.

———. 1995. "Endangered Native American languages: What Is to Be Done, and Why? *Bilingual Research Journal* 19, no. 1: 17–38.

———. 1996. "Seven Hypotheses on Language Loss: Causes and Cures." In *Stabilizing Indigenous Languages,* edited by Gina Cantoni, 51–68. Flagstaff: Northern Arizona University Press.

Cummins, Jim. 1988. "Bilingual Education and Anti-racist Education." In *Minority Education: From Shame to Struggle,* edited by T. Skutnabb-Kangass and Jim Cummins, 69–98. Clevedon, UK: Multilingual Matters.

Deloria, Vine, Jr., and Clifford Lytle. 1983. *American Indians, American Justice*. Austin: University of Texas Press.

Dick, Galena, and Teresa McCarty. 1996. "Reclaiming Diné: Language Renewal in an American Indian Community School." In *Indigenous Literacies: Language Planning from the Bottom Up*, edited by Nancy Hornberger, 45–68. Berlin: Mouton.

Division of Diné Education, Office of Diné Culture, Language, and Community Services. 2003. *Navajo Nation Education Standards with Navajo Specifics*. Window Rock, AZ.

Dunbar-Ortiz, Roxanne. 2014. *An Indigenous People's History of the United States*. Boston: Beacon Press.

Fishman, Joshua. 1991. *Reversing Language Shift*. Clevedon, UK: Longdunn Press.

———. 2001. "Why Is It So Hard to Save a Threatened Language?" In *Can Threatened Languages Be Saved? Reversing Language Shift Revisited: A 21st Century Perspective*, edited by Joshua Fishman, 69–98. Clevedon, UK: Multilingual Matters.

Hinton, Leanne. 2001. "Federal Language Policy and Indigenous Languages in the United States." In *The Greenbook of Language Revitalization in Practice*, edited by Leanne Hinton and Ken Hale, 139–44. Boston: Brill.

———. 2013. "Bringing Your Language into Your Own Home." In *Bringing Our Languages Home: Language Revitalization for Families*, 225–56. Berkeley, CA: Heyday Press.

Holm, Wayne, and Agnes Holm. 1995. "Navajo Language Education: Retrospect and Prospects." *Bilingual Research Journal* 19, no. 1: 141–67.

Hornberger, Nancy. 1997. "Language Planning from the Bottom Up. In *Indigenous Literacies: Language Planning from the Bottom Up*, edited by Nancy Hornberger, 357–66. Berlin: Mouton.

House, Donna. 2002. *Language Shift among the Navajo*. Tucson: University of Arizona Press.

Indigenous Peoples Law and Policy Program. 2012. *The United Nations Declaration on the Rights of Indigenous Peoples: With an Introduction for Indigenous Leaders in the United States*. Tucson: University of Arizona Indigenous Peoples Law and Policy Program, James E. Rogers College of Law. http://unsr.jamesanaya.org/docs/data /UNDRIP-Handbook-USA.pdf.

Johnson, Broderick. 1968. *Navajo Education at Rough Rock*. Rough Rock, AZ: Rough Rock Demonstration School, DINE. Inc.

Johnson, Florian, and Jennifer Legatz. 2006. "Tséhootsoí Diné Bi'ólta'." *Journal of American Indian Education* 45, no. 2: 26–33.

Kappler, Charles J. 1904. *Indian Affairs*, vol. 2, *Laws and Treaties*. Washington, DC: Government Printing Office. https://americanindian.si.edu/static/nationtonation /pdf/Navajo-Treaty-1868.pdf.

Kelly, Lawrence C. 1968. *The Navajo Indians and Federal Indian Policy 1900–1935.* Tucson: University of Arizona Press.

Krauss, Michael. 1996. "Status of Native American Language Endangerment." In *Stabilizing Indigenous Languages*, edited by Gina Cantoni, 116–21. Flagstaff: Northern Arizona University Press.

Lee, Tiffany. 2007. "'If They Want Navajo to Be Learned, Then They Should Require It in All Schools': Navajo Teenagers' Experiences, Choices, and Demands Regarding Navajo Language." *Wicazo Sa Review* 22, no. 1: 7–33.

———. 2009. "Language, Identity, and Power: Navajo and Pueblo Young Adults' Perspectives and Experiences with Competing Language Ideologies." *Journal of Language, Identity, and Education* 8: 307–20.

Lee, Tiffany, and Daniel McLaughlin. 2001. "Reversing Diné Language Shift, Revisited." In *Can Threatened Languages Be Saved? Reversing Language Shift Revisited: A 21st Century Perspective*, edited by Joshua Fishman, 69–98. Clevedon, UK: Multilingual Matters.

Lomawaima, K. Tsianina, and Terersa McCarty. 2006. *To Remain an Indian: Lessons in Democracy from a Century of Native American Education.* New York: Teachers College.

López, David. 1991. "The Emergence of Language Minorities in the United States." In *Language and Ethnicity: Focusschrift in Honor of Joshua A. Fishman on the Occasion of His 65th Birthday*, vol. 2, edited by James R. Dow, 69–98. Philadelphia: John Benjamins.

May, Stephen. 1999. "Language and Education Rights for Indigenous People." In *Indigenous Community Based Education*, edited by Stephen May, 69–98. Clevedon: Multilingual Matters.

McCarty, Teresa. 2002. *A Place to Be Navajo: Rough Rock and the Struggle of Self-Determination in Indigenous Schooling.* Mahwah, NJ: Lawrence Erlbaum.

———. 2003. "Revitalizing Indigenous Languages in Homogenising Times." *Comparative Education* 39, no. 2: 147–63.

McCarty, Teresa, and Tiffany Lee. 2014. "Critical Culturally Sustaining/Revitalizing Pedagogy and Indigenous Education Sovereignty." *Harvard Educational Review* 84, no. 1: 101–24.

Link, Martin, ed. *The Navajo Treaty of 1868: Treaty between the United States of America and the Navajo Tribe of Indians with a Record of the Discussions That Led to the Signing.* Las Vegas, NV: KC Publications.

Meriam, Lewis. 1928. *The Problem of Indian Administration: Report of a Survey Made at the Request of Hubert Work, Secretary of the Interior, and Submitted to Him, February 21, 1928.* https://narf.org/nill/resources/meriam.html.

Parsons-Yazzie, Evangeline. 1997. "Niha'alchini Dayistl'o Nahalin." *Journal of Navajo Education* 14, no. 1/2: 60–67.

Pfeiffer, Anita, and Wayne Holm. 1994. "Laanaa Nizin: Diné Education in the Year 2004." *Journal of Navajo Education* 11, no. 2: 35—43.

Platero, Paul. 2001. "Navajo Language Study." In *The Greenbook of Language Revitalization in Practice*, edited by Leanne Hinton and Ken Hale, 86–97. Boston: Brill.

Reyhner, Jon, and Jeanne Eder. 1990. "A Description of the Rock Point Community School Bilingual Education Program." In *Effective Language Education Practices and Native Languages Survival*, edited by Jon Reyhner, 95–106. Choctaw, OK: Native American Language Issues. http://jan.ucc.nau.edu/~jar/NALI7.html

———. 2004. *American Indian Education: A History*. Norman: University of Oklahoma Press.

Roessel, Robert. A. 1977. *Navajo Education in Action: The Rough Rock Demonstration School*. 1st ed. Chinle, AZ: Navajo Curriculum Center, Rough Rock Demonstration School.

Rosier, Paul, and Wayne Holm. 1980. "The Rock Point Experience: A Longitudinal Study of a Diné School Program (Saad Naaki Bee Na'nitin)." Washington, DC: Center for Applied Linguistics, Papers in Applied Linguistics. Bilingual Education Series: 8.

Skutnabb-Kangass, Tove. 1988. "Multilingualism and the Education of Minority Children." In *Minority Education: From Shame to Struggle*, edited by Tove Skutnabb-Kangass and J. Cummins, 69–98. Clevedon, UK: Multilingual Matters.

———. 1999. "Linguistic Diversity, Human Rights, and the 'Free' Market." In *Language: A Right and a Resource: Approaching Linguistic Human Rights*, edited by Kontra Miklós, Tibor Várday, Robery Phillipson, and Tove Skutnabb-Kangass, 69–98. Budapest: Central European University.

Spicer, Edward. 1981. *Cycles of Conquest: The Impact of Spain, Mexico, and the United States on the Indians of the Southwest, 1533–1960*. Tucson: University of Arizona Press.

Spolsky, Bernard. 2002. "Prospects for the Survival of the Navajo Language: A Reconsideration." *Anthropology and Education Quarterly* 33, no. 2: 139–62.

Spring, Joel. 1992. *Images of American Life: A History of Ideological Management in Schools, Movies, Radio, and Television*. Albany: State University of New York Press.

———. 2005. *The American School: From the Puritans to No Child Left Behind*. 7th ed. New York: McGraw Hill.

Szasz, Margaret C. 1999. *Education and the American Indian: The Road to Self-Determination, 1928–1998*. Albuquerque: University of New Mexico Press.

Thompson, Hildegard. 1975. *Navajos Long Walk for Education: A History of Navajo Education*. Tsaile, AZ: Navajo Community College Press.

Ohannessian, Sirarpi. 1971. "Planning Conference for Bilingual Kindergarten Program for Navajo Children." In *Bilingual Education for American Indians* (Curriculum

Bulletin no. 3). Washington, DC: Office of Education Programs, US Bureau of Indian Affairs.

United States Census Bureau. 2013. *American Survey Reports. Language Use in the United States, 2011.* https://www2.census.gov/library/publications/2013/acs/acs-22/acs-22.pdf.

Young, Robert. 1961. *The Navajo Yearbook.* Window Rock, AZ: Bureau of Indian Affairs, Navajo Agency.

CHRISTINE P. SIMS

[3] Bilingual Education in Pueblo Country

Everyone knew what the marked-off squares on the classroom floor meant. These were the places where empty gunny sacks lay, one in each square, alongside one wall of our classroom. This was where the teacher put you if she caught you speaking in Keres. The punishment was being made to step into the gunny sack, with teacher tying up the top so you couldn't get out. There you sat for hours, tied up in a gunny sack until teacher determined you had learned your lesson: do not speak in Keres, only English.

PUEBLO INTERVIEW [1992]

Among the nineteen Pueblo Indian tribes of New Mexico, five major Pueblo languages indigenous to this state are spoken: Keres, Tewa, Tiwa, Towa, and Zuni. These languages were widely spoken among many more pueblos at the time of first contact with Spanish explorers who entered the southwest in the 1500s. Today, seven pueblos, each with its own distinct dialect, speak the Keres language: Acoma, Laguna, Santa Ana, Zia, San Felipe, Santo Domingo, and Cochiti. Dialects of the Tewa language family are spoken at six pueblos: Ohkay Owinghe, Tesuque, Nambe, Pojoaque, Santa Clara, and San Ildefonso. Tiwa is spoken among four Pueblo communities—Taos, Picuris, Sandia, and Isleta—while the two remaining Pueblo languages, Towa and Zuni, each have the unique distinction of being spoken in only one pueblo—Towa in Jemez Pueblo, and Zuni in Zuni Pueblo.

These Pueblo languages share a common history of having been transmitted over countless centuries as oral-based traditions, enduring as viable spoken languages even as the Spanish, Mexican, and American regimes attempted to stamp out Indigenous cultures and languages of the Southwest. As this chapter reveals, the toll that nineteenth century education policies under the American government had on the vitality of these languages was far reaching, especially among the first generations of Pueblo children who were forbidden to use their languages in government-operated schools. These federal education policies would persist well into the mid-twentieth century, even as public schools were becoming more accessible to Pueblo students.

By the latter half of the twentieth century, Pueblo bilingual programs developed under the umbrella of American national initiatives in bilingual education that formed in the wake of the 1960s civil rights movement in the United States. These national movements influenced the development of some of the first Title VII federal bilingual programs serving American Indian children, directly challenging a long history of suppressing Native languages in federal government schools and recognizing the inequities of public school education in meeting the instructional needs of Native students. Native American bilingual education represented a radical shift in thinking about the use of Native languages in schools. For decades, non-Native educators and policy makers considered Native languages to be a barrier to learning English (Adams 1988). Children in federal government schools were prohibited from using their Native languages—often physically punished for infractions—and forced to learn English. These experiences were common among older generations of Pueblo people from all five of the major Pueblo language groups who attended federal government day and boarding schools in New Mexico in the early 1900s.

Most bilingual programs introduced in the 1970s and 1980s were initially intended to help Native students transition to English-based school curricula as quickly as possible, using the Native language as a bridge for communication and instruction. In New Mexico, the emergence of Title VII bilingual programs in some Pueblo schools created the impetus for orthography development for Native languages that had never been written. The primary purpose for these activities was often linked to the need for bilingual, culturally relevant instructional materials for students, many of whom were still speakers of Native languages.

In New Mexico, the production of stories, topical dictionaries, and other instructional materials were used in bilingual programs in Zuni, Acoma, San Juan, and Santa Clara Pueblos. Much of this work involved Pueblo teachers and educators working in collaboration with linguists who provided technical assistance in language documentation and orthography development. In San Juan Pueblo, for example, field linguists from the Summer Institute of Linguistics based in Dallas, Texas, worked with Tewa speakers such as the late Esther Martinez, who helped document her Native Tewa language. Martínez, along with fellow tribal members, learned to write in Tewa, and together they produced some of the first Tewa literacy materials used in the local Bureau of Indian Affairs (BIA) day school. In Acoma Pueblo, Keres speakers working in their BIA elementary school in the early 1970s engaged in similar efforts, working with Wick Miller, a University of Utah linguist who had conducted his doctoral research documenting the Acoma-Keres language (1965). Other linguists, such as Irvine Davis (1964) and Amy Zaharlick (1977), worked with the Santa Ana-Keres and the Picuris Tiwa languages, respectively. Scholar William Leap (1970) conducted research on identifying patterns of Indian-English language use among Pueblo school children during this time period.

Linguistic documentation activities during the 1970s set the stage for a few initial attempts to develop Pueblo literacy. The intended audience, however, was usually specific to Pueblo students in local schools, where such efforts had the approval of Pueblo leaders. When this type of work was conducted in conjunction with Title VII programs in local BIA schools, or where tribes, such as Acoma Pueblo, were direct Title VII grantees, a measure of local pueblo control over content and materials dissemination was possible because the production was being carried out by Pueblo language speakers, teachers, and program directors from the community.

Producing and disseminating materials for the purpose of introducing widespread Native literacy into Pueblo communities, on the other hand, often did not occur, and only a handful of tribal members (usually Pueblo bilingual staff in the schools) learned to read and write their own language. What was significant in these efforts, however, was that the pioneering work was taken up by Pueblo speakers themselves. Working alongside field linguists on documentation and orthographic development, they learned basic linguistic skills, which enabled them to continue this work in later years on their own. Thus, at the peak of federal bilingual program funding during the 1970s and 1980s, when tribes became eligible to compete for Title VII grants, additional materials were produced in various Pueblo bilingual programs. In some cases, they utilized the new technologies of the time, such as interchangeable fonts in electric typewriters for non-English symbols, and later the first generation of Apple MacIntosh computers utilized for recording and desktop publishing. Topical dictionaries, resource activity books for teachers, newsletters, school calendars, community stories, and other culturally related topics captured in written Pueblo languages were examples of resources produced in the Zuni language, as well as in certain dialects of the Keres and Tewa languages.

As Title VII Native bilingual programs grew and state bilingual funding began to flow into New Mexico public schools, so too did the need for bilingual Pueblo teachers. Title VII funding sources were especially instrumental during this period in the late 1970s as a source of financial support for Pueblo teacher aides in Head Start programs or local elementary schools working to obtain a teaching degree.

In 1973, for example, a major Pueblo teacher education program (PTEP), whose purpose was to produce more state-credentialed Pueblo teachers in New Mexico, was established by the All Indian Pueblo Council (AIPC) and the University of New Mexico. The PTEP supported ninety-five students in its inaugural years, many of whom were teacher aides pursuing associate of arts degrees. One key outcome of the PTEP was that some of these Pueblo graduates (Donna Pino from Santa Ana Pueblo and Rachel James from Acoma Pueblo among them) would eventually become bilingual lead teachers in their respective community schools and participate in the development of Native literacy materials. The PTEP provided financial assistance and academic counseling to participants, encouraging them to pursue their bachelor of science degrees in elementary education and, for some, master's degree at the University of New Mexico. Although this initiative was a joint effort led by AIPC and the University of New Mexico, other support and interagency collaboration was provided through Title VII bilingual and federal Elementary and Secondary Education Act programs, the BIA, Title IV Indian Education Programs, mission schools, New Mexico public school districts, and many other New Mexico agencies and organizations (All Indian Pueblo Council n.d.).

In concert with these emerging developments, one of the first New Mexico–based organizations of Native American bilingual teachers and educators was established in the late 1970s as an outgrowth of linguistic training programs for Native bilingual teachers, initially convened as a collaborative training effort between the BIA, the University of Albuquerque, and field linguists from the Dallas-based Summer Institute of Linguistics. Native American teachers from Title VII programs, including several Pueblo members, participated in these summer institutes. First held on the University of Albuquerque campus in 1976, these programs introduced participants to basic linguistic and bilingual education courses aimed at supporting their work in orthography, Native literacy development, and Native bilingual education.

These institutes continued in subsequent years under the leadership of an independent group of Pueblo and Navajo bilingual educators, who in 1981 formed a non-profit organization, the Linguistic Institute for Native Americans.

Founding members included Gus Keene Jr. (Navajo/Acoma), Rachel James (Acoma Pueblo), Rena Henry (Navajo), Mary Tang (Jemez Pueblo), Teresa Gutierrez (Santa Clara Pueblo), and Christine Sims (Acoma Pueblo). Their efforts to provide training institutes for Native bilingual teachers came to be known as the Summer Institute of Linguistics for Native Americans (SILNA). The organizers of SILNA also collaborated with the University of New Mexico's Linguistics Department and College of Education to coordinate coursework credit and recruit the help of bilingual education professors such as Fred Carillo and Rebecca Blum Martínez. Sandra Johnson from Arizona State University was also recruited to assist with bilingual course instruction. All the core SILNA linguistic courses were taught by veteran linguists from the Summer Institute of Linguistics who had experience working with southwest Native languages, including specific dialects of the Keres, Tiwa, and Tewa Pueblo languages. Linguistic instructors at SILNA included Irvine Davis, a linguist who had worked on the Santa Ana-Keres language; Bea Meyers and Donna Gardner, linguists working on the Tewa and Tiwa languages, respectively; and Hilaire Valiquette and David McNiel, both of whom worked on the Laguna-Keres language. Additionally, former Pueblo students, such as Esther Martínez, who had completed advanced SILNA courses, assisted with tutoring and teaching basic phonetics classes.

Over the course of seventeen years beginning in the mid-1970s, New Mexico pueblos and other participants representing forty-four Native languages across the United States attended SILNA courses. These were held at several New Mexico institutions, including the University of Albuquerque, the Institute for American Indian Arts in Santa Fe, and the University of New Mexico. Notable participants included Esther Martínez (San Juan Pueblo member for whom the 2006 Esther Martínez Languages Preservation Act is named), Wilfred Garcia, (former San Juan Pueblo governor), Gus Keene Jr. (Navajo/Acoma Pueblo member who served as president of the New Mexico Association for Bilingual Education), Richard Little Bear (a Cheyenne tribal member who served as president of Montana's Chief Dull Knife Tribal College), and Lucille Watahomigie (Hualapai teacher who founded the American Indian Language Development Institute at the University of Arizona).

Beginning in 1990, LINA worked in partnership with the College of Santa Fe's Multicultural Education Program (MEP) to establish a permanent home for SILNA. The ongoing need for Pueblo bilingual teachers, combined with SILNA's focus on Native bilingual educators, made the Albuquerque campus of the College of Santa Fe an ideal location for establishing SILNA. Pueblo and Navajo students completing their undergraduate teaching degrees under the MEP could acquire some of their credits by taking SILNA courses in the summer. In the early 1970s, the LINA board, chaired by Christine Sims, in collaboration with the MEP, led by Henry Shonerd at the College of Santa Fe, initiated a proposal to establish a state bilingual certification process for Pueblo bilingual teachers.

The idea for certification, originally explored years earlier by a working group of Pueblo bilingual educators, had identified several issues specific to New Mexico Pueblo languages. Among these challenges was the fact that most Pueblo languages were unwritten, and no language proficiency assessments for Pueblo teachers existed. A key question, therefore, was how to determine the language proficiency of Pueblo bilingual teacher candidates who spoke these languages. This was addressed through the collaboration of LINA members and Pueblo educators, who agreed that New Mexico pueblos should have a say in certifying the language proficiency of Pueblo teacher candidates seeking a bilingual endorsement.

In 1973, a three-part certification process, developed in conjunction with the Multicultural Education Program at the College of Santa Fe. was presented by LINA chair Christine Sims to the New Mexico State Bilingual Advisory Committee. This was subsequently accepted by the New Mexico Bilingual Education Department in 1973, and the process was first utilized by the MEP at the College of Santa Fe, with several Pueblo teacher candidates who were Keres speakers completing their undergraduate teaching degrees. The process comprised three parts: written English responses to general questions about Native American bilingual education; a recorded oral statement in the target Pueblo language; and a videotaped teaching sample in the candidate's native language. The recordings were to be reviewed and verified by members of the candidate's language community, while the written responses and teaching sample were to be reviewed by Pueblo educators knowledgeable about New Mexico Native bilingual education and who spoke the same or a similar dialect of the applicant's Native language. The first Pueblo candidates certified as New Mexico Native bilingual teachers under this new process included individuals from Acoma and San Felipe Pueblos. These first steps in creating a Pueblo bilingual endorsement process for Pueblo bilingual teacher candidates afforded Pueblo peoples the opportunity to be directly involved in determining and verifying the oral proficiency of teachers from their own communities. It also opened the door for Pueblo teachers to obtain a state bilingual endorsement for the first time.

As the national landscape of Native American bilingual education shifted in the late 1980s, Native American language organizations and education groups came together to influence federal legislation in support of Native American languages. They began to coalesce in response to local bilingual program needs and a growing national English-only movement. Some of LINA's board of directors, for example, became involved in state bilingual education organizations. Gus Keene Jr., from Acoma Pueblo, served as president of the New Mexico Association for Bilingual Education (NMABE), as did Christine Sims, who served as NMABE vice president for one term and was later appointed to the New Mexico State Bilingual Advisory Committee.

The increased number of Native American bilingual programs in tribal, government, and public schools also spurred the need for technical assistance resources, especially for Title VII program grantees. The National Origin and Desegregation Assistance Center, for example, provided New Mexico school districts with technical assistance in complying with the *Lau v. Nichols* decision during the early 1980s. At the University of New Mexico, the American Indian Bilingual Education Center (AIBEC) provided a broader scope of training and technical assistance services to Pueblo and other tribal bilingual programs until its closure in 1984. AIBEC also served as an archival repository for some of the first handwritten literacy materials produced in Pueblo (primarily Keres, Tewa, Zuni) and Navajo bilingual programs. The collection was transferred to the University of New Mexico College of Education's Tierman Library after AIBEC closed. Some of these materials are now permanently housed in the resource library of the American Indian Language Policy Research and Teacher Training Center in the College of Education.

By the 1980s, as federal funding began to wane, New Mexico state bilingual funding for Pueblo language programs in public school districts increased. The Bernalillo Public School District, for example, established a multilingual program that included a Keres language component taught by Bill Martin, a Cochiti tribal member and a former SILNA student. With state funding, however, came new requirements for licensed Native bilingual teachers, language curricula, and assessment. For Native languages such as Navajo that had already been introduced into schools on the Navajo Reservation for several decades, written instructional materials were readily available. Cohorts of Navajo teachers had also been trained in bilingual education and were teaching in the Navajo language at least a decade earlier than most Pueblo languages. Nevertheless, bilingual programs serving Pueblo students in Bureau of Indian Education (BIE) schools located in Laguna, Santa Clara, Zia, and Isleta Pueblos, as well as in several public school districts, emerged during this decade.

As the 1980s came to a close, the national pendulum in support of federal education dollars swung more toward science, technology, engineering, and math (STEM) areas, specifically math and science instruction. Bilingual funding was no longer a priority for federal funding, and in local pueblos such as Acoma, the last of federal bilingual funding came to an end by 1985. For most pueblos, securing competitive federal dollars for bilingual programs proved increasingly difficult. The growing pressure of English-only movements also further weakened support for bilingual education, especially during this decade and thereafter.

By the 1990s, Native language communities across the country were seeing a critical language shift in their communities. This shift toward increased English use among school-age children was a phenomenon also emerging in many New Mexico Pueblo language communities (Benjamin, Pecos, and Romero 1997; Sims 2001). Within roughly two decades, between the 1970s and the early 1990s, it was apparent that a radical shift in Native language use had occurred. This shift represented a major reduction in the number of Native speakers among preschool populations and children entering school for the first time. By the early 1990s, Pueblo children in preschool and elementary schools in several pueblos were reported in several community-language surveys as being primarily English speakers (Benjamin, Pecos, and Romero 1997; Boynton and Sims 1997). Many reasons have since been postulated for this critical development occurring in such a short time, including the presence and influence of English-based Head Start programs that had existed in many Pueblo villages since the mid-1960s; the increased presence of English mainstream media (radio and television) in homes; increased time devoted to English-language immersion in school; and overall increased contact between Pueblo people and an English speaking mainstream society resulting from school and work (Benjamin, Pecos, and Romero 1997; Pecos and Blum Martínez 2001; Sims 2001).

In response to this emerging development, concerned Pueblo leaders, Pueblo educators, and advocates of language renewal gathered at the College of Santa Fe's Albuquerque campus in 1995. Organized by LINA organizers and University of California-Berkeley doctoral students from New Mexico pueblos, this meeting was also attended by several members of a small Tlingit community in southeastern Alaska concerned about revitalizing their Native language. The focus of this and subsequent language forums in Pueblo communities in the following years drew attention to the real possibility of Native languages falling into disuse and decline. Over the next several years, with funding support from the New Mexico Office of Indian Affairs, LINA organizers conducted a series of language forums, inviting members of other tribes outside New Mexico to share their experiences in revitalizing and teaching their languages. Karuk tribal members from northern California, for example, came to New Mexico at the invitation of LINA. This tribe, which Christine Sims had visited during her doctoral studies at Berkeley, had only a few remaining speakers. They shared their experiences in learning Karuk and their immersion approach to teaching language to their children and community.

This sharing of experiences and consciousness-raising about language-loss issues brought about a shift in the work of LINA. The organization continued to sponsor the annual summer SILNA programs, but after the mid-1990s, its focus shifted to providing training in language immersion approaches modeled on the Maori and Native Hawai'ian experiences and on the communicative teaching approaches used by the Karuk language community. Thereafter, LINA's training activities received annual funding support from the New Mexico Office of Indian Affairs for summer institutes and training mentorships for Pueblo members involved in community-based language revitalization initiatives. The Chamiza, Lannan, and McCune Foundations also supported this initial training work with Pueblo language speakers. Through this collaborative effort, Pueblo language speakers were introduced to teaching strategies and foundational work in planning community-based language immersion programs. Pueblos such as Acoma and Cochiti were at the forefront of Pueblo communities who developed some of the first summer immersion programs for youth from 1995 onward.

The passage of the Native American Languages Act of 1990/1991 generated renewed interest and advocacy for congressional funding in support of Native American language revitalization efforts. By 1996, competitive grants established through the Administration for Native Americans, a federal agency under the US Department of Health and Human Services, made it possible for pueblos such as Acoma to apply for such grants. These grants helped support the establishment of community-based language programs, materials development, and Native language teacher training in preparation for expansion into public schools in later years. As a new century began, several Pueblo language programs were being implemented in targeted public elementary and secondary schools with approval from local Pueblo leaders. By 2001, Cochiti and Acoma Pueblos had established language immersion classes in the Bernalillo Public School District and the Cibola County School District (Pecos and Blum Martínez 2001; Sims 2001). These efforts, however, did not occur without significant challenges.

In both Acoma and Cochiti Pueblos, efforts to strengthen Keres languages began as community-developed initiatives beginning in 1995. Native speakers from each community had been recruited to help teach the language during summer programs. Other adults, including grandparents, elders, and parents, helped with materials development and organized learning activities in their villages. The core teachings of these programs were based on each pueblo's unique culture and social life, and children who participated were thus immersed in the real-life application of language in their own community. As communities began to see the outcomes of these initial efforts and how children were beginning to learn their Native languages, an increased interest in supporting year-round language programs grew.

School administrators, for whom the idea of offering language immersion classes in local public schools was new, resisted the initiative. They were unprepared, for example, to have Native language speakers without degreed credentials teaching in their schools and to have language immersion classes without fully developed written language curricula—including lesson plans, written instructional materials, and formal language assessments—that were normally required to satisfy school regulations and state educational policies. Initially, it seemed that such requirements would be insurmountable. But by 2002, developments at the state level contributed to several definitive decisions specifically affecting Native language teaching in New Mexico public schools. This set the stage for specific agreements meant to support Pueblo and other tribal languages being taught in public schools that are still in place today.

Meeting the certification requirements for Native language speakers teaching tribal languages in public schools was one of the major hurdles Pueblo peoples faced as they considered allowing their languages to be taught in school settings. This particular challenge was fueled in part by the federal No Child Left Behind Act of 2002 (NCLB). This act required all public schools nationwide to be staffed with "highly qualified" teachers, and the New Mexico Department of Education extended this requirement to Native language teachers. The issue for Pueblo languages was that most fluent speakers did not hold regular teaching licenses, yet they were essential personnel with the skills needed to teach Pueblo language classes in schools.

Linked to this issue was the question of who would verify a Native speaker's language proficiency. This was a process that the state education agency could not do, as they lacked Pueblo staff who could speak these languages. Over the course of nearly two years, between 2002 and 2003, New Mexico tribes and pueblos worked collaboratively to address these issues, challenging the State Department of Education to recognize tribal sovereignty as the basis for working with them to identify and develop solutions to the Native language teaching issue. Ownership of language initiatives in schools was a critical element of tribal concerns, including the determination of language proficiency of Native language speakers who would be teaching in schools. An alternative pathway for certifying Native language speakers to teach in public schools was thus created, with the New Mexico Department of Education agreeing to allow the tribes to verify the language proficiency of their own community members. The Education Department's Certification Unit would then issue a 520 alternative certificate to the Native speaker, who would also need to undergo a background check. Tribes agreed that if they chose to have their language taught in public schools, they would enter into a memorandum of agreement with the Department of Education as a formal government-to-government protocol verifying that the tribe had an internal language-proficiency verification process in place. Additionally, in some local public districts, such as Bernalillo Public Schools and the Cibola County School District, individual pueblos entered into memoranda of understanding or letters of agreement stipulating specific parameters set by the tribe concerning the treatment of their languages in the schools. In these local agreements, decisions about who would teach the Native language, what would be taught, who the recipients of language instruction would be, and who would retain ownership of materials produced for their respective language classes would be determined by the tribe. In the case of Cochiti and Acoma Pueblos, these latter agreements with their local public school districts were just as critical as the state memoranda of agreement in maintaining the fidelity of tribal goals and approaches each had developed for teaching their languages in community-based initiatives that were now expanding into public schools.

Today, some fifteen years later, Pueblo language programs in New Mexico public schools continue to evolve. Some developments, such as the state's recent passage of the 2014 New Mexico Bilingual Biliteracy Seal (NMSA 22–1-9.1), which offers high school graduates the opportunity to earn a special seal on their diplomas, verifying their ability to speak and write in a language other than English, have yet to be assessed. How this will affect the Pueblo languages such as Keres, Zuni, and Tewa now being taught in some elementary and secondary public schools is a new challenge facing Pueblo communities.

Other developments in Pueblo language communities are also emerging in the form of early interventions focused on preschool children through full language-immersion initiatives. A newly established Montessori school for Cochiti Pueblo children, for example, represents an alternative instructional setting supporting children's Keres language development. The Keres Children's Learning Center, founded in 2012 by Trisha Moquino, a Cochiti Pueblo tribal member trained in the Montessori approach, provides a learning environment in which fluent Keres speakers are engaged with the children on a daily basis. The early results of the program are promising, as evidenced by the growing communicative skills in Keres of the four- and five-year-olds enrolled in this school. A second encouraging example is the recent transition of a Head Start program at Jemez Pueblo to a full Towa immersion program. Both these programs exemplify community-driven efforts to realign early childhood and preschool education in support of maintaining and building early foundations in a Pueblo language. While most of these children already know and speak English, the greater challenge is providing a solid foundation in the Native language, strong enough that as these children mature, they will continue to develop speaking abilities in two or more languages.

Critical support for these communities and other Pueblo language initiatives over the last decade has come from the American Indian Language Policy Research and Teacher Training Institute at the University of New Mexico, established in the College of Education in 2008 by Christine Sims, whose role in bringing attention to the critical need for training support and technical assistance to tribal language efforts has been key in her work in New Mexico as well as nationally. Upon invitation from Senator Daniel Inouye, vice chairman of the US Senate Committee on Indian Affairs, Sims testified before this committee in 2003 during public hearings for proposed amendments (S.575) to the 1990/1992 Native Languages Act. In 2006, at public hearings regarding the Recovery and Preservation of Native American Languages, conducted at the Indian Pueblo Cultural Center in Albuquerque by US representative Howard P. "Buck" McKeon, chairman of the US House Committee on Education and the Workforce, Sims again specifically addressed the need for training and technical assistance support for Native language teachers and tribal language programs. These hearings were instrumental in bringing forth Pueblo leaders' support for the Native Languages Act and eventual congressional passage of the 2006

Esther Martínez Language Preservation Act. Christine Sims and Rebecca Blum Martínez, who served as chair of the Department of Language, Literacy, and Sociocultural Studies in the University of New Mexico College of Education at the time, also developed a proposal to request congressional funding support for a Native American Language Center at the university, successfully submitting this as a University of New Mexico Federal Funding Priority in 2007. The proposal was selected and submitted to the New Mexico congressional delegation asking for their assistance.

Shortly thereafter, Sims received notice that seed funding for the American Indian Language Policy Research and Teacher Training Center (AILPRTTC) was being made available through a US Department of Education grant in 2008. Through its staff and graduate students, working with Sims over the years, the center has since developed an important training and advocacy network of Pueblo and tribal language teachers, language program directors, community leaders, and language advocates. They continue to meet and learn from each other's teaching experiences through the annual Native American Language Teachers' Institute, year-round language workshops, community forums, and the recently formed New Mexico Tribal Language Consortium. Together with the AILPRTTC, the consortium received seed funding in 2015 from the W. K. Kellogg Foundation to develop a nonprofit organization of tribal language teachers, program directors and New Mexico tribal members. The AILPRTTC has also developed special projects aimed at support for Pueblo language initiatives through summer training institutes, materials development workshops, and technical assistance for early childhood Pueblo language initiatives with the support of the McCune Foundation of New Mexico and the W. K. Kellogg Foundation.

PERSONAL REFLECTIONS

In reflecting upon the impact of bilingual education on New Mexico's Pueblo language communities over the past fifty-plus years, I am reminded that a major aspect of this history has also been about Pueblo people reclaiming the education of their children. United States federal government schools were the specific tool for implementation of assimilation policies that began in the late 1800s and continued well into the 1950s. These collective stories are still fresh in the memories of many Pueblos families and communities today, including my own. One of my grandfathers, born in 1897, was one of several Acoma Pueblo youth taken to government boarding schools in far-away places such as Chilocco,

Oklahoma, and Carlisle, Pennsylvania. As a result of his school experiences, my grandfather had to relearn his Keres language when he finally returned years later to the pueblo as a young adolescent. Both of my grandmothers also experienced boarding school life at the Albuquerque Indian School in the early 1900s, as did my own mother a generation later. A childhood friend of mine recalls being punished by her teacher for using the only English word she knew on her first day at the village government-run day school in the late 1950s. Her mistake was using the word "red" to refer to a dog she had spotted on the playground.

These recollections often bring to mind thoughts about how different such experiences of past generations of Pueblo children might have been had bilingual education been an acceptable form and policy of education in times past. I have often thought about how the disruption in language transmission over several generations might have been alleviated if only educators knew then about the benefits of being bilingual or perhaps in some cases, multilingual. At the same time, I am reminded about the resiliency and tenacity of past generations who held onto those languages despite early attempts to eliminate them. I think about those elders in different Pueblo villages who were already bi- or multilingual as a result of long years of contact and interaction with speakers of other Pueblo languages. In many of our villages, older generations will recall individuals who possessed these multilingual skills, some even becoming conversant in Spanish, long before the English language entered the picture. Had previous generations with their Native language skills and abilities been more fully embraced by educators and policy makers of the past, might we be in a different place than we are today in many of our communities? With the advent of bilingual education in the 1960s, a shift in thinking about Native languages as being a linguistic and cognitive strength rather than a liability certainly began to take place. A critical consciousness about needed changes in education policy would have far-reaching implications for what was to continue to develop in the latter half of the twentieth century and into the twenty-first century as Pueblo people began to exercise their own self-determination and take their place as educators in schools that had formerly eschewed Native language use.

I believe that this emerging advocacy and a growth in critical consciousness about the importance of maintaining Native languages has been a consistent long-standing perspective for most pueblos, where language has always been an integral part of cultural identity, traditional cultural practices, and Indigenous spirituality. More than ever, language today is one of the most critical foci in almost every Pueblo community, where continued survival of culture is dependent on the mother tongue. The challenge of maintaining, and in some cases re-strengthening, Native language use in the midst of English hegemony in today's society is now at the forefront for many pueblos. For centuries, these oral-based languages have existed within and have been primarily used among members of Pueblo villages. How these languages will continue to thrive among future generations is now the big question in these communities.

Over the years, as I have seen the evolution of bilingual education taking place in Pueblo communities, it is evident that many things could not have happened without a concomitant evolution of self-determination and ownership of education. The vision and goals of Pueblo communities for the education of their children have taken time to develop and come to fruition, often at different paces for various reasons. The one consistency, however, has always been the expectation that not only would future generations need to learn English to be able to navigate through mainstream schools and society, but that they would also one day return to give back to their communities. Learning and knowing how to speak the mother tongue has always been at the heart of this latter expectation. That being said, the work of promoting, advocating, and supporting the development of bilingualism among young Pueblo children today is still an unfinished work. But with recent developments, there are hopeful, promising signs as well. As recently as 2018, I was again invited to testify before the US Senate Committee on Indian Affairs to speak about the need for continuing the reauthorization of the Esther Martínez Language Preservation Act, which has assisted many tribes, including some of our own New Mexico pueblos, in planning and developing new language initiatives aimed at young children.

The hopeful signs I see in these language efforts are pueblos taking control over their local BIE schools and operating these as tribal controlled schools. This has taken place in at least four pueblos (Acoma, Laguna, Isleta, and Santa Clara) as of this writing, including Jemez Pueblo, where public charter schools were established by the tribe more than a decade earlier. Mentioned earlier in this chapter is another example of an independent nonprofit entity formed in Cochiti Pueblo in order to develop a new Montessori school. In Jemez Pueblo, the transformation of a federally funded Head Start program into a full Native language immersion setting has evolved for the last six years. And finally, a former boarding school, the Santa Fe Indian School, once operated by the federal government, is now collectively managed and overseen by the nineteen pueblos of New Mexico.

In each of these examples, Native language support has been a key aspect of exercising local control; in doing so, the intent has been to more fully support the teaching of Pueblo languages. These alternative developments and their future sustainability are important reminders, however, that there will always be a need for advocacy and continued education of policy makers, parents, educational administrators, language practitioners, tribal leaders, and community members regarding the strengths and benefits of bilingualism. I believe that these recent developments also reflect a necessary continuing process of clearly defining education on our own terms, where the possibilities for re-strengthening Pueblo languages are limitless, as long as we keep in mind the basic purpose and function of these languages in the past as well as in the present. These languages have been the foundations for building and maintaining intergenerational relationships, for use in governance and leadership, and for sustaining the cultural and religious life of Pueblo communities. And while public education can play a supporting role in helping Pueblo children learn and maintain these languages through Native bilingual programs, these efforts must always be guided by and implemented in a way that is mindful of and recognizes the necessary active role that Pueblos people must have in determining the teaching and evaluation of these programs. Today more than ever, there is a critical need to bring together all the resources necessary to ensure that Pueblo languages remain viable and that there will continue to be young generations of Pueblo language speakers in the decades to come.

REFERENCES

Adams, David. 1988. "Fundamental Considerations: The Deep Meaning of Native American Schooling, 1880–1900." *Harvard Educational Review* 58, no. 1: 1–28.
All Indian Pueblo Council, University of New Mexico, Pueblo Teacher Education Program. n.d. *Pueblo Teacher Education.* In the private collection of Christine Sims.
Benjamin, Rebecca, Regis Pecos, and Mary Eunice Romero. 1997. "Language Revitalization Efforts in the Pueblo De Cochiti: Becoming Literate in an Oral Society." In *Indigenous Literacies in the Americas: Language Planning from the Bottom Up,* edited by Nancy H. Hornberger, 114–36. Berlin: Mouton de Gruyter.
Boynton, Donna, and Christine P. Sims. 1997. "A Community-Based Plan for Acoma Language Retention and Revitalization." Unpublished paper prepared for the Pueblo of Acoma, Acoma, NM.
Davis, Irvine. 1964. "The Language of Santa Ana Pueblo." *Bureau of American Ethnology Bulletin* 191, no. 69: 52–190.

Leap, William. 1970. "The Language of Isleta, New Mexico." PhD diss., Southern Methodist University, Dallas, TX.

Miller, Wick R. 1965. *Acoma Grammar and Texts*. Berkeley: University of California Press.

Pecos, Regis, and Rebecca Blum Martínez. 2001. "The Key to Cultural Survival: Language Planning and Revitalization in the Pueblo de Cochiti." In *The Green Book of Language Revitalization in Practice*, edited by Leanne Hinton and Kenneth Hale, 75–85. San Diego: Academic Press.

Sims, Christine P. 2001. "Native Language Planning: A Pilot Process in the Acoma Pueblo Community." In *The Green Book of Language Revitalization in Practice*, edited by Leanne Hinton and Kenneth Hale, 251–68. San Diego: Academic Press.

Zaharlick, Ann Marie. 1977. "Picuris Syntax." PhD diss., American University, Washington, DC.

[PART TWO] Experimentation, Policies, and Legislation

This section highlights Nuevomexicano struggles to create a public space for the Spanish language, in particular in the educational realm. In chapter 4, Felipe González describes the history of the many efforts made by Spanish-speaking Nuevomexicanos to protect their language before, during, and after statehood. In early initiatives to establish a public school system during the territorial period, policy makers struggled to strike a balance between the need for the population to learn English and the desire of most Nuevomexicanos to maintain Spanish as a public and educational language. The question of which language would dominate in the schools would persist to the present day. Similar to the policies aimed at Indigenous languages, US legislators held New Mexico statehood hostage until Nuevomexicanos would acquiesce to the use of English in public schools. Given the linguistic reality of the general population and of the teaching staff, however, the sole use of English proved hard to enforce. Further, Nuevomexicano legislators were leery of the federal imposition of English and sought protections for the Spanish language in the state Constitution. Article XII, Section 8 in particular sought to provide Spanish-speaking children with the assistance they would need in learning English by requiring teachers to become bilingual in Spanish and English, and it would play an important role 150 years later.

Time and again, policy makers and educators attempted to include Spanish as an educational tool; notable among these were New Mexico governor Octaviano Larrazolo, Nina Otero-Warren, George I. Sánchez, and Joseph Montoya. Each time, the mostly Anglo boards of education and their Nuevomexicano allies passed educational policies that forbade any language but English in the public schools. These policies were both influenced and supported by national educational movements that sought to "Americanize" students attending public schools. New Mexican educators would encounter this federal influence on multiple occasions and at different time periods, as described in other chapters in this section.

The national civil rights movement of the 1960s and 70s brought opportunities for both Spanish-speaking and Indigenous communities to establish schools that would honor their native languages and assist children to learn English. One outgrowth of these efforts was the experimental Spanish Language Arts program begun in Pecos, New Mexico, in 1963, in which every child in that community was given an opportunity to utilize his or her native Spanish language for reading and writing. This program, developed by Henry Pascual, would become a model for later bilingual education programs in New Mexico and nationally. The presentation of this project at a national conference in 1966 in Tucson, Arizona, that focused on the educational needs of Mexican American students, together with similar presentations from other states, became the impetus for the development of the first national Bilingual Education Act (1968), introduced by Senator Ralph Yarborough of Texas and cosponsored by Senators Morris Udall (Arizona), Joseph Montoya (New Mexico), and others.

Although the national Bilingual Education Act was intended as a remediation for the difficulties faced by children who spoke languages other than English, in New Mexico, educators and policy makers had begun several years earlier creating policies that would allow children to use their linguistic and cultural assets in their education, passing the nation's first bilingual education statute in 1969. Considering New Mexico's struggle through its territorial days to defend and define use of the native languages within instruction, bilingual education seemed a natural fit.

Working closely with Henry Pascual at the New Mexico State Department of Education, Nuevomexicano legislators Roberto Mondragón, John Paul Taylor, Ray Leger, Jerry Apodaca, and many others developed and passed legislation over the years that would promote the use of two languages for instruction in New Mexico schools. Although there were those who opposed bilingual education, the support of the State Board of Education and of educators across the state was critical in establishing an educational reform movement that changed the conception and complexion of schooling.

Aided by these educational reforms and the ideas of the civil and farmworker rights movements, the families in Portales, New Mexico, successfully sued the

Portales School District for national origin discrimination in equal educational opportunities. The plaintiffs in this case highlighted the failure of the district to provide bilingual education. As a consequence, in the judge's decision, and in contrast to the *Lau v. Nichols* case, the district was required to provide bilingual education, an enormous victory for the families and for bilingual education broadly.

The efforts by Nuevomexicanos within the state were aided by the efforts of Senator Joseph Montoya, who served in the US Senate from 1964 to 1977. Montoya coauthored the first Bilingual Education Act and the revisions made in 1973. His professional relationship with Henry Pascual and other New Mexico educators was instrumental in obtaining funding for both Spanish-speaking and Indigenous educators. He was also instrumental in establishing the Presidential Cabinet Committee on Opportunities for Spanish-Speaking People. His leadership at the national level provided many New Mexicans with access to national committees, thereby giving New Mexico a voice in national educational policies.

PHILLIP (FELIPE) B. GONZALES

[4] Promise and Frustration *The History of Spanish-Language Bilingual Education in New Mexico, 1848–1970*

This chapter illustrates aspects of the extended history of Nuevomexicanos (descendants of the former citizens of Mexico) who attempted to establish effective Spanish-language bilingual teaching programs in New Mexico schools, only to be met by local resistance, national obstacles, and wrong roads taken, leading to failure at every turn. This legacy of frustration made for trends of low educational achievement rates among Nuevomexicano youth. It also had a greater effect of stripping Nuevomexicano generations of a right to their Spanish-speaking heritage, sometimes by policy. In my college days in the 1960s, I witnessed the consequences of this policy remiss. English-dominant Chicana and Chicano students yearned for a return to their ancestral culture partly reflected in the ability to speak Spanish. Some succeeded in varying degrees; many more found it too difficult to achieve. It should never have been that way.

The roots of educational inequality run deep in New Mexico. The 1848 Treaty of Guadalupe Hidalgo ended the two-year invasion of Mexico by the United States, gave the US title to New Mexico itself, and made most Nuevomexicanos American citizens. Unfortunately, New Mexico did not have common schools when it belonged to Mexico, that is, no educational foundation to build upon once the transition to American society was done. It would take some time before New Mexicans could build a school system from scratch. As two education scholars note, public education "as we define it today" was almost nonexistent during [New Mexico's] early territorial times" (Mondragón and Stapleton 2005, 133; Wiley 1965, 24).

The federal Organic Act of 1850, which made New Mexico an incorporated territory of the United States, could have provided assistance for school development. Education for the children of upper class Mexicans—large-land holders comprising about five percent of the population—was well provided by the Catholic Church. The schools of Bishop Jean Baptiste Lamy guided their students according to the educational norms of the Vatican in the Spanish language, with English learning included (Bullis 2012; McKevitt 1992; Milk 1980, 215; Read 1911; Steele 2000; Wiley 1965, 21). However, most Nuevomexicanos lived as hardscrabble farming and ranching villagers. Among them, researchers find, "a literary background was almost entirely lacking" (Tireman and Watson 1943; see also Hordes 2005, 199–201).[1] And for them, the Organic Act failed to provide monetary or training aid to establish public schooling (Hemsing 1953, 52).

Both American settlers and Nuevomexicano leaders saw the United States having an obligation to provide federal programs for integrating incorporated Mexicans into America's institutions (Horn 1963, 92; Milk 1980, 215; Sánchez 1940), public schools chief among them. A moral and practical imperative should have inspired Congress to provide schooling for a Spanish-speaking folk that became Americans through military conquest. In an 1853 memorial to Congress, the New Mexico Territorial Legislature, the majority of its members being Nuevomexicanos, pointed out the highly deficient means of education that existed in their territory compared to the rest of the United States (Bullis 1912; McKevitt 1992; Read 1911b, 16). "Time after time," it's been noted, "politicians memorialized Congress for direct appropriations of money to aid in the establishment of adequate free schools" (Nanninga 1942, 8). Virtually all New Mexico territorial governors and territorial legislatures in the first thirty years of annexation appealed to Congress for this purpose (Gonzales 2016; Holscher 2012, 31). The state constitutions that New Mexico citizens wrote in 1850 and 1872 included free education for New Mexico's youth (Cline 1985, 13). Congress denied these petitions for statehood.[2]

Some argue that Congress refused educational aid because the former citizens of Mexico spoke foreign languages, which would require special funds for instruction in English (Hodgkin 1906, 4; Nanninga 1942, 9). Others point to a policy of neglect, unrealistically expecting a compact people from a different culture to adjust to the American way of life on its own (Tireman and Watson 1943, 12–13). The withholding of full citizenship rights for a population forced to become part of the United States contributed to its socioeconomic subjugation, reinforced when settler entrepreneurs from the United States began to use fraudulent schemes to deprive the *nativos* of their large communal land holdings

(Atkins 1982, 2; Gonzales 2003). As Enrique Salazar, editor of the Las Vegas, NM weekly, *El Independiente*, put it in the 1890s, the protection of education that the federal government should have extended to Nuevomexicanos "in the first years after the conquest" was made worse because of the "discord and corruption that American scoundrels" had brought into the territory.[3] The bulk of Nuevomexicanos became Americans as an impoverished, rural proletariat (Deutsch 1987, 21-24).

Nuevomexicano leaders and a smaller group of Euroamericans (so-called Anglos) recognized that they must address the problem of education on their own. The territory's legislative assembly had authority to tax for education. The first attempts were halting. In the 1855-56 session, males whose property value exceeded $250 were taxed at a rate of one dollar. The following session repealed the tax. The 1860 legislature declared the establishment of territorial schools, in 1863 adding the office of territorial superintendent. However, the lack of financial support proved insurmountable. The 1869 session required communities to build schools, but enforcement out on the frontier proved impossible (Wiley 1965, 24-25; Nanninga 1942, 9-11, 12-14; Vaughn 1979, 2-3).

In 1871, at a time when 40,000 Spanish-speakers were illiterate (Bullis 1912), modernist Nuevomexicanos in the territorial assembly passed a meaningful public school bill. Each precinct had to appoint a qualified individual to set up a school. Attendance was made compulsory. Some precincts followed through but most could not, again, for the required local taxes and also for lack of qualified teachers. Moreover, controversy bogged down the process. Both Nuevomexicanos and a growing set of Euroamericans registered strong objection to the fact that Catholic priests were playing central roles in schools that were supposed to be "public" in nature (Everett 1984). In addition, as the largest educational institution in the territory, the Church received support from tax-generated revenues to run their schools. Euroamericans and Nuevomexicanos, most of them Republicans, charged that this violated the separation of church and state. In thrall with the secular public school movement growing in the United States, they pressured the assembly to stop awarding public funds to the Catholic schools. However, the mostly Nuevomexicano legislators voted to continue supporting the Church's educational efforts (see Everett 1984; Garrett 2005).

The rocky road to a public school system had its negative effects. The 1880 census reported 162 schools in the territory but only forty-six school buildings. Many teachers were untrained and ill equipped to deliver adequate instruction, much less utilize an effective bilingual pedagogy. With scant school attendance, over 60 percent of those over ten years of age were unable to read (Mondragón and Stapleton 2005, 135; Nanninga 1942, 17).

The issue of public education arose with considerable intensity in the late 1880s and 1890s in conjunction with a determined effort to have New Mexico become a state. Euroamericans streaming into the territory (Gonzales 2015) believed that Congress would not be receptive to statehood if New Mexico could not show that it had functioning public schools.

However, as New Mexicans persisted in a movement to achieve statehood, the question of what language the youth of the territory should speak arose, not least because the schools continued under Spanish-speaking Catholic influence. In 1889, Euroamericans, most of them Republicans, together with English-language newspapers and Republican Nuevomexicanos, attempted to pass a bill for a non-sectarian school system. Culturally conservative Nuevomexicano legislators, most of them Democrats, defeated it because it included English-only instruction and the appointment of a territorial superintendent of instruction to enforce the language requirement (see Everett 1984, 127–28; Lamar 2000, 162; Larson 1968, 167; Owen 1996, 172–73; Stratton 1969, 104–5). Republicans tried again in 1890 at a statehood constitutional convention. The constitution they drafted included a clause requiring the speaking of English as a requirement for voting. The majority Nuevomexicano electorate defeated ratification of the constitution (Lamar 2000, 165; Larson 1968, 168; Prince 2010, 48–59).

As more Nuevomexicano Republicans got elected to office, their constituencies shifted their attitudes toward secular public schooling. The emergence of unions helped them see its advantages. As one example, a chapter of the Knights of Labor in San José de Chama in Río Arriba County resolved to work for the progress of education for workers and support development of "the arts" for their utility in their trades and the improvement of their work.[4]

In 1891, the territorial legislature passed a comprehensive, non-sectarian public school law. It required that instruction be in the English language only, designed to hasten the assimilation of Nuevomexicano youth to American culture and quicken the prevalence of Anglo-American culture in the territory (Stratton 1969, 143–44; also see Milk 1980, 216–17). Also in 1891, the territorial legislature created the important office of territorial superintendent of public instruction (Cruz 2007).

Indicating the growing importance of Nuevomexicano advocacy for education, the Euroamerican governor appointed Amado Chaves New Mexico's first superintendent of schools.[5] Chaves had matriculated through Catholic schools, but as a Republican figure, he cleaved to American institutions, including secular education. Nine months after inauguration of the territorial public school system, Chaves' first official report affirmed the communities' support for the new school initiative:

> No opposition has been encountered in any part of the territory in the matter of introducing English-speaking teachers in districts where heretofore Spanish alone had been taught. In this connection I have to say that it is very pleasing to me to be able to state from personal observation that the greatest interest is being shown in the Spanish-speaking counties in behalf of the new law, which requires that the English language shall be taught in all the common schools of the territory. (Quoted in Prince 1892, 25).

According to Chaves, county boards of examiners had begun certifying teachers. He had the ""highest degree" of satisfaction in the progress being made by the "native [Nuevomexicano] children." The superintendent saw a bright future on the horizon. Before long, "every one" of the common schools of the territory would have "a competent teacher well versed in the English language and in many cases in both English and Spanish." Soon, no longer would there be a necessity for interpreters in the courts and the legislatures. And, a good business education was within the reach of all classes, "the rich and the poor alike" (quoted in Prince 1982, 26; also Thornton 1893, 379–80).

Chaves no doubt observed a tide of opinion turning toward public education, but his outlook proved too optimistic. The school law initiated what would become an enduring insistence on the part of school powers to give the English language preference in the classroom while restricting the Spanish language. At this early date, for instance, teachers in the rural districts had used Spanish language texts, perhaps because they themselves were Spanish-speakers. However, the school law stipulated that English, or English-Spanish texts had to be used but not Spanish-only books. From now on, school personnel would have to contend with the steady take-over by English in the teaching experience. Indeed, by 1907, no Spanish books would appear on the official list of school texts. At least in 1891, some administrative sensitivity to what language the people spoke obtained. In what one researcher calls "a concession to native Spanish speakers," the school code "ordered schools to furnish all forms, instructions, and explanations about how the schools worked in Spanish—ensuring parents would understand them" (Milk 1980, 217).

The 1891 measure required wholly Spanish-speaking districts to have teachers fluent in both English and Spanish. Educators in the territory promoted the notion that native Spanish-speaking students learned better from bilingual teachers. However, while Spanish remained the people's everyday language, the "pedagogical point of using Spanish," one historian notes, "was not to ensure that children would maintain literacy in their native language but rather served as a transitional process to help the students learn English" (Lozano 2018, 82).

In a major problem, many teachers in village areas lacked sufficient knowledge of English to be able to teach consistently in that language. It was therefore not possible to implement the new regulations even at a bilingual level, for the territory could not recruit native English speakers to work in remote Spanish-speaking pockets (Lozano 2018, 82). The school superintendent's report of 1893 pointed to the obstacle of teachers who were otherwise qualified to teach but not knowing Spanish for instructing Nuevomexicana/o pupils. The territory's normal schools needed to pay special attention to districts where English did not exist, the report argued. Otherwise, it would hardly be possible for teachers to succeed without some knowledge of Spanish. The superintendent made the same plea a year later. The legislature, however, would fail to heed the call for at least another decade (Milk 1980, 217).

Despite the priority of having Spanish-speaking children learn English as rapidly as possible, the first four superintendents of public instruction were Nuevomexicanos—Amado Chaves (1891–1897, 1904–1905), Plácido Sandoval (1897–1899), Manuel C. De Baca (1899–1901), and J. Francisco Chaves (1901–1904)—who sought to safeguard Spanish language learning in the rural schools. Chaves for his part pointed to the "paramount importance" of the language in the whole of the Americas, their being "of far greater practical value to our children than the rest of modern or dead languages." As Chaves noted here, "It is a crime against nature and humanity to try and rob the children of New Mexico of this, their natural advantage, of the language which is theirs by birth-right, to deprive them unjustly of the advantages, great and numerous, which those have who command speech in two languages" (in Lozano 2018, 83).

Professional Nuevomexicanos beyond education keened in on the need for bilingual education. When in 1893 a territorial councilman, Albert Fall, drew up a congressional bill for a "normal" school to train teachers in the southern New Mexico town of Silver City, councilman Félix Martínez amended it to include another normal school in Las Vegas, New Mexico. The journalist Nestor Montoya backed the proposal. For effective English-teaching in the schools, the idea of a normal school deep in the Spanish-speaking region of

New Mexico appeared to Montoya key for training future Nuevomexicana and Nuevomexicano teachers.[6] New Mexico Highlands University, a normal established in 1893, would indeed become an important college for Nuevomexicanos, but not until well after the 1890s.

Enthusiasm for public education surged again in 1898 when Harvey Fergusson, New Mexico's territorial delegate to Congress, guided passage of a bill to set aside public lands in New Mexico for lease to build a permanent school fund (Read 1911b; Smith and Gonzales 2011, 146). J. Francisco Chaves, the fourth superintendent of the Department of Public Instruction, commented wryly that it was "tardy justice" when Congress finally gave New Mexico lands to support the development of its schools (Sánchez 1940, 24).

Still, the problem of supplying schools in Nuevomexicano communities with qualified teachers continued as it would for some time. A 1904 opinion column in the Las Vegas weekly, *El Independiente*, likely by editor Enrique H. Salazar, called attention to a "radical defect" in the high school curriculum recently codified by the territorial department of instruction. Examinations used to hire teachers required exclusive knowledge of English when most of those available to teach were primarily Spanish speakers. The lack of bilingual education deprived the great majority of Spanish-speaking children of adequate language instruction, the essay noted. The writer recommended an amendment to the last school law to allow tests in Spanish for hiring teachers, making them equal to the exams given in English.[7]

It did not happen. Because of the prevailing bias toward English learning, no bilingual proposals passed before New Mexico became a state. The fifth and sixth public school superintendents were Euroamericans who did not support bilingualism, mirroring the national mood of growing xenophobia and pressures for Americanization, backed by US conflicts with Spain. For indeed, another major theme in the history of bilingual education involved dominant ideological currents in the United States acting powerfully to stem the prospects of bilingual education. As an example of how hegemonic perspectives worked to the detriment of education for the Spanish-speaking, Nuevomexicanos at this particular juncture suffered racialized views of themselves back East with the charge that to be a true American, one had to speak no other language than English (Larson 1968, 148).

New Mexico failed to gain statehood at turn of the twentieth century precisely because of this prejudice. In the principal instance, the members of the US Senate's Committee on Territories disdained Nuevomexicanos as a "mongrel" people with primitive customs and the inability to self-govern (Gonzales 2000, 1943, 63; Smith and Gonzales 2011, 6, 11). The Committee's chair, Indiana senator Albert Beveridge, conducted hearings in Las Cruces, Albuquerque, Santa Fe, and Las Vegas, only to find that the Mexicans there spoke Spanish only, or too much, and even used it in the courts and schools (Baron 1990, 98–102; Holtby 2012; Noel 2014, 31–32; Prince 2010, 95–101). Beveridge single-handedly sank New Mexico's bid for statehood. The powerful politician was blind to the fact that Nuevomexicanos had been conducting American style electoral politics and republican government in the Spanish language for over fifty years (Gonzales 2016).

After two decades of New Mexicans intensely lobbying on behalf of statehood, Congress passed the Enabling Act of 1910, which allowed New Mexicans to write a state constitution. The US Senate Committee on Territories made English language exclusiveness a requirement for granting statehood. School instruction should "always be given in English," the Act stated (New Mexico 1911, 37). To some observers, the English-only stipulation appeared "peculiar" among enabling acts for western territories (Moyers 1941, 486). The fact is that New Mexico educators still had rural districts with over 90 percent monolingual Spanish speakers (Lozano 2013, 272) at the same time that the Euroamerican suppression of Spanish continued to be in force, as represented by Senator Beveridge's continuing service as chair of the Senate's Committee on Territories (Larson 1968, 208-225).

The experience of US annexation stunted any hope for a healthy educational development in New Mexico, setting Nuevomexicanos (and indigenous populations) well behind in the struggle for social, cultural, and economic well-being. How best to teach Spanish-speaking children so that they could effectively learn English and standard school subjects would be the difficult question for the educational field in the first decades of statehood.

Article XII, Section 8, of the New Mexico State Constitution seemed to resolve the issue by providing for the training of teachers in the Spanish language at teacher-training schools, such as New Mexico Highlands University at Las Vegas (New Mexico 1911, 29). In the aim, teachers who were proficient in both the English and Spanish languages would be qualified to teach Spanish-speaking pupils, while providing "proper means and methods to facilitate the teaching of the English language and other branches" (New Mexico 1911). It is clear that the provision resulted from the concern of the Nuevomexicano delegates to the constitutional convention to provide for the inclusion of Spanish in the classroom against the hostility of Euroamericans to that goal (Gonzales-Berry 2000, 174–75;

Montez 1973, 371; Moyers 1947, 497). Still, interested parties interpreted the provision differently. In the eyes of one Nuevomexicano journalist, it did not mean the exclusion of Spanish as a language in and of itself, suggesting that a bilingual education could come out of a system of parallel language immersions.[8] On the other hand, it provided fuel for making English the only legitimate language of instruction. One Nuevomexicano response called it *"un insulto gratuito y un atentado de intervención en nuestros sagrados derechos"* (a gratuitous insult and an attempt to intervene on our sacred rights).[9]

It seems patently clear in hindsight that Spanish-speaking children needed instruction to kick off of a Spanish-language platform. Many in New Mexico believed this. The assumption aligned with the insight of Joshua Fishman, one of the most important sociocultural linguists, concerning language rights. "Every mother or father had the right to have his or her children grow up in his or her cultural tradition," Fishman declared, "to enact it, to be ennobled by it [and] to foster it." As Fishman continued, "That is a basic right, a natural right, an ordinary human right."[10] In New Mexico's public discourse following statehood, this approach meant advocating for what would be called "the bilingual method" (Lozano 2013, 278).

Advocacy would not come easy, however. In 1915, the State Board of Education (as it was called before becoming the New Mexico State Board of Education; Gonzales 2001, 126), held ultimate authority over the public schools (Wiley 1965, 42, 43), and it decided to hold the line in resistance to a clear and well-defined bilingual means of teaching English to Spanish-speaking children. Reinforcing this strategy, a language nationalism continued to course through the country. The so-called "language panic" around World War I, triggered by the German language prominently spoken in certain parts, equated language with national spirit. Foreign languages prevented assimilation, it was popularly believed, and worked against patriotism, a form of nativism that Theodore Roosevelt had effectively boomed while president (Baron 1990, 107–12; Gonzales-Berry 2000, 178).

Nuevomexicano politicians, whose percentage in the legislature saw a decline, attempted to pass laws to meet the teacher training provisions in the state constitution such as to suit bilingualism. In 1915, HB 198 allowed the teaching of Spanish as a separate subject in elementary and secondary schools (New Mexico Department of Education 1915, 104). Most members of the New Mexico Board of Education supported it, but only if a majority of county boards of education would direct the program, a difficult goal to attain. English-language textbooks were still required, but at least Spanish could be used orally to explain the meaning of English words (Getz 1997, 31; Moyers 1941, 496). It tended to subordinate Spanish into a foreign language and failed to address the problems of Spanish-speaking students in the classroom (Gonzales-Berry 2000, 177).

In 1917, Nuevomexicano legislators tried again to circumvent English-only with HB 51, which proposed to facilitate the teaching of English and Spanish by the bilingual method in the first, second and third grades (New Mexico Department of Education 1917, n. p.). HB 51 was strengthened by HB 155, passed in 1919, which required rural teachers to be proficient in the reading, writing, and speaking of both Spanish and English. In the concept, teachers could help Spanish-speaking pupils translate their English-reading lessons into Spanish (Getz 1997, 31; Moyers 1941, 497; New Mexico Department of Education 1919, 300). In the actuality of the classroom, instruction tended to be in Spanish with English studied incidentally, "if at all." As a result, the all-Euroamerican board of education returned to enforcing English-only, arguing that the wording of HB 155 allowed them to require this policy. The problem remained of how to give effective instruction in English to Spanish-speaking classmates in the early grades in a workable bilingual fashion (Moyers 1941, 534).

University of New Mexico Spanish professor D. B. Morrill criticized the school board's conformity to the national climate of excluding foreign languages. Taking Teddy Roosevelt's language ideology to task, he argued for teaching Spanish-speakers in their heritage language. Dealing with Spanish-language illiteracy would facilitate pupil's ability to read in English, Morrill posited. He challenged the teaching of English directly without Spanish aids, for, he maintained, if students picked up English through that procedure it would be only "incidentally." As Morrill concluded, the pupil's failure to learn substantial English would be "as complete as the theory [of direct English instruction] is ridiculous" (quoted in Gonzales-Berry 2000, 179–80).

In line with Morrill's position, Republican Governor Octaviano Larrazolo, who served in office in 1919–20, put Spanish instruction in territorial education front and center of his administrative agenda (Gonzales 2007). Hailing the teaching laws of 1915 and 1917, Larrazolo sent a request to the state legislature for a provision to require teachers in rural areas to speak and write in both languages. In the practical aim of the governor's plan, teachers would instruct their pupils such that they could translate their English reading into the Spanish language, "to the end that they may understand that which they read" (Gonzales-Berry 2001, 181).

Larrazolo, who was an immigrant from Mexico, had a greater vision: a truly bilingual state. In still another major theme in New Mexico's linguistic history, proponents advanced the argument that Nuevomexicanos belonged to the greater field of Latin America, and should therefore fully participate in it. Larrazolo kicked off the notion. To have New Mexico assist the United States compete with Europe for the commercial trade with Latin America, he proposed compulsory Spanish instruction for all students in all high school grades and in the four levels at colleges and universities with the compulsory use of bilingual textbooks. He called for tests to ensure that teachers be fully qualified to read, write, and speak Spanish.[11] One of Larrazolo's measures would have added the requirement of textbooks with English and Spanish pages facing each other. He even sought the penalty of withholding salaries of teachers who did not comply with bilingual instruction requirements (Gonzales-Berry 2001, 181–82).

The Spanish-language press and state legislators from his political party praised the governor's proposal. However, partisanship reared its head and in such a way as to reveal the inherent handicap of Nuevomexicanos having differing views on bilingual education. Democrats had always tended to balk at bilingual education, and here they cursed compulsory Spanish on the thought that it held back the Americanization of Nuevomexicanos. Antonio Lucero, the pro-assimilation former secretary of state, accused Larrazolo's program of reducing the importance of English, the language that, as he put it, "should always stand first because it was the language of government and because it was absolutely necessary for the individual's advancement in life." Teach Spanish in a subsidiary fashion, Lucero demanded. Administratively, Lucero felt that making the teaching of Spanish a state requirement served to undermine the autonomy of the local school district, and, in any case, he did not believe there to be a sufficient number of Spanish-qualified teachers in New Mexico to comply with Larrazolo's program.[12]

In *La Bandera Americana* in Albuquerque, the Republican editor Nestor Montoya resented the Democratic Party implication that speaking Spanish meant a lack of patriotism, charging it with only wanting to discredit the governor. Republicans hailed the instruction in Spanish being provided by the Christian schools of Santa Fe, claiming that it produced "the most expert and educated linguists, as much in English as in Spanish, that the state had ever known." Students came out maintaining both their patriotism and capability, Montoya argued. "It's not the language that produces patriotism," he editorialized, "but rather, the heart [that does], and the *Neo-Mexicanos* are patriots of the heart, as much in one language as the other, or in both. Witness the registry of the past and present wars written with the blood of our youth."[13]

Republican state senators Antonio Sedillo and R. P. Barnes worked to have Larrazolo's program implemented. Their bill would have made Spanish compulsory for students in all the state's institutions of higher education, and require them to take Spanish each year they were in college up to four years. It did not help that some Nuevomexicano educators rejected the proposal. The State Senate Education Committee redesigned the bill to require high schools and colleges to provide instruction in the reading, writing, and speaking of Spanish as an option for students. The legislature amended a section to have all branches of study in the schools taught in the English language while permitting Spanish reading for monolingual Spanish pupils. Another revision to the bill provided for the employment of Spanish-speaking teachers in schools where the majority of pupils were Spanish speaking.[14]

It differed from what Larrazolo envisioned for a dyed-in-the-wool bilingual state. Even then, the New Mexico Board of Education took a dim view of the new law. Flexing its power, the board announced a continued commitment to the Americanizing mission of America's public schools regardless of the bill's intent (Gonzales-Berry 2000, 183). Waging the good fight, Larrazolo sponsored a conference to focus on the "pedagogical phases and the literary value of the Spanish language." In his opening address, the governor posed English and Spanish as not antagonistic to one another. A linguistic expert from the University of Illinois emphasized the need of Spanish acquisition in the context of a growing interest in pan-Americanism. A prominent set of New Mexicans—including the Nuevomexicanos Atanasio Montoya, Antonio Lucero, and Adelina Otero-Warren—debated methods of Spanish language instruction. One session featured the experimental instructional techniques of a teacher in the northeastern New Mexico town of Raton. A group of teacher participants decided to organize a New Mexico branch of the American Association of Teachers of Spanish.[15]

The discourse over language education spilled onto the public forum. Larrazolo publicized his views on the proper ways to carry out bilingual instruction, emphasizing the need for teachers to translate English terminology into Spanish.[16] Citizens weighed in on total English instruction versus bilingual approaches for Americanizing foreign-language groups. The National Educational Association pledged its support of Larrazolo.[17]

Larrazolo won a split decision, but only in the short run. The State Department of Education reluctantly and half-heartedly implemented the bilingual laws.

However, their weak guidelines did little to provide professional guidance to Spanish-speaking or English-speaking teachers needing training in Spanish. Many New Mexico educators used bilingual teaching on their own in their local schools. One researcher says it represented "a means of treating Hispano children with dignity, thus enhancing the learning process" (Getz 1997, 38, 32). However, countervailing arguments justified the practice of promoting assimilation Americanism in the schools.[18]

In 1923, the New Mexico Board of Education overturned Larrazolo's bilingual initiatives. In addition, a reactive legislature repealed the law of 1917, which provided for the teaching of reading in Spanish and English (considered a bilingual method), and even nullified Spanish as a separate curricular subject. The aim was clearly to reinforce the mission of holding English up as *the* language of instruction and learning, rejecting any suggestion that the child should also become literate in Spanish (Getz 1997, 31; Moyers 1941, 497). Making English dominant in the classroom proved more effective in the urban areas where English prevailed in the community (Lozano 2013, 275).

The contention did not end there. Liberal teachers and professional educators pressured the board of education to have English taught from a Spanish startpoint, not the faulty "direct method." The board, however, stood by the prevailing national sentiment that language in the schools should serve as an instrument of Americanization. Neglect of the special problem of teaching English to Spanish-speaking children followed from the national movement to have school curricula standardized in favor of common American culture. By 1930, the Department of Education's Course of Study pushed English instruction solely, except with regard to the first grade, with monolingual Spanish-speakers teaching in a separate classroom. Nuevomexicanos who spoke English proceeded directly to the regular first grade. Meeting the special needs of Spanish-speaking students meant separating them for a customized course and withholding them from their respective chronological age group, thereby consigning them to over-age status in their grade level throughout their school careers (Getz 1997, 34, 36–37, 39).

In the 1930s, the concept of the "community school" became the rage. In one of the first instances in New Mexico, Santa Fe County school superintendent and Nuevomexicana Adelina Otero-Warren turned to cultural preservation to perfect the curriculum of the schools in her district. Otero-Warren was a core member of the Nuevomexicana teaching element, representing the "feminization of the Hispanic teaching force" (Deutsch 1987; 67-68; Nieto-Phillips 2004, 200). It was, Otero-Warren held, the way for Nuevomexicano youth to attain the life advantages of the United States while preserving modicums of their home customs. Based on John Dewey's progressive principle of connecting school and community through daily activities, Otero-Warren sought to preserve and teach the Spanish language as the way to bring closer cooperation between school and home. She strongly believed that the schools had a responsibility to help Nuevomexicano children achieve fluency in both languages, and that the legislature should endorse the idea of teaching Spanish in elementary schools. Otero-Warren reinforced the argument that poor instruction in English in the primary grades held Spanish-speaking children back and contributed to high dropout rates. The untrained teacher was the greatest handicap the non-English speaking child endured, she argued. The teaching of English to Spanish-speakers required sympathy and familiarity with students' personal experiences, including home life. Developing "comradeship, friendliness, and mutual belief'" would free the child from embarrassment and self-consciousness (Getz 1997, 39-41).

Few New Mexico educators favored the use of Spanish in the classroom, however. State officials pressured teachers to instruct students in English and to discourage or suppress the use of Spanish while teaching. A defiant Otero-Warren urged her teachers to employ Spanish in school through songs, plays, and games, informally imparting the important message to students that their language was worthwhile. While Otero-Warren offered a model for curriculum reform, few state officials took notice. Otero-Warren's work as superintendent thus failed to change the dominant pattern of education for Spanish-speaking youth (Getz 1997, 40–45).

Yet the notion of the community school remained alive in New Mexico, another instance to be described below. At the same time, the public schools in the Southwest began to rely on the Stanford-Binet intelligence quotient (IQ) for gauging school success. University of New Mexico psychologist B. F. Haught conducted IQ testing among Nuevomexicano and Anglo youth. From the resulting distribution of scores, he concluded that, "the native intelligence of the average Spanish child was lower than that of the average Anglo child." Haught found that the IQ scores of older children, who presumably knew English better because of greater exposure to the English-speaking world and contact with Anglo counterparts, were no better than those of children in the lower grades. He therefore concluded that a "language handicap" could not account for the low school performance among Nuevomexicano pupils (Haught 1931).

Two unwarranted suppositions followed from Haught's findings. In one, Spanish-speakers were vulnerable to the stereotype of being inferior in intelligence "as a *race*" (Getz 1997, 46, 50). In the other, bilingual education appeared ineffective as a means of educating Spanish-speaking children. The activist scholar George I. Sánchez, working in the Bernalillo County school district, conceded that heredity could possibly serve as a partial explanation of intergroup differences on mental tests and therefore special problems in Anglo-dominant schools. However, he strongly recommended controlling for environmental and linguistic factors, as well as differences in personal, social, and cultural histories and milieu. In particular, he highlighted linguistic differences in the home environments by ethnicity. For example, eighty-four words appeared in the wording of the Stanford-Binet test for grades three through eight that, he said, did not appear in the every-day vocabulary of Nuevomexicano children. Sánchez, who became an important early critic of culture/class biases in standardized tests (Blanton 2014), pointed out that a lack of comprehensive English terminology hurt Spanish-speaking youth. A lack of English vocabulary may have hampered Mexican American schoolchildren, but in addition, their poor development in Spanish made education doubly detrimental. He concluded that IQ testing in and of itself was culturally detrimental to Spanish-speaking students (Sánchez 1934a, 1934b; for a review, see López and Samora 1977, 107–9).

The kind of biological determinism that Haught promoted did not pause to consider whether extra-psychological factors contributed to the unsatisfactory scores on standardized tests among Nuevomexicano and Mexican-American youth. The League of United Latin American Citizens and progressive education colleagues agreed with Sánchez, arguing that a language-intensive kindergarten classroom for Spanish-speakers would help struggling students. However, the organization also wondered if it could make up for the effects on education of deep levels of social inequality (Blanton 2014, 30–31).

One community school effort for dealing with the problem of poor Nuevomexicano reading attempted to control for environment in light of standardized IQ measurement of school performance. University of New Mexico education professor Loyd S. Tireman counted himself among the nation's progressive education reformers (Bachelor 1991, 3–8). In 1930 he established the San José Training School, an elementary school experiment, in San José, a Spanish-speaking, working-class community south of Albuquerque. The first San José cohort consisted of 524 students up to grade eight. Many were over-age for their grade placement. In his brand of progressivism, Tireman explicitly rejected the bilingual method of using Spanish in order to get students to transition to English, especially in the first year of school. The research literature did not support the effectiveness of such a procedure, he stated. Instead, he initiated modest Spanish-language instruction, involving one thirty-minute period of Spanish a day, in grades one through five and making it an elective in grades five through eight (Bachelor 1991, 40; Tireman 1951, 76).

In his key policy, Tireman seems to have followed the one notion of George Sánchez that Spanish-speaking children were hampered by lack of exposure to everyday English. The San José curriculum thus relied on a specially enhanced English-language curriculum to compensate for the observation that Spanish-speaking homes did not have sufficient English-language materials to enable everyday English learning compared to the typical Anglo home. Spanish-speaking children were placed before a host of English-language books, newspapers, recreational pamphlets and other published materials. Specially trained teachers, a number of Nuevomexicanas, provided individualized tutoring in English and minimal Spanish language development. The experiment included the pre-first concept, which, in actuality, added to the over-age problem. Tireman eschewed training in formal reading in favor of English-talking exercises, play exploration, and child-development activities around Anglo-assumed norms such as promptness, hygiene, and neatness, before taking pupils on to intensive reading. Eventually, a community school design worked with families to encourage the kinds of home activities thought to enhance school learning while encouraging participation in such community agencies as health committees. Hispanic arts and crafts played in, although in an English-language format (Tireman 1936, 4–7, 32; 1951, 28, 83–84, 105–8; Bachelor 1991, 73–77).

Tireman's focused, ambitious, and well-funded project (by the General Education Board, the University of New Mexico, and Senator Bronson Cutting) drew the praise of educators, school administrators, and politicians (Tireman 1936, 5; Moyers 1941, 563–67). For indeed, school attendance improved such that a state education program adopted San José's teacher training component. However, the substantive effects of the experiment proved disappointing (Bachelor 1991, 49–53). Standardized school proficiency tests (Stanford Achievement and Gates Reading) across five years for five thousand Spanish-speaking children, and compared to a couple of control schools, showed mixed results. While group achievement and English-proficiency grew steadily up to three years (including pre-first), the scores scattered out significantly in the middle and higher grades. In Tireman's disconsolate conclusion, "San José has reason to be deeply concerned over the fact that with all the effort put forth and with all the emphasis on reading, the grades above the second are below norm" (Tireman 1936, 32). Tireman did not know why, as he conceded. He called for further instructional experimentation, insisting that "we must improve the teaching procedure" (Tireman 1951, 36, 29).

Just as the San José experiment wound down with low enrollments (Bachelor 1991 61), another opportunity fell onto Tireman's lap. In 1937, Cyrus McCormick III, heir to a harvest machine fortune, funded a new school in the village of Nambé, eighteen miles north of Santa Fe. He and Joseph Granito, Santa Fe County superintendent of schools, asked Tireman for assistance in developing a curriculum for the Nambé school. Called *La Comunidad* (The Community), the facility was founded on the concept of "community cooperation." "Grave concern" over the education of Nambé children led Granito and McCormick to ask if there were some way to "bring a more practical program" to the school. Tireman agreed to direct the work of adjusting the school's curriculum "to better fit the needs of the people and the children." Nambé parents, not happy with the content of the curriculum their children had been receiving, approved of the proposal to recruit Tireman. Granito would take responsibility for recruiting teachers, and McCormick committed to completely subsidizing the school for five years (Bachelor 1991, 64–66; Tireman and Watson 1943, 8–9).

In this endeavor, Tireman rejected the standard academic principle that schools should gear students toward higher education. Such an approach did not work for children like those in Nambé, Tireman opined. As he declared, "The curriculum must be made to fit the needs of the child." Tireman and Granito saw the majority of the folks remaining in Nambé, as their parents had before them, in spite of a lack of sufficient acreage to allow their plots to thrive. Consequently, the Tireman team reported, "we said quite frankly that our job is not to prepare these children for college but to live happier and more efficiently in this community" (Tireman and Watson 1943, 14, 15), a quite strong notion of "community school" indeed.

Even though three of its six teachers were Nuevomexicanas (Tireman 1939, 2), *La Comunidad* retained the overbearing emphasis on the English language. It was a pedagogy that had ruled in the San José experiment. In the key difference, the Nambé approach had students take the English language out of doors. Adapting reform efforts from other rural regions of the country, it involved two aspects: the inclusion of "other agencies of education which are ordinarily relegated to the hours outside of the schoolroom," and relying on "outdoor laboratories," that is, the natural environment. Having the students educated while assisting in community development formed a hallmark of *La Comunidad* (Tireman 1951,

232, 234–36). Language instruction tied into objects found in the community (Bachelor 1991, 84–88).

La Comunidad ended in 1942 over parent dissatisfaction with the educational progress of their children and the disruptions of an educated activist who called the school an example of Anglo control of the Nuevomexicano people. At this point, Tireman's efforts to revolutionize Nuevomexicano education ended (Bachelor 1991, 97–102).

One education historian sees Tireman as well intentioned but embodying the blind spots of Anglo progressivism: over-reliance on strict scientific methods, statistical measurement, quantifiable proof, and "teaching to the test." In his rapid assimilation approach, the gap between emphasizing the community and forgetting native language was too wide (Getz 1997, 85–86). In his pronounced bias toward the English language, Tireman considered it important for English-speaking students to effectively learn Spanish in the early years, but the reverse did not hold. As he wrote, "For Spanish-speaking children, the problem is different. If the child is struggling to acquire English, there is quite a possibility that a period of Spanish each day will be detrimental." Tireman justified this position based on research in Puerto Rico, which he interpreted to mean that it was unhelpful to have students speak only English for a time and then have them switch to Spanish-only for a shorter period. He felt that the most reasonable compromise, until further data came in, was to begin Spanish in the upper grades. He chose to go along with the view in New Mexico that English instruction "must come first," not for patriotic reasons, but for the science of learning (Tireman 1948, 174, 175–76). In the end, Tireman's failure derived from his inability to translate culture into academic learning.

The Great Depression posed the danger of New Mexico school closures. The New Deal, President Franklin Roosevelt's program to provide federal relief for the whole country, provided resources for the nation's schools. To New Mexico, the Federal Emergency Relief Act provided teacher relief funds in three allotments from 1933 to 1935. The grants allowed schools to remain open in Taos, Rio Arriba, Union and Sandoval Counties. In addition, Governor Clyde Tingley leveraged federal support to launch a major school construction project (Forrest 1989, 107, 109-110). The resulting schools were linked to the new vocational programs that the New Mexico Department of Education built with funds from the Emergency Education Program. In Nuevomexicano communities, the vocational program, headed by Brice Sewell, state supervisor of vocational trade and industrial education, focused on traditional arts-and-crafts. The specialization in "hand trades" (tanning, leatherwork, weaving, cabinet making, farming) would provide for "self-improvement" in the production of "traditional" Hispanic arts. Participants were educated in small business practices. The plan called for the workshops to become independent economic resources for localities (Sewell 1935, 1936).

The New Deal vocational schools served adult education, but they became remarkably successful in northern New Mexico, not least because youngsters were also included. As one historian finds, "The classes were extremely popular with students of all ages. In one Hispanic community a grandfather and grandmothers, father and mother and their four children all enrolled in the same class to learn to read and write." A modicum of bilingualism operated. In one school, for example, instruction in the practicalities of farming was in English, but "class discussions were in Spanish and the evening concluded with the singing of Spanish folk plays" (Forrest 1989, 110-111). The project held promise for community education. But of course, the program would soon be interrupted by World War II.

By the late 1930s, Nuevomexicano spokespersons, including editors of Spanish weeklies, were reawakening to the necessity of school classes to prepare rural youth for college and bring teachers, doctors, dentists, and pharmacists to the villages (Getz 1997, 87, 110–11, 116–17). Educators, legislators, and other interested parties highlighted school bilingualism just as they did right after statehood.

In 1938, for example, the Taos County Teachers Association issued a call to the state education administration to incorporate English classes in the primary schools in a graduated immersion and to teach Spanish grammar and composition separately. As it was thought, this method of putting English and Spanish on an equal footing would result in perfectly bilingual students. Association members stressed the shame that Nuevomexicano children felt over their home language due to its lack of legitimacy in the schools. As they noted, "Spanish speaking students should take pride in the ability to use correct Spanish as well as English, and they should be proud of their historical and cultural heritage" (Nieto Phillips 2004, 202-03).

Of course, a substantial amount of training and supervision would be required for such a shift in curriculum, one that the state was not prepared to institute. Yet the desire for bilingual education among Nuevomexicano legislators did not subside during World War II. In 1941, state senators Joseph M. Montoya (D-Bernalillo) and Ralph Gallegos (D-Rio Arriba) submitted SB 3, requiring courses in the subject of Spanish for all fifth through eighth graders in schools with at least three teachers or ninety regularly attending students. Teachers would have to complete substantial Spanish coursework across three years. (Lozano 2013, 282–83).

Once again, a heated debate sparked up among stakeholders in Santa Fe, Albuquerque, and Las Cruces. To many, SB 3 appeared too strong. Some Spanish-speaking state representatives opposed it as antithetical to wartime Americanism. Two legislators from southern New Mexico countered SB 3 with the weaker HB 24, requiring only a single Spanish course prior to high school graduation, based on the opinion that compulsory Spanish in the elementary schools lacked popular acceptance. For bilingual stalwart Nina Otero-Warren, still the Santa Fe school superintendent, SB 3 appeared too weak. The teaching of Spanish had to involve all the elementary grades, Otero-Warren argued. In the assessment of the presidents of four state universities, SB 3 would have little impact without sufficient teacher training, financial support, and preliminary educational studies of Spanish instruction (Lozano 2013, 280–283).

SB 3 passed after US senator Dennis Chávez campaigned for it at a joint session of the New Mexico legislature. The New Mexico Board of Education had responsibility for enforcing the act. Under its administrative reign, "compulsory" turned out to be relative. District boards of education granted exceptions to some of their schools. The program was greatly undermined when the school board allowed objecting parents to pull their children out of Spanish courses if they chose to do so (Lozano 2013, 282–83; 2018, 238–39).

Taking up the charge, New Mexico Highlands University professor Antonio Rebolledo teamed with elementary teachers from throughout the state to produce a series of bulletins with instructional suggestions and materials for best practice Spanish-teaching (Tireman 1948, 171). The Rebolledo proposal focused on teaching native Spanish-speaking youth to read in Spanish and understand vocabulary, pronunciation, and grammar. However, support for improving the rate of high school graduation was not the point, but rather, the retrograde aim that Lloyd Tireman introduced at Nambé, having students gain some literacy so that, when they dropped out of school, it would help them gain employment in their ancestral environments. A job as an inheritance of parental lands seemed to be the value (Getz 2005, 96–97; Lozano 2018, 225).

Ironically, Rebolledo recommended stronger Spanish language practices than those in SB 3. In his plan, instruction in Spanish would occur in the first three grades, with English introduced slowly after students had adequately learned to read and write. Students would secure literacy in the language they understood. Introduction to the foreign English language would follow. It seems now like a sound and appropriate procedure, even though the anti-segregation laws in the state constitution would be violated by permitting separate language instruction in schools with a majority of native Spanish speakers. It was justified on the idea that a heterogeneous classroom hindered effective curriculum change and benefitted Anglo students mostly. In 1943, the legislature failed to adopt Rebolledo's plan, but it did create the new position of state supervisor of Spanish instruction (Lozano 2013, 289–90).

That seems to have been the extent of it in the early 1940s. As an effect of the war, New Mexico came increasingly to reflect the curricular patterns of mainstream schools nationally. Another wave of education nationalism landed. Historian Lynne Marie Getz (2005, 98) finds New Mexico coming under the propaganda influence of United States commissioner of education John Studebaker. Studebaker had exhorted Americans to turn to a "new learning" based on "truly democratic process" to ward off totalitarian doctrines. The commissioner stressed the responsibilities of adult citizenship, and emphasized the public forum as the site of developing critical independent thinking and objective analysis (Kunzman and Tyack 2005, 326, 337). His views had their lingering effects during the war. Educators in the various states were hit by the necessity of inculcating democratic values in the classroom such as to meet Studebaker's standards. To the New Mexico State Board of Education, the whole emphasis on civic unity in "The American Way" (Kunzman and Tyack 2005, 328) included strong attention to English in the schools. The board informed teachers of the need to adjust their curricula to an entirely English format while dropping courses not essential to the war effort and civic mobilization (Getz 2005, 98).

While holding true to Americanism and the value of English for the nation, Senator Dennis Chávez exalted Spanish as a "priceless" cultural heritage. However, in something of a shift from his previous strong stand on the value of bilingualism for youth development, he now highlighted Spanish for its utility in foreign and wartime policy. Georgia Lusk heard the tune and used it in her role as New Mexico superintendent of public instruction. To her, Spanish instruction and development of proficiency in speaking and reading Spanish helped children appreciate "other peoples' culture." In truth, the perspective that a better understanding of Latin Americans via knowledge of their language deflected from the importance of Spanish for school performance. The phrase "English-speaking culture" stood superior to Spanish-speaking culture. The nation's hemispheric relations superseded Spanish's intrinsic value for a student's cultural background (Lozano 2013, 271–72, 290–91).

It did not help that, with Nuevomexicanos, now a clear minority in the state population, a severe teacher shortage emerged. Many of the Nuevomexicanas who composed the backbone of the teacher corps in the northern villages left for better paying jobs or to serve in the Good Neighbor program. "Back-to-the-land" initiatives became obsolete in the schools as New Mexico's economy shifted to technology. Teachers from out of state did not really understand Nuevomexicano culture, and as the war waged, even they were not of sufficient number to meet school demands. Meanwhile, one-third of Nuevomexicano men under twenty-five went to war and most of them had not finished high school (Getz 2005, 98–102).

The 1950s Cold War era shifted the national perspective on public education. An explosion of interest in education emanated from the initial explorations of outer space. A focus on science excellence opened up a "hysterical cry" over the inadequacy of America's school systems (Wiley 1965, 153). Economy-minded interests demanded concentrations in science and mathematics to the detriment of the "soft" social sciences and humanities. School officials tightened requirements, raised the minimum number of credits for graduation, and rewarded the "gifted" student. Passage of the National Defense Education Act in 1958 subsidized the teaching of science and math in public school districts (Wiley 1965, 86, 88, 89), leaving projects like bilingual education by the wayside.

New education facilities supported by the federal government helped New Mexico materially, but the war disrupted educator careers. Energies and attention were siphoned out of reform initiatives, including bilingual education (Getz 2005, 109). Increases in Anglo immigration caused New Mexico to embrace standardized curricula more thoroughly than before. But also, the patriotic weight of the war encouraged upwardly mobile Nuevomexicanos to value assimilation for themselves and their children. To take advantage of new opportunities in science, technology, and business, middle-class Nuevomexicano parents tended to think the time right to demand an education that prepared their children alongside Anglo counterparts. In doing so, "they might have been prepared to sacrifice certain aspects of their own cultural heritage" (Wiley 1965, 109).

Indeed, up to the late 1960s, Nuevomexicano children and Mexican Americans in the Southwest encountered strict prohibitions on speaking Spanish in the schools. Teachers inflicted corporal punishment or detention on children for speaking Spanish informally in the classroom or schoolyard (Carter 1970, 97–98; Zamora 2009, 80). Speaking Spanish could bring on fines for parents or even expulsion to students (Baron 1990, 166). As one observer at the time noted, "Children have been taught to forget the 'foreign' ways of their fathers. Children have been cajoled, enticed, threatened, and punished for speaking Spanish. Children have been beaten" (Steiner 1967, 209). At least the National Education Association sounded the alarm regarding the harm in self-worth handed to Spanish-speaking youth at the hands of punitive practices in the schools (Montez 1973, 377).

The "problem" of teaching English and core courses to Nuevomexicano pupils persisted into the late 1960s. The US Commission on Civil Rights found 36 percent of New Mexico's Mexican-American first-grade pupils not speaking English as well as average Anglo peers. One of every four such students left school, and among those who remained, 54 percent scored below reading grade level. The commission recognized that New Mexico's largest minority group, the Spanish speaking, had educational problems nurtured greatly by a language communications tension, which, a contemporary critic noted, "an educational system must learn to understand and rectify" (Montez 1973, 364, 365).

Spurred in part by the Supreme Court's *Brown v. Board of Education* decision of 1954, forces for social reform in the Sixties led to federal intervention in public schooling.[19] For a change, the national trend proved encouraging, not repressive, for bilingual education. The era of Civil Rights extended to the 1970s with an array of congressional enactments meant to improve the education of women, minorities, the poor, and handicapped. Significant resources from federal and foundation agencies helped New Mexico deal with the problem of educating minorities. The Elementary and Secondary Education Act of 1965, mandating education funds to deal with poor children enrolled in each public school district, exemplified such laws (Colton and Baca 1994, 209). Head Start, for three- to five-year-olds provided important early childhood learning as well as child care for working-class parents. The non-profit Southwestern Cooperative Educational Laboratory (1968) disseminated information on the latest techniques for dual language skills development. The quest for suitable bilingual education programs for Mexican Americans returned. Nuevomexicanos and Mexican Americans generally went full circle to an appreciation of their vital heritage (Getz 2005, 109).

A consciousness around civil rights brimmed among Mexican Americans throughout the Southwest and beyond. It evolved the Chicano movement. In the nation's universities and colleges, students did the most to advance *el movimiento*. As they set out to conceptualize Chicano studies programs and departments, they may not have been sufficiently attentive to the specific need for bilingual education, including those at the University of New Mexico (United

Mexican American Students 1969; Chicano Coordinating Council on Higher
Education 1969). Yet it was more generally significant that student militancy
adopted "self-determination and empowerment" and that it exposed the "limits of
'Americanization' ideals" (Galicia 2007, 33). Educators embodied such principles
as they founded the Cultural Awareness Program and Upward Bound at the
University of New Mexico.

The Chicana and Chicano movement's spirit of struggle for rights, equal access, and democracy led Mexican American professional educators and parents
to move away from assimilation preferences toward a plural vision of the place
of their children in society. Educators, politicians, students, and parents affected
higher education with their educational reform initiatives. The current ignited a
renewed interest in bilingual education (Galicia 2007, 33, 57–58).

The passions of social change at local levels were partly responsible for passage of the Congressional Bilingual Education Act of 1968 (CBEA), proposed
originally by Texas Senator Ralph Yarborough (Lyons 1995, 2–3). One assessment deemed CBEA relatively weak and its aim vague. It may have been so
purposely. For it proved effective in providing tangible means for addressing
concerns of Nuevomexicanos, Mexican Americans, and Latinos in general. In
particular, it afforded a potential way for measuring progress toward educational equity (Blum Martínez, chapter 6 this volume; Gándara and Contreras
2009, 11; Habermann López, chapter 5 this volume). Now the stage was set for
a truly new era in the historical struggle for bilingual education. Interested
educators, politicians, policy makers, and parents in New Mexico jumped in
with both feet. And as ever before in the history of educating Nuevomexicano
and Nuevomexicana children, more bouts in the "bilingual wars" would follow
(Gándara and Contreras 2009, 123).

NOTES

1. An 1850 census has seven-eighths of the adults not able to read and write; Vaughn
1931, 213; also, Larson 1968, 65. For the high illiteracy rates among Nuevomexicanos and
Native Americans in the early years of the twentieth century, see Seyfriend 1934.

2. The potential spread of slavery to the western territories prior to the Civil War
was one reason. After the war, disagreements within the territory over New Mexico's
readiness for statehood were primary reasons, as were partisan considerations. For 1850,
see Gonzales 2017, 223–28.

3. "*Si Nuevo México no ha recibido protección del gobierno para fines de educación,
cuando más la necesitaba, que era en los primeros años despues de la conquista, ha sido por*

causa de las cizañas que han metido los 'chiflados.'" "Nuevo México y los 'Chiflados," *El Independiente*, August 4, 1898, 1.

4. Alejandro García, resolutions of a meeting to form a chapter of the Knights of Labor, in "Comunicado," *La Voz del Pueblo*, April 4, 1891, 1. The community came to be called Hernandez.

5. "Un Nombramiento Acertado," *La Voz del Pueblo*, February 21, 1891, 2; Ogden 1974, 80–81.

6. "La Legislatura," *La Voz del Pueblo*, February 11, 1893, 2.

7. "Los Institutos de Condado," *El Independiente*, September 1.

8. Untitled editorial column, *La Voz del Pueblo*, July 9, 1910, 2.

9. "Respuesta," *El Independiente*, November 3, 1910, 2.

10. Joshua Fishman. "The Struggle for Cultural Democracy." National Association of Bilingual Education. Keynote address. April 1, 1992, Albuquerque, NM.

11. Larrazolo's message was published as "Message to the Fourth New Mexico Legislature," in "Governor Urges Educational and Social Reforms," *Santa Fe New Mexican* (hereafter *New Mexican*), January 15, 1, 4. See also, Getz (1997, 31); Gonzales-Berry (2000, 180).

12. See, "El Mensaje del Gobernador," [Las Vegas, NM] *Voz del Pueblo*, January 18, 1919, 2.

13. "No es la Lengua la que Hace al Patriota Sino el Corazón." [Albuquerque] *Bandera Americana*, February 28, 1919, 2.

14. See, for example, "Baca and Armijo Rival Sponsors for Larrazolo Legislation; Good Part of Program Now in Form of Bills," *New Mexican*, January 21, 1919, 2; "Governor's Bill on Education Is Given Revision," *Albuquerque Morning Journal*, March 11, 1919, 3.

15. See, for example, "Governor Larrazolo's Interview," *Albuquerque Morning Journal*, July 6, 1919, 2; "Montoya Head of N. M. Branch of Spanish Teachers," *Albuquerque Morning Journal*, July 4, 1919, 2; "Governor, Back from Las Vegas Conference, Emphasizes Stand on Language Question," *New Mexican*, July 7, 1919, 3.

16. "Governor Larrazolo Makes Clear Statement Regarding the New Mexico School Law." *Albuquerque Morning Journal* in 6 July 6, 1919, editorial section, 1.

17. See, for example, Linquista, "Bilingual Method of Teaching Is Condemned by Educator Who Has Had Practical Experience," *Albuquerque Morning Journal*, July 20, 1919, 3; Juan J. Clancey, "Juan J. Clancey Contributes Strong Article on Public School Problem," *Albuquerque Morning Journal*, July 25, 1919, 6; "Language Study Should Begin in Junior High School Classes, Is National Federation's View," *New Mexican*, July 8, 1919, 4; "A Vicious Bill," *New Mexican*, July 15, 1919, 4.

18. See the complaints registered by "A New Mexican" to the *New York Times*, February 25, 1919, 10.

19. Brown v. Board of Education of Topeka, 347 US 483 (1954).

REFERENCES

Atkins, Jane. 1982. "Who Will Educate? The Schooling Question in Territorial New Mexico 1846–1911." PhD diss., University of New Mexico, Albuquerque.

Bachelor, David L. 1991. *Educational Reform in New Mexico: Tireman, San José, and Nambé.* Albuquerque: University of New Mexico Press.

Baron, Dennis. 1990. *The English-Only Question: An Official Language for Americans?* New Haven: Yale University Press.

Blanton, Carlos Kevin. 2014. *George I. Sánchez: The Long Fight for Mexican American Integration.* New Haven: Yale University Press.

Bullis, Don. 2012. "A Brief History of Education in New Mexico. Triple-A Livestock Report." Sponsored by *New Mexico Stockman and Livestock Market Digest.* https://aaalivestock.wordpress.com/2012/07/27/a-brief-history-of-education-in-new-mexico-by-don-bullis/.

Carter, Thomas P. 1970. *Mexican Americans in School: A History of Neglect.* New York: College Entrance Examination Board.

Chicano Coordinating Council on Higher Education. 1969. *El Plan de Santa Bárbara: A Chicano Plan for Higher Education.* University of California Santa Barbara.

Cline, Dorothy I. 1985. *New Mexico's 1910 Constitution, A Nineteenth Century Product.* Santa Fe: The Lightning Tree.

Colton, David L., and Luciano Baca. 1994. "Governing New Mexico's Schools." In *New Mexico Government,* edited by Paul H. Hain, F. Chris Garcia, and Gilbert K. St. Clair, 207–32. Albuquerque: University of New Mexico Press.

Cruz, Lynn Carrillo. 2007. "'No Cake for Zuni:' The Constitutionality of NM's Public School Capital Finance System." *New Mexico Law Review* 37 (Spring): 308–56.

Dargan, Marion. 1943. "New Mexico's Fight for Statehood, 1895–1912, VI: Advertising the Backyard of 'the United States.'" *New Mexico Historical Review* 18 (January): 60–96.

Deutsch, Sarah. 1987. *No Separate Refuge: Culture, Class, and Gender on an Anglo-Hispanic Frontier in the American Southwest, 1880–1940.* New York: Oxford University Press.

Everett, Dianna. 1984. "The Public School Debate in New Mexico, 1850–1891." *Arizona and the West* 26, no. 2 (Summer): 107–34.

Forrest, Suzanne. 1989. *The Preservation of the Village: New Mexico's Hispanics and the New Deal.* Albuquerque: University of New Mexico.

Galicia, Laura. 2007. "Americanization." In *Latino Education in the U.S.,* edited by Lourdes Díaz Soto, 31–35. Lanham, MD: Rowman & Littlefield Education.

Gándara, Patricia, and Frances Contreras. 2009. *The Latino Education Crisis: The Consequences of Failed Social Policies.* Cambridge, MA: Harvard University Press.

Garrett, Clarke. 2005. "French Missionary Clergy Confront the Protestant Menace in New Mexico, 1851–1885." *Journal of the Western Society for French History* 33: 292–307.

Getz, Lynne Marie. 1997. *Schools of Their Own: The Education of Hispanos in New Mexico, 1850–1940.* Albuquerque: University of New Mexico Press.

———. 2005. "Lost Momentum: World War II and the Education of Hispanos in New Mexico." In *Mexican Americans and World War II*, edited by Maggie Rivas-Rodriguez, 93–113. Austin: University of Texas Press.

Gonzales, Phillip B. 2000. "La Junta de Indignación: Hispano Repertoire of Collective Protest in New Mexico, 1884–1933." *Western Historical Quarterly* 31: 161–86.

———. 2001. *Forced Sacrifice as Ethnic Protest: The Hispano Cause in New Mexico and the Racial Attitude Confrontation of 1933.* New York: Peter Lang.

———. 2003. "Struggle for Survival: The Hispanic Land Grants of New Mexico." *Agricultural History* 77 (2, Spring): 293–324.

———. 2007. "Race, Party, Class: The Contradictions of Octaviano A. Larrazolo." In *Noble Purposes: Nine Champions of the Rule of Law.* Edited by Norman Gross, 95–125. Athens, OH: Ohio University Press.

———. 2015. "New Mexico Statehood and Political Inequality: The Case of Nuevomexicanos." *New Mexico Historical* Review 90, no. 1: 31–52.

———. 2016. *Política: Nuevomexicanos and American Political Incorporation, 1821–1910.* Lincoln: University of Nebraska Press.

Gonzales-Berry, Erlinda. 2000. "Which Language Will Our Children Speak? The Spanish Language and Public Education Policy in New Mexico, 1890–1930." In *The Contested Homeland: A Chicano History of New Mexico*, edited by Erlinda Gonzales-Berry and David R. Maciel, 169–89. Albuquerque: University of New Mexico Press.

Haught, B. F. 1931. "The Language Difficulty of Spanish-American Children." *Journal of Applied Psychology* 15, no. 1: 92–95.

Hemsing, William Moyer. 1953. "The History and Trends of Indian Education in New Mexico." PhD diss., University of New Mexico, Albuquerque, NM.

Hodgkin, Charles. 1906. *Early School Laws of New Mexico.* Albuquerque: University of New Mexico Bulletin 1, no. 41.

Holmes, Joseph. 1975. "Bilingual Education: *Serna v. Portales Municipal Schools.*" *New Mexico Law Review* 5: 321–33.

Holscher, Kathleen. 2012. *Religious Lessons: Catholic Sisters and the Captured Schools Crisis in New Mexico.* Oxford: Oxford University Press.

Holtby, David V. 2012. *Forty-Seventh Star: New Mexico's Struggle for Statehood.* Norman: University of Oklahoma Press.

Hordes, Stanley M. 2005. *To the End of the Earth: A History of the Crypto-Jews of New Mexico.* New York: Columbia University Press.

Horn, Calvin. 1963. *New Mexico's Troubled Years: The Story of the Early Territorial Governors.* Albuquerque: Horn & Wallace.

John, Vera P., and Vivian Horner. 1971. *Early Childhood Bilingual Education*. New York: MLA.

Kunzman, Robert, and David Tyack. 2005. "Educational Forums of the 1930s: An Experiment in Adult Civic Education." *American Journal of Education* 11 (May): 320–40.

Lamar, Howard W. 2000. *The Far Southwest 1846–1912: A Territorial History*. Albuquerque: University of New Mexico Press.

Larson, Robert W. 1968. *New Mexico's Quest for Statehood*. Albuquerque: University of New Mexico Press.

López, Richard E., and Julian Samora. 1977. "George Sánchez and Testing." In *Humanidad: Essays in Honor of George I. Sánchez*, edited by Américo Paredes, 107–15. Los Angeles: Chicano Studies Center, Monograph No. 6.

López, Thomas R., Jr. 1972. "Prospects for the Spanish American Culture of New Mexico." PhD diss., University of New Mexico.

Larson, Robert W. *New Mexico's Quest for Statehood 1846–1912*. Albuquerque: University of New Mexico Press, 1968.

Lozano, Rosina A. 2013. "Managing the 'Priceless Gift': Debating Spanish Language Instruction in New Mexico and Puerto Rico, 1930–1950." *The Western Historical Quarterly* 44, no. 3 (Autumn): 271–93.

———. 2018. *An American Language: The History of Spanish in the United States*. Berkeley: University of California Press.

McKevitt, Gerald. 1992. "Italian Jesuits in New Mexico: A Report by Donato M. Gasparri, 1867–1869." *New Mexico Historical Review* 67, no. 4 (October): 357–92.

Milk, Robert. 1980. "The Issue of Language Education in Territorial New Mexico. *Bilingual Review/La Revista Bilingüe* 7, no. 3 (September–December): 212–21.

Mondragón, John B., and Ernest S. Stapleton. 2005. *Public Education in New Mexico* Albuquerque: University of New Mexico Press.

Montez, Ray R. 1973. "Education and the Spanish-Speaking—An Attorney General's Opinion on Article XII, Section 8 of the New Mexico Constitution." *New Mexico Law Review* 3 (Rev. 364): 364–80.

Moyers, Robert Arthur. 1941. "A History of Education in New Mexico." PhD diss., University of Tennessee, Knoxville, TN.

Nanninga, S. P. 1942. *The New Mexico School System*. Albuquerque: University of New Mexico Press.

New Mexico. 1911. *The Constitution of the State of New Mexico: Adopted by the Constitutional Convention Held at Santa Fe, N. Mex. from Oct. 3 to November 21, 1910*. Washington, DC: US Government Printing Office.

New Mexico Department of Education. 1915. *Compilation of the Public School Laws of New Mexico*. Santa Fe: New Mexico Department of Education.

———. 1917. *Compilation of the Public School Laws of New Mexico*. Santa Fe: New Mexico Department of Education.

———. 1919. *Compilation of the Public School Laws of New Mexico.* Santa Fe: New
Mexico Department of Education.

Nieto-Phillips, John M. 2004. *The Language of Blood: The Making of Spanish-American
Identity in New Mexico, 1880s–1930s.* Albuquerque: University of New Mexico.

Noel, Linda. 2014. *Debating American Identity: Southwestern Statehood and Mexican
Immigration.* Albuquerque: University of Arizona Press, 2014.

Ogden, Raymond. Historical Sketch of St. Michael's College. Santa Fe: College of
Santa Fe, 1974.

Owen, Gordon R. 1996. *The Two Alberts: Fountain and Fall.* Las Cruces, NM: Yucca
Tree Press.

Prince, L. Bradford. 1892. *Report of the Governor of New Mexico to the Secretary of the
Interior.* Washington, D.C. Government Printing Office.

_____. 2010 (1910). *New Mexico's Struggle for Statehood.* Santa Fe: Sunstone Press.

Read, Benjamin M. 1911. "Paper Read before the New Mexico Educational Association
at its 26th Annual Meeting at Santa Fe, N.M., Nov. 15, 1911." In *History of Education
in New* Mexico, edited by Benjamin M. Read, 8–18. Santa Fe: New Mexican
Printing Company.

Rosenfelt, Daniel M. 1976. "Toward a More Coherent Policy for Funding Indian
Education." *Law and Contemporary Problems* 40, no. 1 (Winter): 190–223.

Sánchez, George I. 1934a. "Bilingualism and Mental Measures." *Journal of Applied
Psychology* 18 (December): 765–72.

———. 1934b. "The Implications of a Basal Vocabulary to the Measurement of the
Abilities of Bilingual Children." *Journal of Social Psychology* 5 (August): 395–402

———. 1985 (1940). *Forgotten People: A Study of New Mexicans.* Albuquerque:
University of New Mexico.

Sewell, Brice H. 1935. "What Our Vocational Schools are Doing." *New Mexico School
Review,* 15 (October): 49–50.

———. 1936. "New Los Lunas Vocational School Building." *New Mexico School
Review* 15 (January): 6.

Seyfried, J. E. 1934. "Illiteracy Trends in New Mexico." *The University of New Mexico
Bulletin* 8, no. 1 (March 15): 3–38.

Smith, Chuck, and Stephanie Gonzales. 2011. *The New Mexico State Constitution.*
Oxford: Oxford University Press.

Southwest Cooperative Educational Laboratory. 1968. *Classroom Strategies: Culture and
Learning Styles.* Albuquerque: The Laboratory.

Steele, Thomas J. 2000. *Archbishop Lamy: In His Own Words.* Albuquerque:
LPD Press.

Steiner, Stan. 1967. *La Raza: The Mexican Americans.* New York: Harper & Row.

Stratton, Porter A. 1969. *The Territorial Press of New Mexico 1834–1912.* Albuquerque:
University of New Mexico Press.

Thornton, W. L. 1893. "Report of the Governor of New Mexico." In *Report of the*

Secretary of the Interior, vol. 3, 357–87. Washington, DC: US Government Printing Office.

Tireman, Loyd. 1936. *We Speak English: A Preliminary Report of the Achievement of Spanish-Speaking Pupils in New Mexico/ San Jose Experimental School*. Albuquerque: University of New Mexico.

———. 1939. *Nambe: A Community School*. Santa Fe: Santa Fe County, New Mexico.

———. 1948. *Teaching Spanish-Speaking Children*. Albuquerque: University of New Mexico Press.

———. 1951. *Teaching Spanish-Speaking Children*. Rev. ed. Albuquerque, University of New Mexico Press.

Tireman, Loyd S., and Mary Watson. 1943. *La Comunidad: Report of the Nambé Community School 1937–1942*. Albuquerque: University of New Mexico Press.

———. 1948. *A Community School in a Spanish-Speaking Village*. Albuquerque: University of New Mexico Press.

United Mexican American Students. 1969. "The Chicano and UNM." Albuquerque: University of New Mexico.

United States Commission on Civil Rights. 1971. *The Unfinished Education: Outcomes for Minorities in the Five Southwestern States*. Mexican American Educational Series Report II. Washington, DC: US Government Printing Office

———. 1972. *The Excluded Student: Educational Practices Affecting Mexican Americans in the Southwest*. Washington, DC: US Government Printing Office.

Vaughn, John H. 1931. *New Mexico History and Government*. Las Cruces, NM: State College.

Wiley, Tom. 1965. *Public School Education in New Mexico*. Albuquerque: Division of Government Research, University of New Mexico.

Zamora, Gloria. 2009. *Sweet Nata: Growing up in Rural New Mexico*. Albuquerque: University of New Mexico Press.

[5] The Pecos Project

Henry W. Pascual often talked about the treatment Hispanic and Native American children received in many classrooms. He once said:

> The one element, which beginning in 1963, was insulting to me and ego damaging to the children was the fact that they were forbidden to speak their home language. The penalty for speaking Spanish anywhere in school was one 'whack' with a ruler for each word spoken. This was a policy condoned by our agency as well as local districts. I began a war against this practice."[1]

The children and their parents had been given an inferiority complex about themselves because of their language and their origin, and in many cases the schools reinforced it. This created what he called "psychological baggage" that he believed hindered their success in school.

▢ ▢ ▢

I first learned of the Pecos project while employed by the New Mexico State Department of Education (SDE, now the New Mexico Public Education Department) as a bilingual education specialist in the Title VII Bilingual Education Unit, directed by Henry W. Pascual from 1978 to 1982.

We traveled many miles across New Mexico to observe instruction in Title VII bilingual education classrooms as we monitored the implementation of the program. Pascual, who had been hired at the SDE as a foreign language specialist in 1962, often talked about the early days of bilingual education in the state.[2] Central to his view about how to best educate New Mexico's Spanish and Native American students was the use of the children's home/native language as mediums of instruction. Educating the students in their mother tongue would give them the same opportunity to learn concepts as English-speaking students have.

Born in Puerto Rico and honorably discharged from the US Army Air Corps in 1946, Pascual first came to New Mexico as an air traffic controller, having worked in the Panama Canal Zone and in Santa Fe from 1946 to 1953. Graduating from the University of New Mexico in 1958, he taught French, English, and Spanish in Albuquerque until he was offered the position at the SDE.[3] As he began his work, he became aware of early English as a second language (ESL) programs, which had been implemented in districts with large Native American populations from 1958 to 1962.[4] Teaching English as a second language (TESL) was a relatively new concept in elementary public education, having previously been used in the 1930s to respond to the enrollment of diplomats and foreign students in US universities (Crawford 1989). This new approach to teaching English was incorporated into the first Spanish-English bilingual education program in the nation in 1963 in Dade County, Florida, in response to the large influx of the children of Cuban immigrants who were seeking US asylum from the dictatorship of Fidel Castro.

As a consultant to the Dade County Ford Foundation Project on the Miami Linguistic Readers from 1964 to 1967, Pascual learned about a new series of English readers that were being developed in Miami for Cuban refugees to teach reading to students learning English as their second language as an alternative to the basal readers that were in use at the time. They introduced minimal pairs of phonemically regular words (fat/cat/mat/hat) and then taught reading by controlling the sentence pattern, such as "The fat cat sat on a mat"(Criscuolo 1970). Pascual field tested the *Miami Linguistic Readers* in five schools in New Mexico, including West Las Vegas and Albuquerque in 1964. While the teaching of English as a second language to the nation's large Hispanic and Native American students in the public schools was certainly a "new approach for English instruction," a "bilingual" education would indeed become an educational innovation.

Pascual's official charge at the SDE was to determine how districts were implementing the 1941 law requiring the teaching of Spanish (see Gonzales, chapter 4 this volume). In that capacity, he conducted on-site reviews of foreign language instruction in New Mexico schools, which were unsettling. "After visiting many, many classrooms in the state as an official of the Department of Education, I found many disparities in the treatment of Hispanics and Native

Americans in comparison with Anglos."[5] At that time, Spanish and seven Native American languages were the lingua francas in many communities across New Mexico.

An August 2001 interview with Pascual after his retirement from the SDE and a number of his papers described what he saw across New Mexico's classrooms. In one location in the southeastern part of the state, a student was ridiculed because of his Spanish name, Jesus Maria Aguilar. "The teacher said, 'Is your name Jesus Mary?' (with English pronunciation) and all the children laughed."[6] In another observation in a school serving fifth-grade predominantly Navajo students, the teacher had ten sentences on the board. "Sentence number seven read, 'The early pioneers had to fight the Indian savages as they marched toward the West.' I took the teacher out to the hall and told him, 'What the heck is the idea of making these children read out loud and copy such an insulting statement? Answer: That's what's in the book.' I said . . . 'Get in there and erase that sentence.'"[7]

His conclusion after many visits was alarming: districts either did not implement the law or implemented it poorly. Most importantly, teachers taught Spanish as a foreign language, an approach designed for those who had no command of the language. Pascual used to say that New Mexico's school practices effectively removed Hispanics' use of Spanish at the elementary level and then offered it back to them in high school as a foreign language. Spanish was far from being "foreign" in New Mexico.

At that time, common instructional practice saturated and bombarded Hispanics and Native American students with English. Spanish and the seven Native American languages—Keres, Tewa, Tiwa, Towa, Zuni, Navajo, and Mescalero/Jicarilla Apache—were vital to the daily lifeways, cultural practices, and long-standing traditions in their homes and communities. Additionally, many schools prohibited students from speaking their home/native languages (see Gonzales, chapter 4 this volume). The intensive English practices had little if any impact, and underachievement was rampant throughout the Southwest (United States Commission on Civil Rights 1971).

This all-English approach of the early 1960s robbed students of the opportunity to learn about and see their culture and heritage reflected in the curriculum. Textbooks portrayed father smoking a pipe after a day at work while mother took care of a house that had all the modern conveniences of the United States in 1950s and 1960s. The language of the school, the teachers, and the textbooks was schoolbook English, which many Hispanic and Native American children barely understood. These texts portrayed a life and a language that were a far cry from the lives and languages of the children of rural New Mexico at that time. Many children could not relate to the content, the context, or the language used in these materials. Additionally, all-English instruction gave students and their parents an inferiority complex about their native language and culture.

These visits motivated his vision for a "bilingual" education as conceived in the experimental Pecos project. For Pascual, bilingual education would give these students an equal educational opportunity to learn through the medium of their mother tongue, equal footing with their Anglo counterparts, and "the return of language and culture that belong to the people."[8] His view is reminiscent of the struggle of language stakeholders in Pascual's native Puerto Rico, who advocated the use of Spanish as a medium of instruction after the country became a territory of the United States in 1899 (see Gonzalez, chapter 4 this volume). He expressed the power of this view in his preface to the Pecos project report when he described one of the outcomes of the project as "an awareness of the vastness and richness of the Hispanic cultural heritage through the study of geography, children's literature and Hispanic society" (Digneo and Shaya 1998, 7)

In his 1973 paper, "Bilingual Education for New Mexico Schools," Pascual stated, "If bilingual education is to contain the study of the language, the history and the culture of the children who are linguistically and culturally plural, then it should call for a continuous process and a planned program at elementary and secondary schools which will develop bilingualism and biculturalism as a positive factor in the education of these children."[9] The paper was written the year the state law was passed and seems to reflect fundamental values he acted upon throughout his tenure at the SDE.

THE NATIONAL CONTEXT

The early 1960s saw the beginning of profound changes in the United States that would come to affect many if not all the nation's institutions. In New Mexico, these changes would particularly impact its Hispanic and Native American population and propel the state's educational system into a new era. Federal law, the nation's changing demography, and the US Supreme Court shaped a legal framework that spawned an innovative educational framework encompassing race, ethnicity, language, and culture in the ensuing decades. The Landmark 1957 Supreme Court Decision *Brown v. Board of Education of Topeka* and the 1964 Civil Rights Act set the groundwork for the civil rights movement, which had a profound impact on people and institutions as the country struggled to first define and later ensure equal rights for all its citizens.[10]

As *Brown v. Board of Education* was being deliberated in the highest court of the land, foreign language instruction was gaining a new momentum in the schools of the United States.

> When the Soviet Union launched Sputnik, the first satellite, in 1957, the United States saw the study of foreign languages as important to security and defense and passed The National Defense Education Act in 1958. This Act provided a focus and national funding opportunities for experimentation in instruction in foreign languages. (Andersson 1971, 5)

In the 1960s, the Chicano movement spoke to the needs of Mexican Americans, encompassing "a broad cross section of issues—from restoration of land grants, to farm workers' rights, to enhanced education, to voting and political rights, as well as emerging awareness of collective history."[11] During this time period as well, various national studies on the education of the children of the Southwest documented the cultural, linguistic, socioeconomic, and achievement abyss that existed between Hispanics and Mexican Americans and their Anglo American counterparts.[12]

In Florida, well-educated Cubans had fled their homeland to Miami. "Proud of their language and culture, they brought with them education and job skills. . . . Many had taught schools in Cuba " (Crawford 1989, 36). The Dade County schools introduced a new method of instruction called "bilingual education" in 1961 by introducing Spanish for Spanish speakers classes. By 1963, a Ford Foundation grant paved the way for a full-fledged bilingual program at Coral Way Elementary, the first bilingual education program in the country (Crawford 1989, 36). This experimental bilingual education program was offered to approximately equal numbers of English speakers and Spanish-speaking Cuban children (Andersson 1971). Other programs followed soon after. For Henry Pascual, however, it was not just about immigrant children; in New Mexico, it was largely about the native-born children whose families had been there for centuries.

THE PECOS CONTEXT

Having begun his work at the SDE, Henry Pascual sought funding for the SDE under a Ford Foundation grant "to explore effective and innovative programs of instruction."[13] The objectives of the grant were "(1) to increase oral fluency in Spanish, (2) to begin instruction in Spanish reading and writing, and (3) to develop appreciation and awareness of Spanish culture" (Digneo and Shaya 1998). For Pascual, the grant authorized the go-ahead for "instruction in Spanish language arts and reading (as) a medium to achieve two things: (1) to develop a positive self-image for Hispanic , and (2) to transfer language and skills to English programs."[14] By learning to read fluently and with comprehension in their native language, children would be able to transfer these skills to English.

Instruction in Spanish was to become an integral part of daily classroom activities in the elementary school. "It also helped to try out teacher prepared units and to demonstrate the feasibility of offering a language arts block in Spanish in grades 1–6" (Digneo and Shaya 1998, 6, 7). According to the director, Ellen Hartnett Digneo, "The entire staff at Pecos showed an interest in the program and assisted wherever possible" (4).

Formally titled "The Teaching of Spanish to the Spanish Speaking Child," the Pecos project was initiated at West Pecos Elementary School in grades one through six in the little town of Pecos, New Mexico, near Santa Fe.[15] The village of Pecos was similar to many Spanish hamlets in northern New Mexico in that its people were rooted in their Spanish language, heritage, and culture. The oral tradition knit the people together while also conveying long-standing cultural traditions and values. The Spanish language in the north constituted "a mixture of Spanish dialects with an additional influence in the language coming from indigenous roots and other cross cultural contacts" (Arreano 1978, 45). Because of northern New Mexico's isolation from the rest of the Spanish speaking world, its language was—and is to this day—seasoned with the archaic characteristics and expressions used in sixteenth century Spain, along with borrowings from the Nahuatl language of the Aztec Indians such as *chocolate, tomate, atole, guacamole, guajolote, chante,* and *petaca* (Arrellano 1979, 57).[16] Although the language of instruction in the school was schoolbook English, the children spoke and understood this northern New Mexico Spanish, an integral part their historical and linguistic legacy.

In order to accomplish the goals of the project, the teacher would need to teach completely in Spanish. "I went out of my way to find a teacher who could not speak English just to see if the base, the linguistic base of New Mexico Spanish, would hold out in a teaching-learning situation."[17] To prove his point, Pascual hired a teacher from Chile who "could not even understand English." The teacher, Olivia Pincheira, had taught for six years at the elementary level in Chile prior to being hired for the project. Before Pincheira began her assignment in Pecos,

Pascual provided her training and an orientation to the American system of education as well as background on the oral nature and particular usage of the Spanish spoken in northern New Mexico.[18]

According to the 1968 report "Teaching Spanish to the Spanish Speaking Child, 1965–1968," Pincheira delivered thirty minutes of daily Spanish instruction to 325 students in grades one through six over the duration of the project. She started with first grade students and added a grade each year of the project. A professional film was made of the third-grade instruction, which was later shown at the 1966 Tucson Symposium (see Blum Martínez, chapter six this volume).[19]

The project selected basic readers from the series *Por el mundo del cuento y la aventura*, published by Laidlaw and whose authors were from Puerto Rico. These materials contained Hispanic cultural content as one vehicle to accomplish the project objectives (Digneo and Shaya 1998, 8). Pincheira enriched instruction by incorporating audio-lingual materials, records, reference books, periodicals, library materials, and tape recorders, and she developed the four skills of listening, speaking, reading, and writing as she taught. "Reading included subjects of science, social studies, art, literature, and arithmetic. . . . Science lessons constituted a very innovative activity during the three years of Spanish. This was done on all grade levels and proved to be a very enjoyable educational activity" (Digneo and Shaya 1998, 10), As noted by Pascual in the introduction to the project report, there was "a concerted effort to put meaningful content into each lesson, for language without tangible content becomes an insignificant code" (Digneo and Shaya 1998, 6)

Since there were no accompanying workbooks for practice in writing, vocabulary development, and other critical skills associated with reading, Pincheira developed many supplementary resources on her own. These included charts, word cards, pictures, picture charts, and special exercises to give the students needed practice in the skills of the language and the concepts taught and to help her evaluate their progress. Activities included dramatizations, declamations, listening projects, and oral and written reports, including paragraphs expressing the students' personal opinions about the lessons being taught and daily narrations on "topics of family life, county affairs, or world news. Also, they liked to talk about their dreams" (Digneo and Shaya 1998, 16). All grades participated in special programs entirely in Spanish given at the end of the school year, and these were attended by parents and the rest of the school staff. Digneo and Shaya indicated that the end-of-year programs "proved to be a contributing factor in self-identification and the development of a sense of pride in their native language" (1998, 17).

As students progressed through the program, their advancement in Spanish became evident. The report indicates teacher-made written exercises and informal tests measured word recognition; comprehension of concepts taught; exactness of language production in reading, speaking, and writing; and tests of comprehension and interpretation of the content being taught. The project evaluation also documented the expansion of new vocabulary that the students had acquired (see the chart at the end of this chapter).

On January 19, 1968, in the village of Pecos, the program hosted a statewide conference called "Teaching Spanish to the Spanish-Speaking Child" to share its outcomes and special features. There is little documentation on who attended, but by that time, Las Cruces and the West Las Vegas schools were carrying out new, experimental bilingual-education programs (see Calvo, chapter 9 this volume). West Las Vegas schools began their program in 1965 under Superintendent Ray Leger.[20] Interest was growing, both in New Mexico and nationally, with passage of the national Bilingual Education Act in 1968 (see chapter 9 this volume).

In 1965, the National Education Association (NEA) sponsored the Tucson Survey on The Teaching of Spanish to the Spanish Speaking. Leading educators from the Tucson area conducted onsite visits across the Southwest and West— Arizona, California, Colorado, New Mexico, and Texas—to explore innovative and experimental approaches that could possibly remedy the academic failure experienced by many of the 1.75 million Spanish surnamed children in the schools. Teachers with insight and expertise teaching Hispanic students had recommended two distinct ways to help them. They attributed the students' lack of interest in school and their underachievement to their limited experience with American culture; thus, acculturation models became popular. Next, they sought to foster pride in the students' own culture and origin, believing that to be critical to their academic success. By valuing the students' Spanish-speaking abilities as a "distinct asset to build on," their language could also serve as a useful bridge to learn English (National Education Association 1966, iv; San Miguel 2004).

The NEA-Tucson Survey teachers visiting West Pecos Elementary School in September 1965 described what they saw in the classroom: "We watched her in action in the classroom. The linguistic sophistication of the Latin-American-trained teacher was amply evident. Mrs. Pincheira used a wide variety of charts and illustrations which were obviously her own. She employed clever exercises and games. And she was enormously effective. . . . It was obvious that something extremely important, bearing tremendous promise for the future had been introduced into the education system at Pecos. It was called 'bilingualism'" (National Education Association 1966, 20).

The NEA-Tucson Survey led to its Tucson symposium, titled "The Spanish-Speaking Child in the Schools of the Southwest," in October of 1966, which provided the stimulus for the national law (see Blum Martínez, chapter 6 volume). The symposium publicized the efforts in education for the Spanish-speaking children of the Southwest reported in the survey, comprising various experimental programs of bilingual education, including the Pecos project. Pincheira and Pascual described the program before an audience of national, state, and local policy makers attending the symposium. They shared the seventeen-minute film that documented the performance of third-grade students in the program. New Mexico senator Joseph Montoya and US senator Yarborough of Texas saw the film and became interested in the feasibility of writing a National Bilingual Education Act (See Blum Martínez, chapter 6 this volume). When Montoya saw the film at the symposium, he pulled Pascual aside and said, "Henry, that's great. Help us with a bill we are presenting to promote the proper education of Hispanics."[21]

PROGRAM OUTCOMES

The 1968 report on the Pecos project states that one of the "very special outcomes in our program has been the favorable attitude of the parents who began to realize that their language was accepted" (Digneo and Shaya 1968, 18). In his introduction to *Teaching Spanish to the Spanish Speaking Child* (Digneo and Shaya 1968), Henry Pascual added to that, saying, "An inestimable and perhaps immeasurable outcome of this project has been the positive psychological impact the program has had on the children, for they are no longer shy and ashamed to use their mother tongue. They are most anxious to show off their ability to read in Spanish" (Digneo and Shaya 1968, 6–7).

The report listed six fundamental outcomes (Digneo and Shaya, 1968):

1. A change in community and administrative attitude toward the use and place of Spanish in the school

2. Development of reading skills that enable students to read easily material designed for native speakers of Spanish at the various levels (grades 1–6)

3. Development of writing skills for self-expression

4. Acquisition of an extended oral vocabulary (Latin American Spanish) to complement the basic home-acquired Spanish language

5. A positive attitude from the students toward the study of Spanish

6. An awareness of the vastness and richness of the Hispanic cultural heritage through the study of geography, children's literature, and Hispanic society

The Education Service Center of Albuquerque conducted the evaluation of the West Pecos Spanish program. It stated, in part:

> Here is a splendid example of the advantages of teaching Spanish in the elementary level from the first through the sixth grades. A master teacher, who not only knows subject matter but understands the youngsters in her classes, exists in this classroom. . . . While the room being used in carrying out the program was a 'reactivated' room, through the ingenuity of Mrs. Olivia Pincheira, it has been transformed into a most inspiring area where one immediately feels a Spanish environment. (Digneo and Shaya 1968, 20)

In retrospect, the program was significant for a number of reasons. First, it showed the importance of the mother tongue as vital to learning and literacy and created a way to revitalize the Spanish language in New Mexico among its people and its institutions. With very limited mother-tongue education, the Spanish language had slowly eroded since statehood in 1912, even though many attempts had been made to preserve it (see Gonzales, chapter 4 this volume). Second, in the ensuing years as national and state bilingual education legislation unfolded, the program offered a perspective on how to educate the large Hispanic and Native American populations of the Southwest (Andersson 1971).

CLOSING THOUGHTS

As I look back today at the innovative experiment termed "bilingual education" that was the Pecos project, I clearly see how very difficult school was for the Indigenous and Spanish-speaking students prior to the advent of bilingual education. Immigrant and New Mexico Hispanic and Native American children struggled to make sense of instruction given in a language they could not comprehend. The curriculum did not reflect their culture other than to portray the "discovery of America" by Columbus and depict the Native peoples of the

New World as hostile "savages." In some respects, the actions of the early bilingual education leaders and scholars of New Mexico—at the policy, legislative, and university levels—effected a permanent change in many communities and school districts of the state. Today, bilingual education teachers can benefit from the lessons of those early scholars and practitioners who had the vision and courage to challenge the ubiquitous view that one's native or heritage language and culture were detriments to learning.

The practices described in the Pecos project report were child-oriented and enjoyable. In the test-driven consciousness of education practice today, teachers do not always have the luxury to make learning come alive as they could in the past, fearing that students may not succeed on the state achievement test and therefore testify to an inability to teach effectively and to a failure of the school to educate them—in my view a flawed practice. Pincheira's approach and practices were new at the time; today, those practices have become part of the past, reminiscent of a time when thematic learning, creativity, and teaching content across the curriculum—to name but a few of the practices—were commonly part of instruction.

When the Pecos project began, learning through one's native tongue was a new approach; today, there is abundant research demonstrating its academic, linguistic, and cultural value. We who play a significant role in teaching Hispanic and Native American youth must be ever vigilant of the political winds of change that move education toward a punitive English-only approach. The *Lau v. Nichols* Supreme Court decision clearly explains why in its majority opinion: "There is no equality of treatment merely by providing students with the same facilities, textbooks, teachers and curriculum . . . Those who do not understand English are effectively foreclosed from any meaningful education."[22]

If we are not persistent in advocating how and why native and heritage languages and cultures make learning feasible, successful, self-empowering, and a meaningful expression of a given community's wishes, the hard work done in the past can become but a historical reflection of "how it used to be," when language and culture were integral to instruction. I was fortunate to sit on the shoulders of early leaders in the state, such as Henry Pascual, Maria Spencer, Miguel Encinias, Cecilio Orozco, J. Paul Taylor, Mela Leger, and many others too numerous to include here. I continue to learn from my colleagues today who have furthered this important work with groundbreaking actions in the schools, professional development, policy, and new legislation.

George Santayana's well known saying is appropriate here: "Those who cannot remember the past are doomed to repeat it."[23] I hope that this text provides some inspiration to those who follow.

APPENDIX

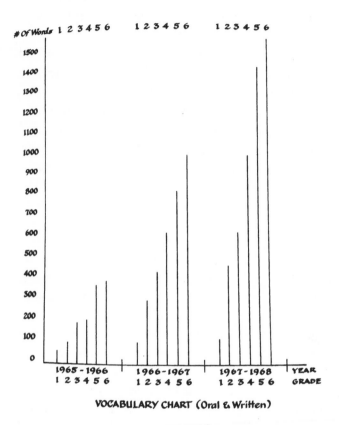

VOCABULARY CHART (Oral & Written)

NOTES

1. "Bilingual Education Recollections," talk prepared for National Association for Bilingual Education Conference in Albuquerque, NM, January 20, 1991. Unpublished transcript in Habermann López's private possession. Much of the information in this chapter has been culled from interviews with Henry W. Pascual on January 20, 1991 and August 11–12, 2001, and from his unpublished papers.

2. Title III of the National Defense Education Act funded such positions as Pascual's across the nation as a part of a national effort to improve the teaching of foreign languages, among other areas.

3. Henry W. Pascual, biographical profile, in the personal collection of Mary Jean Habermann López.

4. Henry Pascual, personal communication, January 20, 1991.

5. Ibid.

6. Henry W. Pascual, interview by Rebecca Blum Martínez, Mary Jean Habermann López, and Julia Rosa López-Emslie, August 11–12, 2001, at Pascual's home. DVD and partial transcript in the personal collection of Mary Jean Habermann López.

7. Henry Pascual, personal communication, January 20, 1991.

8. Pascual interview.

9. Henry W. Pascual, "Bilingual Education for New Mexico Schools," 10, unpublished SDE report prepared on January 2, 1973. In the personal collection of Mary Jean Habermann López.

10. Brown v. Board of Education of Topeka, 347 US 483 (1954). "The case involved an eight-year-old girl named Linda Brown who had to cross Topeka, Kansas, to go to school, while her white friends attended a public school nearby. Even while the two schools were apparently equal, Brown's parents argued that the schools were inherently unequal and that segregation has deleterious effects on children based on 'intangible' factors" ("Civil Rights Movement," http://www.u-s-history.com /pages/h2876.html). The courts ruled against segregation based in the Fourteenth Amendment.

11. Wikipedia, s.v. "Chicano Movement," https://en.wikipedia.org/wiki/Chicano _Movement.

12. United States Commission on Civil Rights 1971, 1972.

13. Henry Pascual, personal communication, January 20, 1991.

14. Ibid.

15. There are conflicting dates about when the project actually began. Materials from Henry Pascual's papers and history records say it began in 1963. The actual report says it began in 1965.

16. Anglicisms first found their way into New Mexico Spanish after Americans entered the area in 1846 and continued as more and more English terms were incorporated into New Mexico Spanish through the years (Arrellano 1978, 46–50). For deep study of the Spanish of New Mexico after statehood, see Espinosa, "Studies in New Mexico Spanish"; and Kercheville and McSpadden, *A Preliminary Glossary of New Mexican Spanish*. For a current and comprehensive study of the linguistic complexity of Spanish in the region, see Cobos, *A Dictionary of New Mexico and Southern Colorado Spanish*.

17. Pascual interview.

18. Pascual, personal communication, January 20, 1991.

19. The only available information about the actual instruction in this early bilingual education program is this descriptive 1968 report, a filmstrip with accompanying audio,

and a film made about the students and the program itself. The film cannot be viewed until it is digitized. I have used the available material and references from Henry Pascual's documents to tell the story of the program.

20. Ray Leger, the longest serving superintendent in the West Las Vegas Schools, immediately saw the value in bilingual education because Spanish was the primary language of most of the students. He was elected senator in the early 1970s and helped champion passage of the Bilingual Multicultural Education Act of 1973. *Albuquerque Journal*, Obituary of Ray Leger, October 15, 2009, http://obits.abqjournal.com/obits /2009/10/15; M. J. Habermann López, personal collection, 2009 and 1986.

21. Henry Pascual, personal communication, January 20, 1991.

22. Lau v. Nichols, 414 US 563, 94 S.Ct. 786, 39 L.Ed.2d 1 (1974).

23. George Santayana, *The Life of Reason*, vol. 1, *Reason in Common Sense* (New York: Scribner's, 1905), 284.

REFERENCES

Andersson, Theodore. 1971. *Bilingual Education and the American Experience*. Paper presented at the Conference on Bilingual Education at the Ontario Institute for Studies in Education under the auspices of the Southwest Educational Development Laboratories at the University of Texas in Austin. Toronto, Canada. https://eric.ed.gov/?id=ED048581.

Arreano, Anselmo F. 1978. "New Mexico Spanish." In *La Tierra Amarilla: The People of the Chama Valley*, edited by Anselmo Arreano, 42–59. Chama, NM: Chama Valley Public Schools.

Bloomfield, Leonard, and Charles Barnhart. 1961. *Let's Read: A Linguistic Approach*. Detroit: Wayne State University Press.

Cobos, Reuban. 2003. *A Dictionary of New Mexico and Southern Colorado Spanish*. Rev. ed. Santa Fe: Museum of New Mexico Press.

Criscuolo, Nicholas P. 1970. "A Look at Linguistic Readers." *Reading Horizons* 10, no. 3: 115–19. http//scholarworks.wmich.edu/cg/viewcontent.cgi?article=2714andcontext = reading_horizons.

Crawford, James. 1989. *Bilingual Education: Politics, Theory and Practice*. 4th ed. Trenton, NJ: Crane.

Digneo, Ellen Hartnett, and Shaya Eila, eds. 1968. *Teaching Spanish to the Spanish Speaking Child*. http://files.eric.ed.gov/fulltext/ED026183.pdf.

Espinosa, Aurelio. 1909. "Studies in New Mexico Spanish." PhD diss., University of Chicago.

Kercheville, Francis Moore, and George E. McSpadden. 1934. *A Preliminary Glossary of New Mexican Spanish*. Albuquerque: University of New Mexico Press.

Lozano, Rosina A. 2013. "Managing the 'Priceless Gift': Debating Spanish Language

Instruction in New Mexico and Puerto Rico, 1930–1950." *Western Historical Quarterly* 44, no. 3: 271–93.

National Education Association. 1966. *The Invisible Minority: Report of the NEA-Tucson Survey on the Teaching of Spanish to the Spanish-Speaking.* https://eric.ed.gov/?id=ED017222.

———. 1973. *Report of a National Bilingual Bicultural Institute. A Look at Tucson '66 and Beyond.* http://files.eric.ed.gov/fulltext/ED101923.pdf.

San Miguel, Guadalupe, Jr. 2004. *Contested Policy: The Rise and Fall of Bilngual Education in the United States 1960–2001.* Denton, TX: University of North Texas Press.

Schmidt, Jorge R. 2014. *The Politics of English in Puerto Rico's Public Schools.* Boulder, CO: First Forum Press.

United States Commission on Civil Rights. 1971. *The Unfinished Education: Outcomes for Minorities in the Five Southwestern States.* Washington, DC: US Government Printing Office.

———. 1972. *The Excluded Student: Educational Practices Affecting Mexican Americans in the Southwest.* https://eric.ed.gov/?id=ED062069.

REBECCA BLUM MARTÍNEZ

[6] Initial Policies, Legislation, and Decisions

PROLOGUE

In 1960, I entered kindergarten speaking no English. I was the only one in my class who didn't understand English, and all my classmates were aware of this. I didn't want to stand out in any way, so I would copy whatever my classmates did. During art, my classmates drew a big X on their paper, making four triangles, and colored each triangle a different color. I did the same. During art one day, I made the big X on my paper and started coloring. My teacher stood over me and started scolding me. Apparently, she had told the class that we needed to draw something new, but I didn't understand. I was afraid and ashamed.

The Spanish Speaking Child in the Schools of the Southwest Symposium, at the University of Arizona at Tucson (hereafter Tucson symposium), organized by the National Education Association in 1966, was a watershed moment for New Mexicans. Conference discussions on the education of Mexican Americans included such topics as parent-school relationships, the roles of school boards, legislative needs, and teacher education. New Mexico was well represented at this conference (Hart 1966) (see chapters 5 and 8, this volume). In 1967, inspired by the success of the New Mexico State Department of Education's Pecos project, the reception to his presentation about that project at the Tucson symposium, and the discussions throughout this conference, Henry Pascual began crafting the first bilingual policy statement for the New Mexico State Board of Education. "I prepared a policy statement for the state school board of education because I wanted something that I could prove to people that was approved by the state department of education—a nice one page of the advantages of being bilingual and multicultural."[1] The statement began by stating five objectives: "1) Developing the abilities of rational thought; 2) Developing a positive self-image; 3) Fostering a student's individual talents; 4) Developing fundamental skills; and 5) To achieve maximum development of ability and desire in each individual to make the greatest possible contribution to his own society."[2] Citing the percentages of Spanish-surnamed and American Indian students, the statement acknowledged that the standard curriculum "may not meet the needs of bilingual children," and urging local school personnel " to study the educational problems of their bilingual children with a view towards effecting necessary changes for the full education of these students."[3]

In this policy statement, the New Mexico State Board of Education established a Division of Bilingual Education to "assist local schools in formulating and implementing programs for bilingual students." Implied in this statement was the fact that many common educational practices would have to change. These practices included teacher education/reeducation, materials selection, lesson planning, course offerings, and reappraisal of administrative responsibilities. Emphasis was placed on the changes needed in the language arts programs for approximately 40 percent of the state's students that "should include instruction in the mother tongue and English for children who have not acquired fluency in the English language" (2).

Early pioneers were already implementing these needed changes in the state. At the time of the policy adoption, the Pecos project had been functioning for four years. Utilizing Title I funding, the West Las Vegas schools had begun a maintenance bilingual program in 1965, under the direction of Ray Leger.[4] And in the same year as the policy adoption, John Paul Taylor had just established a dual language program, with the aid of Title III, NDEA funds.[5] It should be noted that these programs were focused on Spanish-speaking Nuevomexicanos, most of whom had been in New Mexico for several generations.

Two State Board of Education members were instrumental in the adoption of this policy statement: Virginia Gonzalez of Santa Fe and Joe Romero, who represented several school districts in northern New Mexico. With their assistance, the board passed this policy unanimously. Given the growing interest in and the positive results from these early bilingual programs, it is not surprising that the state board would approve of this policy.

This policy statement came a full year before the national Bilingual Education Act of 1968 and may well be the first such statement from any state board of education in the nation. After its approval, Henry Pascual sent the policy to

Senator Joseph Montoya. Montoya responded, "I greatly appreciate your bringing this to my attention for as you know the formation of bilingual education
is one of my primary efforts."[6] Further, Montoya referenced the newly formed
Mexican American Affairs Unit of the US Office of Education, with which he
was working to promote the teaching of Spanish.

With this policy, the State Board of Education, as the entity charged with
the education of all public school children, admitted for the first time that current educational practices had failed 40 percent of the public school students
and called for changes in those practices. While the statement held no legal
requirements, it allowed those educators who wished to make changes to do so
with the support of the state school board. Further, this statement served as the
springboard for the first bilingual education act of the state that was proposed
in 1969 by then state representative Roberto Mondragón (D-Bernalillo). "Bob
Mondragón came into my office and said we should make a law. Let's go and
present it to the committee."[7] Representative Mondragón sponsored House Bill
75; the same bill was sponsored in the New Mexico Senate (Senate Bill 270)
by Senator Jerry Apodaca, who would later become governor in 1974. It was
approved April 1, 1969.

This first bill did not include any funding for bilingual programs, but it did
support the creation of such programs as established by a local school board that
"may establish as a part of its regular school program in the school district the
teaching of approved courses of instruction in a language other than English"
while giving the state school board the authority to establish guidelines for
these programs. The act allowed for initial experimentation and the possibility
for schools to expand the program to different grade levels and for all students.
Moreover, these programs could "incorporate techniques and materials that
provided learning opportunities outside of a formal classroom, and could utilize
instructors not formally certified but who had the language abilities to teach in
the target language."[8] The fact that the bill allowed languages other than English
was meaningful not only to Spanish speakers, but also to those who spoke an
Indigenous language. Moreover, providing learning opportunities outside of a
formal classroom and with instructors who were not necessarily certified opened
the door for both Native American and Spanish-speaking community members to
participate in educational programs. One important caveat was that such programs
could not segregate children "by virtue of cultural or linguistic backgrounds."[9] In
this respect, New Mexico was the first state to declare that such programs were
open to all children, not just those who struggled with an all-English curriculum.

One year before this bill was passed in New Mexico, Title VII of the Elementary and Secondary Education Act (the Bilingual Education Act) was passed nationally. In contrast to New Mexico's law, the national law did not propose the establishment of bilingual education, nor was there an expressed warning about segregation:

> In recognition of the special educational needs of the large numbers of children of limited English-speaking ability. . . . Congress hereby declares it to be the policy of the United States to provide financial assistance to local educational agencies to develop and carry out new and imaginative elementary and secondary programs designed to meet these special educational needs. (PL 90–247 in Garcia, 2009, 169)

In essence, the federal law allowed schools to develop any kind of program that would address the students' "special needs." The laxity of this legislation led to many English as a second language (ESL) and English-only programs across the nation that Senator Montoya of New Mexico (one of the cosponsors of this federal legislation) would critique seven years later (see below).

These educational reforms at both the state and national levels added justification to some of the first bilingual programs in New Mexico—the dual language program in Las Cruces and the bilingual program in the West Las Vegas schools (see chapter 9, this volume). Each of these programs received funding from different sources: Title I, Elementary and Secondary Education Act, funded the West Las Vegas program; Title III, National Defense Education Act, funded the program in Las Cruces (more details about these programs are provided in chapter 10).

As discussed previously, the first bilingual programs that were established focused on the children of Nuevomexicano families who had resided in the state for generations. It is important to distinguish these programs from those that resulted from federal legislation. The Bilingual Education Act at the federal level was conceived of as remediation for those students who did not know English, and it supported the use of Spanish (or other non-English languages) only in service of English. Early New Mexico programs were focused on both languages, further expanding children's Spanish while also developing English.

Despite the New Mexico focus on both English and Spanish, as the idea for bilingual education grew in popularity, even those politicians in more conservative areas of the state became interested in funding sources for their districts.

So it was that in 1971, Senator Jack Eastham (R-Bernalillo) approached Henry Pascual for assistance in developing a bill that would fund bilingual education for grades one through three as essentially a transitional bilingual program. Senator Eastham was especially concerned with the growing numbers of immigrant students enrolling in the Albuquerque public schools. Senate Bill 155, named the Bilingual Instruction Act, was approved April 8, 1971. Similar to the national law, the state bill cited the large numbers of children who had special needs because of their limited speaking ability in English, especially those children who were in grades one through three. However, the purpose of the bill included the development and use of two languages:

> The purpose of this act is to help children in these grades to develop greater competence in English, to *become more proficient in the use of two languages* and to profit from increased educational opportunity.[10]

In keeping with New Mexico's long history of advocacy for the native language, Section 4 of the bill stipulated:

> "Such programs must use two languages as mediums of instruction for any part or all of the curriculum of the grade level or levels within the program." (2)

By including the term "mediums of instruction," the aim was that each language would have an instructional purpose in the curriculum, thereby avoiding the common practice of using the non-English language as mere translation. And for the first time, the law required teachers "who have specialized in elementary education and who have received *special training in bilingual education which was conducted through the use of two languages* [author's emphasis]" (2). Teachers also needed a professional development program conducted in two languages to assist those who had never had an academic experience in Spanish and therefore did not have advanced literacy skills in the language (see Hannum and Salazar, chapter 10 this volume). As for the curriculum, the bill specified that the history and culture associated with the students' mother tongue was to be an integral part of the instructional program."[11] Although this bill was transitional in its conception (providing bilingual instruction until third grade), the requirements for instruction in two languages and the inclusion of the history and culture of the students demonstrated the state's commitment to a bilingual and bicultural program.

The implementation of the state-funded programs that required special preparation of teachers and instructional materials that reflected children's linguistic and cultural backgrounds called for changes in teacher preparation and for new materials. Moreover, the social reforms demanded by the Chicano movement added new urgency to these educational reforms (see Gonzalez, chapter 4 this volume).

In the same year, 1971, Roberto Mondragón was serving as New Mexico's youngest ever and first Chicano lieutenant governor. Having been raised in large part by his grandfather in La Loma, close to Anton Chico, Mondragón learned the language and traditions of Nuevo México as he helped his grandfather with the animals and crops in his small farm. This upbringing instilled in Mondragón a great love for the language and culture that would become the focus of much of his life's work, including his work on behalf of the Chicano movement.[12]

In 1971, neither Lieutenant Governor Mondragón nor Governor Bruce King enjoyed large support staffs, and when Mondragón received a call from Tony Armijo, an intern with the National Management program under the US Health, Education, and Welfare Department who was looking for a placement in his home state of New Mexico, Mondragón jumped at the chance, telling Armijo to "come on down."[13] In a meeting with Representative Ben Luján Sr., Mondragón, and Governor King, Armijo said his goal during his internship was "to stop the punishment of kids for speaking Spanish on school grounds." Luján concurred with this goal, saying that the punishments were being meted out in northern New Mexico as well. Armijo's request was approved by all present, and he began by studying the 1848 Treaty of Guadalupe Hidalgo and the documents that led to New Mexico's becoming a state. It was when he was studying the New Mexico State Constitution that he "figured out that the punishment for speaking Spanish or Navajo or any other [language] . . . was an abridgement of free speech." Armijo's contention was further supported by Article 12, section 8, of the New Mexico Constitution:

> The legislature shall provide for the training of teachers in the normal schools or otherwise so that they may become proficient in both the English and Spanish languages, to qualify them to teach Spanish-speaking pupils and students in the public schools and educational institutions of the state, and shall provide proper means and methods to facilitate the teaching of the English language and their branches of learning to such pupils and students.[14]

Armijo requested an opinion from the state attorney general, in the lieutenant governor's name, asking:

1. Does Article XII, Section 8 . . . require that the Legislature provide for the training of New Mexico teachers so that they may become proficient in both the English and Spanish languages?

2. If the answer to question No. 1 is in the affirmative, what has been done, should be done or could be done by the New Mexico Legislature to comply with the constitutional mandate?

3. What was the intent of the founding fathers of our State in enacting Article XII, Section 8:21?

Attorney General David Norvell responded on August 26, 1971. With reference to the first question, he stated that "the wording of this section 'clearly indicates' that the Legislature provide training in order that state teachers become proficient in both languages." In reference to what had been done in the past, Attorney General Norvell referred to past legislation and appropriations, specifically the Bilingual Instruction Act of 1971 and the policy passed in 1969. As to what should or could be done in the future, Norvell suggested that "a determination should be made of the number and areas of concentration of Spanish-speaking pupils . . . in the state. Based on these figures the state should calculate how many teachers would be required and then the Legislature should require that the "colleges and universities provide training for a sufficient number of teachers."

For the final question, the attorney general opined:

The intent of the founding fathers was to require the Legislature to provide trained teachers proficient in both Spanish and English.[15]

In addition to referencing the two bilingual education laws, the attorney general also based his opinions on *Serna v. Portales* (see Sosa-Provencio and Sánchez, chapter 7 this volume).[16]

Norvell's decision became the foundation for much of what has occurred in the New Mexico bilingual education field since that time. The preparation of teachers, materials, programs, and program models have all found their legal standing in his decision. Henry Pascual and other leaders often cited this decision as being critical to the bilingual education movement.

But none were more elated with this decision than Tony Armijo. Armijo had grown up in the 1950s in Magdalena, New Mexico. As a boy in that school district, he and his classmates had been paddled for speaking Spanish or Navajo. In 1959–1960, Armijo's father, Justiniano Armijo (Mi'justi), Abraham Sánchez, and a Mr. Monte from Alamo (the small adjoining Navajo reservation) were all elected to the school board and vowed to do away with the punishments for speaking a language other than English, and the word got out to the community. During the school board meeting where the resolution to do away with these punishments was passed, the superintendent, a Mr. Thompson, declared that he would not enforce the resolution, claiming that it was unconstitutional. "Mi'justi, who was a little dude . . . and Thompson, who was like 6'1.' Mi'justi said, 'I'll show you who's not going to carry this out,' and they actually came to blows."[17] Their disagreement continued outside, where they were joined by the "Mexicans and Indians on one side, and the *gringada* [a derogatory term for whites] on the other." The Magdalena School Board Rumble, as it was called, led to the administrative takeover by the State Board of Education for one year, during which time Tony Armijo and his relatives "were in exile" in the schools of Socorro for one year. "All I remember was we came back and we had to take Spanish I and Spanish II in order to qualify to graduate. First they punish us for speaking Spanish, and then they tell us to take Spanish."[18]

During the interview with Tony Armijo, he heard for the first time of the tremendous impact that the Norvell decision had had on bilingual education in the state. Based on the Norvell decision, schools, universities, and curriculum specialists begun the arduous task of conceiving of a new way to teach Spanish-speaking and Native American language–speaking children. Program models had to be developed. New methodologies were tried, materials reflecting children's backgrounds and languages had to be researched and written, and teacher preparation needed to be overhauled. Although Tony Armijo went on to other successes—among which were the development and establishment of the New Mexico Public School Insurance Authority and the New Mexico Risk Management Authority—it is for his initiation of and role in the Norvell decision for which he is most proud and by which he would most like to be remembered.[19]

In the same year as the Norvell case, several educators and politicians began making plans to expand the 1971 act. Junio López (R-San Miguel County), a young senator running for reelection, proposed a bilingual education bill based on the Massachusetts bill passed in 1968. Henry Pascual, who by then was the director of the Bilingual-Bicultural Communicative Arts Unit, analyzed the proposal for his supervisors. In his analysis, Pascual found that the proposed bill was "practically the same as that of Massachusetts" and that the intent of this bill was to establish transitional programs, saying "transitional programs may equal 'tokenism' (not good)." Further, if Anglo children did not choose to participate in bilingual programs, "it will be segregationist."[20] On the positive side, the bill proposed to extend the programs through the twelfth grade. Nevertheless, the bill was never introduced because Senator López was not reelected.

One year after the Norvell decision and the failed attempt by Senator Junio López, Senator Matías Chacón (D-Rio Arriba) proposed a new bilingual multicultural education law that would provide funding for programs K–6. This bill described the purpose of bilingual education as "insur[ing] equal educational opportunities for students in New Mexico" and providing "cognitive and affective development of students by utilizing the cultural and linguistic backgrounds of the students in the curriculum; providing students with opportunities to expand their conceptual and linguistic abilities and teaching students to appreciate the value and beauty of different languages and cultures."[21] As mandated in the 1971 bill, two languages were required to be used by teachers with specialized training, and emphasis was placed on the history and cultures of the students. Further, the bill required the state board to develop guidelines for these programs and charged the State Education Department with the approval of program plans, administration, and enforcement of the provisions of the bill. Notably, this was the first bilingual bill to include Indigenous children as possible recipients of funding.

Senator Matías Chacón worked with Henry Pascual and his office; Senator Ray Leger (D-Las Vegas), former superintendent of the West Las Vegas schools (and founder of the 1965 bilingual program in that district); and other bilingual educators in the state, including Cecilio Orozco, professor at New Mexico Highlands University, Grace Gutiérrez from Santa Fe, and Mela Leger, who was the director of bilingual education in the West Las Vegas schools and also of the Bilingual Teacher Demonstration Center in Las Vegas on the bill. Pascual recalled, "I emphasized to Matías Chacón that it had to be a permissive law not a law that forced local districts into the idea of bilingual education because otherwise it is very difficult and he said to me, I'll never forget: 'If we want money, we have to identify need.'"[22] Educators and legislators were to face this situation repeatedly throughout this time and into the present. While they were in agreement that bilingual education could be the best educational experience for the children of New Mexico, they had to justify this program on the basis of poor academic outcomes tying the idea of bilingual education to remediation rather than as a legitimate, progressive, and internationally regarded education.

On February 23, 1973, the Senate Education Committee heard SB 421, and later that day, a press release was issued that called the bill "one of the most historically significant bills to come before the legislature since New Mexico became part of the United States." The press release described the testimonies:

> Questions were raised about the fact that if children are taught through more than one language, they may be missing out on some aspects of the curriculum. For those present at the hearing the testimony dispelled those fears because it was clearly explained that learning through two languages expands rather than limits the intellectual development of the children."[23]

The bill was lauded for assisting Mexican-American, Indian and Black children as a:

> vehicle through which many of these deficiencies can be erased; but most important, bilingual education gives a promise to the people that the languages and cultures of our state will be preserved and made part of the education of our children.

Further, though the bill was not a mandate to every school, it "is a most important step in alerting and allowing the people to have their language and their culture as part of the education of their children"[24]

While the February hearing was a positive one, in the March 2 hearing, the tenor was often contentious. Pascual's office was instrumental in collecting and summarizing the need in the state. In a memo to bilingual directors, the administrators responsible for bilingual programs, dated March 6, 1973, he thanked the directors for all of the data they had sent to them:

> The Friday, March 2 session was long and at times unpleasant, but even if no action is taken on the bill, the legislators know that many of us care about our language and culture and more important yet, they know we care about the education and the lives of the children.[25]

The hearing for this bill must have been difficult as noted not only by Pascual, but also by Orozco, who wrote in Spanish to Senator Chacón:

> *Todo me pareció bien hasta que el tema se deterioró y se empezó a hablar de ESL en vez de educación bilingüe y multicultural. . . . Lo que proyectamos es un programa para el niño de descendencia india e indohispana al cual el sistema le ha negado su lengua y su cultura"* [Everything seemed to go well until the topic deteriorated and they began to talk about ESL. What we propose is a program for the Indian

and Indo-Hispanic child who has been denied his language and culture by the system].[26]

Despite the difficulties the champions of this movement faced, the bill was passed and signed into law on March 14, 1973. On March 29 of that same year, Senator Chacón wrote to Henry Pascual thanking him for his work on Senate Bill 421. "I want you to know that I have nothing but respect for the hard work, knowledge and dedication of the people in your profession. You have certainly fortified my belief that you have nothing but the interest and welfare of our children in mind."[27]

Indeed, the 1973 Bilingual Education Law was a giant step forward. The legislature appropriated $700,000 to fund the bill's programs, and in contrast to the 1971 law, the bill opened participation to all students in the state, regardless of linguistic or cultural background.

In 1975, two years after the passage of SB 421, Henry Pascual, Senator Chacón, and others suggested amending the bill so that students in grades K–12 could participate in bilingual programs. Unfortunately, these suggestions were rejected, although they would be reintroduced by Representative John Paul Taylor in 1987.

In late November and early December 1973, a conference sponsored by the National Education Task Force de la Raza and the National Education Association was held in Albuquerque. Titled "A look at Tucson 66 and Beyond," the conference had six objectives:

1) To review the rationale and the recommendations made during the Tucson conference

2) To review important activities in bilingual education since 1966

3) To demonstrate exemplary bilingual bicultural programs

4) To review present and pending state bilingual education legislation and appropriations

5) To review present and pending national bilingual education legislation and appropriations

6) To develop new directions for bilingual education for the 1970s that would lead to national legislation (National Education Task Force de la Raza and the National Education Association 1973).

Speakers included a welcome from Governor Bruce King and a keynote from Senator Joseph Montoya. In his speech, Senator Montoya spoke frankly about the challenges of transitional bilingual programs that had been the thrust of the first federal Bilingual Education Act:

At six or seven years of age they (children in transitional bilingual programs) were asked to perform a kind of mental miracle—and when that miracle didn't happen those around them too often pretended it was the children's failure instead of ours. Of course it was our failure because we did not understand the values of the languages and cultures we were asking those children to leave behind. Most of the programs we offered did not have the goal of bilingualism, but simply offered a change in the brand of monolingualism the children used. We tried to turn a 'limited English speaking ability' into a child with 'limited Spanish-speaking ability or a 'limited Indian language ability. (National Education Association 1973, 11)

Despite these challenges, Senator Montoya remained committed to bilingual education stating:

We must see that every citizen in the United States understands that when children are asked to forget their own identity and their own traditions they do not miraculously turn into something better—instead they shrink inside, and when that happens our whole nation shrinks too. (National Education Association 1973,12)

Other speakers covered such topics as "Growth pains in bilingual bicultural education since 1966"; and "The Role of the Teacher in Bilingual Bicultural Education." Working groups were formed to discuss specific issues in bilingual education: state legislation action, national legislation action, administrative action, association action, court action, community action, and exemplary programs that included university teacher preparation programs. Participants in these working groups from New Mexico included Senator Matías Chacón (D-Española) in the state legislation action group and Dolores Gonzales and Miguel Encinias in the exemplary programs group. Recommendations were made by each work group and written into the final recommendations of the conference. The recommendations for state legislative action included having state legislatures appropriate adequate funds to implement bilingual bicultural programs "not on a compensatory or remedial basis for some children, but on a continuing basis to ensure equal educational opportunity for all children" (National Education Association 1973, 43).

It is not surprising, given the work that had gone on in New Mexico in the previous ten years and over its longer history, that some of the participants at this conference were important leaders in New Mexico and, in the case of Senator Montoya, nationally. Senator Matías Chacón, the sponsor of the 1973 Bilingual

Multicultural Education Act, had significant experience as an advocate and legislator. Dolores Gonzales was one of the first professors of bilingual education and had been instrumental in the establishment of the bilingual education teacher preparation program at the University of New Mexico. Moreover, she was the principal author of the *Tierra del Encanto* reading series (see López-Emslie, chapter 11 this volume). At the time of this conference, Miguel Encinias was working with Henry Pascual. Later, Encinias became the director of the University of Albuquerque's Bilingual Multicultural Teacher Preparation Program, which focused on preparing teachers through the Spanish language and highlighting the cultures of Spain and New Mexico. He cofounded the Compañía de Teatro de Albuquerque, a bilingual theater company, and after retirement, the Zarzuela de Albuquerque (see Calvo and Gonzalez, part I of chapter 13 this volume).

CONCLUSION

This chapter has detailed the first policies, legal decisions, and legislation providing for bilingual education in New Mexico. In contrast to the state's earlier history (Gonzales, chapter 4 this volume), in the 1960s and 1970s, we see Nuevomexicano and other Latino actors in leadership positions making educational and policy decisions that supported the languages and cultures of the state's residents. Although full bilingual bicultural education through the twelfth grade was not available until 1987, the first initiatives laid the groundwork for programs that would support both the growth of the first language and the development of English, in contrast to federal legislation. Further, teacher preparation was also of concern during this period, given that few if any teachers at that time had the appropriate educational and linguistic coursework that would have allowed them to adequately support their students. Finally, we see New Mexico hosting the next iteration of the Tucson symposium, providing ongoing leadership at the national level.

REFLECTIONS FROM THE AUTHOR

When I began working in bilingual education in 1975, the passage of the 1973 Bilingual Multicultural Education Act was a scant two years in the past, and the fervor for bilingual education was growing. I was hired by Miguel Encinias to teach in his Bilingual Multicultural Teacher Education Program at the University of Albuquerque. My initial role was to teach pedagogy classes in Spanish. My role evolved, however, as Encinias developed a whole series of cultural activities to accompany the teacher education classes (see Calvo, Habermann López, Blum Martínez, chapter 13 this volume).

After receiving my BA in Latin American Studies, I had decided to study for an MA in TESOL (teachers of English to speakers of other languages) from the University of New Mexico. As a second-language learner of English myself, I could relate to those who were experiencing English for the first time. Coming from a family of teachers, I knew I wanted to teach, but becoming involved in a bilingual multicultural education program allowed me, for the first time, to find a true professional home. I did not have to separate my Spanish-speaking self from my English-speaking one. I could be my whole self in a professional setting, and this was truly liberating.

I was honored to have worked with Miguel Encinias, a native Nuevomexicano and brilliant and driven educator, who introduced me to Henry Pascual, equally brilliant, who, as a native Puerto Rican, understood the need for developing a bilingual citizenry. Working with both of these pioneers, who introduced me to other wonderful and committed educators—several of whom have authored chapters in this volume—has been one of the most significant experiences of my life.

Although I had heard stories about the Pecos project and the first initiatives, I had never really studied them. Researching and writing this chapter has brought a renewed respect and admiration for these early pioneers. Miguel Encinias, former Lieutenant Governor Mondragón, Tony Armijo, Senator Matías Chacón, and so many of those who worked with them were raised in the small towns and villages of rural New Mexico, where they were immersed in the language and culture of their ancestors. Their love for and commitment to the language and the culture are reflections of the efforts of countless others who came before them and those who followed. Many, like Tony Armijo, suffered for their commitment. Nevertheless, despite the punishments, the oppression, and the historical movements that opened or closed their possibilities, they persisted. In a very profound sense, their commitments to a way of life are tightly woven into the fabric of this state.

NOTES

1. Henry W. Pascual, interview by Rebecca Blum Martínez, Julia Rosa López-Emslie, and Mary Jean Habermann López, August 11, 12, 2001, at Pascual's home. DVD and partial transcript in the private collection of Mary Jean Habermann López.

2. "Bilingual Education," New Mexico State Board of Education, 1967, 2. Habermann López, personal collection. The first objective—developing the abilities of rational thought—was needed to counter the prevailing idea at that time that bilingualism led to confusion and a cognitive disability.

3. Ibid.

4. Ray Leger, the longest serving superintendent in the West Las Vegas schools, immediately saw the value in bilingual education because Spanish was the primary language of most of the students. He was elected senator in the early 1970s and helped champion passage of the Bilingual Multicultural Education Act of 1973 (*Albuquerque Journal*, October 15, 2009, Mary Jean Habermann López, personal collection).

5. Pascual interview.

6. Correspondence from Joseph Montoya to Henry Pascual, October 9, 1967. Box 176, Folder 8, University of New Mexico Center for Southwest Research and Special Collection.

7. Pascual interview.

8. *Providing for Bilingual-Bicultural Programs and Enacting a New Section 77–11–12* NMSA1953. Senate Bill 270. Approved April 1, 1969, Chapter 161, 554.

9. Ibid., 2.

10. *Providing for Bilingual Instruction Programs in Grades One, Two and Three; Providing Eligibility, Approval and Distribution; And Making an Appropriation*. Senate Bill 155. Approved April 8, 1971.

11. Ibid., 2.

12. "Mondragon Lauds Life in Village for Values," *Albuquerque Journal*, August 18, 1970, 3.

13. Tony Armijo, interview by Rebecca Blum Martinez, June 6, 2017, at Armijo's home, Bosque Farms, NM

14. New Mexico State Constitution, Article XII, Section 8.

15. Montez, *Education and the Spanish-Speaking*, 369.

16. Serna v. Portales Municipal Schools, 351 F. Su 1279 (1972).

17. Armijo interview.

18. Ibid.

19. Ibid.

20. Henry Pascual, memo to Mr. Ready, October 2, 1972, Mary Jean Haberman López, private collection.

21. *Providing for Establishment of Bilingual Multicultural Education Programs in the Public Schools*. Senate Bill 421. Approved March 14, 1973, 3. *New Mexico Law Review* 364 (1973).

22. Pascual interview.

23. New Mexico Department of Education, press release, February 23, 1973, 1. Mary Jean Haberman López private collection.

24. Ibid., 2.

25. Henry Pascual, memo to all bilingual directors, March 6, 1973. Mary Jean Habermann López private collection.

26. Cecilio Orozco, letter to Senator Matías Chacón, March 5, 1973. Mary Jean Haberman López private collection.

27. Matías Chacón, letter to Henry Pascual, March 29, 1973. Mary Jean Haberman López personal collection.

REFERENCES

García, Ofelia. 2009. *Bilingual Education in the 21st Century. A Global Perspective.* West Sussex, UK: Wiley Blackwell.

Montez, Ray R. *Education and the Spanish-Speaking: An Attorney General's Opinion on Article XII, Section 8, of the New Mexico Constitution*, 3 N.M. L. Rev. 364 (1973). https://digitalrepository.unm.edu/nmlr/vol3/iss2/8.

Hart, Elinor, ed. 1966. *Las voces del sudoeste (New voices of the Southwest) Symposium: The Spanish-Speaking Child in the Schools of the Southwest.* Tucson, AZ: National Education Association.

National Education Task Force de la Raza and the National Education Association. 1973. Report of a National Bilingual Bicultural Institute. *A Relook at Tucson'66 and Beyond.*

[7] *Serna v. Portales,* 1974 *Changing the Music and Asserting Language Rights for New Mexico's Children*

Before the suit was filed, they had no teachers with a Spanish surname . . .
no principals, no vice principals . . . none! It was all Anglo. All of it. And these
kids were coming in from a background where they spoke Spanish at home,
and they come in and boom, right off the bat to English, where Spanish wasn't
favored. It was English that was favored and they couldn't identify with their
environment.

DAN SOSA JR. [2004, Elizabeth Galligan Oral History Collection]

New Mexico has long been a crossroads where peoples
of distinct cultural and racial backgrounds have met, clashed, accommodated,
and developed complex strategies to ensure cultural survival.

GONZALES-BERRY 2000 [169]

Bilingual education is not just linguistic, but political.

EVANGELINA ENCINIAS [2003, Elizabeth Galligan Oral History Collection]

New Mexico has a long history of both admonishing and protecting bilingualism in public schools. By 1910, nearly all traces of Spanish were removed from
schools (Milk 1980). This shift in power over the education of a Spanish-speaking
majority population into the hands of a minority Anglo population reflected
a larger power shift that still reverberates today. Reflected in the microcosm
of schooling politics, New Mexico's Spanish-speaking population struggled
to maintain political voice in their own land, which had been promised by the

1848 Treaty of Guadalupe Hidalgo (Gomez 1999; San Miguel 1999). Public schools increasingly used a heavy hand in segregating Spanish-speaking children and imposing cultural and linguistic assimilation practices (Gonzales-Berry 2000). Within Spanish-speaking Nuevomexicano communities, arguments as to the cultural and utilitarian value of bilingualism continued to gain ground in newspapers and public discourse, largely to the exclusion of arguments over Native-language rights, which are still politically contentious. This assertion of the value and economic legitimacy of the language and its speakers exists within a historical context of a people who struggled sixty-six years for statehood amid accusations of racial, linguistic, economic, and religious inferiority by a nation that has long struggled with anti-immigrant and racist sentiments and policies (Gomez 2008; Nieto-Phillips 2004; Noel 2011). This battle raged for years. It burned at the heart of civil rights battles in Portales during the mid- to late 1960s, and manifests especially in the landmark bilingual education case *Serna v. Portales Municipal Schools* (1974), which upheld Mexican American's right to language, to Spanish-surname educators, and to a meaningful education.

THE RACIAL CLIMATE OF PORTALES, NEW MEXICO, IN THE 1960S

As late as the 1950's, Portales had a sign on each end of the town
which said, "N . . . don't let the sun go down on your back in Portales."
. . . I heard that from men from Portales. "Keep them in their place."
REVEREND FARREL ODOM [2003, Elizabeth Galligan Oral History Collection]

Prior to World War II, the Spanish-surnamed population of Portales, a town in Roosevelt County in eastern New Mexico, was nearly nonexistent.[1] Located about twenty miles from the Texas state line, the town's primary industry was peanut farming (Polese 1978). One of the first documented Spanish-surnamed families of Portales was the Trujillo family, who arrived in 1942. In a memoir, Agapito Trujillo describes Portales: "The atmosphere, unlike the rest of New Mexico, is strictly Texan" (Trujillo and Elder 2015, 16). Trujillo was a member of one of several such families arriving from Encino to harvest the peanut crop as seasonal workers. With little left for them to return to in drought-stricken Encino, the Trujillo family stayed. Over time, other Hispanic families settled the area permanently (Trujillo and Elder 2015). Some accounts describe that by 1965, the Hispanic population constituted nearly one-third of the population (Penrod 2005). According to the

1970 US census, the city of Portales, New Mexico, had 10,554 residents, of which 136 people were reported as foreign born.[2] United States census data (1970) indicate that in 1970, 16 percent of Portales residents were Hispanic.

Though the Hispanic population was a sizeable percentage of the local population by the 1960s, discrimination against Hispanics was overt and persistent. Portales belonged to a region of New Mexico dubbed "Little Texas" for its geographic proximity to Texas and because cultural and identity politics more closely resembled those of Texas than Santa Fe (Polese 1978; Trujillo and Elder 2015).[3] For example, it was not until 1970 that the Roosevelt County Courthouse hired its first employee with a Spanish surname (Penrod 2005). While Spanish-surnamed families were more engrained in the power structures of northern New Mexico, in Portales, families of similar heritage continued to experience exclusion and marginalization. In local business and city services, the Hispanic population was nearly invisible. Most Spanish-surnamed residents of Portales could only secure employment as farm workers (Penrod 2005; Trujillo and Elder 2015).

The town of Portales was also shaped by an institution of higher learning that would play a significant role in the civil rights movement in the second half of the century. Eastern New Mexico University, initially founded as Eastern New Mexico Community College, was legislated in 1927, opened in 1934, and transitioned to a full four-year university in 1940.[4] Over time, the presence of a university attracted other kinds of "outsiders" to Portales, including academics and students from diverse populations.[5]

In the 1960s and early 1970s Spanish-surnamed residents of Portales were subjected to racism and discrimination in their daily lives. For Frank I. Sánchez, founding member of Eastern New Mexico University's student groups Association to Help Our Raza Advance (AHORA) and the Chicano Youth Organization (CYA) and principal community organizer behind the *Serna v. Portales* case, the racism and economic disparity between whites and Mexican Americans was most evident on the "Mexican side of town." According to Sánchez, North Portales had "unpaved roads [while] everything was paved on the Southside, and so you know, you clearly could see the disparities and in talking to African Americans, they talked about how in some restaurants they weren't even served. . . . We felt pretty isolated. . . . Most Mexican Americans just, we stuck to ourselves."[6] Isidro González, a classmate of Frank I. Sánchez at New Mexico University and cofounding member of AHORA and CYA, describes Portales in the following way: "I knew my place. And I wasn't going to make waves. . . . We were powerless."[7]

An unpublished manuscript by local Portales historian Dolores Penrod (2005) recounts different types of discrimination that impacted the minority population of the community. People with a "Hispanic" phenotype were routinely picked up and hassled by police. Young Hispanic males were often targeted by police for nonexistent crimes when merely walking in the community; the police would "just pick them up on the street and lock them up, for no reason."[8] Once in jail, the jailer often shaved their heads. Not only was this punishment unjustly exercised, it was humiliating and shaming. Many young men who were unjustly shaved were reluctant to return to school once released (Penrod 2005). In other instances of aggression, female shoppers at a white-owned grocery store in North Portales were regularly harassed (Penrod 2005). Intimidation tactics were used in court cases and white males composed a majority of juries (Penrod 2005). Spanish-surnamed families were routinely denied access to basic services in the community such as healthcare. Christine Sánchez Cantrell noted how in Portales, "those babies were dying without prenatal care."[9] For Spanish surnamed families in Portales, every facet of life was impacted by discriminatory attitudes and practices. The educational system of the town was also not immune.

THE PORTALES SCHOOL DISTRICT

It was a very difficult time, because of seeing our people so downtrodden,
and knowing how far we had to bring them up, and knowing
that they finally had a resource through the legal system to do it.
CHRISTINE SÁNCHEZ CANTRELL [2017]

The Portales School District replicated the discriminatory racial practices of the larger community. The district did not employ Spanish-speaking teachers. Not only were they lacking Spanish-speaking teachers, they did not have any teachers or employees with Spanish surnames working in the district. A 1966 newspaper column reported that in that year alone, Portales High School had sixty-six dropouts, a large number of whom were Spanish-surnamed youth who were often admonished with harsh punishments and provided inadequate educational experiences.[10] Juvenile officers routinely sent Hispanic boys and girls to reform school in Springer, NM, and Girl Houses in Albuquerque with little to no cause (Penrod 2005).

In 1970, the Portales School District was still punishing students with "licks for speaking Spanish." In one particular instance, a parent named Isabel Gonzales notified local activist Dolores Penrod about a punishment issued to her son, Jake. After speaking Spanish to a peer, Jake was sent to the principal's office and given the choice of suspension or licks. Jake refused the licks and was suspended. Penrod contacted the national civil rights advocacy group, Mexican American Legal Defense and Educational Fund (MALDEF) in Albuquerque, which became involved in the case. A MALDEF attorney phoned the superintendent and requested that the student get reinstated in school. When the superintendent refused to reinstate the student, MALDEF called again with a threat to deliver a file to the federal court house against the Portales School District. The threat of legal action forced the superintendent to relent (Penrod 2005, 84). The school board continued to support the use of corporal punishment in schools, despite the fact that a presentation had been made to them on the detriments of this type of punishment.

Before that time, white teachers commonly expressed racial resentments and even disgust toward Mexican American families and students of Portales. Evangelina Encinias, a bilingual teacher who was brought into Portales after *Serna*, recalls teaching her class next to one white teacher of white students who pushed the school to keep "Mexican" kids out of "their" restrooms, claiming they were dirty and that "those kids don't know how to use the bathroom." Melinda González, former student at Eastern New Mexico University and later a bilingual educator in Portales, recounts when a white fifth-grade teacher asked her a question that had been bothering her for years: "Why do you people name your children Jesús!?" For Melinda, this teacher's tone of condemnation signaled a grave loss of educational opportunity for generations of students whose teacher, for cultural misunderstanding, "harbored that resentment all these years against these bright kids" and "you people," their families and community.[11] During her student teaching practicum as an undergraduate at Eastern New Mexico University, Christine Sánchez-Cantrell noted linguistic misunderstandings resulting in over-identification of Spanish-speaking children in special education classrooms. In an oral history interview (2017), Christine recounts a particular student deemed to have no language skills and placed in special education. Once Christine began working with her, she recognized that the girl was a fluent Spanish speaker, likely placed because she didn't respond in English.

Infuriated by the treatment of their children, parents began to organize. In 1969, many mothers with Spanish surnames were elected to serve as PTA officers in local schools (Penrod 2005). Based on the pattern of discrimination occurring throughout the district, a group of Eastern New Mexico University students and North Portales community members in 1970 issued a statement to the Portales School Board with seven demands (Penrod 2005), which would eventually form the core of the *Serna v. Portales* lawsuit. When initially presented with the demands, one of which was a request that the district offer bilingual education, the board argued that they did not have sufficient funds to provide bilingual education. They refused to end corporal punishment, and a mandate to fire the middle school principal was ignored, but the board could not stop the agency or the momentum that was building among stakeholders.

THE STUDENTS OF EASTERN NEW MEXICO UNIVERSITY

These struggles for equity and justice sustained by the Portales families and community members of *Serna* were preceded by several events in the late 1960s that fortified student resistance to racial and linguistic oppression. Minority students at Eastern New Mexico University, activated by the larger national civil rights movement, organized around local injustices. Isidro González notes, "I could relate to the farm workers because of my dad . . . the problems they were going through and the injustices that they suffered. . . . Martin Luther King and César Chavez were people that you would admire because they gave you an opportunity to get beyond the oppression."[12] When González began at Eastern New Mexico University, there were few Chicano and Mexican American students. By the late 1960s, Mexican American numbers had grown, largely a result of the federally funded Upward Bound program, which supported underrepresented minority students to attain secondary education. Young people of Portales, who had been expected to "know their place," found solidarity with other Mexican American students from around the state. In line with universities such as Ohio's Kent State and the University of California, Berkley, students at Eastern New Mexico held marches decrying the Vietnam War, police brutality, sexual harassment, and campus racism. They staged protests, marches, and sit-ins, pressing university administration for Chicano and ethnic studies and for recruitment of Mexican American students and professors.

WORKING TO CHANGE THE MUSIC IN PORTALES

During these years, Mexican American students would no longer accept "how things were and that that's the way they were always going to be," González contends. "That's when we started seeing and admitting to ourselves: Why? Why are we allowing this to happen? And how come you're allowing the CUB [Campus Union Building] not to put any Mexican songs on the jukebox?"[13]

Melinda González, also a student at Eastern and later Isidro's wife, describes the significance of one event in which Mexican American students demanded a change to the Anglo music that had dominated in the CUB: "It was just a big victory. Just the music in the jukebox . . . just a small thing that kind of galvanized people together [to] say, 'Why don't we?' . . . So at 9:00 in the morning, I mean people skipped classes and everything when the guy went and changed the music. . . . It empowered us to not be afraid to do these things." To Isidro, changing the music was a way for Mexican American students at Eastern to "show the rest of the people in the CUB that we were there." This difficult racial climate and students' desire and newfound voice for change would play out in the lives of Mexican American children in Portales, who alone did not have this power to change the music.[14]

SERNA V. PORTALES MUNICIPAL SCHOOLS

[Portales] had four elementary schools. . . . Lindsey was located on the north side of the tracks where the Hispano lived . . . up to 87–88 percent Hispanic . . . but when you went to the junior high, it dropped to 27 percent. . . . Then when you went to the high school it dropped to 17 percent. So our kids were flunking out, dropping out, being disgusted and cutting out

DAN SOSA JR. [2005, Elizabeth Galligan Oral History Collection]

We made . . . demands on the Portales School System . . . a community effort . . . a whole lot had gone on. . . . We went to the school board. . . . We demanded that they quit punishing our kids for speaking Spanish. . . . We demanded they establish a bilingual program. . . . We demanded that they hire Mexican American teachers. They had zero at the time. . . . We wanted school board members. . . . This was before there was a lawsuit.

FRANK I. SÁNCHEZ [2003, Elizabeth Galligan Oral History Collection]

Like I say, this [lawsuit] was done pretty quietly and it kind of surprised us.

SUPERINTENDENT L. C. COZZENS [2003, Elizabeth Galligan Oral History Collection]

In the 1971–1972 school year, the Portales Municipal School District of Eastern New Mexico comprised four elementary schools, one junior high, and one high school. Thirty-four percent of elementary school students were Spanish-surnamed Spanish-speaking children. By middle and high school, Spanish-surnamed enrollment declined to just 29 and 17 percent, respectively. A 1969 report by the Portales Municipal Schools to the US Commission on Civil Rights revealed that the four elementary schools—Lindsey, James, Steiner, and Brown—were racially and linguistically segregated. At Lindsey Elementary in particular, 86 percent of students were Spanish-speaking children of Nuevo-mexicano/Mexican American descent, while in the other three schools, those students were nearly absent.

On July 2, 1971, a US marshal delivered a summons to the superintendent of schools and four Portales principals. The summons contained six causes of action within a class-action suit filed by the family of Judy Serna, a kindergartener in the Portales Municipal Schools. Judy, who was seven years-old at the time of the suit, recalls the words of her late mother, Ramona, explaining it to her years later: "Mija . . . If these attorneys ever come looking for you this is the reason why. . . . I put a lawsuit because they wouldn't let you start school because you didn't speak English."[15] The suit eventually involved other families of Portales's Spanish-speaking Lindsey Elementary community and Eastern New Mexico University's CYA (Holmes 1975). On August 19 of the same year, the suit was narrowed to include only the children as appellees.

When *Serna* was initially filed, conservative community members, educators, and members of the school board dismissed the activism leading up to the case as fomented by outside radicals, an assertion based on the national legal counsel of MALDEF, which in fact had strong ties to New Mexico. MALDEF provided the following attorneys: Vilma Martinez, Sanford Jay Rosen, Alan Axelrod, and Michael Mendelson, all of San Francisco, as well as David Bonem of Clovis, New Mexico, and Dan Sosa Jr. of Las Cruces, New Mexico.

The grassroots leaders of *Serna* began their activism in 1967 as New Mexican students at Eastern New Mexico University involved in AHORA, Upward Bound, and the Black Student Union, which culminated with the efforts of multi-generational New Mexican families connected to the North Portales Community Association and the Chicano Welfare Rights Organization. Principal families named in the suit likewise bore multigenerational ties to New Mexico. Attorneys filed on behalf of plaintiffs, citing discrimination on grounds of national origin manifesting as linguistic and racialized discrimination that inhibited Spanish-speaking, Spanish-surnamed students' access to meaningful education.[16]

Three families at the heart of the momentum and the organizational know-how of *Serna* included the Serna, Meza, and Aragón families, who had encountered the United Farm Workers in California while working the circuit of migrant labor. According to Frank Sánchez, these families "moved back to the community so they had some, some connection . . . to social movements and social justice. . . . They were familiar with the issues. . . . They had also lived in the Portales area. So clearly they knew the, the injustices and discrimination."[17] Judy recalls the activism of her grandmother, Simona Meza,

> My grandma did a lot. . . . I remember them doing a lot of *huelgas*. . . . They would get in groups and go to the courthouse and protest. . . . I remember my grandma would always be like, "Don't let them spank you, if they spank you, let us know. . . . My grandma pushed her to say enough is enough. . . . When it came to me, and they told her again, "You need to teach them English before they come," I think she was just like, "No." It was maybe at that point that she decided that this wasn't right.[18]

Serna publicly exposed Portales's long history of racism, educational segregation, social stratification, and stark economic disparities between Mexican and white populations. Recalling the deposition of one boy who testified that his Anglo shop teacher disparaged his project, telling him it was "a typical Mexican job," Dan Sosa Jr. notes, "This is one of the things that knocked them down. That if it was Mexican, it was no good . . . [the Anglo shop teacher] told him that! . . . Can you imagine how he must have felt when he went home? This is second rate."[19] Janie Flores, who grew up in Portales, was a founding member of AHORA and the CYA and was later a Spanish teacher, likewise contends that racism shaped her schooling:

> Lindsey School was the "Mexican school." And everybody that went to Lindsey School flunked at least one grade. . . . That was the norm. . . . My parents really didn't want me to go to Lindsey. They knew what it was like. . . . We used to be tracked at Portales High School. . . . Most of the Mexican kids that made it to high school were in track three . . . vocational. . . . All the kids that I started school with by the time we finished, there was so few of us left.[20]

Janie goes on to describe the climate of resistance surrounding *Serna*:

> I remember the time that Serna was going on . . . there was a man named Mr. ___ who had been a junior high history teacher and he was a real redneck, you know. . . . And he said, "I don't know where all these kids are getting these wild ideas about they have to be taught in Spanish. . . . We didn't teach you guys

in Spanish and you did just fine." And I just looked at him and said, "Maybe it's because we didn't know any better." And he didn't like that very much. He turned around and walked off.

Even two decades after the Red Scare (Schrecker 1994), the collective advocacy of these groups was painted by many as being that of radical communist outsiders and not the inevitable uprising of generations of people who had endured decades of racial/linguistic oppression.

POSITING AND LEGAL QUESTIONS OF THE CASE LEGAL ARGUMENT—SERNA ET AL., PLAINTIFFS-APPELLEES

National origin discrimination in equal educational opportunities was the alleged basis for the lawsuit. The suit that appellees brought against the Portales Municipal Schools alleged discrimination against Spanish-surnamed families and students under the following claims: 1) failure to provide bilingual instruction; 2) failure to hire bilingual educators of Mexican American descent; 3) failure to provide a curriculum attending to the particular educational needs of Mexican American children; 4) failure to provide a curriculum highlighting the historical contributions of people(s) of Mexican and Spanish descent in New Mexico and nationally; and 5) failure to hire Mexican Americans in upper administration and truancy officer positions (Serna v. Portales, 1974). Appellees argued that a substantial number of Spanish surnamed students had been denied their constitutional right to an equal educational opportunity under the Civil Rights Act SEC. 601, which states:

> No person in the United States shall, on the ground of race, color, or national origin, be excluded from participation in, be denied the benefits of, or be subjected to discrimination under any program or activity receiving Federal financial assistance.

MALDEF attorneys presented the following evidence. Until 1970, not one of the teachers in the Portales District was Spanish surnamed, not even those who taught Spanish at the high school level. Additionally, there had never been a Spanish-surnamed principal or vice principal, and there were no Spanish-speaking staff. Further evidence indicated that across the four elementary schools, great educational disparities existed between Mexican American and Anglo students, which over time resulted in low attendance and school dropouts.

These Spanish-speaking elementary students, who on the whole did not speak English—save four bilingual students—were at the time of the lawsuit enrolled in a language arts program that was delivered exclusively in English. According to a New Mexico Department of Education evaluation entered into evidence, the class was "below average and not meeting the needs of those children" (499 F.2d 1147, 2). Appellees argued that despite the district's knowledge of the un-disputed evidence of disproportionately low academic outcomes, high dropout rates, lack of bilingual educators and staff, and low quality programs for Spanish surnamed children, they neither applied for funds under the federal Bilingual Education Act (20 US C. § 880b) nor accepted funds that were offered by the state to ameliorate the situation.

Attorneys brought expert witnesses to testify on behalf of plaintiffs. According to official court records for the United States Court of Appeals, Tenth Circuit (499 F.2d 1147) these included long-time educator Maria Gutiérrez Spencer and child psychologist Estevan Moreno. Gutiérrez Spencer testified on the grounds of her personal, cultural, and professional experience as a native New Mexican who herself received punishment as a child in Las Cruces for speaking her mother tongue of Spanish and as an educator who pioneered education for Native/Heritage Spanish speakers across grades decades before it was nationally recognized as a field (L. Gutiérrez-Spencer, personal communication, August 15, 2017). Maria Gutiérrez Spencer's testimony signified a turning point in *Serna*. According to MALDEF attorney Dan Sosa Jr., Gutiérrez Spencer's testimony underscored that "if you pounce a kid down, have him lose his sense of identity and he loses his dignity and he looks around and becomes frustrated, it doesn't matter if you have a good curriculum. He's not going to learn it."[21]

The testimony of Maria Gutiérrez Spencer and Estevan Moreno established the low pedagogical effectiveness of English-only curricula for Spanish-speaking children. Additionally, thrusting Spanish-speaking Mexican American children into an English-only environment to the exclusion of their home culture has emotional, psychological, intellectual, behavioral, and academic impacts that culminate in feelings of low self-worth, invisibility, and frustration, which inhibit their participation in community and school life.[22] Another key witness for the plaintiffs was Henry Pascual, who later became one of the chief organizers of the New Mexico Association for Bilingual Education. As director of the New Mexico Communicative Arts Division, Pascual was asked by the New Mexico Department of Education to conduct a routine evaluation of Portales district schools. Years later, in an interview conducted by Mary Jean Haberman López and Julia Rosa López-Emslie, Pascual recalls what he saw at Lindsey:

It was a totally segregated school. . . . Instruction was absolutely lousy. It was bad. The [Spanish-surname] kids, they didn't know what they were doing, they couldn't read, the teachers, they didn't give a #s@ percent one way or another.[23]

Pascual asserts that the evaluation filed with the state,

specifically stated . . . Lindsey school should not be funded for the following year until it was desegregated and that a significant instructional program, including the proper instruction of English as a second language and possibly instituting a bilingual program to give the students a sense of belonging and not of identity destruction.[24]

The Pascual report was central to MALDEF's victory, both in 1972 and on appeal.

LEGAL ARGUMENT—PORTALES MUNICIPAL SCHOOLS, DEFENDANTS-APPELLANTS

Lead attorney for the Portales Municipal Schools was Archibald H. McCloud, who chiefly called upon the testimony of Superintendent L. C. Cozzens. Cozzens testified that a lack of district funding inhibited efforts toward bilingual education and likewise that a lack of Spanish-surnamed applicants across the district impeded the hiring of Mexican American principals, vice principals, teachers, secretaries, and truancy officers. He further testified that during the 1971–1972 hiring cycle, only one Spanish-surnamed applicant was identified out of nearly eighty total elementary teacher applicants. Cozzens's testimony described actions the district had taken when *Serna* was filed in 1972 to ameliorate the opportunity and achievement disparities it alleged. Preemptive actions included hiring six Spanish-surnamed teachers, initiating a high school ethnic studies course, and mandating cultural awareness training for teaching, which one third attended. Cozzens further asserted that an ESL program was now offered to Mexican American first grade students at Lindsey.

During cross examination, defense attorney for the district asked Henry Pascual to reference his report with specific reference to the Lindsey school. Although the final report compiled by Pascual and his team (consisting of educator Mela Leger and Bob White of the University of New Mexico) and referenced in the *Serna* (1974) legal briefing uncontrovertibly cited gross educational inequities at Lindsey, the authenticity of the actual evaluation submitted into evidence by the Department of Education came under scrutiny during the

1972 court proceedings. As Judge Mechem read from the report in evidence, Pascual recognized that the state had submitted a doctored version omitting committee findings and recommendations. Pascual immediately alerted the judge to his realization and began reading from his own copy of the report, which was originally submitted:

> I got halfway through [my] report and the lawyer for MALDEF called to the judge and said, "I request a recess. Henry lets go have a cup of coffee." And when we sat down, he said "Henry, we just won the case."[25]

This rather dramatic courtroom revelation demonstrated to many the lengths to which the state would go to conceal the educational injustice Spanish-surnamed children and families endured. The lower court relied heavily upon Pascual's evaluation to rule that strict measures were insufficient in addressing the low test scores and discrimination brought to light in *Serna*.

LOWER COURT RULING

In 1972, the court ruled for declaratory and injunctive relief against the Portales Municipal Schools for discrimination against Spanish-surnamed students. District Judge Edwin L. Mechem found in favor of appellees, citing discrimination on the part of the district under the Equal Protections clause of the Fourteenth Amendment and ordered a plan of relief which encompassed areas of curriculum, recruitment/hiring, and funding. Regarding curriculum, the following actions were ordered: 1) all students in grades one through six were to receive thirty to forty-five minutes per day of bilingual instruction which included establishing a Title III self-contained classroom for first grade students; 2) a testing system would be instituted to determine adequacy of bilingual programming; 3) a bicultural outlook would be taken in as many subjects as is possible and/or practical; 4) a high school ethnic studies course would be established in the 1973–1974 school year as an elective funded through the State Department of Education though with local school board control. Regarding recruitment, the plan mandated special efforts be made to fill vacancies with qualified bilingual teachers. It also ordered the district to investigate state and federal funding to provide equality of educational opportunity for Spanish surname children.

The district immediately appealed this ruling, challenging the evidence that a lack of bilingual education precluded a meaningful education for

Spanish-surnamed Spanish-speaking children. The district likewise challenged appellees' right to bring a class-action lawsuit, arguing that this collective of school-age children, families, and community members could claim personal stake in the outcome of district actions. Appellants argued that "even if the school district were unintentionally discriminating against Spanish surnamed students prior to institution of this lawsuit, the [preemptive] program they present to the trial court in compliance with the court's memorandum opinion sufficiently meets the needs of appellees." The New Mexico State Board of Education, in their amicus curiae brief, supported the district's appeal, citing that the trial court's decision and the relief granted "constitute unwarranted and improper judicial interference in the internal affairs of the Portales School district."[26] Judges for the United States Court of Appeals for the Tenth Circuit struck down this appeal, ruling again in favor of plaintiffs.

TENTH CIRCUIT COURT OF APPEALS: CIVIL RIGHTS LANGUAGE BEYOND THE NEW MEXICO CONSTITUTION

While Judge Mechem decided *Serna v. Portales* in 1972 on the legal precedent set by the 1954 *Brown v. Board of Education of Topeka*, which found the Board of Education in violation of Section 1 of the Fourteenth Amendment, *Serna* on appeal was in fact decided upon the legal precedent established in the 1974 US Supreme Court case *Lau v. Nichols*.[27] *Lau* ruled that the San Francisco Unified School District violated the Civil Rights Act, Section 601, which bans discrimination "on the ground of race, color, or national origin [in] any program or activity receiving Federal financial assistance."[28] Six months prior to the 1974 *Serna* decision, justices in *Lau* ruled in favor of Chinese non-English speaking students who alleged that the San Francisco Unified School District precluded them from a meaningful education on the grounds of a lack of allowances for their particular linguistic and educational needs. *Lau* established legal precedent for *Serna* (1974) in that the inability to speak and understand English had prohibited national origin and/or minority group children from effective and meaningful participation in a program offered by the school district. Judges in both *Lau* and *Serna* ruled that in cases where language becomes a barrier to educational access, the district must take action. Judges on appeal in the Tenth Circuit *Serna* ruling found that Mexican American students were deprived their statutory rights under Title VI of the 1964 Civil Rights Act by virtue of the district's failure to attend to their language needs and offer a meaningful education.[29] Court of Appeals judges found that the lower court's plan was indeed feasible and that the district's preemptive efforts did not sufficiently remedy *Serna*'s claims of discrimination. In his final ruling, Judge James R. Durfee wrote:

> The evidence shows unequivocally that appellants had failed to provide appellees with a meaningful education. There was adequate evidence that appellants' proposed program was only a token plan that would not benefit appellees. Under these circumstances the trial court had a duty to fashion a program which would provide adequate relief for Spanish surnamed children. . . . Under Title VI of the Civil Rights Act of 1964 appellees have a right to bilingual education.[30]

THE YEAR IN HELL AND PAVING A WAY TO HEAVEN

Upon the 1974 *Serna* ruling, the district under federal mandate hired more Spanish-surnamed teachers from across the state. Evangelina Encinias describes her move to Portales to accept a kindergarten position as both personally and professionally difficult:

> I know why I was hired. . . . I've always called myself the token Mexican for Portales . . . there were several other Hispanics that were hired that year . . . with federal money. . . . It was difficult to come here. . . . Teachers would come by and slam their door shut on the bilingual classroom because they didn't want to hear them [students]. . . . They're shunned, teachers are not supported. . . . I had nothing. . . . There were no books . . . nothing. . . . My background was not in early childhood, and was certainly not in English as a second language, but I had to teach those little guys something. [31]

Melinda González, also hired in Portales post *Serna*, describes the difficult situation she encountered when her new position disrupted established district power structures:

> They had to hire someone. . . . They were under the gun to hire bilingual teachers and Mrs. Cozzens [superintendent's wife] was named in the suit [as] Judy Serna's teacher. . . . I walked into her room and she was packing up her things and all the teachers were in there . . . all crying. And I walk in saying, "Hi. I'm the new teacher!" Not a good reception [laughing]. . . . They were forced to have us there. We were not welcome. . . . The principal did not give us any support . . . [It] really makes me mad because they really didn't care if we had the skills as long as they had the name to give to it—we were sort of tokens.[32]

Although the new hires note the lack of support and rejection they received from white colleagues and the blatant racism against Mexican American students culminating in what Melinda González calls "the year in hell," she says these teachers also "paved our way to heaven with it."[33] The "heaven" that González notes was being able to serve Mexican American students who, like themselves, had experienced economic and linguistic challenges in schools that did not want them and were not invested in their success. Judy Serna, who became one of Melinda's first students, similarly evokes this "heaven" they found: "Mrs. González . . . and her husband were . . . like guardian angels . . . It was just one year, but it was like a lifetime to me. . . . She just protected us and took care of us. . . . She really just kind of put us under her wing."[34] Evangelina Encinias describes her resolve as an educator who understood the challenges her students and families faced: "I had kids that had to get up, get themselves cleaned, make their own breakfast, and get to school. And when they came in dirty, you just kind of overlooked it because you knew that mom and dad had to leave at five o'clock in the morning."[35]

The "way to heaven" was also paved by these teachers' ability to connect with Mexican American families and to support them socially and educationally. Evangelina remembers that "parents felt a little freer. . . . I had a lot of parents come to my classroom . . . two of them are now teachers . . . she decided that, 'Hey, I can do this,' because she had been a part of our classroom . . . [it] had a big impact. It was very meaningful to them."[36] Teacher advocacy extended outside the classroom as well. Christine Sánchez Cantrell worked with teachers to lead an afterschool *ballet folklórico* troop, which affirmed the cultural heritage of the children by engaging the practice and history of Mexican dances. Families, too, became involved in costume design and sacrificed greatly for their children's attendance.

THE LEGACY OF *SERNA*

In thinking about Serna's legacy, several things become salient:

    1. Women were central to the initiation, organization, and enactment of advocacy leading up to the *Serna* decision as well as in the remedies resulting from it.

    2. Student activism was a powerful and potent factor in Portales, New Mexico, and was ultimately a decisive factor in provoking the legal change at a state and

national level. While legal precedent set forth by *Lau* (1974) established that non-English speaking Chinese students could not be precluded from a meaningful education by English-only policies and practices, Judy Serna's words reveal the magnitude of *this* case: "We were *born* here. . . . People tell me *oh you are Mexican*. . . . My *mom* was not born in Mexico, my *dad* wasn't born in Mexico, I don't know if my *grandfather* was even born in Mexico.

3. I'm from *here*." *Serna* forced the nation to recognize that in New Mexico, Spanish is *not* a foreign tongue.

4. The battle over language in US schools and public spaces is not linguistic— it is politically inextricable from battles involving land, power, belonging, and the dignity of all marginalized and minoritized people(s) of color that continue to this day.

This legacy is ours as a state, as New Mexicans across identity and as Spanish-speaking Nuevomexicanos who have collectively inherited it and are entrusted to carry it forward. *Serna*'s legacy touches us as Nuevomexicanas, as female educators, and as the descendants of two people in particular—Christine Sánchez Cantrell and Dan Sosa Jr.—who were brought into Portales during the same historical moment to offer educational and legal remedy to the children, families, and community struggling for racial and linguistic equity there.

REBECCA: YOU GUYS CAN DO IT

I think one of the greatest things I've done in my life was that clinic that's still there, that we were able to start that clinic for all those people and it's been there for 40 years. And it wasn't easy because . . . we knew that the authorities for whatever infraction that we had would be out to get us.
CHRISTINE SÁNCHEZ CANTRELL, 2017

My colleague and lifelong friend Mía Sosa-Provencio, knowing of my interest in New Mexico history and my commitment to bilingual education, invited me to work on the *Serna* chapter after her own invitation from Rebecca Blum Martínez. I was initially drawn to the project for just that reason; I looked forward to excavating the history of the *Serna* case in order to amplify its significance and to more deeply understand the history of my home state, a place I cherish. Because I was interested in the topic and also because of my regard for the work of the late Justice Dan Sosa, I eagerly jumped into the research. I couldn't have imagined the numerous other personal connections that would reveal themselves in the research.[37]

My *herencia* is a set of ideals and commitments rooted in social justice, education, and equity. In my family, we joke that education is the family business. My grandfather, Albert N. Sánchez, was an advocate for bilingual education in Guadalupe and San Miguel counties from the onset of his career in the 1950s, and two of my father's siblings who attended Eastern New Mexico University in the 1970s and both became bilingual teachers. To this day, I can still hear my grandfather telling his children, grandchildren, and me—and anyone in his path—"You can do it." That mantra was a fortification that motivated all of us to stay committed in perilous times. After mentioning in passing the research for this chapter to my aunt, Christine Sánchez Cantrell (formerly Christine Sánchez Brandl), I learned that she was one of the bilingual teachers hired by the Portales School District to remedy the discriminatory practices of the district. Throughout her time in Portales, my grandparents supported her work, telling her regularly, "You can do it."

As I combed through old newspaper articles and the unpublished Penrod (2005) manuscript, I found my cousins Bernice Garcia and Ernest Sánchez listed as heroes of the "struggle for justice." There I noted cousins from both sides of my father's family who, like Christine, had engaged in activism to improve the lives of our people. I have since shared numerous conversations with my aunt about life in Portales at that time, and she has described the abhorrent conditions the families were up against. In emotional accounts, my aunt recalled the racism, the lack of services, and the indignities thrust upon the children and families with Spanish surnames at that time. I learned that in her long career as an educator, her most significant accomplishment was assisting in the creation of a health clinic in Portales while working there as a bilingual teacher. Even then, she connected the work with the clinic to my family story by mentioning that my father, Albert T. Sánchez, helped acquire medical supplies for the clinic. Every conversation, every bit of historical evidence from oral history collections, newspapers, and primary documents, connects me more intimately to the *Serna* case and to the cause.

To me, the case is about organizing, about women coming together, and about students having a hand in shaping the future. Frank Sánchez, in reflecting on how change came about in Portales, commented, "It was always the women." My aunt echoed this when she said:

So it was a great time. I didn't know I would get so emotional but it's hard to remember back because we cried a lot together you know, we had to stay strong together and that's why I can remember all these ladies that I worked with because we were all together saying *this has to be done*. They don't want us here, the board and the superintendent, they don't want us here. But we're going to show them that it can be done for our people so we did. I'd go home and cry to papa and mama and Bob and papa and mama and Bob [my husband] would say you guys can do it. Just keep at it. They were good times and they were hard times. And that's what we do. We gave them a lot of heart.[38]

I have deep roots in activism, education, and New Mexico. The research process connected me more deeply to my own lineage and *herencia*. As I consider the challenges we face as bilingual educators in New Mexico, I will call upon the wisdom of my grandfather and summon the phrase that has propelled our work and been passed through the generations. You can do it.

MÍA: CASTING BREAD UPON THE WATERS

I was sitting in the dentist chair the other day. . . . I started reflecting about my life . . . What meaningful thing have I done? . . . I can truly say that the most meaningful time in my life was from 1965 to 1975 . . . Working with MALDEF at its inception. . . . Success in life isn't the accumulation of money . . . [but] how you have lived life to help people.
DAN SOSA JR. [2004, Elizabeth Galligan Oral History Collection]

I have been deeply moved by happenings in this work that could be perceived as coincidences but which I instead receive as evidence of the interconnectedness and blessings that are had when we accept the good work before us and do so toward a greater purpose. I am not a historian, legal scholar, or a scholar of bilingual education. My work lies in youth engagement and teacher preparation, especially for Mexican American/Latina/o students. The editors of this book, colleagues of mine at the University of New Mexico's College of Education, invited me to write this chapter principally because Dan Sosa Jr.—*Serna* attorney, former Supreme Court justice, and one of eight founders of MALDEF—is my maternal grandfather. As our family continues to bear his loss on September 4, 2016, at the age of ninety-three, this chapter brings him back to me in profound ways. It leads me toward his history, our family history of struggling for generations to hold onto our beloved Spanish, and toward others who lived these events and who knew and loved *him* long before I did. This chapter revealed where my family history merges with others', including that of Rebecca Sánchez, my colleague and coauthor here. Working to uncover the history of *Serna*, Rebecca and I, childhood friends from Las Cruces, discovered that her aunt was one of the teachers hired in Portales as per federal mandate. I also had the pleasure of meeting Frank Sánchez, wise rabble rouser and community organizer at the heart of *Serna's* student activism. Here was this man whom I had never met, who knew my grandpa since his youth, and who had maintained a friendship decades after *Serna*. I am certain it brought a smile to my grandpa's face to see Frank, Rebecca, and me sitting at the Frontier Restaurant that morning discussing this case.[39]

Though Dan Sosa Jr. was conviction-in-the-flesh for maintaining our Spanish amid discrimination and keeping the flame of justice alive in New Mexico, one of my biggest regrets was not documenting his recollections surrounding *Serna's* legal implications or his personal connection as a boy from Las Cruces reared on the "Mexican" side of town who did not have access to the bilingual education he helped ensure in *Serna*. I was initially discouraged by the lack of academic literature pertaining to the topic, but I could feel my grandpa's gentle hand guiding me. Upon calling Eastern New Mexico University's library in Portales, I was given the phone number of a retired professor, Elizabeth Galligan, who I was told "had done work on *Serna*." I was able to reach Galligan, who told me of her multiyear oral history project. With the passage of time, however, she could not say if she had met or interviewed my grandpa. She graciously welcomed Rebecca and me into her home and into her research. As I sat on her floor next to boxes of meticulously organized folders, there it was—a glorious thirty-two-page document transcribed verbatim. Grandpa's voice rained down on me. Lines thundered with his language, his sharp memory for names and dates that remained intact until his death, and the way he punctuated sentences with laughter and seasoned quips that were his alone. He spoke to me through those pages, as if to say, "I will never be lost to you. I am in all that you do." He is with me now, even as I write this with the help of his great-grandchild, growing and kicking inside me. In the transcript, he says *Serna* "made me feel glad I'm alive; I'm glad I'm able to do something for my people. . . . [It] had such an impact on my life." The lessons he infused into my mother and her six siblings rise sharply: Honor your people. Fight fiercely with others for what is just. Make yourself available to the Almighty and your strength will be renewed. Make way for those who follow. One story he relays to the researchers from the campaign trail underscores these lessons:

I saw a kid and I knew he was an attorney. . . . I saw him blowing up balloons that said "Sosa Supreme Court" in Albuquerque. Then I'd see him up there in Farmington. . . . So I went over there to talk to him. . . . "I don't know I can ever repay you." He said, . . . "You're one of the founders of MALDEF, and I'm one of the recipients of your scholarship. I went to law school . . . because of MALDEF."

I have heard him tell this story many times, so I know his open-mouthed "¡¿*Fí-jate*?!" expression of satisfied disbelief that followed. He then adds solemnly, "Bread that you cast upon the waters comes back to you." He says these words without biblical reference, but because I know my grandpa, I sought them there first. Indeed: Ecclesiastes 11:1 reads, "Cast your bread upon the waters, for you will find it after many days." My deepest wish is that the lionheartedness of all the players of *Serna* come back to us like bread cast upon the waters in these trying times during which embers of hate seek to divide us as brothers and sisters. Even these many days later, we must look upon the waters for *their* bread as nourishment for the journey that lies ahead.

NOTES

1. Although many labels are utilized by the Spanish-surnamed population of New Mexico, such as *Hispanic, Nuevomexicano, Latino, Mexican American, Hispano*, this chapter will use the term *Spanish-surnamed*, consistent with language in the lawsuit. Authors also refer to this population using the language and terms of the individuals providing oral histories and historical accounts. As such, if *Hispanic, Mexican American*, or *Mexican*, for example, are used, it is because that is the term utilized in the research sources.

2. The first census with a reporting category of *Hispanic* defined the term as follows: "People who identify with the terms 'Hispanic' or 'Latino' are those who classify themselves in one of the specific Hispanic or Latino categories listed on the decennial census questionnaire and various United States Census Bureau survey questionnaires—'Mexican, Mexican Am., Chicano' or 'Puerto Rican' or 'Cuban'—as well as those who indicate that they are "another Hispanic, Latino, or Spanish origin." This census has been discredited for underestimating the total number of Hispanics in the nation. See US Census Bureau, *1970 Census of Population*, vol. 1, *Characteristics of the Population*, part 33, *New Mexico*, https://www.census.gov/library/publications/1973/dec /population-volume-1.html#par_list_29.

3. Christine Sánchez Cantrell, interviewed by Rebecca M. Sánchez, July 25, 2017, at

private residence in Albuquerque, NM, in private collection of Rebecca Sánchez. See also the Elizabeth Galligan Oral History Collection, Serna v. Portales Oral History Project, Eastern New Mexico University, Portales, NM.

4. Eastern New Mexico University website, http://www.enmu.edu/about/general-information/enmu-history-traditions. References to Eastern New Mexico University as *Eastern* are common in the Elizabeth Galligan Oral History Collection.

5. Sánchez Cantrell interview.

6. Elizabeth Galligan Oral History Collection, 2003.

7. Ibid.

8. Sánchez Cantrell interview.

9. Sánchez Cantrell interview.

10. "By the Way-Dropouts," *Portales New Tribune* January 27, 1966.

11. Elizabeth Galligan Oral History Collection, 2002.

12. Ibid.

13. Ibid.

14. Ibid.

15. Judy Serna, phone interview by Rebecca M. Sánchez and Mía A. Sosa-Provencio, September 6, 2017.

16. Serna v. Portales Municipal Schools, 351 F.Su 1279 (1972); Serna v. Portales Municipal Schools, 499 F.2d 1147 (1974). The original 1972 *Serna* lawsuit ruled against the district and in favor of the plaintiffs. This decision was appealed by the district, which then led to the second and final lawsuit that again ruled in favor of plaintiffs in 1974.

17. Elizabeth Galligan Oral History Collection, 2003.

18. Cantrell Sánchez interview.

19. Elizabeth Galligan Oral History Collection, 2005.

20. Elizabeth Galligan Oral History Collection, 2003.

21. Elizabeth Galligan Oral History Collection, 2005.

22. Serna v. Portales Municipal Schools, 499 F.2d 1147 (1974).

23. Henry W, Pascual, interview by Rebecca Blum Martínez, Mary Jean Habermann López and Julia Rosa López Emslie, August 11, 12, 2001 at Pascual's home. DVD and partial transcript in the personal collection of Mary Jean Habermann López.

24. Ibid.

25. Ibid.

26. Serna v. Portales Municipal Schools, 499 F.2d 1147 (1974), 6.

27. Brown v. Board of Education of Topeka, 347 US 483 (1954); Lau v. Nichols, 414 US 563, 94 S.Ct. 786, 39 L.Ed.2d 1 (1974).

28. 42 US C. § 2000d.

29. 499 F.2d 1147.

30. Ibid., 6.

31. Elizabeth Galligan Oral History Collection, 2003.

32. Elizabeth Galligan Oral History Collection, 2004.

33. Elizabeth Galligan Oral History Collection.

34. Serna interview.

35. 2003, Elizabeth Galligan Oral History Collection.

36. Ibid.

37. Dan Sosa Jr. was born in 1923 in Las Cruces, New Mexico. He graduated from the University of New Mexico School of Law in 1951. Sosa practiced law in Las Cruces for twenty-four years and ultimately served on the New Mexico Supreme Court for sixteen years beginning in 1975. In 1968, Dan was one of the eight founding members of the Mexican-American Legal Defense and Education Fund (MALDEF). In *Serna v. Portales* (1974), Dan acted as one of MALDEF's six attorneys who fought to ensure the language rights of New Mexico's Spanish-speaking Nuevomexicana/o and Mexicana/o People.

38. Cantrell Sánchez interview.

39. Frank I. Sánchez interview by Rebecca M. Sánchez and Mía A. Sosa-Provencio. June 3, 2017, at Frontier Restaurant in Albuquerque, NM.

REFERENCES

Gómez, Laura E. 2008. *Manifest Destinies: The Making of the Mexican American Race.* New York: New York University Press.

González, Gilbert. 1999. "Segregation and the Education of Mexican Children, 1900–1940." In *The Elusive Quest for Education: 150 Years of Chicano/Chicana Education,* edited by José F. Moreno, 53–76. Cambridge, MA: Harvard Educational Review.

Gonzales-Berry, Erlinda. 2000. "Which Language Will Our Children Speak? The Spanish Language and Public Education Policy in New Mexico, 1890–1930." In *The Contested Homeland: A Chicano History of New Mexico,* edited by Erlinda Gonzales-Berry and David R. Maciel, 169–90. Albuquerque: University of New Mexico Press.

Holmes, Joseph M. 1975. "Bilingual Education: Serna v. Portales Municipal Schools." *University of New Mexico Law Review* 5, no. 2: 321.

Milk, Robert. 1980. "The Issue of Language in Education in Territorial New Mexico. *Bilingual Review/La Revista Bilingüe* 7, no. 3: 212–21.

Nieto-Phillips, John M. 2004. *The Language of Blood: The Making of Spanish-American Identity in New Mexico, 1880s–1930s.* Albuquerque: University of New Mexico Press.

Noel, Linda C. 2011. "'I Am an American': Anglos, Mexicans, Nativos, and the National Debate over Arizona and New Mexico Statehood." *Pacific Historical Review* 80, no. 4: 430–520.

Penrod, Dolores. 2005. *Standing There: The Struggle for Justice in Roosevelt County*

1965–1980. Unpublished manuscript. Dolores Penrod Papers (Special Collections). Archives at Eastern New Mexico University Library, Portales, NM.

Polese, Richard. 1978. "New Mexico's 'Little Texas.'" *El Palacio: Quarterly Journal of the Museum of New Mexico* 84, no. 1: 1–132.

San Miguel, Guadalupe, Jr. 1999. "The Schooling of Mexicanos in the Southwest, 1848–1891." In *The Elusive Quest for Education: 150 years of Chicano/Chicana Education*, edited by José F. Moreno, 31–51. Cambridge, MA: Harvard Educational Review.

Schrecker, Ellen. 1994. *The Age of McCarthyism: A Brief History with Documents.* Boston: Bedford.

Trujillo, Agapito, and Donald C. Elder. 2015. *Hispanics of Roosevelt County, New Mexico: A History.* Charleston, SC: History Press.

REBECCA BLUM MARTÍNEZ
AND MARY JEAN HABERMANN LÓPEZ

[8] New Mexico's Role in Federal Policies

PROLOGUE

"The schools have sometimes been like a gardener who buys an expensive rose
bush and cuts its roots. He plants it and lavishes care on it and is surprised that
he has only produced a stump. For in his enthusiasm for change he has killed
the plant. The schools in trying to make us what we are not have often killed
our spirit, stunted our curiosity and deadened our feelings."
MARÍA GUTIÉRREZ SPENCER

The United States after World War II was a prosperous nation. New technology
in the kitchen and in the workplace created for many Americans unprecedented
material comfort and a sense of uniformity in society, along with something the
country's forebears had precious little of: leisure time. Yet this prosperity was not
enjoyed by all, and many people—among them nearly all of America's non-white
citizens, including African Americans, Latinos, and Indigenous peoples—lived
lives of struggle and widespread discrimination and segregation in all corners
of American society, in public spaces, employment, housing, and education.

The levels of poverty among Hispanics displayed in the 1960 US census lent
a lie to the prosperity being touted by politicians. In the Southwest, the total
population had a poverty rate of 19.7 percent. However, Spanish-surnamed
families' levels of poverty were twice that of whites, 34.8 percent to 15.9 percent.
In urban areas, Spanish-surnamed families had a poverty rate of 30.8 percent,
and in rural areas, the differences were even greater—50.2 percent of Spanish-
surnamed families lived in poverty in contrast to 24.2 percent for whites.[1]

The differences in educational attainment between white and Latinos in the
Southwest were also stark. Whereas the median years of schooling for whites was
twelve years for persons fourteen years of age and over, for Spanish-surnamed

individuals, the median was 8.1. The percentage of the Spanish-speaking males in each of the five southwestern states with no schooling added to the despairing profile. In comparison to 27.7 percent of the total population, in Arizona, 52.1 percent of Hispanic males had had no schooling. In Texas, the figures were even more dismal; there, 64.7 percent of Hispanics had no schooling, as compared to 29.2 percent of the general population. In New Mexico, the differences were 44.4 percent of Hispanics to 23.1 percent of the total.[2]

For America's ethnic language minorities, society's long-held doctrine of manifest destiny and the great immigration surges in the early 1900s had spawned an assimilationist philosophy. Under this view, it was believed if all those who spoke a language other than English learned English and surrendered their native language, they would successfully become part of the giant "melting pot," the symbol of the United States at the time. "Traditional theory had argued that ethnicity in general and ethnic minority languages and cultures in particular would disappear over time as a result of ethnic group assimilation into American life" (San Miguel 2004, 7). To "Americanize" Native Americans, children were removed from their parents and thus denied access to their language and culture, a practice that would exorcise them of what was viewed as the harmful influences and deprivation suffered in their home environments (see Werito, chapter 2 this volume). Continued segregation of blacks in the public schools through the "separate but equal doctrine" (*Plessy v. Ferguson*) supported the widely held public belief that segregation was in the best interest of all. These views also impacted many Latino communities where children were schooled in separate and impoverished school settings (as was made evident in the 1931 Lemon Grove incident in California, which led to the first successful school desegregation case in the United States). A common reeducation practice in the schools attended by Latinos was to severely physically punish and shame the students for speaking their native Spanish language (Santa Ana 2004).

National actions in the late 1950s questioned such societal views. The 1957 *Brown v. Board of Education of Topeka* Supreme Court decision struck down the doctrine of segregation of black and white children in public education. The Civil Rights Act that same year (see Gonzales and López, chapters 4 and 5 this volume) established the federal Civil Rights Commission, which paved a way for Congress to support the desegregation of public schools under *Brown*. "In effect, Brown vs. Board of Education established the precedent that when it came to education, same was not always equal, a principle that was later to be sued for the education of language-minority students" (García 2009, 169).[3]

In the 1960s, New Mexico was primarily a rural state, and many of its children experienced early life in small villages and farming communities. Statewide, 951,023 people lived in New Mexico, and approximately 21 percent were living in Albuquerque.[4] The larger cities of Roswell, Santa Fe, Las Cruces, Hobbs, Carlsbad, Clovis, and Farmington comprised an additional 19 percent of the total population. The ethnic profile for the state in 1967—Spanish surnamed 40.7 percent, Native Americans 7.7 percent, black 2.2 percent, Asian .2 percent, others (Anglo-American) 49 percent—made New Mexico a "majority-minority" state, as it is to this day.[5] (New Mexico State Board of Education 1969).

As stated previously, large portions of the Hispanic and Indigenous populations lived in poverty. Nevertheless, there was a rich family and community life that relied heavily on an oral tradition. The majority of Hispanic and Native American children lived in small villages or in isolated family compounds and spoke their languages and practiced the traditions that had been handed down to them from their forebears for generations. It was in just such a small village—Peña Blanca—that Senator Joseph Montoya was born. Peña Blanca is located in Sandoval County, and borders the Pueblo de Cochiti reservation. Senator Montoya's father was a sheriff, and his mother was a schoolteacher, and like so many others, he was raised in a Spanish-speaking home. After graduating from Bernalillo High School, Montoya attended Regis University in Denver. Thanks to the sponsorship of then-senator Dennis Chávez, Montoya was admitted to Georgetown Law School. In 1936, at the age of twenty-two, Montoya became the youngest person elected to the New Mexico House of Representatives. Later, he was elected lieutenant governor of the state three times. In 1957, he was elected to the US House of Representatives, and in 1964, he became a US senator.[6]

From the time he served in the New Mexico legislature, Montoya was dedicated to the maintenance of the native languages of New Mexico. In 1941, he had sponsored a bill that would allow require Spanish instruction "in schools with at least three teachers or ninety regularly attending students" (Lozano 2013, 283) in the fifth through eighth grades (see Gonzales, chapter 4 this volume). Senator Montoya's interest in and advocacy of the Spanish language would remain a constant in his professional life.

In 1965, the National Education Association (NEA) sponsored "The Tucson Survey on the Teaching of Spanish to the Spanish Speaking" to find out how best to help the 1.75 million Spanish-surnamed students in the schools of Arizona, California, Colorado, New Mexico, and Texas succeed in school. According to the survey, "many of these young people experience academic failure in school. At best, they have limited success. A large percentage become school dropouts."

According to the 1960 census, there were "nearly 3.5 million people of Spanish surname" in this part of the country. The NEA built a team of Spanish-speaking educators from the Tucson area to survey instruction in the five-state area of the Southwest. Aware of the magnitude of the problem, the NEA recognized that "some teachers and some school systems were developing forward-looking solutions built on this base of bilingualism." The team visited schools where novel approaches using new materials and new techniques were employed, especially those programs that were utilizing bilingual approaches. They "observed student groups in action, talked with teachers and administrators and prepared detailed written reports of their visitation experience." The survey team hoped the report would kindle action and programs that would better serve Spanish surnamed students of the southwest (National Education Association 1966, iv–v). In New Mexico, the team visited Albuquerque High School, Rio Grande High School, and Pecos Elementary School (see Habermann López, chapter 5 this volume)

The NEA-Tucson Survey produced five recommendations:

- There is a need for a well-articulated program of instruction from the preschool level to the high school level in the student's native language.
- The preparation of teachers for bilingual programs must be based on: (a) the personal qualities of the teacher. (b) their knowledge of children and appreciation of the cultural environment of the community from which these students derive, (c) skill in the teaching process, and (d) bilingual fluency.
- Teachers must be recruited from the Spanish-speaking population and young Mexican Americans must be encouraged to pursue teaching as a career. English must be taught as a second language, using appropriate techniques and materials.
- Curriculum models must be characterized by their diversity so that the needs of students will be met rather than continue to fit the children to the curriculum.
- English must be taught as a second language, using appropriate techniques and materials. (National Education Association 1966, 3)

The following year, NEA convened a follow-up symposium on October 30–31, 1966, at the University of Arizona at Tucson, titled "The Spanish-Speaking Child in the Schools of the Southwest." Needs that were identified in the survey became the catalyst for further actions. "This Symposium served as a sequel to the Survey and was rightfully qualified as a prologue to action" (National Education Association 1966, 3). Senators Ralph Yarborough of Texas, Morris Udall of

Arizona, and Joseph Montoya of New Mexico were in attendance. Henry Pascual, foreign language specialist at the New Mexico State Department of Education (SDE), was invited to speak. He discussed the results of the Pecos project that had begun in 1963 and that focused on developing children's literacy skills in their first language. Pascual showed a videotape of the Pecos children learning to read and write in Spanish (see Habermann López, chapter 5 this volume). In a 2001 interview, Pascual recalled the sequence and impact of the presentation:

> I went to the podium and I explained all that I had done to create this project
> . . . the proposal, the [Ford] Foundation, the system that I had followed, the
> teacher I had hired. Then I introduced the teacher and told the audience that she
> had some preliminaries to talk about and then I would show the film. I did. It
> was like an atomic bomb. Everybody said, "That's what we want," including New
> Mexico's own Senator Joseph Montoya.[7]

Senator Montoya's comments at this conference displayed his commitment to bilingual education:

> Our nation can no longer indulge in the luxury of letting its human resources go
> to waste. We must take advantage of what heretofore has been a disadvantage,
> turning liability into an asset . . . We must bring two distinctive cultures
> and languages together in our schools . . . Think of it—both heritages, both
> histories and both languages producing tens of thousands of productive, stable
> and capable personnel utilizing the finest offered by both worlds." (National
> Education Association 1966, 19)

Other leaders in attendance included Bruce Gaarder of the federal Office of Education; Theodore Andersson; chair of the Modern Languages Department at the University of Texas; Hershel Manuel of Texas; and many NEA educators from the five states. Many of those present would become friends and allies of Pascual throughout his professional life.

Upon their return to Washington, Senator Yarborough and his colleagues, including Senator Montoya, began the task of putting together a bill that would promote bilingual education for Spanish-speaking students. Several views of bilingual education were advanced. In the Senate's debate two contrasting views of bilingual education were discussed: a comprehensive education using both English and children's native language; and one that was transitional, using a child's native language only until she or he learned English. Senator Montoya, a cosponsor of Yarborough's bill, promoted for the first view, arguing,

"Comprehensive bilingual education programs are to my way of thinking, one way we can give to all the best of both worlds in terms of language, culture and cooperation in daily life' (Crawford 2000, 110). Other senators preferred the transitional view, arguing that they had learned English without the assistance of their native language.

In the end, Senator Yarborough, the chief sponsor of the bill, opted for a view that would be more palatable to the greater society, stating, "It is not the purpose of the bill to create pockets of different languages throughout the country. It is the main purpose of the bill to bring millions of school children into the mainstream of American life and make them literate in the national language of the country in which they live: namely English" (Crawford 2000, 110–11). Moreover because of the interests of Puerto Rican, Native American and Asian American language groups who also lobbied for the bill, other language groups were included.

In all, thirty-seven bilingual education bills were introduced in the 19th Congress (Crawford 2000). However, Senator Yarborough's bill prevailed. The Bilingual Education Act was enacted by Congress in 1967 and signed into law by President Lyndon Johnson in January of 1968 (San Miguel 2004). Eighty-five million dollars was authorized for a three-year period to accomplish the bills primary mandates: "to encourage the recognition of the special educational needs of limited English speaking children; and to provide financial assistance to local educational agencies to develop and carry out new and imaginative public school programs designed to meet these special educational needs" (San Miguel 2004, 16–17).[8]

New Mexican school districts immediately applied for funding and called on Senator Montoya to assist in garnering those funds. In 1969, the US Office of Education approved proposals of five New Mexico educational agencies—Española, Albuquerque, Grants, Las Cruces, and Artesia.[9] These grants included support for bilingual education in Navajo and Acoma/Laguna as well as Spanish. Senator Montoya commented, "I am pleased indeed to see that the bilingual education bill which I co-sponsored is now producing results in meeting the special needs of educationally deprived children with limited English-speaking ability; and I intend to press for expansion of this important educational program."[10] In December of that same year, $15 million was added to the original $85 million, thanks to the work of Senator Montoya, who was serving on the Senate Appropriations Committee.[11]

In the same year that Congress enacted the Bilingual Education Act, President Johnson, mindful of the growing activism of Latinos, established the Inter-agency Committee on Mexican American Affairs, a federal task force established to ensure that Mexican Americans received a fair share of federal government services and programs, and named Vicente Ximenes of Texas as committee chair. Both senators from New Mexico, Anderson and Montoya, were invited to the announcement of the creation of the committee.[12] Montoya enthusiastically supported the plan. In June 1969, he proposed a bill to permanently establish the Inter-agency Committee on Mexican American Affairs and amended the name to Inter-agency Committee on Hispanic American Affairs in order to ensure that Puerto Ricans and other Latinos would be included. This agency would comprise the US attorney general and the secretaries of Agriculture, Commerce, Labor, Health, Education and Welfare, Housing and Urban Development, and Treasury. Moreover, administrators and directors from federal agencies and departments would also be called upon to serve. This agency's role would be to provide advice and guidance to the federal departments and agencies that would support Spanish-surnamed Americans.

In his lengthy testimony, Senator Montoya presented the historical narrative of Spanish-surnamed Americans and the often dismal statistics regarding their education, employment, health, and poverty levels. He began his testimony with a potent statement:

> "I like to make a particular statement, which I usually tell in jest, but which often upon reflection has much truth in it. . . . When the Pilgrims landed at Plymouth Rock, the Spanish were there to feed them pinto beans."[13]

Montoya continued his narrative by describing the explorations of the Spanish in the Southwest, long before the Pilgrims arrived. He pointedly described the treatment of American Indians as the "blackest mark on our history" and then proceeded to ask, "But what of those of our citizens that that were here on this land second only to the Indian?" Recounting the history of the Mexican American War and its aftermath, Montoya stated:

> But unlike the Anglo American, the Spanish-speaking American had to give way, as did the American Indian. He lost lands which he had held for centuries. He lost his footing in his community. He became the governed in his village. His language, which had been the tongue of commerce, became the mark of the "foreigner." Suddenly, this was no longer his land or home.[14]

Clearly, Senator Montoya was describing the history of New Mexico and the Southwest, perhaps even that of his home village, Peña Blanca.

Montoya's bill was approved by Congress in December 1969. At that time, Senator Joseph Montoya declared, "[As] the only US Senator of Spanish heritage, I pledge to my people that I shall keep careful watch, that I shall keep careful surveillance over the activities of this new Cabinet-level committee to insure that it carries out its work in the dedicated spirit I know it is capable of."[15]

Indeed, Senator Montoya remained actively involved in issues that related to Hispanic Americans. In 1973, he, Senator Alan Cranston of California, and Senator Edward Kennedy of Massachusetts worked together to revise and strengthen the Bilingual Education Act. As they worked on the revisions, Senator Montoya sought the advice of Henry Pascual, writing, "You have been recommended to this office as 'one of the very best people in the country in bilingual education."[16] In his letter to Pascual, Montoya requested Pascual's comments on the funding of teacher-training institutes, citing the excellent Teacher Training Institute at New Mexico Highlands University:

> I would be very interested in hearing your suggestions for legislation which could support teacher-training institutes nationwide in an effort to close the gap between schools which are ready to go ahead with bilingual teaching and the preparation of teachers, materials, testing etc., for use by those schools. It is obvious that we are never going to achieve the goals of the Bilingual Education Act unless we do a better job of preparing the teachers and course materials.[17]

In characteristic fashion, Pascual responded with both editorial and substantive suggestions: "If politically feasible, delete 'children of limited English-speaking ability.' Change this to bilingual-bicultural children. The word limited relegates bilingual education to the remediation category only." Further, he recommended including a provision for state education agencies to maintain adequate staffing, and complained that the independent auditing of accountability under Title VII "has not operated satisfactorily."[18]

One month later, on October 31, 1973, the Senate Subcommittee on Education met to hear testimony on Senate Bill 2552, a bill to improve bilingual and bicultural educational opportunities for children of limited English-speaking ability. Senator Montoya testified before the subcommittee, although his appearance was early and brief because of his and Senator Kennedy's obligations on the Judiciary Committee, which was concerned with the Watergate affair. Montoya thanked the subcommittee and introduced five New Mexicans who would provide testimony: Henry Casso, executive secretary of the National Education Task Force de la Raza; Cecilio Orozco, director of the Institute for Bilingual Education at the New Mexico Highlands University; Henry Pascual, director of the Cross Cultural Unit, New Mexico Department of Education; and María Gutiérrez Spencer, director of teacher training, Deming Demonstration Center. Senator Montoya also recognized a delegation from the Navajo Nation who were in attendance. Although the delegation was not called to testify, it is clear from the correspondence between his office and the Indigenous communities of New Mexico that Senator Montoya was concerned that the Indigenous groups of New Mexico should also receive bilingual education dollars to assist them in their efforts.[19]

In their testimonies, Pascual and Orozco urged the subcommittee to utilize the term "culturally and linguistically different child" instead of the pejorative term then in use: "Children of limited English ability does not recognize the potential for full binguality and biculturalism that children from bilingual communities have."[20]

Gutiérrez Spencer's testimony focused on in-service teacher training:

Nowadays it is quite common for a superintendent to find himself bowing to public pressures to come up with a bilingual program. He casts about for a teacher with a brown face or a Spanish name to head the experiment. This particular teacher may not know anything about the rationale, the methodology or the materials."[21]

She went on to describe the ways in which the in-service training occurred in New Mexico:

In New Mexico, the State Department of Education asked the State legislature to establish a network of demonstration centers where . . . teachers can observe master teachers [and] have the opportunity to discuss rationale. . . . They are videotaped to encourage self-evaluation. Later, the network staff visit the trainees in their own classrooms and offer further assistance.[22]

The focus of Orozco's testimony was on teacher training: "I think we cannot go on with teacher preparation or teacher trainer preparation unless we do identify what is to take place in the bilingual classroom."[23] In the written portion of his testimony, Orozco elaborated three models of bilingual education—transitional, maintenance, and dual language immersion. Based on these models, Orozco identified four general areas that needed to be included in any teacher training program:

1. In-depth knowledge of the history and historical problem solving of the target community. Including its contributions to the world and the USA.

2. Knowledge of the minorities' present problems in the USA, including a historical knowledge of American education's failure to meet the needs of the particular group.

3. Knowledge of the problems of learning English that the target group has, coupled with . . . (New methods in TESOL with specific instruction in particular linguistic groups).

4. Knowledge of the language, literature and tradition of the target group as well as that of the group's ancestors.[24]

Orozco also made a special plea for the subcommittee to include children from bilingual communities in the bill, "children who have not necessarily been born out of the country, children who do speak English and another language and whose communities often speak English in the public life, yet Spanish or an Indigenous language in the home."[25] With this request, Orozco made the case for many of the children of New Mexico and other parts of the Southwest.

In Pascual's written testimony, he provided a report on successful international bilingual programs and the particular needs of children in New Mexico. He also responded to specific questions about teacher preparation that Senator Kennedy had posed him, Orozco, and Spencer:

Colleges and universities still are not implementing significant teacher training programs nor programs for counselors and administrators. . . . The colleges have picked people who cannot speak or read the non-English language to do the training.[26]

Further, he detailed three general competencies all bilingual teachers should possess.

1. Language
   a. Fluency in the local dialect—to be measured by observation in the field experience and practice.
   b. Extended functional vocabulary

    c. Classroom terminology (instructional language)

    d. Literacy skills—Degree of proficiency to be determined by an acceptable instrument when applicable.

2. Culture

    a. Fundamental aspects of ethnic group cultures of the Southwest

    b. Monumental aspects of cultures with pre-requisite preparation so that these courses may be taught in the language of the culture.

3. Methodology

    a. Practicum to be conducted in bona fide bilingual setting.

    b. There shall be three minimum components in the practicum: Language Arts, Social Studies and Fine Arts which should be taught in the language of the culture.[27]

Pascual's oral testimony focused on the need for Native American teachers:

> In my state, New Mexico, we have over 22,000 Indian children in public schools but only 114 teachers representing them. Bilingual bicultural education for our Indian students is a critical need. The training of teachers from the Navajo Nation and the Pueblos is so critical that I have proposed to various state and federal agencies that teacher training centers be established in the Indian communities rather than the college campuses. . . . The frustration of the community is so great that in our tribes in our state a study revealed a drop-out rate of 53%.[28]

In his written testimony, Pascual proposed twenty objectives for a possible pre-service and in-service training center for Native American teachers, among them to provide a teaching-learning center, to develop materials, to study the learning styles of Keres and Navajo people in the teaching-learning environment, to bring professional preparation (university training) to the site, and to recruit senior high school Native American students as teacher-apprentices to recruit future teachers.[29]

As a consequence of this hearing and additional lobbying by bilingual educators and Indigenous leaders, the National Network of Centers for Bilingual Education was established in 1977 to create supports for bilingual education. Within this network, several important centers were developed: the National Clearinghouse for Bilingual Education, which collected and disseminated research and educational materials pertaining to bilingual education; materials development centers; evaluation dissemination and assessment centers; and bilingual education service centers (BESC).

The American Indian Bilingual Education Center (AIBEC), a badly needed BESC for American Indian students as attested to by Pascual, was established in Albuquerque, New Mexico. The main office for this center was at the University of New Mexico, and a field office was established in Window Rock. The center was staffed with Pueblo and Navajo educators and served all the seventeen Title VII American Indian programs in New Mexico and the Navajo Nation. It also served the five universities in the state and coordinated with all twenty-two tribal nations. Their specific activities included conducting needs assessments, providing in-service and pre-service training for educational personnel, assisting with pilot-testing of materials, and maintaining and improving communication among all stakeholders. This center and others like it became critical to the development of quality bilingual programs and bilingual teacher development, and in this particular case, supported up and coming Indigenous educational leaders. Senator Montoya's support for AIBEC, and the network of bilingual centers was critical. He continued to actively support bilingual education until his defeat in 1976 and played a pivotal role in paving the way for other New Mexicans to be recognized as leaders in bilingual education.

Pascual, Gutiérrez Spencer, and Orozco, who had testified at the 1973 bilingual education hearings, had hoped to change the way in which emergent bilingual children were viewed. It is clear that unfortunately, they were not successful in changing the federal term "children with limited English speaking ability." This term morphed first into "limited English proficient" (LEP), and then to the present "English Language learner," or "English Learner" (ELL or EL). Nevertheless, their request to change these terms signals an important distinction between federal policy and the intent of New Mexico bilingual programs. In New Mexico, bilingual education was viewed as "a vehicle for developing and expanding the richness of languages and cultures in this country."[30] Most New Mexican bilingual educators and communities had long lobbied for the recognition and presence of their languages in the schools and other public spaces (see chapters 2, 3, and 4 this volume). Generally, what they sought were the spaces where they could continue to utilize their languages without oppression, punishment, or shame. They saw bilingual bicultural education as an answer to their long and historic struggles. It was for these reasons that each enactment of the state bilingual education laws stated unequivocally that bilingual education meant "a program of education by which students learn through two languages to understand and participate in the cultures of their environment."[31]

Henry Pascual maintained an active national role throughout his career. In 1975, President Gerald Ford invited him to attend the White House conference for leaders in bilingual education to prepare accountability guidelines for Title VII (Pascual, personal communication). On August 25, 1981, Pascual and a group of Hispanic educator leaders requested and were granted a meeting with Education Secretary Terence Bell to discuss concerns "about the quality of education for Hispanics at all levels of the educational system in the nation, . . . employment opportunities in all federal and state agencies, the continued existence of Title IV training and technical assistance centers, the future of bilingual education; the status of the Spanish language in American education and the negative representation of Hispanics in all media; and access to higher education and research."[32]

The group that met with Secretary Bell included professors of education such as Sara Meléndez, University of Hartford; Rosa Feinberg, University of Miami; Macario Saldate, University of Arizona; Leonard Valverde, University of Texas; and Henry Trueba, San Diego State. Also attending were directors of bilingual and multicultural education across the country. As their chosen spokesperson, Pascual prepared a report of the discussion with the secretary in which he outlined the group's concerns. Specifically, the group requested that Hispanics be involved in planning and implementing any initiatives that would impact Hispanic communities, such as those directing Title III programs and those reading Title III proposals; that Hispanics be represented fairly and honestly in the US Department of Education's media outlets; and that there be Hispanic representation in the Division of Post-Secondary Education.[33] The group also called for a director of the Office of Bilingual Education and Minority Languages who was bilingual themselves, had expertise in bilingual education, represented a large linguistic group, provided diversity in gender and geographic area, and above all held an appropriate philosophical orientation. The group also proposed more research on Hispanic populations and funding for Hispanics pursuing higher education.

One of the major concerns of this group was the threat of funding cuts to Title VII, given the growth in numbers of immigrant English learners who were now joining the ranks of those English learners who were native born. The report and communication from Pascual requested a follow-up meeting with Secretary Bell in November of that same year. Unfortunately, this meeting did not take place.

Nevertheless, other New Mexicans continued to play important roles at the national level. Rudy Córdova served in the Office of Bilingual and Multicultural Education from the early 1970s through 1984.[34] This afforded many bilingual directors in New Mexico more direct access to federal initiatives. Rudy Chávez and Paul E. Martínez provided leadership to the National Association of Bilingual Education in the early 1990s; their ability to work with federal officials and to include the voices of parents, students, teachers, and other stakeholders was a hallmark of their leadership.

There were many other remarkable educators who contributed to bilingual education at the national level. Unfortunately, time and space do not permit the inclusion of their stories here. The authors hope that other individuals will be able to tell their stories in subsequent publications. What is clear from the history recounted here is the stellar reputation that New Mexico had in this field.

NOTES

1. S.740 Hearings before the Subcommittee on Executive Reorganization of the Committee on Government Operations, United States Senate, 91st Cong (1969), 8. Testimony of Joseph Montoya.

2. Ibid.

3. See also Alan Brinkley, "The Fifties," https://www.gilderlehrman.org/history-by -era/fifties/essays/fifties.

4. New Mexico Secretary of State, *New Mexico Blue Book 1965–1966*, 9, 81.

5. New Mexico State Board of Education, 1969. Policy on Bilingual Education. Copy in possession of Mary Jean Haberman López.

6. For a complete political history, see https://www.loc.gov/rr/hispanic/congress /montoyaj.html; and Vigil and Luján 1986.

7. Henry W. Pascual, interview by Rebecca Blum Martínez, Mary Jean Habermann López, and Julia Rosa López-Emsli, August 11–12, 2001, at Pascual's home. DVD and partial transcript in the personal collection of Mary Jean Habermann López.

8. See also the American Presidency Project, "Lyndon B. Johnson XXXVI President of the United States: 1963–1969," http://www.presidency.ucsb.edu/ws/index .php?pid=28292.

9. *Santa Fe New Mexican*, "5 Districts to Receive Bilingual Funding," June 11, 1969.

10. *Santa Fe New Mexican*, June 11, 1969.

11. *Albuquerque Tribune*, December, 1969. These articles are found in the Special Collection of Joseph Montoya, Box 176, Folder 8, University of New Mexico, Center for Southwest Research and Special Collections.

12. See https://www.eeoc.gov/eeoc/history/35th/milestones/1967.html; and http://www.presidency.ucsb.edu/ws/index.php?pid=28292.

13. S.740 Hearings before the Subcommittee on Executive Reorganization of the Committee on Government Operations, United States Senate, 91st Cong (1969), 3, Testimony of Joseph Montoya.

14. Ibid., 4.

15. "Montoya, Joseph Manuel," History, Art and Archives, United States House of Representatives, http://history.house.gov/People/Detail/18432.

16. J. Montoya to H. Pascual, April, 1, 1973, Joseph Montoya Papers, University of New Mexico.

17. Ibid.

18. H. Pascual to J. Montoya, September 17, 1973, Joseph Montoya Papers, University of New Mexico.

19. Correspondence, Joseph Montoya Papers, University of New Mexico.

20. S.1539: Amendment and Extension of Certain Acts Relating to Elementary and Secondary Education Programs, 1973, Orozco, 2857.

21. S.1539: Amendment and Extension of Certain Acts Relating to Elementary and Secondary Education Programs, 1973, Spencer, 2769.

22. See chapters 4, 5, and 9 this volume. US Department of Health, Education and Welfare National Institutes of Education (August, 1974) *Alternatives: A Survey of Title III, ESEA, Projects in New Mexico*, 25–31, 72. http://files.eric.ed.gov/fulltext/ED 109273.

23. S.1539: Amendment and Extension of Certain Acts Relating to Elementary and Secondary Education Programs, 1973, Orozco, 2845.

24. Ibid., 2853.

25. Ibid., 2845.

26. S.1539: Amendment and Extension of Certain Acts Relating to Elementary and Secondary Education Programs, 1973, Pascual, 2844.

27. Ibid., 2841.

28. Ibid., 2783.

29. Ibid., 2836–37.

30. Ibid., 2782.

31. New Mexico Senate Bill 421. An Act Relating to Education. Providing for Establishment of Bilingual Multicultural Education Programs in the Public Schools; Repealing Certain Sections of NMSA 1953.

32. Henry Pascual, Summary of Concerns Presented to Secretary Terrel H. Bell on August 25, 1981. Mary Jean Habermann López, personal collection.

33. Title III was the innovations component of ESEA. Successful innovations went on to become part of the National Diffusion Network, the federally sponsored effort that spread transformative practices to America's schools

34. Paul E. Martínez, phone interview by Rebecca Blum Martínez, October 9, 2018.

REFERENCES

Crawford, James. 2000. "Language Politics in the United States: The Paradox of Bilingual Education." In *Politics of Multiculturalism and Bilingual Education: Students Caught in the Cross Fire*, edited by Carlos Ovando and Peter McLaren, 106–25. Boston: McGraw Hill.

Lozano, Rosina A. 2013. "Managing the 'Priceless Gift': Debating Spanish Language Instruction in New Mexico and Puerto Rico, 1930–1950." *Western Historical Quarterly* 44, no. 3: 271–93.

MacLean, Nancy. 2015. "The Civil Rights Act and the Transformation of Mexican American Identity and Politics." *Berkeley La Raza Law Journal* 18: 123. http://scholarship.law.berkeley.edu/blrlj/vol18/iss1/10.

Montoya, Joseph. 1967. *Las Voces Nuevas del Sudoeste (New Voices of the Southwest)*. Symposium: The Spanish-Speaking Child in the Schools of the Southwest (Tucson, Arizona, October 30, 31, 1966). Washington, DC: National Education Association, Committee on Civil and Human Rights of Educators.

National Education Association. 1966. *The Invisible Minority*. Washington, DC: Department of Rural Education. Library of Congress Catalog 66–26858.

National Education Association and National Education Task Force de la Raza. 1973. *Report of a National Bilingual Bicultural Institute: A Relook at Tucson '66 and Beyond*. Washington, DC.

New Mexico University. College of Education. 1980. *American Indian Bilingual Education Center Handbook*. Albuquerque: University of New Mexico.

San Miguel, Guadalupe, Jr. 2004. *Contested Policy: The Rise and Fall of Federal Bilingual Education in the United States, 1960–2001*. Denton, TX: University of North Texas Press.

Santa Ana, Otto. 2004. *Tongue Tied: The Lives of Multilingual Children in Public Education*. Oxford, UK: Rowman and Littlefield.

Valdés, Guadalupe, and Richard A. Figueroa. 1994. *Bilingualism and Testing: A Special Case of Bias*. Norwood, NJ: Ablex.

Vigil, Maurilo, and Roy Luján. 1986. "Parallels in the Career of Two Hispanic US Senators." *Journal of Ethnic Studies* 13, no. 4: 1–19.

PART THREE

Innovations,
Preparation, and Leaders

In this section, we focus on bilingual education programs—those innovative
programs that served children and those that helped to better prepare teachers,
the materials used, and the notable leaders who helped shape the practice for
both Spanish and Indigenous languages. It is important to remember that in
the early days of bilingual education, many educators, even those who were
committed to the ideals of bilingual education, had not had much actual experience teaching and working in a bilingual setting. Teaching materials were
limited or inadequate, teachers who spoke Spanish at home were not prepared
to use Spanish in instruction, and few policies and procedures were in place to
guide educators. Navajo communities at Rough Rock and Rock Point began
groundbreaking work in community-based education, as did Zuni Pueblo. It
was a time of excitement, great possibility, and significant challenges.

In the early 1960s, few educators had had direct experiences with bilingual
education nationally. In New Mexico, however, as described by Argus-Calvo,
Habermann López, and Blum Martínez in chapter 9, the programs established
by John Paul Taylor in Las Cruces, and in Las Vegas by Ray Leger, in addition
to the Pecos project (chapter 5) were critical in modeling sound bilingual practices. These pioneering public-school programs had three enormous challenges:
developing a curriculum for the particular populations they served, developing
culturally and linguistically responsive materials, and supporting teachers in the
practice of bilingual education.

The success of the Pecos project allowed the Las Cruces School District to
attempt the first two-way dual-language program for Spanish- and English-
speaking students in the state in 1965. As stated above, this project faced the

challenges of finding bilingual and biliterate teachers and adequate materials. John Paul Taylor, who was the administrator and cofounder of this program, understood that his teachers needed time to plan, to create materials, and to study—needs that still exist today. The schools' relationships with families and the community became a critical part of their success.

The successful bilingual school in West Las Vegas, the Armijo School, not only became a positive educational site for children, but also functioned as the base for the Bilingual Teacher Training Network in northern New Mexico. A similar network was begun in southern New Mexico, under the direction of María Spencer, who ran a successful bilingual program in Silver City. The two sites served different students. The northern site served Spanish-speaking Hispanos whose families had lived in the region for several centuries. The southern site served the many students who were children of Mexican immigrants and other Spanish-speakers who had a great deal in common culturally and linguistically with Mexico, their immediate southern neighbor. For this reason, there was a greater focus on English as a second language in the south, whereas in the north, there was more concern about conserving the variety of Spanish spoken there and introducing children to the Spanish of books and general literacy. Both sites were used essentially as lab schools for practicing teachers to learn how to better teach in a bilingual setting. These sites were critical in helping teachers in this task. The methods that were used—observation, practice, critique, videotaping, and continuous monitoring of teachers—all assured that teachers were supported in changing their practice.

The Guadalajara Institutes were important in providing teachers with the linguistic and cultural development needed to better understand the cultural and linguistic issues that they would eventually face in the classroom. Having an international experience allowed teachers to better understand their own culture and the similarities and differences between Mexican language and culture and their own.

Recognizing the challenges that bilingual teachers faced, New Mexico Highlands University and the University of Albuquerque established teacher preparation programs that focused on critical elements of bilingual pedagogy, on the development of Spanish for professional purposes, and on Keres for specific Pueblo communities. The focus on language and culture in both university programs addressed the ongoing concern with teacher candidates' base knowledge, while at the same time providing them with much needed confidence and self-concept.

The results of such programs can be seen in the comments of its graduates and in the work of the late Carlos Chávez, who began a bilingual certification program before it existed in any state nationally. Utilizing the lessons he learned in his teacher preparation program at the University of Albuquerque, Chávez created a safe but challenging environment for his students that highlighted and honored their linguistic and cultural assets.

In chapter 10, Salazar and Hannum describe the dilemma of many Spanish-speaking teachers. Several had been raised in Spanish-speaking homes but had never been given the opportunity to develop professional uses of Spanish. In the early days of bilingual programs, finding teachers who could conduct classes in Spanish was difficult.[1] Out of ignorance, and in a rush to obtain bilingual funding, many school administrators hired Spanish-surnamed teachers to staff their programs, many of whom did not speak Spanish or spoke it with difficulty. Bilingual educators were concerned that this practice would ultimately harm both their cause and the children they served. For this reason, ensuring bilingual education teachers' Spanish language ability became one of the primary concerns in the field. The authors also tell the story of how and why the Four Skills Test (the first Spanish language test for bilingual teachers) was developed and how the present test, Prueba, came to be. As native Spanish speakers who did not have the privilege of studying their language in their school careers, Hannum and Salazar bring an important perspective to this work, and one that mirrors the experiences of many bilingual teachers who have had to formally study Spanish at the university.

In chapter 11, Julia Rosa López-Emslie shares her experiences in materials development. Her story begins in Albuquerque, where she and her colleagues, realizing that the Spanish language materials developed for second/foreign language learners were not helpful to native speakers, worked to develop classroom materials that would support the students' linguistic abilities. This experience served her well in her later work at the Spanish Curricula Development Center (SCDC) in Miami, an important curriculum project that served the nation, including New Mexico. The SCDC hired curriculum writers from many backgrounds to ensure that the particular Spanish language varieties spoken by Cuban, Puerto Rican, South American, Mexican, and New Mexican children, as well as the children's cultural and experiential backgrounds, would be reflected in the materials that would be used. During this same period, Dolores Gonzales, a beloved and highly respected bilingual educator, one of the first bilingual education professors at the University of New Mexico, and her students created the *La Tierra del Encanto* series that featured the experiences of many northern Nuevomexicano students, particularly those living in rural areas. Both of these curricular and materials development projects were created by non-profit organizations, which is in sharp contrast to the materials that are available today. At that time, having little or no materials to use in bilingual classrooms, these two projects attempted to fill the gap, and they were perhaps more responsive to the lives of Nuevomexicano children than those produced today commercially and for a wider audience.

Chapter 12 describes the critical role of the State Bilingual Advisory Committee (SBAC), which guided much of bilingual education policy and practices since its establishment in 1970. The SBAC was a committee of volunteer bilingual educators, experts, and community leaders who assisted the New Mexico State Department of Education in developing many of the policies and legislation that still exist today. In the early period of bilingual education, there were no formal requirements for bilingual teachers or teachers of English as a second language. There were no state requirements for the different elements of a bilingual program, for example, how many subjects to teach in each language, what standards to follow for the different content areas taught in the Spanish language, and how to assess student progress.

Many Spanish-speaking and Indigenous language leaders served on this important committee throughout its fifty-year span. This committee developed criteria for bilingual teacher preparation and guidelines for implementing bilingual programs. Importantly, a special subcommittee of the SBAC also developed criteria for Native American bilingual teacher certification. Because this process was led by Indigenous educators, the criteria reflected the reality of Indigenous communities and respected the rights of the tribes to ultimately certify the linguistic abilities of their teachers.

Members of the SBAC also testified at various legislative committees and were instrumental in developing revisions to existing educational policy to accommodate the needs of bilingual and English learning students. Much of the work to create these policies was done in partnership between the State Department of Education and the SBAC. The mutually beneficial relationship between the two entities is an important element of the bilingual education story in New Mexico.

We end this section and our book with chapter 13, in two parts. The first, authored by González and Calvo, describes the biographies of six Spanish/English pioneers whose work runs through many of the chapters of this book. These individuals were instrumental in the many successes that were achieved during the time that they worked in bilingual education. They mentored many educators who have continued their work, and who in turn have mentored younger bilingual educators who are the future of our profession.

In the second part, Blum Martínez highlights the Navajo and Pueblo innovators who have worked tirelessly on behalf of their languages and cultures and to the appropriate inclusion of these in educational settings. The Navajo were the first to develop community-run schools based on their language and worldview. These programs have become outstanding examples of bilingual education, and the leaders who were involved in establishing these programs have inspired younger Indigenous bilingual educators.

Many Pueblo innovators withstood the pressure of modeling their programs on Spanish programs, focusing instead on their own conceptions of language, culture, and the most appropriate ways of passing these on to future generations. Some programs have been established in public schools; others have remained in their communities, depending always on the wishes of the community. A common theme in the lives of these leaders is the preservation and maintenance of language and a way of life.

Time and space have not allowed us to include all the many valiant and brilliant educators who worked tirelessly on behalf of the children of New Mexico. It is our hope that this first book will inspire others to highlight other pioneers and continue the story.

NOTE

1. Finding teachers who can teach content in Spanish continues to be challenging. Because of the sociopolitical situation in New Mexico and nationally, the arguments against bilingual education have continued to cast doubt on this educational reform and have discouraged bilingual teacher candidates from pursuing bilingual education as a career. Moreover, the accountability movement that has only accepted English language standardized test scores has pushed school districts to adopt English-only programs. Ironically, these movements have happened in the decade (1993–2003) during which the numbers of English learners has doubled nationally.

BEVERLY ARGUS-CALVO, REBECCA BLUM MARTÍNEZ,
AND MARY JEAN HABERMANN LÓPEZ

[9] Innovations in Bilingual Education in New Mexico

The successful Pecos project in New Mexico created new enthusiasm and interest among many educators wishing to include language and culture in instruction.[1] Numerous elementary bilingual education programs quickly followed Pecos.

The enthusiasm was contagious after so many attempts by New Mexicans to include their native languages in school. As detailed by Felipe Gonzales in chapter 4 of this volume, New Mexico had seen uneven support for Spanish instruction since territorial days. Native American tribes had long struggled to ensure that their languages could survive within both federal and state public school contexts (see Werito and Sims, chapters 2 and 3 this volume) Hispanics had long suffered educational neglect as documented in national and state statistics on dropout and achievement (National Education Association 1966).

A bilingual approach to educating students gave hope to those who understood its intrinsic and educational value. In and of itself, bilingual education became an educational innovation in New Mexico and across the nation. How to implement it, however, was the question on everyone's mind.

This chapter will discuss stellar innovations in bilingual education both at the K–12 and university levels in New Mexico beginning in 1967.

INNOVATIONS IN K–12 PUBLIC SCHOOL SYSTEMS: A SUSTAINED PRIMARY PROGRAM FOR BILINGUAL STUDENTS, 1967–1980

In 1967, Henry W. Pascual worked with John Paul Taylor for over a week writing a proposal that was initially funded by Title III of the US Office of Modern and Classical Languages. No other funding source for this new and innovative approach was available at the time. The program offered half a day of instruction in English and half a day in Spanish to Spanish speakers, bilingual students, and English speakers at Mesilla and Washington Elementary Schools.[2] Beginning in kindergarten in 1967, the program added one grade level every year through the twelfth grade. The 1980 graduates were to become *la primera y única clase bilingüe de graduantes de preparatoria, K–12 en la nación* (the first and only high school graduates receiving bilingual education K–12 in the nation; Las Cruces Public Schools 1980) and were recognized by Josué Gonzales, director of bilingual education at the US Department of Health, Education, and Welfare, the New Mexico Department of Education, and the New Mexico Association for Bilingual Education, years later. It became a prototype for other programs to emulate, specifically what is known today as two-way bilingual education.[3]

Staffing the Project

One of the first and major challenges was finding the best teachers for this project who were fully bilingual. The then-new concept was that a teacher was to teach in both languages, and there was not to be any mixing of the languages. Pascual commented about the Las Cruces project, "Two aspects were key: the teachers were excellent both in English and in Spanish and the attitude was incredibly positive, the psychology of it was natural."[4]

John Paul Taylor recruited teachers who he knew were both bilingual and excellent teachers. Refugio (Cuca) Medina, a master bilingual educator and cornerstone of this program, recalls, "I was anxious when he first asked me to teach in the program."[5] It was a daunting task to think of all that had to get done. Another teacher, Angie Morgan, reminisced that Taylor had approached her to teach in the program, even though she had been teaching in another district.[6]

Curriculum Development

The greater part of curriculum development took place during the summer months at the project office. Margarita Mestas, a bilingual curriculum specialist, was hired to write the Spanish curriculum with the program's teachers, who played a major role. The academic calendar was adjusted to allow them time to develop curriculum and materials in both Spanish and English. Although they used books from the different Spanish speaking countries, there were concepts particular to the United States and the New Mexico region that could not be "translated." Thus, the word "development" carried a special meaning. It meant creating and having peers review each other's work.[7] The 1980 program report indicated "121 persons from 11 New Mexico cities, 14 states, and 7 foreign countries had ordered teacher curriculum guides and materials created by the project" (Las Cruces Public Schools 1980)

Professional Development

The program also offered continual professional development to teachers and paraprofessionals via coursework at New Mexico State University, as well as monthly training sessions on site. By the end of the program in 1980, 60 percent of the teachers had their master's degrees. Paraprofessionals participated in a weekly class delivered in Spanish on topics related to mathematics, history and Spanish, and Mexican and New Mexican literature.

Implementation of the Project

There were numerous aspects to this program that made it innovative. One included the practice of having teachers follow the same group of children for two years. "Students felt that teachers knew them, and teachers understood and could address the needs of the children from one year to the next."[8] Another innovation was the level of parent involvement. Parents were kept informed of each of the program's unique features as well as any and all changes. They received a monthly newsletter in Spanish and English that contained all curricular developments, which teachers had attended the professional development and where, and the names of every staff member. *Mirasol*, the newsletter developed by the teachers for the parents, even included any special happenings with the families. Thus, the newsletter contained information that brought the program alive and into the homes of the students they served.[9] It was circulated to 810 homes and covered topics on history, culture, heritage, student activities, and the visitors to the program (Las Cruces Public Schools, 1980).

THE EXPERIENCED TEACHER FELLOWSHIP IN BILINGUAL EDUCATION (THE GUADALAJARA INSTITUTES) 1970–1973

The Summer Training Institutes in Mexico were born of the needs that Henry Pascual observed in his extensive statewide school visits. It was clear that teachers required support and training in the Spanish language to ensure that Hispanic students could develop literacy in their first language, build a positive self-image, be successful in the curriculum, and learn English well.[10] The teachers could speak Spanish but had not had "training of any kind and they were unable to read

Spanish. . . . If we were going to do a language culture maintenance program, which is what we wanted, we needed to have the training for teachers, and not just pick a 'Valdez' and put him up there because his name was Valdez."[11]

In the early 1970s, new federal funding offered bilingual education professional development opportunities for teachers through university summer institutes in Mexico. Unfortunately, most training was delivered in English, a concern of Bruce Gaarder, director of language research in the US Office of Education, who was in charge of these grants. A native of New Mexico, Gaarder discussed his concern with Pascual and invited New Mexico to submit a proposal. The summer institute that Pascual had designed in Guadalajara, Mexico, responded to the need for trained literate teachers in the Spanish language.[12]

Pascual's proposal was funded for $300,000, and the thirty teacher-students selected would be granted eight credit hours through the University of New Mexico. As director of the institute, "I took leave from my work to do this. I was lucky to have Cecilio Orozco as my assistant director since he was from Guadalajara and was studying at the University of New Mexico."[13]

The Experienced Teacher Fellowship Program in Bilingual Education, later referred to as the Guadalajara Institutes, became very well-known across the state.[14] A total of sixty bilingual teachers from New Mexico and Colorado participated the first two years. "[It was] probably the best training anyone could get," stated Emma Armendáriz.[15] She highlighted how critical this experience had been in developing their own understanding of the history of Mexico and for their Mexican counterparts to understand them, "because most of us as being Hispanos were known as *Pochos* [derogatory term in Mexico for Mexican-Americans]—they got to know us and that we were a striving people in the US."

Institute Content

The purpose of the institutes was to immerse the teachers in the Spanish language and to develop firsthand knowledge of the cultures of the peoples of Mexico. "We developed a rigorous course of study and cultural travels . . . and had a most successful experience."[16] Students took classes in anthropology and the history of Mexico, participated in demonstration classes, and had daily language practice with three teachers and one tutor, with a focus on oral and written language development. Henry Pascual was unable to direct the third year institute, but he invited María Spencer, who "came to the rescue and the summer session was conducted at Highlands University and on-site in Santa Fe."[17]

The momentum and success of these institutes created the impetus for bilingual teacher development within the state via the demonstration centers, discussed next.

THE BILINGUAL BICULTURAL TEACHER–TRAINING NETWORK, 1971–1974

In the early 1970s, universities were hard pressed to meet the local demand for well-prepared teachers in the emerging field of bilingual education. There were few professors of education who could deliver instruction through Spanish, and there was little experience with teaching through two languages. State certification criteria for bilingual education would not be created until 1973. Twenty-three districts were operating bilingual education programs via federal and state funding sources; many needed help with curriculum, bilingual delivery of the curriculum, and program models.[18]

Having experienced such success with the Guadalajara institutes, Henry Pascual sought a solution via Title III funds that had become available to the state:

> In 1971 or 1972 I was called by the New Mexico Department of Public School Finance to see if there was some use for extra funds they had. Immediately, I wrote up a proposal to establish a training center for northern New Mexico. My format was accepted and the West Las Vegas District accepted—Ray Leger was Superintendent and Mela Leger became the director.[19]

The Armijo School in West Las Vegas and the Bicultural Orientation and Language Development in Silver City had been carrying out demonstrations for district bilingual teachers. Knowing of their quality, Pascual selected these sites for the network. A third center was created the following year (1972) at Roswell. In a 2002 interview, Pascual noted, "These centers were precursors to the many centers funded by the Office of Bilingual Education and Minority Languages Affairs later. The work done by the teachers and trainers was spectacular!"[20]

THE ARMIJO BILINGUAL BICULTURAL DEMONSTRATION CENTER IN WEST LAS VEGAS

Using the Pecos project model, the West Las Vegas schools began a bilingual education program in 1965 with Title I funds. The district subsequently built successful programs in other schools as state federal funds became available. As

Pascual mentioned in his 2002 interview, "West Las Vegas was tremendously successful because the spirit was there."[21]

Three main objectives guided the teaching at the Armijo Elementary School bilingual program: Improving self-image by teaching students the positive elements of their culture; teaching English using English-as-a-second language techniques; and teaching thinking skills using Spanish in science, math, social studies.

The teachers were "committed to teach . . . some of the content areas besides the language arts."[22] In other words, they had the Spanish skills for content instruction and thus played an active role in making the demonstration project successful. It was their work that trainees observed and emulated. As a district bilingual education demonstration site, the Armijo school was ideal as a site for network teacher training.

Unique Aspects of the Supervision

Mela Leger, the district's director of bilingual education who had helped to write up the plan for the demonstration center at Armijo Elementary, oversaw its expenditures and implementation. At that time, Leger was serving as director of bilingual education and housed at Las Vegas West Schools Central Office. Master teacher Lupe Castillo, a former bilingual education teacher from the school, became the coordinator of the Network Teacher Training Center. Castillo received continuous support and guidance from both Henry Pascual and Mela Leger, a welcome departure from the more typical lack of support and guidance afforded to support staff who are hired to coordinate externally funded projects. According to Castillo, Leger

> "supervised the application and . . . during the week when the teachers were there, or after it was over, then she would meet with me and say how do you feel about how the week went? Or how did it go with the teachers, did they have any problems?"[23]

Castillo also described the supportive role that Henry Pascual played, an indication of his full commitment to the program. Pascual would go to Las Vegas to conduct classroom observations with Castillo and then compare their findings. Castillo recalls Pascual explaining to her that "if you run into any problems throughout this program you give me a call and I'll help you out. So . . . he just made sure that things were running smoothly and that things that needed to be addressed, were addressed."[24]

Selection of Trainees

The purpose of the demonstration project at West Las Vegas was to help teacher trainees from northern New Mexico who were having difficulties delivering instruction or implementing any aspects of their programs. Henry Pascual and Lupe Castillo observed instruction and selected trainees who had self-identified areas of need. This was important because having had their university preparation in English, many had difficulty using Spanish as the medium of instruction. Districts sent the trainees to observe and to "try out" effective teaching practices demonstrated at Armijo; the SDE managed the distribution of funding via local administrators.

Micro-Teaching at the Demonstration Site

Teacher trainees committed to working in Armijo Elementary for an entire week as follows.

MONDAY The visiting teachers identified areas of need, "mainly the objectives of the program, the strategies to be used, . . . the activities they were going to include in order to teach those objectives, and how they were going to find out if the objectives had been addressed and the students had acquired them." The objectives they wrote followed a format. Castillo recalled that "the students will be able to do such and such after my lesson . . . . It was well framed. I remember thinking if everyone was able to do this they would have a top notch program."[25]

TUESDAY Participants observed multiple lessons taught by master teacher Castillo and then by the Armijo teachers in fifteen- to twenty-minute time allotments, which were videotaped. Utilizing the observation checklist for each lesson they observed, teachers wrote the objectives they had observed, how they were being met, and what strategies teachers were using to teach the objectives. That evening, the participants prepared a fifteen- to twenty-minute lesson plan that they would deliver the following day.

WEDNESDAY AND THURSDAY Teachers observed their fellow participants teach small groups of Armijo children while their lessons were videotaped. Then, using the same observation tool, the visiting teachers critiqued each lesson in a group session guided by Castillo. After that, each teacher critiqued her own lesson. The group also discussed recommendations for improvement.[26]

FRIDAY During final discussions and evaluation, teachers outlined what they had learned and how they would apply this to their local classrooms.

CONTINUOUS FOLLOW-UP The process did not end there. Lupe Castillo followed up by traveling to the districts to spend half a day with each of the teachers in their classrooms. Sometimes she gave a sample lesson. She also observed their instruction and wrote up the observations for each teacher, with a copy provided to the principal. Castillo explained the process: "And the reason we did it like that was because we wanted the teachers to feel the importance of their role in the classroom and the principal of course was included because we wanted for them to cooperate in the endeavor."[27]

In the spring, the teachers returned to Armijo for the final week of training to determine how trainees were progressing with the ideas that they themselves suggested. The training also included another videotaping with critiques. Most of the teachers had problems using the technical language in Spanish; some had problems writing it. Lupe Castillo was clear about the obvious need for further teacher training in Spanish: "It is a common mistake to assume that just because you can speak two languages, you can teach bilingual classes."[28]

When asked about the success of the demonstration project, Castillo had this to say:

> The best part about that, all of that work and everything is the fact that the teachers themselves when we didn't have the program anymore they were coming to me and saying, how come you don't have that program? I wanted to attend it. The other teachers got a lot of help."[29]

BICULTURAL ORIENTATION AND LANGUAGE DEVELOPMENT: THE BOLD DEMONSTRATION CENTER IN SILVER CITY

The second demonstration center—the Bicultural Orientation and Language Development Program (BOLD)—was directed by María Spencer, a heroic and dynamic bilingual educator who dedicated her work in bilingual education to a highly segregated student population. The program, which included a teacher training component, offered an exemplary bilingual education program for 150 Hispanic students in first, second, and third grades. Spencer's approach was highly innovative and revolutionary for Silver City. The unique aspects of this program involved the use of technology. In describing the Sixth Street School program, the lab school for this project, Emma Armendáriz recalled that "the school had been wired for closed captioned TVs, and one of the classrooms was a language lab that had individual listening stations—*cabinas*, carrels—where each student listened to audiotapes at their level. They could practice pronouncing words in English, privately." When educators came from across the country to learn about the BOLD program, they "could either observe the classrooms from a TV or a two-way observation room."[30] The local newspaper stated that "Mrs. María G. Spencer, director of the Demonstration Center reported that 78 teachers from California, Texas, Colorado, Arizona and New Mexico spent from one to five days observing classes in the Center. One hundred and ninety high school and university students also visited the program."[31]

Spencer administered a non-verbal intelligence test to Hispanic children, and taught them a bilingual curriculum half the day and a non-bilingual curriculum the other half. According to her daughter, Laura Spencer, who heads the Chicano Program at New Mexico State University, within three years, Spencer's students were outperforming those in the "regular" curriculum.[32] The program focused on cultural strengths and the languages students brought to school while quickly developing skills in English. "From the time I was a child," Laura Spencer recalled, "and she was starting the BOLD program, she would explain to me the advantages I had and how the culture of poverty is not about economics, it's about how you see the world and how you plan your life, how you survive."[33] Emma Armendáriz stated, "So that was the start of bilingual ed. We were inventing it!"[34]

Seeking professional development for her teachers and staff was paramount for Spencer. She provided opportunities for them to travel to one of the first conferences in the country where people convened to consider such critical questions about bilingual education as, "Okay what about these children who come in speaking a language other than English? What is the value, and what importance are you going to give it and so forth?"[35]

THE MASTER'S PROGRAM IN ELEMENTARY BILINGUAL EDUCATION AT NEW MEXICO HIGHLANDS UNIVERSITY 1971–1976

After Cecilio Orozco received his doctorate in 1971 from the University of New Mexico, he went to New Mexico Highlands University, where he pioneered the first MA program for elementary bilingual education teachers, and in 1973 secured one of the early Title VII ESEA professional development grants. This was the first such MA program in the state.[36]

Innovative Program Features

The interdepartmental design of the program gave students the opportunity to take non-language subject-matter courses in Spanish. Departments whose faculty could teach in Spanish offered MA program students classes such as Spanish for Science for the Elementary Classroom, Mathematics in English and Spanish, and a Spanish linguistics course.[37]

Master's program teachers learned about the cultural lifeways of New Mexico Hispanics and the nature and history of the vernacular of Spanish New Mexico. For example, the course Socio-Cultural Factors Affecting Education—taught first in English and later in two languages—incorporated New Mexico's heritage, folklore, and the oral tradition that were common to Hispanic students in the homes and communities of the state.

Orozco taught a course in which teachers collected and classified Spanish language usage in northern New Mexico into categories such as *anglicismos, arcaísimos,* and *mejicanismos,* (anglicisms, archaic aspects of the language, and vocabulary and expression influenced by Mexican Spanish), and the peculiarities of New Mexican Spanish (such as *suidad* versus *ciudad, onde* versus *donde, pa que* versus *para que,* and *jita* versus *hijita*). Students identified words and expressions of foreign origin and examples of other linguistical elements and collected and shared examples of *dichos, adivinanzas, cuentos, chistes* (sayings, riddles, stories, and jokes) used in the oral tradition in the communities of New Mexico. This work validated both the vernacular and standard forms of Spanish for instruction as important for students' self-concept. It also explained the linguistic evolution of northern New Mexico Spanish.

Another innovation was the use of a language laboratory for Spanish oral language development. For example, the course Story Reading, Telling, and Writing in Spanish emphasized language arts and literature for the elementary classroom. Students read children's literature in Spanish, wrote synopses, collected new vocabulary, and wrote definitions and synonyms, all in Spanish. They were given various storytelling and reading tasks in paired configurations with their peers. Students also collected and shared local New Mexico *cuentos* (stories) and organized these into teacher-made instructional materials, providing a useful example of how to incorporate local culture into elementary language arts instruction.

An agreement between the West Las Vegas Schools and the university gave West Las Vegas High School's bilingual program students access to the language lab. In one language development activity, students viewed slides depicting local scenes in West Las Vegas—its people, local community events, fiestas, landmarks, school activities—and after being given a prompt, they were asked to discuss these scenes in paired groups (what happened right before the depicted event, why the photo was taken, who the characters were, how they would describe the photo to a blind person, a young child, and so forth). Similar methods and activities took place with teachers in the MA program, such as inventing stories they would tell their students. These and other activities like them extended their comprehension, vocabulary, and control of the Spanish language.

Another lab activity involved language analysis through music. As a graduate assistant for Orozco's program, Habermann López transcribed lyrics from a variety of popular, classical, Mariachi, and local New Mexican songs in Spanish and underlined words and phrases that might be said differently in the vernacular. For local New Mexican songs, the vernacular would be highlighted, and students would then identify the standard written form. This created oral and linguistic awareness in oral and written form without disparaging the native New Mexican Spanish dialect. The instructor pointed out these distinctions as part of the lesson. Often, the entire class would be singing out loud with their headsets on. As students listened and read the lyrics, they came to identify both vernacular and standard Spanish usages and built needed literacy skills in Spanish for the classroom.

The Spanish content developed teachers' capabilities in all four skills of the language—listening, speaking, reading, and writing—with practical classroom and bilingual program application. Further, it built teachers' knowledge about the culture and history of Spanish New Mexico and Mexico. Lastly, there was an emphasis on both standard Spanish and the vernacular of northern New Mexico.

Habermann López recalls how the program was equally rich for Anglo students such as herself: "As a student who learned Spanish as my second language, the MA program courses taught me about New Mexico Spanish, how and why it evolved as it did. With this knowledge I was able to incorporate the vernacular into my teaching. . . . My students and their parents could see their language and culture reflected in the curriculum."[38] Roberta Marquez mentioned how it strengthened her sense of identity. "The whole program changed my worldview, my experience, to actually teach in Mexico and study there and learn about our, my history, because we did take New Mexico History there, too. It developed my self-confidence as a Chicana."[39]

This program became a model for university MA preparation in bilingual education in the state.

Title VII ESEA MA Bilingual Education Program Institute

Beginning in the fall of 1973, Title VII funds offered bilingual teacher fellows a master's degree via intensive university study at Highlands University and the Universidad Autónoma de Guadalajara, in Guadalajara, Mexico. Cecilio Orozco and Henry Pascual interviewed elementary bilingual education teacher applicants from across the state and Southern Colorado and selected thirty teacher fellows. Participants attended the Autónoma during the winter quarter. The year-long program consisted of coursework (described above) at New Mexico Highlands University in the fall, immersion in Guadalajara (described below) in the winter, and student teaching in the spring at the West Las Vegas schools elementary bilingual education program at the Armijo elementary demonstration center overseen by Mela Leger. During the spring, while they did their student teaching, they also studied Mexican folk dances, guitar, and traditional children's songs and finger plays for the elementary classroom.

Immersion in Guadalajara (Winter)

Teacher fellows spent the first half of the day teaching English as a second language with Mexican children in the schools. During the afternoon, they attended two classes at the Autónoma—the History of Mexico and a course on the Aztec calendar taught by Rivas Salmón, one of Orozco's mentors and fellow researchers. Marquez recalls, "Dr. Salmón believed the Aztec Calendar was not really a calendar at all but the story of the four migrations of the native people who settled in the valley of Mexico now known as Mexico City."[40] Orozco took an interest in this work and continued studying the migrations claiming that one was in the United States Southwest.

The preparation in Spanish was comprehensive, rich and useful for elementary classroom instruction. Márquez described the impact of the program:

> [It] really changed my life. I was a little kid coming from Tucumcari who
> struggled in Spanish in an English speaking environment, using it [Spanish]
> with my grandparents. The intermediate Spanish classes at the undergraduate
> level were super challenging, but I don't recall them helping my Spanish. Those
> classes were excellent but there was nothing about them that reflected my dialect
> and my culture. But Cecilio's classes did. [The Institute] gave me what no other
> school experience gave me in my life. Not that I didn't get a good education,
> I got very good basic training. But, there is something about getting to know

who you are, learning about your culture, history and language that is really empowering.[41]

Around this same time, Lieutenant Colonel Miguel Encinias, recently retired from military service, returned to his native New Mexico and became involved in bilingual education. He enrolled in the bilingual education doctoral program at the University of New Mexico, worked with Henry Pascual at the New Mexico State Department of Education, and served as a member of the New Mexico Bilingual Advisory Committee, which helped develop teacher certification standards for bilingual education. From 1974 to 1979, Encinias directed the University of Albuquerque's Bilingual Multicultural Teacher Preparation Program, which became renowned for its innovative format.

In his doctoral dissertation, Encinias wrote:

> As I learned more about the literature written in Spanish, and about Spanish linguistics I became more and more convinced that the best way to educate Hispanic children was to allow them to learn through Spanish about the many different Hispanic cultures and literatures.[42]

THE BILINGUAL MULTICULTURAL TEACHER PREPARATION PROGRAM 1974–1979

The University of Albuquerque's teacher preparation program in bilingual-bicultural education was funded by Title VII in 1976 and housed on campus in a remodeled dormitory. The program, designed by Miguel Encinias contained several unique features that focused on the language and culture of two distinct New Mexico groups: the Pueblo People and the Keres language, the Spanish/Hispanic group. Here he sums up his rationale for building the program:

> What the teachers must do in order to acquire Spanish proficiency is to gain a deep appreciation for Hispanic culture. They must be inspired to continue studying and reading in Spanish and to develop a curiosity about Hispanic society and civilization which will culminate in such activities as travel in Spanish-speaking countries and other participation in Hispanic life. . . .
> If enough interest, or better, excitement is generated in Hispanic culture to permit it to permeate the community, bilingual-bicultural education will have been a success. (Encinias 1976, 179–78)

In his dissertation, Encinias clearly laid out his classically based teacher preparation program, which included all relevant historical, theoretical, and research available at the time. His objective was to provide the best academic preparation for bilingual-bicultural teachers while incorporating the Spanish language and cultures. He was able to provide an innovative program that included support for the teachers in the development of their own language within a strong cultural component. In his dissertation, Encinias stated:

> Culture and language are given short shrift in most bilingual education programs. It is difficult to pinpoint reasons, but one fact is clear: the preponderance of such programs are developed by the colleges or departments of education who quite naturally place their kind of stamp or emphasis on them, often to the detriment of the language and cultural components. (Encinias 1976, 108)

Instructional Staff

A group of highly educated staff members were hired as instructors in the program. In the Native American component of the program, for example, Amy Zaharlick, a graduate from Georgetown University's anthropology linguistics program, taught alongside Donna Pino Martinez, from Santa Ana Pueblo. Martinez was a respected New Mexico educator from a Pueblo community whose work in the area of Native American linguistics and language was important.

For the Hispanic component, Rebecca Blum Martínez, who later became a professor of bilingual education, and Fred Carrillo, a well-known Spanish-language educator, taught courses in Spanish and provided Spanish-targeted language development for the participants. Blum Martínez described the instructional dilemma at the beginning of the program:

> Initially, the students were overwhelmed by having to read and write their papers in Spanish and while Dr. Encinias was understanding of their stress, he insisted on continuing (solely in Spanish). In order to ensure that they had sufficient support in Spanish, we had special classes where we incorporated specific aspects of the Spanish language with oral and written practice based on the kinds of activities that teachers would develop and lead in their classrooms. All of this was innovative, given the kinds of bilingual teacher training programs that existed in some other universities.[43]

Student Enrollment

The program was designed for educational assistants who were working with students who spoke either Spanish or Keres languages in their home but had

never undertaken any formal studies in their native language. The program provided scholarships and stipends to each participant. The group was composed
mainly of non-traditional students, with three students under the age of twenty
making the program intergenerational. Even with their differences in age and
experience, the group became a strong community of learners, which students
considered one of the benefits of the program. A participant explained that
"looking back on it forty years later, I think of it with joy. . . . There was always
a major connection among the participants, a sisterhood, a brotherhood."[44]

Innovative Program Features

There were various features that were intended consequences of the program
and others that simply were added benefits. This section will mainly rely on the
voices of three individuals directly involved in the program: Miguel Encinias;
Rebecca Blum Martínez, former program instructor; and Anne Marie Ulibarrí,
a program participant and former principal of a full-immersion dual-language
program in the Albuquerque Public Schools. It was through active learning
that the cultural activities were built into the program. In the Spanish/Hispanic
component of the program, all classes were taught exclusively in Spanish. As
Blum Martínez relates, "No other university program offered all coursework
in Spanish for bilingual teachers. They were exposed to courses in Spanish but
not limited to teaching and learning [pedagogy]. Spanish for Spanish speakers,
science, mathematics, and the like."[45]

Another feature was that history was used as a building block to optimally
prepare these teachers. Miguel Encinias justified including history in bilingual-
multicultural teacher preparation programs in the following manner:

> The study of history reveals a great deal: the great public accomplishments, the
> great discoveries, the momentous diplomacy and more, and it is important to be
> well acquainted with the record of the group. As the epigraph by Unamuno at
> the beginning of Chapter 1 reads, 'In order for an individual or a people to know
> themselves, they must in one form or another study their history.' There can be
> little disagreement that history should be part of the curriculum at any university.
> It is of particular importance to bilingual-bicultural education with its concern
> for balanced sociological perspectives.[46]

It is interesting to note that Encinias also taught one of the history courses,
History of Mexico, which was specifically designed to educate teachers about
the country from which their students and their families came. Another feature

that was considered essential by Encinias was the building of self-esteem in the teachers. The idea that self-esteem is critical in teaching, especially in the much disputed area of bilingual-bicultural education, demands that teachers be well-grounded not only in knowledge, but also in self-worth, which is challenged so continually by society. In turn, their self-worth and self-esteem will transfer into their teaching of children in a non-dominant language and culture. "There are . . . other sources of the kind of knowledge," Encinias asserted, "which can bring prestige, pride and, above all, self-awareness."[47] Ulibarrí, once a student in the program, explained how the program impacted her self-concept: "I felt a certain pride when I heard him (teach). I felt I needed to listen."[48]

Another important and innovative feature in teacher preparation was the inclusion of the arts. Blum Martínez explained that "Miguel Encinias found any means possible to expose the student to every aspect of culture and language."[49] Through these activities, the students found the connections between culture and art, culture and language, and culture and life. In Encinias's words, the art forms were a justifiable part of a teacher's preparation:

> Not only should the history and the sociocultural significance of art forms such as literature, painting, music, and architecture be studied, but those forms which lend themselves to ready demonstration in a university should be experienced firsthand, if possible by participation, as in a choir or a play [dramatic arts]. There is no better way to learn and appreciate an artistic element of a culture. In view of the tasks required of bilingual-bicultural education: the sociological task, the pedagogical task and the principal one, the learning and appreciation of the culture, a concentration of required courses should form the core of a bilingual teacher education program."[50]

As a result of these beliefs, culturally intact performing arts activities were built into the program. For example, Encinias found a company from New York that would rent films, and Rebecca Blum Martínez would select movies that were shown on Fridays to the participants as part of their program.

Dramatic arts were also included. The focus was on plays originally written in Spanish. Encinias contracted with the Spanish language theater company Repertorio Español de Nueva York to present *La vida es sueño* to students and the general public. When he met José Rodríguez, the lead actor—an effusive and gifted Puerto Rican who had studied at the Royal Academy of Dramatic Arts in London—he invited him to come to New Mexico for a year, and teach theater to our students. And once again, we all participated. At the end of that year, the students presented two short plays written by Federico García Lorca: *Los Títeres de Cachiporra* and *Don Perlimplín con Belisa en su Jardín*. That was how La Compañia de Teatro began.[51]

Encinias enhanced the performing arts programs with yet another cultural activity—El Coro (choir). First taught by Padre Cuesta, a Spanish priest, directorship of the El Coro was later transferred to a student in the program, Mary Frances Reza, who had previous experience with choral groups. The songs were all original Spanish songs.

There were two other features to the program that Anna Marie Ulibarrí remembered from her own days as a student in the program. While she feels that "the fight continues whether bilingual education is viable," her preparation program taught them to defend bilingual education and keep it alive. She described how "the political piece was a requirement, and students were expected to be strong advocates and take it to the political level." Students were required to attend both district school board meetings and state educational board meetings. In fact, through the years after completing the program, the participants have met again at meetings and events to defend bilingual education.[52]

One feature that built on the participants' teaching skills was Saturday School. On Saturdays, children from the community came to the university, where they were taught by the university participants to build on their Spanish vocabulary through hands-on learning. Ulibarrí remembered working with children and building their Spanish repertoire. Although these lessons were designed to be engaging and relevant, not dull and boring, the activities were not to be "just fun and games but they had to have intensity."

Blum Martínez and Ulibarrí considered the program a success. Both mentioned one of the students, Emmalou Rodríguez, who was a stalwart of bilingual education and went on to serve on the State Board of Education. Ulibarri and Blum Martínez also described independently how the vast majority of the participants became active players in teaching, and how many moved on into leadership positions beyond the classroom. Ulibarrí and Blum Martínez have become quite successful in their own right. Ulibarrí is currently a principal in the only full-immersion language school in the Albuquerque Public Schools, where open enrollment is an option to any student who lives within the district.

Ulibarrí described how the Encinias program prepared her to serve children: "The lessons I learned there have sustained me to this day as an educator." In discussing her daily practices as principal and its connection with the program, she added that "now excellence is the key—to hold high expectations but to share support for children with the community, the parents, and the staff." She also felt that "this program was transformational. It was an awakening for me, and I became proud of who I am."[53]

Blum Martínez is a researcher and advocate of bilingual education and is tireless in her efforts to continue impacting the public school bilingual education classroom through her programs in higher education. She described the impact that Encinias had on the public schools :

> [Encinias] became the director of the Albuquerque Public Schools' Cross Cultural Center. . . . Dr. Encinias was able to envision smaller aspects of the program he had developed at the University of Albuquerque, particularly at Albuquerque High, where Carlos Chávez, a former student from University of Albuquerque began teaching US, and World History in Spanish. He recruited Dr. Fábrega to teach Spanish Language Arts to the Spanish-speaking students and he recruited another Spanish-speaking teacher to teach drama in Spanish. Today, thanks to Dr. Encinias vision, we continue to have high school courses taught in Spanish which in turn has resulted in the Bilingual Seal. So you can see that in that program, he was able to put many of his ideas into practice.[54]

THE GOLD SEAL OF BILINGUALISM ON HIGH SCHOOL DIPLOMA: 1998

In 1998, several bilingual students at Rio Grande High School (RGHS) in Albuquerque, New Mexico, graduated with the very first gold seal of bilingualism placed on their diplomas—the first such seal in the nation.[55] Rio Grande High School students hailed from the largely Spanish-speaking South Valley, and many were children of Mexican heritage. The school began building its secondary-level bilingual program in the Albuquerque district beginning in mid-1980s.

Carlos Chávez, a former student in Encinias's program, was hired as the Title VII secondary bilingual program coordinator. Chávez recognized the efforts of his students who were taking content courses in both English and Spanish. He argued that one of the goals of the program should be a recognition of students' bilingual abilities. He established the first bilingual seal for proficiency in two languages on students' high school diplomas—a golden opportunity to recognize the gift of bilingualism for students. It was no small challenge, however.

Chávez had always held high expectations of and standards for his students. He demanded students' best, but he also acknowledged their challenges. Robert

Cisneros, the former community liaison at Rio Grande High School who worked with Chávez, recalled his teaching:

> He assigned a very difficult project to his [students] in his class and they had to do a lot of research on the computer. A lot of the [students] were immigrants and they had no access to computers. But he did not let up. [Students] would come to me and say, "You know, I don't have a computer." . . . Afterward, he [Chávez] told me, "You know, it breaks my heart that I have to tell these kids that they have to do it some way; they have to find a way to get this research done. I know they don't have a computer but they have to find one." . . . And you know those students, they came through, they produced.[56]

Chávez intervened on behalf of his students with parents as well. "There was this young lady who had a scholarship to New Mexico Highlands University. It was a Mexican family; the father didn't want to let her go. So here go Carlos and I to the house. . . . Carlos convinced him. That young lady attended and graduated from NMHU."[57]

As a teacher, Chávez believed that his students had great potential. Sally Brown Martínez, Spanish teacher at RGHS said, "He adored the community, all of his [children] graduated from there. He was proud of his school and his students, and he never let up. He had lots of lunchtime conferences with (students) trying to straighten them out. (He was) so familiar with growing up in the Valley, he would take no excuses. He held a high standard for the kids. He required lots of projects speaking in front of the class."[58] Cisneros described numerous graduates of the program who went on to do very well, some creating local businesses, others going on to college, and even one student who today is a testing engineer for IBM. Many of Chávez's students emulated their mentor, becoming bilingual teachers.

How the Seal Program was Built

Carlos Chávez started the seal process by first bringing a team of teachers in the Spanish curriculum together—Sally Brown Martínez, Gloria Barrata, Gordon Douglas, Robert Cisneros, and the community liaison—who together produced a process to validate student achievement in two languages at the highest level on the high school diploma. Seniors applying for the seal had to prepare two essays, one in Spanish and one in English. If they passed, they would then be invited to interviews, conducted by two staff members, during which the students had to respond to five questions in Spanish and five in English. Staff used a rubric to determine the level of fluency, and this, combined with the essay score, was the basis for awarding the bilingual seal.[59]

Seal Success

The bilingual seal offered exceptional preparation for students seeking this recognition. Students enrolled in advanced placement Spanish language and literacy classes taught by Gloria Barrata, and they passed the rigorous process with an 80–90 percent rate. Rio Grande High School Spanish teacher Sally Brown Martínez recalled how Barrata would take her seniors to sit in on 300- and 400-level Spanish classes at the University of New Mexico, where they would actively participate. The bilingual program eventually offered a Spanish theatrical component, created by Brown Martínez, called Río Gigante, a take-off on the Spanish TV Program *Sábado Gigante*, which ran for six years. Students were involved in every aspect of the program production, from selling and creating video ads to performing, dancing, singing, engaging the audience with games, awarding prizes, and bringing in groups such as *folclórico* dancers and University of New Mexico's mariachi.

Carlos Chávez spearheaded it all. In addition to instituting the RGHS bilingual seal policy, he made a point of organizing a breakfast reception for students and families, inviting well-recognized keynote speakers who honored their accomplishment.[60] Over time, the recognition became a school-wide event involving more and more teachers and students. For example, students in the Home Economics Department catered the event at local venues and made the sashes students wore at the breakfast, and the Technology Department designed and printed all the invitations.[61]

Current Seal Status

The Albuquerque Public Schools later adopted a regulation for the seal that specified coursework and GPA requirements. The number of RGHS seal applicants dropped. "The result was we had only a dozen apply," Brown Martínez recalled. "We went from ninety to a dozen and what got most of them was the [required] grade-point average. You know, a lot of our kids, they weren't scholars, but they went to school . . . but they couldn't make the grade-point average.[62] Cisneros concurs: "Something he [Carlos Chávez] was totally against in later years [was] when they started putting the bilingual seal requirements into writing. . . . What Carlos used to say was, 'What does a GPA have to do if the student is fluent in both English and Spanish. . . . He can master both languages in reading writing and speaking."[63] The district currently requires a total of sixteen credits in Spanish language arts, English language arts, and core content in Spanish and in English. Students must maintain a minimum 2.0 GPA in all coursework in both English and Spanish. Finally, they must create and present a written and oral portfolio consisting of an oral presentation delivered in each language and written reflections with work samples in both languages before a panel of community and staff members.[64]

It is no small wonder Mr. Chavez was able to bring this goal of the Title VII grant to fruition. The seal was the forerunner of those that are now given in various states, including the New Mexico State Seal of Bilingualism.

REBECCA BLUM MARTÍNEZ'S CONCLUDING REMARKS

As a professor of bilingual education charged with the preparation of bilingual teachers, I am struck by the vision of the innovations that were developed fifty years ago. So much of what they attempted is still viable, and badly needed today.

Presently, among the five New Mexico universities, the programs that prepare bilingual teachers and teachers of English to speakers of other languages (TESOL) are working together to strengthen our coursework in TESOL and bilingual education so that students receive a rigorous set of courses, and if needed, can transition easily from one university to another. An in-service or pre-service program that would allow teachers to observe master teachers, prepare lesson plans, and then be visited by master teachers to improve their practice would assist teachers in providing the best pedagogy for their bilingual students.

Preparing teachers adequately in the Spanish language has been of concern since the early days of bilingual education, and continues today (see Guerrero and Guerrero 2017 for a deeper discussion). There are still school districts that hire teachers who have only a conversational level of Spanish. For this reason, many states have instituted Spanish-language tests that must be passed by a teacher before she or he can teach in a bilingual situation. New Mexico universities have tried several ways to incorporate the use of the Spanish language into our teacher preparation programs. Some have relegated this aspect of the program to the Spanish departments because of a lack of faculty with advanced levels of oral and written proficiency within the schools of education. Others have developed summer Spanish immersion programs where teachers take coursework in Spanish that prepares them for their future professions.

Nevertheless, as early pioneers pointed out, the challenge of finding education professors who can utilize Spanish in academic settings remains, especially in the age of shrinking university budgets, paltry federal aid, and the mischaracterization of bilingual education as remedial education and unnecessary.

The attitudes of many mainstream university and public-school educators and administrators has remained unchanged. There is a grudging acceptance of the need for teachers to have TESOL preparation. For the most part, the education of emergent bilingual students is left up to the TESOL teacher—or worse, to the remedial reading teacher—while other teachers, administrators, and policy makers absolve themselves of any responsibility. In 2014, Judge Sarah Singleton of New Mexico's First District found in favor of Latino and Native American families who had sued the state for providing an insufficient and unequal education for their children. Many Latino and Native American children are bilingual and in need of a bilingual education or a sound English-language development program. Testimony on behalf of the families indicates that there are insufficient numbers of TESOL-endorsed teachers to serve these students and that both the New Mexico Public Education Department and school districts have not put the appropriate programmatic structures in place to protect English learners from educational malpractice.[65]

The waxing and waning of political support for bilingual education at both state and federal levels has wreaked havoc with the lives of bilingual children. In one administration, children can receive bilingual education, only to be placed in ESL classrooms in the next. The lack of a consistent and pedagogically sound approach to educating bilingual children has had deleterious effects. New Mexico bilingual students struggle both to achieve English language proficiency and to maintain their mother tongues. While New Mexico bilingual educators have consistently advocated for bilingual education, federal policy, funding, and politically conservative governors have made their mark.

Those of us who started our careers in bilingual education in the 1970s are now seeing many of the same damaging policies and practices reappear. While it is at times discouraging, it is also instructive to look back at the pioneers who are the reason for this book. We had the great advantage of being able to observe and be mentored by these wonderful visionaries. Our task is to continue the struggle and to bring the next generation of bilingual educators along with us so that they can be the leaders in the future.

NOTES

1. As a result of the NEA Tucson Survey (see Blum Martínez, chapter 6 this volume) the Pecos bilingual education project (See Habermann López, chapter 5, this volume) became a recognized and well-documented education innovation in New Mexico as well as in the United States (National Education Association 1966).

2. Henry W. Pascual, interview by Rebecca Blum Martínez, Mary Jean Habermann López, and Julia Rosa López-Emslie, August 11,12, 2001, at Pascual's home. DVD and partial transcript available and in the possession of Mary Jean Habermann López.

3. US Department of Health, Education and Welfare National Institutes of Education 1974.

4. Pascual interview.

5. Refugio (Cuca) Medina interview by María Luisa González on February 17, 2017, in Las Cruces, NM.

6. Angie Morgan interview by María Luisa González on March 17, 2017, in Las Cruces, NM.

7. Refugio (Cuca) Medina, Angie Morgan, Victoria Oliver Escalante interview by María Luisa González on March 17, 2017 in Las Cruces.

8. Medina, Morgan, Oliver Escalante interview.

9. Refugio (Cuca) Medina, personal archives, March 17, 2017.

10. Mary Jean Habermann López interview by María Luisa González on August 1, 2017 in Albuquerque, NM.

11. Pascual interview.

12. Ibid.

13. Henry W. Pascual, "Bilingual Education Recollections," talk prepared for the National Association for Bilingual Education Conference in Albuquerque, NM, January 20, 1991, unpublished transcript in Mary Jean Habermann López, personal collection.

14. Newspaper clippings from across the state attest to the widespread awareness of the institute: "Louis Brady Taking Special Courses in Mexico School," *Hagerman Star*, June 10, 1971; "Isabel Abeyta to Attend Bilingual Education Program," *Grant Beacon*, June 9, 1971; "Local Teachers to Attend Bilingual Classes in Mexico," *Tucumcari Daily News*, June 10, 1971; "30 Elementary Teachers Join Bilingual Program," *New Mexico Lobo*, June 11, 1971; *The Taos News*, June 16, 1971; "Mrs. Abeyta Chosen for Training Project," *Las Vegas Daily Optic*, June 16, 1971; "Hurley Teacher Chosen for Bilingual Program," *Silver City Daily Press*, June 9, 1971; "Rosa Anaya in Bilingual School Training Program," *Portales News Tribune*, June 9 1971; "Bilingual Institute Slated in Las Vegas," *Albuquerque Journal*, June 10, 1971.

15. Emma Armendariz interviewed by María Luisa González on July 26, 2017 in Las Cruces, NM. Emma Armendáriz participated in the Institute and taught in the

Silver City Bilingual Demonstration Center, discussed further on in this chapter. She dedicated her entire career to bilingual education, serving as a teacher trainer in federally funded state and regional centers and later as principal of one of the first dual language education schools in Albuquerque, NM.

16. Pascual interview.

17. Ibid.

18. This information was culled from a SDE non published report on 1971–1972 Title VII and state funded bilingual education programs, January 21, 1972. Report in possession of Mary Jean Habermann López.

19. Pascual interview.

20. Ibid.

21. Ibid.

22. Lupe Castillo interview by Mary Jean Habermann López, April 13, 2016, at Castillo's home in Santa Fe, NM.

23. Ibid.

24. Ibid.

25. Ibid.

26. Ibid. The Armijo teachers were pilot-testing the new SCDC materials from Miami. Castillo notes, "They were so happy then because they had the vocabulary. They did not have to go searching for it. Everything was mapped out for them." They also used the Dolores Gonzales Spanish materials and the Miami Linguistics readers for English language development (see López-Emslie, chapter 11 this volume).

27. Ibid.

28. Ibid.

29. Ibid.

30. Emma Armendáriz, interview with the author, July 24, 2017.

31. *Silver City Daily Press*, "TESOL Children, Staff, Entertain Parents at Meeting," June 12, 1973, section 2, page 6.

32. "Silver City Teacher's Contributions Recognized in Las Cruces," *Silver City Sun News*, September 7, 2015, https://www.scsun-news.com/story/news/local/2015/09/07 /pioneer-teacher-honored-with-historical-sign/72294738/.

33. Jocelyn N. Apodaca, "Historical Marker at NMSU to Honor María Gutiérrez Spencer," New Mexico State University website, https://newscenter.nmsu.edu/Articles /view/11190/historical-marker-at-nmsu-to-honor-María-Gutierrez-Spencer.

34. Armendáriz interview.

35. Ibid.

36. Information on this master's degree program depends heavily on the insights and experiences of two program graduates: Mary Jean Habermann López, who also worked as a graduate assistant for Cecilio Orozco; and Roberta Márquez.

37. The innovations described in this section evolved over the duration of the

program, 1971–1976. The intensive study in Guadalajara occurred with Title VII fellows only.

38. Mary Jean Habermann López, interview with María Luisa González on communication, September 30, 2017, in Albuquerque, NM.

39. Roberta Márquez, telephone interview with Mary Jean Habermann López, October 1, 2017.

40. Ibid.

41. Ibid.

42. Encinias 1976

43. Rebecca Blum Martínez, interview by María Luisa González, July 31, 2017, Albuquerque, NM.

44. Anna Marie Ulibarrí, phone interview by María Luisa González and Beverly Argus-Calvo, August 26, 2017.

45. Blum Martínez interview.

46. Encinias 1976, 125.

47. Ibid., 126.

48. Ulibarrí interview.

49. Blum Martínez interview.

50. Encinias 1976, 128–29.

51. Blum Martínez interview.

52. Ulibarrí interview.

53. Ulibarrí interview.

54. Blum Martínez interview.

55. The first seal recipients were recognized by the NM State Board of Education. See State Bilingual Advisory Committee chapter, this edition, for more information.

56. Robert Cisneros interview by Mary Jean Habermann López, October 26, 2017, at Cisneros's home. Copy in possession of Mary Jean Habermann López.

57. Ibid.

58. Sally Brown Martínez interview by Mary Jean Habermann López, October 2, 2017, at Martínez's home. Copy in possession of Mary Jean Habermann López. .

59. Ibid.

60. Keynote speakers included former US ambassador to Spain Ed Romeo, former US ambassador to Honduras Mari Luci Jaramillo, former lieutenant governor Roberto Mondragon, *Bless Me Ultima* author Rudolfo Anaya, high-ranking district and state officials, and dignitaries such as the Mexican consul and the director of the Resource Center of Spain.

61. Brown Martínez interview.

62. Ibid.

63. Cisneros interview.

64. State of New Mexico Diploma of Excellence Bilingualism and Biliteracy Seal

Guidance Handbook, 2017, 7. Retrieved from https://webnew.ped.state.nm.us/wp
-content/uploads/2017/12/State-of-New-Mexico-Diploma-of-Excellence
-Bilingualism-and-Biliteracy-Seal-Handbook-Final-8.15.16.pdf
  65. See Yazzie v. the State of New Mexico; Martinez v. the State of New Mexico,
2017.

REFERENCES

Andersson, Theodore. 1971. "Bilingual Education and the American Experience."
  Paper presented at the Conference on Bilingual Education at the Ontario Institute
  for Studies in Education (Toronto, Canada) under the auspices of the Southwest
  Educational Development Laboratories at the University of Texas in Austin.
  https://eric.ed.gov/?q=Andersson%2c+Theodore&ff1=subBilingual+Education
  &ff2=autAndersson%2c+Theodore&ff3=locCanada.
Encinias, Miguel. 1976. "Teacher Education: Hispanic Bilingual-Bicultural Education
  in New Mexico: A Study of Teacher Preparation." PhD diss., University of New
  Mexico.
Guerrero, Michael, and Maía Consuelo Guerrero. 2017. "Competing Discourses of
  Academic Spanish in the Texas-Mexico Borderlands." *Bilingual Research Journal* 40
  (1): 5–19.
Habermann López, Mary Jean. 1992. "Pioneers: Summary of NM Pioneers in
  Bilingual Education," prepared for National Association for Bilingual Education
  National Conference in Albuquerque. Copy in possession of Mary Jean
  Habermann López.
Las Cruces Public Schools. 1980. *Escuelas Oficiales de Las Cruces, Nuevo México Proyecto
  Demonstración 1–12 Bilingüe (Español/Inglés) Multicultural, 1967–1980.* Copy in pos-
  session of Mary Jean Habermann López.
National Education Association. 1966. *The Invisible Minority: Report of the NEA-
  Tucson Survey on the Teaching of Spanish to the Spanish-Speaking.* Washington, DC:
  Department of Rural Education, National Education Association.
Orozco, Cecilio. 1990. *Pyramids of Air.* In *Social Science Perspectives* 4, no. 6: 93–102.
US Department of Health, Education, and Welfare National Institutes of Education.
  1974. *Alternatives: A Survey of Title III, ESEA, Projects in New Mexico,* 25–31, 72.
  http://files.eric.ed.gov/fulltext/ED 109273.

THOMASINA PAGÁN HANNUM
AND LORETTA C. SALAZAR

[10] Assessing the Spanish Language Proficiency of Bilingual Teachers

PROLOGUE

We often wondered, even after years of teaching, why students chit-chatted in Spanish in the hallways and around campus, with each other and even with us, their instructors, yet in the college classroom they hesitated to utter *any* Spanish.

In the early 1970s, as a new teacher from out of state in a small rural district in northern New Mexico, I witnessed students being scolded and punished for speaking Spanish on the playground during recess. This occurred while teachers, aides, and administrators were talking with each other—in Spanish! No surprise that our students grew up concerned about what would happen if they used their home language in class. It would be hard for them to overcome this early training/conditioning. Still, many wanted to become bilingual teachers.

During territorial times, long before statehood, as New Mexicans were beginning to acquire English, the maintenance of Spanish was a topic of concern. Back then, writers actively expressed their reservations regarding the overpowering influence of English. The nineteenth- century poet Jesús María Alarid wrote a poignant piece expressing his concerns about the linguistic status of the two languages. In his 1889 poem "El idioma español," Alarid shares his deep emotional attachment to his mother tongue while confirming the need to attain proficiency in English. In this poem, Alarid appeals to the importance of acknowledging the equal worth of each language and urges us never to diminish the importance of either (Alarid 1990).

This advice is something we have both taken to heart, and as we wrote this chapter, we reminisced about our childhood languages and their impact on our career paths.

As a native Nuevomexicana whose mother tongue is Spanish, I feel the deep
sentiments connected with maintaining and developing my first language.
My Spanish is my childhood; my earliest memories are indelibly expressed
in Spanish. In my grandmother's gentle and caressing voice, I heard my first
prayers and melodies in Spanish. Her *cuentos*, or stories, all in Spanish, lulled me
to sleep. I awakened each day with the sweetness of mother earth and the soft
sounds of my grandmother's voice embracing me, always in Spanish. My early
years in the Valdez valley north of Taos shaped my future as an educator in love
with my Spanish. My Spanish—yes, it is mine—passed to me as a precious gift
from those who came before me. At age six, I started first grade (no kindergarten
back then), all in English. Taken out of my idyllic valley to an urban boarding school, my first teacher (bless her!) made me feel special, naming me her
"Spanish helper."

Somehow, magically, I learned English, liked school, and did well, following
my grandmother's and mother's orders, though I missed my innocent life and
especially my grandmother's gentle New Mexican Spanish voice. She praised my
learning English, but quickly and often would add, "*Pero no te olvides tu español,*"
but don't forget your Spanish. My Spanish! I was captivated with my language.
I thought the conjugation patterns were exciting, and I became a word nerd.
While peers struggled to speak in Spanish, I felt great using my "new" vocabulary
and iterating grammatical structures that had been mine since childhood. The
literature and the linguistics all beckoned to me!

   Pero no te olvides tu español. These sage words resound in me still today. Little
did I imagine back then the strength of my grandmother's counsel and how far
my mother tongue would carry me. (LS)

Well, I'm not a native New Mexican, although I've lived here almost fifty years.
I was born in New York City, and my first language was Nuyorican Spanish, a
very cool version of the Spanish spoken in my Puerto Rican family, with lots of
code switching. Some of my aunts, uncles, and cousins lived within a block of
our tenement just south of Harlem on the Upper West Side of Manhattan and,
most importantly, my non-English speaking grandmother, *abuelita* Tomasa, lived
with us. She took care of me, my brothers, and our cousins while our parents
worked. Needless to say, we all grew up speaking Spanish. When I got to school,
I realized that I was not the only one who was not a fluent English speaker.
There were Polish, German, Japanese, French, and Spanish speakers in my classes

who challenged the imagination and ingenuity of our teachers. Before the advent of ESL and bilingual education, our teachers taught us with a devotion that is hard to explain. I wanted to be like those teachers. My education was important to me and to my parents. Even my *abuelita* acted as a cheerleader as I continued through junior high. I still spoke mostly Spanish at home, although all the cousins whispered in English if we did not want *abuelita* to understand.

By high school, I was taking Spanish classes with an amazing teacher, also from Puerto Rico. She did not let us rest on our laurels, and she demanded excellence from us, so my academic Spanish skills really took off, and I realized that what I wanted to be was a Spanish teacher. Later, I came to New Mexico for graduate school and it was here that I found people who had similar experiences with Spanish as their first language. I got to study, teach, and learn about New Mexico Spanish. What an exciting time! I am still learning, and it still fascinates me. (TH)

So here we are, two old friends and colleagues, still pursuing our dreams and still learning, remembering what has brought us to this writing. Our university classes with our beloved professor, Sabine Ulibarrí, were nothing short of divine. His delight and joy in the Spanish language was contagious. As he entered our University of New Mexico classroom, he cast a spell over us with his lecture in and about Spanish, whether it was language or literature. "Uli" flavored his lectures with New Mexican regionalisms, adding to the comfort and intrigue of both native and non-native speakers. This *caballero* from Tierra Amarilla had mastered the academic world in and outside of New Mexico and referred to us all as his *hijitos*, exuding a sense of *familia*. Years later, around 1996, Dr. Ulibarrí gave us permission for the following words to be used as the prologue to the new exam, Prueba, being developed:

El que habla dos lenguas vale dos. Vale dos porque cada una de sus lenguas representa una manera distinta de identificar y analizar los fenómenos de la creación. Cada una de sus lenguas es una visión única del mundo y de la vida. Así es que la persona bilingüe puede enfocar la realidad con dos puntos de vista, dos ángulos de percepción y llegar a una mejor comprensión del mundo que le rodea. [One who speaks two languages is worth two. He/she is worth two because each of the languages represents a distinct way of identifying and analyzing creation. Each of his/her languages presents a unique view of the world and of life. Thus, the bilingual person is able to focus his/her reality through two points of view, two perspectives and arrive at a better understanding of the world around him/her.]

A century after Alarid's poem, we still can appreciate Ulibarrí's eloquent confirmation of the profound value of knowing two languages.

Through its state constitution, New Mexico has been a leader in advocating for and ensuring appropriate access to education for its children. Key in Article 12, Section 8, and germane to this discussion, is the preparation of teachers in the Spanish language. Then, very soon after statehood in 1912 and as early as 1915, the New Mexico legislature proposed a bill requiring that all teacher candidates be tested on their abilities in Spanish before receiving their teaching credentials. Though this condition in the 1915 bill did not pass, the notion of Spanish language proficiency for teachers surfaced then and continues to the present time (Arellano 1974).

The civil rights movement of the 1960s drew particular attention to the education of language minority students. Of special national concern was (and still is) the adequate access to instruction in English. One major avenue toward this access was bilingual education, through which instruction was delivered in English and in the students' home language. The New Mexico State Department of Education (SDE), in 1963, received a three-year grant from the Ford Foundation to "explore effective and innovative programs of instruction. The 'experimental' programs taught the language arts and social studies in Spanish to Hispanic Spanish-speaking students in the small village of Pecos" (Habermann López 2011, 5). New Mexico's first bilingual education director, Henry W. Pascual, championed bilingual education and the associated verification of the Spanish language skills of educators serving the state's children. As Pascual stated, "It is impressive to see that most states emphasize competence in the non-English language, culture, and history of the students. However, very few states require verification of that competence through objective measurement" (Pascual 1979, 20). Pascual brought to New Mexico the national narrative of teachers' linguistic competence in the non-English language (in this case, Spanish). Decades later, these issues continue to be discussed across school districts and within state and national policy-making entities.

In 1974, Leonard J. De Layo, state superintendent of public instruction, issued a certificate "prescribing minimum standards for prescribing program requirements for approved teacher education programs in bilingual education." Within this regulation (No. 74-1), there is an expressed minimum requirement of eight-grade proficiency in Spanish. Sadly, in 1978, as Valdés (1989) points out, an article in the *Albuquerque Journal* reported on the results of a fourth-grade Spanish reading and writing test administered to 136 bilingual educators, none of whom passed. Valdés had cautioned that native New Mexican Spanish-speaking teachers who self-identified as bilingual were often excused from the university course requirements in Spanish (Valdés 1989, 2). Comprehensive discussions regarding use of the vernacular typical of New Mexico Spanish speakers had not taken place. Neither had discussions occurred regarding what would be expected of teachers in the school setting. Further exacerbating this situation, it appears that at this time, each teacher preparation program interpreted the eight-grade level of proficiency without statewide uniformity and, frankly, haphazardly.

It is important to remember the plight of Spanish-language bilingual teachers who had suffered punishment and embarrassment during their own schooling for using their mother tongue, not only in class but also on the playground. Now, as teachers, they were being expected to teach in the very language that had been suppressed during their formative years. Many school districts, administered by mostly ill-prepared and English monolingual leaders, had little notion of the level of Spanish that was needed in classrooms. Nor had they been prepared to recognize and be sensitive to the value of local varieties of Spanish. These leaders were ignorant of the sheer strength of a mother dialect that "nurtured" a sense of identity and personal worth. This negligence created an atmosphere of disregard and profound disrespect for the Spanish language and for the linguistic rigor required in the preparation of teachers for bilingual programs. The result of this regrettable history was that bilingual teachers were not sufficiently prepared in the academic aspects of the Spanish language (Valdés 1989, 1). Pascual understood that teacher preparation was also problematic. He boldly stated, "We must insist that the university personnel who are to educate the teachers have themselves a measure of competence and scholarship in the language. We must insist that they read and write that language using some standard of selectivity and excellence" (Pascual 1979, 23). Pascual and other educational leaders were determined to improve both the school bilingual programs and bilingual teacher preparation.

In 1979, the SBE issued specific requirements for a bilingual education endorsement that highlighted Spanish language proficiency in the four domains of listening, speaking, reading and writing. Equally important was that teachers in New Mexico were also expected to recognize and accept the varieties of Spanish used in communities throughout the state. Through a grant from Title VII of the Elementary and Secondary Education Act, the New Mexico

SDE, with the University of New Mexico, developed a test that addressed the language requirements for the bilingual endorsement (Habermann López 2011, 7). In a memorandum to school superintendents on August 4, 1981, Pascual announced that "the title of the test is The Four Skills Exam: A Spanish Language Examination for the Certification of Bilingual Teachers, Grades K–8." He also stated in this memorandum, "The Department of Education endorses the use of this test which, in our opinion, will serve the needs of our bilingual certification endorsement criteria." Pascual, in this same memo, summarized the test as follows:

> The exam is divided into two principal parts. The first part tests listening comprehension and the ability to speak Spanish. It is approximately one hour long, it is controlled through a tape, and must be administered in a language laboratory. The second part tests reading and writing and is an hour and a half long. Attention has been paid to New Mexico Spanish in all aspects of the test. Generally the content centers on activities that bilingual teachers would be required to do in the normal performance of their duties. (Pascal 1981)

It should be noted that the test was intended to assess Spanish language proficiency at the eighth-grade level, as stated in the criteria for bilingual endorsement. Nevertheless, in Valdés's overview of the Four Skills Exam, she specifically included that "examinees read passages taken from materials used in bilingual classrooms in grades 1–3 " (1989, 18). It is important to recall that in 1978, bilingual educators who were tested were not able to pass a test at the fourth-grade level. So at the time the Four Skills Exam was developed, it would have been unreasonable to impose a high-stakes assessment at the eighth-grade level. At the same time, at the universities, faculty in bilingual teacher preparation programs were just beginning to recognize their responsibility for addressing Spanish language proficiency development within the curricula. In ensuing years, innovative programs at the University of Albuquerque and New Mexico Highlands University ensured that students seeking the bilingual education endorsement received comprehensive instruction in Spanish (as detailed in Argus-Calvo, chapter 9 this volume).

In 1992, years after the adoption of the Four Skills Exam, Rebecca Benjamin (now Rebecca Blum Martínez) and Cecilia Navarette of the Evaluation Assistance Center reviewed it in light of statewide concerns regarding various aspects of its design, administration, and scoring.[1] This review was reported to the Legislative Education Study Committee (LESC) on June 6, 1992. Several major concerns were articulated:

- Knowledge of the New Mexican Spanish vernacular/regionalisms were not taken into account.
- The facilities available across the state for language testing did not meet uniform standards regarding acoustics and/or language laboratories.
- Testing personnel at each university were not provided appropriate training for this type of assessment.
- The administration manual lacked the necessary detail to facilitate the examinees' understanding of the format and scope of the test.
- There was no study guide available to prospective examinees.
- Detailed rubrics were not included to assist in scoring nor to inform examinees.
- Though it was recommended that three scorers grade each test, it was always graded by two for lack of funding.

Despite these critical concerns, the Four Skills Exam was a forerunner in the arena of language proficiency testing. At the time that the Four Skills Exam was developed, the majority of the bilingual education programs existed at the elementary level. In 1988, the passage of Representative J. Paul Taylor's (Las Cruces) House Bill 5 expanded the bilingual education programs through the twelfth grade. Consequently, teachers were required to demonstrate a higher level of proficiency verified by an approved measure. The bill phased in the expansion over a four-year period, from 1988 to 1991. As Guerrero points out, "The Four Skills Exam appears to have outlived its usefulness owing to its original design. . . . Even with its shortcomings, [the exam] represents a noble effort on the part of the test development team to protect the rights of students to a meaningful education" (1994, 172).

The aforementioned concerns about the Four Skills Exam were brought to the attention of legislators.[2] In 1992, the LESC included in its agenda a discussion item pertaining to the Four Skills Exam. Upon hearing credible testimonies from statewide bilingual education stakeholders and psychometric analyses (Benjamin and Navarette 1992), the LESC recommended that funds be appropriated to initiate a task force within the State Bilingual Advisory Committee to study these concerns and offer a possible solution. Representative Taylor sponsored House Bill 224 to fund this effort. The bill passed, and funds were allocated to address the concerns about the Four Skills Exam outlined above. As a result, the task force recommended to the director of bilingual multicultural education at the SDE that the Four Skills Exam be replaced.

Under the SDE bilingual education directorship of Mary Jean Habermann López, a coordinator, Walter Archuleta, was selected to support the development of the new test. Archuleta convened a writing team composed of experts in linguistics, statistics, the Spanish language, bilingual education, and with public school teaching experience to develop a new Spanish proficiency test. These consultants, well-versed in vernacular Spanish, reflected a range of public school and higher education experiences, as well as an academic proficiency in Spanish.

It should be noted again that the 1979 endorsement requirements specified eighth-grade minimum Spanish language proficiency. Yet as designed, the Four Skills Exam addressed the Spanish language proficiency at only the fourth-grade level. Later, in 1987, the SBE moved to a competency-based licensure system whereby each university designed its teacher preparation program to address the stated competencies in the regulations. Significantly, licenses and endorsements were no longer recommended by the universities. Now the credentialing process was the responsibility of the SDE. Higher education institutions provided coursework and granted degrees; SDE issued credentials based on degrees, coursework, and tests meeting the competencies.

The SBE approved the competencies for teachers of bilingual education on June 19, 1987. This included a set of "Native Language Competencies" (see Appendix), which went into effect almost ten years after the Four Skills Exam was developed and used. Under the competency, "communicates effectively orally and in writing (where the written form exists and is allowed)," teachers had to demonstrate "at least a minimum eighth grade level of proficiency in the native language."

Michael Guerrero (University of Texas, Rio Grande Valley) designed the new exam, assuring that state competencies were addressed in an integrated manner. The internationally renowned sociolinguist Eduardo Hernández-Chávez (University of New Mexico) was included to safeguard the language registers (or formality levels) used in the exam and to assure that Spanish varieties (dialect and/or regionalisms) used by examinees in their responses would be accepted and not be counted against an examinee's score. Loretta C. Salazar (New Mexico Highlands University), who had public school experience, along with Thomasina Pagán Hannum, a retired public school teacher, author, and Spanish instructor at the University of New Mexico, completed the core writing team. Hannum was one of the authors of the Four Skills Exam and served as its principal grader; Salazar also had assisted in grading the Four Skills Exam.

This core team worked tirelessly to address the state's Native language competencies, integrating the Spanish language within a situational school context.

A true sense of earnest camaraderie prevailed, with the intent of producing an exemplary assessment that met all design expectations, coupled with an integrated approach to language testing. The writing team was also responsible for creating all of Prueba's ancillary materials and paid particular attention to addressing the concerns that existed with the Four Skills Exam.[3] The team worked cohesively—challenging, discussing, critiquing, writing, and rewriting—until full agreement with the entire exam and its ancillary materials was reached.

Voices for the exam's recordings also had to be selected. Considerations such as native-like fluency and natural voice qualities were taken into account. Needless to say, repeated recordings were often required. University of New Mexico's language lab was commissioned for this task, with assistance from the lab's director, Neddy Vigil. Hernández-Chávez was also intricately involved with this aspect of the test development and directed the filming of the video and wrote its associated test items. Salazar and Hannum were largely responsible for writing the classroom-based situations and related test items. Archuleta coordinated activities, acquired all copyright approvals, and held the writing team to a timeline. On occasion, he was called upon to assist in determining specific language usage. It bears repeating that the writing team worked together diligently, reacting to each other's observations and concerns, with a focus on constructing an integrated and linguistically sound assessment, keeping New Mexico varieties of Spanish at the forefront of all deliberations.

At this juncture, the topic of New Mexico Spanish merits consideration. Rubén Cobos states that the Spanish language varieties of New Mexico are characterized by "borrowings from English, local and regional vocabulary, words and idiomatic expressions peculiar to the Spanish of Mexico, indigenous Rio Grande Indian terms, Mexican Indian vocabulary (mostly from the Nahuatl), and archaic sixteenth-and seventeenth-century Spanish " (2003, xv). In light of the multitude of linguistic influences on Spanish, Cobos goes on to say that the survival of Spanish in New Mexico "testifies to the strength of the language of Cervantes (xvi)." Cobos reminds us of the power that Spanish has exhibited for many generations in the face of an ever more English-dominant community. Therefore, it was essential that Prueba assess the Spanish language employed by teachers in school settings while accepting and affirming vernacular usage.

It was incumbent upon the authors of Prueba that scorers give due consideration to examinees who displayed fluency in the communication skills (oral and written) required in the test. The scorers' decision regarding such usage became dependent upon accurate spelling and comprehensibility, since the assessed language should communicate with ease with students and parents within school settings. At times, varied pronunciations might occur. Again, the key was whether an expression or utterance was understandable. Thus, the scorers play an important role in the decision as to whether certain terminology and utterances are accepted. After all, Prueba is an assessment of the Spanish language of New Mexico bilingual teachers who will communicate on a daily basis with students and parents in New Mexico. We mention here a few examples of lexicon, verbs, or expressions, with the more formal register in parentheses (we highly recommend Cobos's dictionary, in which the description of New Mexico Spanish is more fully referenced):

alcojol (alcohol)	espeletear (deletrear)	puela (sartén)
apearse (bajarse)	grados (calificaciones)	resultos (resultados)
arrear (manejar/conducir)	hablates (hablaste)	tecolote (búho)
asina/ansí (así)	jumo (humo)	truje (traje)
brecas (frenos)	muncho (mucho)	túnico (vestido)
cajete (tina)	naide/naiden (nadie)	volver pa'tras (regresar)
espauda (fr. yeast powder)	principal (director/a)	zacate (césped)

Chris Nelson (New Mexico Highland University) was the statistician charged with directing, piloting, and monitoring; documenting the test's validity and reliability; ascertaining the equivalency of the final three versions; and assuring graders' inter-rater reliability, all of which is noted in the test's technical manual. Many other contributors were recruited to participate in this meticulous process. A complete list of consultants is found in Prueba's administrator's manual (New Mexico Public Education Department 2006).

As mentioned, this exam is supported by multiple ancillary materials, including a study guide, a scoring and interpretation manual, a technical manual, and an administrator's manual.

Following is a description of the exam and its ancillary materials.

The exam itself consists of four principal parts and fifteen subsections. The entire exam, including all instructions, written and oral, is in Spanish. The examinee listens and responds to recordings in a language-lab setting. The voice of the recordings is that of a proficient New Mexican Spanish speaker. While the exam acknowledges the use of regionalisms, the examinee must also demonstrate control of an academic/school register. Throughout the exam, as noted by Archuleta, "each test section takes an integrated approach in the evaluation of oral production, listening and reading comprehension, oral reading and writing/ editing in Spanish" (2002, 48). The overarching characteristic of the exam is its situation-based structure emphasizing authentic classroom situations along with New Mexico language and culture. The four major parts of the exam are described below:

PART ONE, LANGUAGE AND CULTURE | *Primera Parte, Lengua y Cultura*

This part includes a video depicting a New Mexican craftsman describing and showing the family's artistry with multiple choice items, and it requires the examinee to write a composition on a topic related to the video. These activities evaluate listening and reading comprehension and writing accuracy.

PART TWO, SCHOOL-BASED COMMUNICATIONS | *Segunda Parte, Comunicaciones Escolares*

This part requires the examinee to identify and correct errors in a letter, review a report card (in English), explain it to monolingual Spanish-speaking parents, and write a response in Spanish to a phone message from the parents. This part evaluates reading, writing, and listening comprehension.

PART THREE, SOCIAL STUDIES | *Tercera Parte, Estudios Sociales*

This part requires a silent reading of a social studies text, giving an oral presentation (recorded) of the main ideas to students, and asks the examinee to write discussion-type questions based on the reading. These activities evaluate reading comprehension, speaking, and writing.

PART FOUR, SCIENCE | *Cuarta Parte, Ciencias Naturales*

This part involves reading a science text aloud (recorded), a dictation on the same science topic, and a fill-in-the blank exercise on the same topic, for which the examinee must provide a word that maintains the meaning of the text. This part evaluates reading comprehension, coupled with appropriate pronunciation, rhythm, intonation, fluency, and writing accuracy.

The writing team carefully selected Spanish-language reading materials from eighth-grade-level texts in order to meet the stated minimum competencies (see appendix).

The *Study Guide*, or *Manual de Estudio*, offers a general review of Spanish-language norms often encountered in school settings. It is intended to build on an already well-established formal preparation in the Spanish language. This indispensable guide presents practice materials, including grammatical exercises, proofreading activities, readings for comprehension on a variety of topics, and suggestions for writings and oral presentations. Included is a *prueba modelo*, or sample exam that presents much of the format of the exam itself. The general rubrics are included to inform the examinee about how sections of the exam are evaluated.

The *Scoring Booklet*, or *Libreta de Evaluación*, is used by a grader to correspond to a specific examinee's test. The grader also uses rubrics found in the *Scoring and Interpretation Manual*, which guides in evaluating all sections of the test.

Prueba has a statewide team of graders with specific qualifications. Each has a minimum of a master's degree, years of classroom experience, a native or near-native proficiency in Spanish as determined by the director of the Bilingual Multicultural Education Bureau of the New Mexico Public Education Department (PED, formerly the State Department of Education), and represents one of the major regions of New Mexico (north, central, south). A grader must be knowledgeable about and respectful of the New Mexico regionalisms when evaluating the examinee's usage.

The administrator's manual outlines in detail:

> procedures for administrators to follow in advance of the examination date,
> including handling of the test materials and preparation of the testing
> site. It also discusses pre-test procedures on the day of the examination,
> including registration and seating, general instructions to examinees, and
> testing of equipment. Finally, the Manual presents specific instructions for
> the administration of the Prueba and for the maintenance of records and the
> submission of reports. (New Mexico Public Education Department 2006, 3)

As described by Nelson (2006), the "*Technical Manual* overviews the history of the *Prueba* and summarizes information regarding the technical adequacy of the three alternate forms, including evidence of the exam's validity, and reliability data collected from a standard setting sample" (1).

At this writing, Prueba is administered through Eastern New Mexico University's Testing Center.[4] Great care has been taken to assure that Prueba is administered in language labs that meet uniform standards across the state, one of the concerns about the four skills.

In order to share the development process, the task force team made presentations at various regional and national professional conferences. The team presented at the Linguistic Association of the Southwest Conference in Puebla, Mexico, in 2000 and at the National Association for Bilingual Education in Phoenix, Arizona, in 2001. Presentations were also made at state conferences, such as the New Mexico Association for Bilingual Education in 2006. Other professional development workshops were conducted at school districts throughout the state by members of the writing team.

Culminating the development process, Prueba and its ancillary materials were reviewed by a team of nationally recognized experts in the field of language assessment. The team was led by Eugene García (University of California, Berkeley) and included Elena Izquierdo (University of Texas, El Paso) and Leslie Grant (Central Michigan University). This review lauded the exam, noting its unique format capturing the bilingual classroom situation while assessing language proficiency in all four domains. This team also made several recommendations that were integrated into the current versions.

The development of Prueba, which aligned more closely with the state competencies, impacted the preparation and the ongoing professional development of bilingual teachers. It became critical that the teachers' Spanish-language skills be expanded and refined to more adequately address the competencies. Universities and colleges throughout the state have become more aware of their roles in providing this necessary preparation. Some institutions amended their bilingual education academic programs to include additional coursework in Spanish. University faculty in bilingual education programs were urged to use Spanish in instruction when possible and to make field placements in schools where Spanish was in use for instruction. Some institutions called upon faculty in Spanish departments to assist in teaching and/or designing coursework addressing bilingual teachers' Spanish language development. Highly proficient bilingual teachers were also tapped to offer valuable professional development. Professional organizations such as the New Mexico Association for Bilingual Education and Dual Language Education of New Mexico sought presentations and workshops in Spanish for their annual conventions.

As referenced by Archuleta et. al. (2001), "In 1994, in response to concerns regarding teacher preparation for bilingual education, the state legislature appropriated funding (HB 224) to hire three part-time coordinators for university immersion institutes" (2). These immersion institutes were designed as intensive reviews of the Spanish language in preparation for the Prueba exam. Though each university decided its own format for the institute, each included proof-reading, orthography and accents, practices in writing on a variety of school related topics, and exposure to New Mexico's Spanish language varieties. The emphasis continues to be on maintaining the use of Spanish throughout the entire institute. After all, as with the Four Skills Exam, Prueba is a high-stakes exam whose success determines a teacher's eligibility for the bilingual education endorsement required in state-approved bilingual education programs.

As posed by Eugene García:

> The state of New Mexico, like many states, has recognized the need to ensure that the education of its children is implemented by the most qualified teachers. The evidence that high quality teachers directly influence the quality of instruction and learning in their students is unquestioned, particularly in classroom circumstances that require the use of Spanish as a mode of instruction in Bilingual Education. (García, Grant, and Izquierdo 2002, 1)

As described, assessment is a dynamic process reflecting the latest trends in testing. Despite the eighth-grade proficiency requirement, the Four Skills Exam mainly addressed the Spanish language demands of lower elementary bilingual programs. Coupled with this discrepancy, higher education's lax interpretation of proficiency, with little attention to language development, led to inadequate preparation. After years of utilizing the Four Skills Exam, the expansion of bilingual programs stretched further to include additional K–8 and, later, the secondary levels through the twelfth grade. The Four Skills Exam no longer adequately addressed the greater language skills demanded by these higher levels. Designs of language assessments have become more sophisticated in or-der to evaluate integrated language, not solely discreet skills. At the same time, greater adherence to state competencies came into play. In complying with these competencies, the SDE had to develop a new exam (Prueba), which would have greater fidelity to the stated competencies. At the same time, higher education was pressured to address these competencies in the programs of study leading to degrees, licensure, and endorsement.

Bilingual programs have continued to evolve into the secondary schools. Many high schools currently offer content courses such as science, math, lan-guage arts, and social studies in Spanish. Prueba does not necessarily assess the greater and more refined academic proficiency required of teachers instructing in Spanish at these upper levels. Interesting discussions have occurred posing a possible need for another assessment or an expansion of the current Prueba to account for more specific and advanced subject matter; additional competencies may be needed that describe content-specific Spanish language proficiency. It is important to remember that the current bilingual education endorsement is a K–12 endorsement, regardless of the license. Current discussions allude to the need for a bilingual license, not just a bilingual endorsement. Challenges will inevitably arise as language proficiency and its accompanying assessment advance.

New Mexico, cognizant of its linguistic legacy and the demands for a more proficient citizenry, is well aware of the economic benefits that will accrue if the state continues to value the education of its youth through the quality preparation of its teachers. A recent article in the *Albuquerque Journal* praised the efforts of a local high school that offers remarkable opportunities, inspiring students to attain high linguistic prowess:

> Albuquerque High School has been named the national high school of the year by the Embassy of Spain for excellence in bilingual immersion programs. . . . Albuquerque High offers high-level classes in Spanish . . . including two Advanced Placement courses, with over a dozen subjects taught in Spanish, from U.S. History to biology and algebra . . . to create bilingual-biliterate students for our global economy.[5]

Other New Mexico high schools offer similar opportunities for their students. In 2014, through legislative action sponsored by Representative Rick Miera (HB 330), New Mexico approved an official bilingual-biliteracy seal for those graduates meeting certain coursework and proficiency requirements. This recognition brings prestige to students' achievements and underscores the state's commitment to prepare students and their teachers.

CONCLUDING REFLECTIONS

At this moment in our elderly lives, we find ourselves among scholars, poets and authors, still moved by the call of the Spanish language, by the vivid recollections of our childhoods, by the hopes and dreams shaped by our language. As our grandmother's voices and our professors' teachings still resound deep within us, the Spanish language defines each of us, knowing that our passion for this precious gem is ever present. We have sincerely and fervently dedicated our professions to maintaining, protecting and nurturing this Spanish language.

We feel honored to have participated in the task of developing an assessment for bilingual teachers and, in writing this tale, we are trusting it will contribute to quality instruction for the greater benefit of our New Mexico children.

In conclusion, we share Sabine Ulibarrí's wise and profound words that appear in the prologue to the Prueba test, which strike at the heart of the matter regarding the worth, dignity, and responsibility of Bilingual Education in New Mexico:

> *Para comprender a un pueblo y su historia es necesario aprender su lengua. La lengua es la novela viva del pueblo.* [In order to understand a people and their history it is necessary to learn their language. Language is the living story of a people.] (Authors' translation)

And we pose a question for all: Is New Mexico up to the challenge of honoring its linguistic legacy and responding to the tremendous need for a bilingual-biliterate citizenry serving the global community?

APPENDIX

Minimal Distribution of Native Language Competencies: Measured by the Prueba de Español para la Certificación Bilingüe:

1. The teacher communicates effectively orally and in writing *(where the written form exists and is allowed) in the language other than English.
   a. The teacher *demonstrates at least a minimum of an eighth grade level of proficiency in oral and written language (where the written form exists and is allowed), necessary to deliver content K-12 in the language other than English.
   b. The teacher demonstrates a high level of accuracy and fluency in spoken language.
   c. The teacher utilizes vocabulary appropriate to the broad range of functions, topics and genres in speech.
   d. The teacher demonstrates competency as a participant in ordinary social situations in which the language other than English is spoken.
   e. The teacher *responds adequately to written material by exercising the processes of comparing, contrasting, categorizing, summarizing, inferring, analyzing, synthesizing, hypothesizing, and evaluating.
   f. The teacher *reads with comprehension a broad range of literary forms (folk, technical, classic, etc.) across the content areas.

g. The teacher *writes sentences, paragraphs, and essays, utilizing formal language models which express individual thought, communicates and accomplishes complete and well-organized ideas, and accomplishes a full set of written functions.

2. The teacher carries out instruction in content areas of the curriculum to attain the Standards and Benchmarks for the content area in a language other than English.[6]

NOTES

1. The Evaluation Assistance Center-West was one of two Title VII ESEA federally funded centers established to assist Title VII bilingual education programs with evaluation.

2. Rebecca Blum Martínez interview by Thomasina Pagán Hannum and Loretta C. Salazar on July 7, 2017, at Blum Martínez home in Albuquerque, NM

3. The Spanish certification exam for endorsement in bilingual education (Prueba de Español para la certificación bilingüe) is often referred to simply as "Prueba."

4. See www.enmu.edu/testing for more information.

5. Kim Burgess, "Embassy of Spain Recognizes Albuquerque High," *Albuquerque Journal*, March 17, 2017, C1, https://www.abqjournal.com/970970/embassy-recognizes -albuquerque-high.html.

6. Title 6, Chapter 64, Part 10, Section 9 of the State of New Mexico Education Code, native language competencies mandated by the New Mexico State Board of Education effective July 1, 1989.

REFERENCES

Alarid, Jesus Maria. 1990. "El idioma español, the Spanish Language." In *Mexican American Literature*, edited by Charles M. Tatum, 254–59. Orlando, FL: Harcourt Brace Jovanovich.

Archuleta, Walter R. 2002. "Prueba de español para la certificación bilingüe." PhD diss., University of New Mexico, Albuquerque, NM.

Archuleta, Walter, Thomasina Hannum, Sara Harris, Eduardo Hernández-Chávez, Merryl Kravitz, Alice Menzor, Chris Nelson, and Loretta Salazar. 2001. "Prueba de español para la certificación bilingüe: A Process." Paper presented at National Association for Bilingual Education, Phoenix, AZ.

Arellano, Anselmo F. 1974. "Don Ezequiel C. de Baca and the Politics of San Miguel County." Master's thesis, New Mexico Highlands University, Las Vegas, NM.

Benjamin, Rebecca, and Cecilia Navarette. 1992. "Review of New Mexico State Spanish Proficiency Test For Bilingual Teachers." Unpublished document.

Cobos, Rubén. 1983. *A Dictionary of New Mexico and Southern Colorado Spanish.* Santa Fe: Museum of New Mexico Press.

De Layo, Leonard J. 1974. State Superintendent of Public Instruction, Certificate No. 74–1, State of New Mexico, Department of Education, January 25. Mary Jean Habermann López, private collection.

García, Eugene, Leslie Grant, and Elena Izquierdo. 2002. "Evaluation of New Mexico Spanish Language Instruments for Bilingual Teacher Endorsement: Report for the Bilingual/Multicultural Education Bureau." Copy in possession of Walter Archuleta.

Guerrero, Miguel D. 1994. "A Critical Analysis of the Validity of the Four Skills Exam." PhD diss., University of New Mexico, Albuquerque, NM.

Habermann López, Mary Jean. 2011. *History and Importance of Bilingualism and Bilingual Education in New Mexico.* Unpublished manuscript.

Harris, Sara, Merryl Kravitz, Alice Menzor, Chris Nelson, and Loretta Salazar. 2000. "Spanish for Bilingual Teachers: Preparation and Assessment." Paper presented at the Annual Meeting of the Linguistic Association of the Southwest, Puebla, Mexico.

Nelson, Chris. 2006. *Technical Manual for Prueba de Español para la certificación bilingüe.* Unpublished manuscript. School of Education, New Mexico Highlands University, Las Vegas, NM.

New Mexico Public Education Department. 2006. *Prueba de español para la certificación bilingüe and Ancillary Components* [Administrator's manual, grader's manual, scoring manual, study guide, technical manual]. Limited circulation instrument. Portales, NM: Eastern New Mexico University, Testing Division.

Pascual, Henry W. 1979. "Clients and Teachers in Bilingual Education Programs." Paper prepared for the National Conference on the Education of Hispanics. National Dissemination and Assessment Center, California State University, Los Angeles, CA.

———. l981. Memorandum to superintendents re: Bilingual endorsement certification. State of New Mexico, Department of Education. Mary Jean Habermann López, private collection.

Valdés, Guadalupe. 1989. "Testing Bilingual Proficiency for Specialized occupations: Issues and Implications." In *Test Policy and Test Performance: Education, Language and Culture,* edited by Benjamin R. Gifford, 207–29. Norwell, MA: Kluwer Academic Publishers.

JULIA ROSA LÓPEZ-EMSLIE

[11] Development of Instructional Materials for Bilingual Education Programs

PROLOGUE

Henry Pascual would say that being bilingual gave you two handles on the world. Studies have demonstrated the cognitive advantages of bilingual education. What about the affective domain? How does bilingual education contribute to the self-concept of children?

My aunt, Margarita López de Mestas, coordinator of the bilingual education program in Las Cruces, New Mexico, would describe the children in the classrooms before the implementation of bilingual education as being very quiet and uncomfortable, almost afraid, definitely unsure of themselves. These behaviors were indicative of a low self-concept. Once bilingual education programs were implemented, the children began to smile, enjoy the classroom, laugh, and speak freely—all indications of a high self-concept brought about by acceptance and reflection of their language and culture in the curriculum and the reading materials. When researchers would ask her how to measure the affective domain, she would say that they would have to count the smiles on the children's faces.

In the period between 1960 to 1975, a group of Hispanic educators in New Mexico, myself among them, defined their careers in bilingual education and laid the foundations of a transforming curriculum. Born during the Chicano movement and the civil rights era, the use of Spanish language and culture for instruction in bilingual education programs in the United States broke new ground. The curriculum materials and strategies these educators designed, piloted, and perfected overturned earlier techniques. They empowered Hispanic students to value their own language and culture as they learned English. These educators used assessment and research to refine their materials, fought for professional development for all teachers to address the needs of English language learners, and overcame the resistance of districts and colleagues to support the students who had no voice. They went on to teaching and administrative careers and mentored the next generation of bilingual educators. They worked to shape public policy so that students' educational needs would never be overlooked again.

This chapter addresses the historical development and use of instructional materials for bilingual education programs and records my involvement in language education in the United States and the professional lives and friendships of committed educators who became friends as they recognized a common cause.

In a 1975 editorial that appeared in the first issue of the National Association for Bilingual Education (NABE) journal, children's book author Alma Flor Ada addressed the need for materials and publications in multiple languages of the United States that were vital to the successful life and maintenance of languages and cultures. Her comments are as true today as they were in 1975. She wrote in part:

> When we look at people from other cultures who have been educated in the United States we are confronted in almost all cases with the fact that even those people fortunate enough to retain the use of their language and a respect for their home culture possess a very unbalanced bilingualism and an equally unbalanced biculturalism. They feel more secure when they function in English, especially at the professional level, and their degree of information about United States Anglo-Saxon culture (literature, history, art, geography, sociology) is by far more extensive than their knowledge of their home culture. If bilingual bicultural education is to fulfill its goal this extreme imbalance must disappear. We must be able to provide future generations with a command of their language and culture as adequate as the command we are demanding they obtain of the dominant language and culture. (Ada 1975)

What Alma Flor Ada so eloquently expressed here is the reason my colleagues and I dedicated our lives to bilingual education and to developing instructional materials for bilingual programs.

I had a very strong bilingual/bicultural experience growing up on the border, though I understand Alma Flor Ada's concepts well, as I know my experience was not universal among my peers growing up. I came to the United States from Ciudad Juárez, Chihuahua-México, after graduating from high school in El Paso, Texas. I attended elementary school in Juárez and then commuted daily to school in El Paso. Since my aunt was the coordinator of the bilingual education program in Las Cruces, I was somewhat familiar with New Mexico. She recommended that my sister and I attend the College of St. Joseph on the Rio Grande in Albuquerque, and that is where I received a bachelor of science degree in education, majoring in secondary education with an emphasis in Spanish and French.

I began my career in bilingual education at Albuquerque High School (AHS), where I worked with audio lingual method (ALM) materials. In 1967, I was hired as a French and Spanish teacher at AHS. Rita Minkin was the Foreign Languages Department chair there and was also the lead teacher and supervisor of the Spanish and French student teachers from the University of New Mexico. Minkin was my mentor and role model—she taught me how to teach. She would model a lesson and I would take notes. The next class period, I would teach the lesson while she observed me. Afterward, we would discuss my performance, my strengths and weaknesses, and ways to improve my teaching.

At that time, partly in response to the Russian launch of Sputnik, the first human-made Earth satellite, there was a national push for foreign language instruction; the ALM system grew out of this initiative. In New Mexico, Minkin and Enrique LaMadrid were involved in the development and field testing of the ALM material, which was published by Harcourt, Brace & World in 1961. The ALM methodology emphasized listening and speaking before reading and writing, using dialogues as the principal form of language presentation and drills as the main teaching technique. Use of English in the classroom was discouraged. The teacher would utter a sentence and the students were asked to repeat without having the printed page before them.

At AHS, most of the students in the Spanish classes were native Spanish speakers born in New Mexico; they and the few immigrants from Mexico in the school were already fluent in oral Spanish. This was not unusual; an National Education Association Tucson Survey on teaching Spanish to Spanish speakers noted that this practice was a southwestern phenomenon and not unique to AHS or New Mexico. The administration and counselors, unfamiliar with the students' language and culture and unprepared to address this new kind of learner, considered these students "discipline" problems. Minkin, a native New Mexican from Encino, and I knew that these students were engaged and eager to learn. The problem was that they were not being engaged in their classes. We realized that the oral/aural method of the ALM materials was not appropriate for these students. They needed to learn how to read and write in the target language, and memorizing dialogues and practicing drills without seeing the printed word was not conducive to learning. Together, we modified our instruction and our use of the ALM materials.

This was my first experience designing successful strategies for language instruction for native speakers. I learned that we needed to include the students' culture and cultural history if we to successfully engage them in their learning. Because Rita and I believed in an interdisciplinary approach to language teaching, we collaborated with the Social Studies Department to integrate students' history and culture into our classes. I also learned to incorporate New Mexican Spanish into my curriculum to show students its historical development and linguistic richness. Students now were able to see themselves reflected in the classroom curriculum. Their lives and experiences were valued.

In 1972, I was contacted by Rosita Apodaca, a national consultant for bilingual education, about a special assignment for the Dade County Schools in Florida working with the Spanish Curricula Development Center (SCDC) and the center's materials. Rosita, originally from Palomas, Chihuahua, was a longtime friend who recognized my strengths as an educator and the contributions I could make to the profession. She and I both attended the College of St. Joseph on the Rio Grande. She graduated in 1966 and went to live in El Paso, Texas. My experience with the SCDC ignited my passion for bilingual education and served me well as a university professor.

During a telephone interview, Rosita explained how her teaching career led her to become a leader in bilingual education. When a teacher friend in Gadsden, New Mexico, invited her to visit the schools in 1969, she immediately accepted a job at Gadsden Junior High to teach a class of eighteen students, ages twelve to eighteen, who spoke only Spanish. Most of the students had been schooled in Mexico, coming north when their parents sought work in agriculture. Rosita was very frustrated at the lack of professional development available to teachers to help them teach Spanish-speaking students effectively. She began to teach US history in Spanish with textbooks she bought in Juárez using second-language strategies to help students transition from Spanish to English. She collaborated with the English language arts teacher and other teachers to help them incorporate these strategies into their teaching, meeting with them after school and on weekends. Other teachers did not understand the rationale for teaching content in Spanish to transition students into English, and they were upset because she was teaching the students in Spanish. When they complained to the principal, Rosita believes that only her husband's family connections kept her from being fired.

Her situation changed dramatically during a visit from the New Mexico State Department of Education (SDE) to Gadsden Junior High in the early 1970s. Henry Pascual visited her classroom, and he was impressed with her teaching and asked if she would consent to be filmed. He spoke with Maria Spencer, the director of the Teacher Training Center in Silver City, New Mexico, about using the film to train other teachers throughout the state. The training film also showed highlights of Rosita's work with parents' groups, explaining curriculum, providing educational and community resources, and giving parents an opportunity to share their concerns. (See Calvo, Habermann López, and Blum Martínez, chapter 9 in this volume, for a detailed history and description of the New Mexico Teacher Training Network.)

Based on the expertise that Rosita exhibited in the training film, Pascual invited her to join the curriculum-design team at the Spanish Curricula Development Center in Miami. Pascual also served as the state coordinator for the SCDC'S five field-testing centers in New Mexico. Rosita's family situation did not permit her to relocate to Miami, but she did visit and was excited to work on a project to create instructional materials developed in and for the United States (at this time, all bilingual teaching materials were published in Spain and Latin America and did not reflect US culture and language). She told Ralph Robinett, project director at the SCDC, that something was missing in this impressive project: the curriculum writers were from Cuba and Puerto Rico, but there were no writers from Mexico. Robinett agreed but had been unable to hire Mexican writers. Rosita said she could help. She contacted teachers in El Paso and set up interviews. Two teachers were hired. Then she contacted me in Albuquerque and encouraged me to go to Miami.

Rosita continued to serve as consultant for the SCDC while helping teachers in her region and continuing her work in the Southwest. She faced a challenging opportunity when she was contacted by the El Paso Independent School District (EPISD) to work with teachers following the *Alvarado v. EPISD* desegregation case of 1976, which was filed by the Mexican American Legal Defense and Education Fund. The court found in favor of Alvarado, and the EPISD was ordered by the Office of Civil Rights to put in place a desegregation plan. It was a difficult situation for teachers unprepared to teach linguistically and culturally diverse students. But as a result of the court case and with the support of the EPISD administration, Rosita was able to start the first bilingual education program in El Paso.[1]

Recruited by Rosita for the SCDC, I had moved to Miami in the summer of 1972 with my mother and my children to begin my new role as a curriculum writer representing Mexico's and New Mexico's languages and cultures. My ten years of experience with Spanish language teaching in college as a teaching assistant and as a teacher at Albuquerque High School had prepared me well for this assignment.

The SCDC had been charged with developing and producing instructional materials for Spanish/English bilingual education programs, the first Spanish language materials developed in the United States for bilingual education programs. The project was funded by Title VII and directed by Ralph F. Robinett, a linguist and curriculum expert with many years of experience in curriculum development focused on language minority students. Robinett was a major contributor to the formation of the SCDC. Before it was formed, Robinett worked with the Dade County Public Schools to address the influx of Cuban refugee families into Miami that began in 1959. As a result, in 1963, under his leadership with Pauline Rojas, the Coral Way School in Miami began teaching in English and Spanish and was a pioneer in the field of bilingual education in the United States.

That same year, the Dade County Public Schools also started a Spanish for Spanish speakers program. With help from the Ford Foundation, the program was modified into a full bilingual education curriculum. It quickly became an unqualified success. In the article "Coral Way Elementary: A Success Story in Bilingualism," Pellerano, Fradd, and Rovira noted that "a 1973–1974 report by the Department of Program Evaluation for the Miami-Dade County Schools revealed that the students who attended the dual language programs continued to show progress on standardized testing" (1998).

Robinnet's success on behalf of Coral Way Elementary's bilingual education program made him the perfect choice to direct the Title VII grant that created the SCDC. The SCDC had three goals for the development of curriculum: "(a) to utilize the resource of children who are bilingual by providing materials that reflect their language and culture; (b) to make available a curriculum written in the United States for limited-English-speaking students who are in programs where the basic skills and content areas are being developed in Spanish as the students learn English; and (c) to provide curriculum for non-Spanish speakers who benefit from the enrichment experiences of a bilingual instructional program" (Hartner 1977, 42). Developing and teaching these new bilingual instructional materials was meant to be a collaborative process that would engage teachers, administrators, community representatives, theorists, and practitioners.

All materials and related activities were structured to extend the students' experiences and language beyond the comfort of their homes and to show them how those experiences and language could be applied to and were related to their community and the world at large. Instructional materials were developed for language arts, social science, science/health, Spanish as a second language, and fine arts at the elementary level. Each area had an additional set of specific instructional goals. For example, in language arts, "the main goals are to develop comprehension and interpretation skills related to a basal reading program; develop language analysis skills; and develop creative expression at the verbal, nonverbal, and written levels" (Hartner 1977, 44).

The language arts strand included structured reading and writing activities that were addressed in the pupil's book and seatwork. Activities also included oral language development and language experience reading, both oral and written. Aural and oral listening activities were key areas of instruction. Each activity included a focus, an objective, and support materials, which were comprehensive. Teachers would follow a detailed script for implementation. To help teachers accomplish the goals of the materials, a teacher's guide provided them with a written account of the intellectual content and all that had to be done to carry out the suggested activities. A supplement that accompanied the guide provided the teacher with all the visuals needed to effectively introduce and reinforce the structures, vocabulary, and concepts in the activities. With the guide and supplement was a packet of material to be used by individual students to support the successful implementation of the activities. The pupil's reading books contained visual stimuli for the development of reading skills.

Criterion-referenced tests accompanied each unit of instruction These tests could be used by classroom teachers for placement, evaluation of pupils' progress, and as part of a diagnostic prescriptive approach (Hartner 1977). My first assignment at the SCDC was in the evaluation department. We would analyze the materials and compile a frequency table of objectives that we would use to develop test items for the criterion-referenced tests.

Once the initial SCDC materials were completed, they were disseminated to teacher-training centers in the United States, and detailed, systematic review processes were conducted. Four editions were published—Southwest, Midwest, Northeast, and Southeast—to accommodate different Spanish linguistic groups in the United States. For the Southwest edition, materials were sent to the demonstration teacher training center in Las Vegas, under the direction of Mela Leger, the regional director for the state. Mela would receive the materials from the SCDC and then distribute them to teachers and provide them with in-service training. After using the materials, participating teachers would complete surveys assessing the materials' suitability for the children in New Mexico and noting what changes they would like to see. Feedback was sent back to the SCDC for review and recommendations, and regional directors such as Mela Leger attended review sessions four times a year in Miami. Regional state directors for the Mexican American student populations would also meet as a committee. Representatives from New Mexico, Texas, California, and Illinois discussed feedback from the teachers and regional directors to assess relevancy of materials to students and to make recommendations for improvement. At the same meetings, regional state directors would receive instruction on the new material that had been developed.

Leger was an invaluable member of the committee. She was very knowledgeable about students, teachers, and programs in New Mexico as well as regional linguistic and cultural variations. Her extensive knowledge and experience helped make the case for New Mexico's unique vocabulary. I participated in these committee meetings with other Mexican American members of the staff. Experiences with users of the materials were very encouraging. Teachers reported that students looked forward to the stories and activities. They attributed this interest to the relevance of the content presented (Hartner 1977).

My time in the evaluation department made me well versed on all the material content and structure. I was then assigned to write the third-grade social science materials. the social science concepts were the threads connecting the language arts, science/health, and fine arts instructional strands. Each activity, regardless of area of instruction, would address at least one social science concept taken from the disciplines of history, sociology, anthropology, geography, political science, and economics (Banks 1977).

The activities I prepared were based on Hilda Taba's model of curriculum development and the inquiry strategies she developed. These included concept development, interpretation of data, application of generalizations, and analysis of values, feelings, and attitudes. Taba (1902–1967) contributed to the theoretical and pedagogical foundations of concept development and critical thinking in social studies curriculum. Her influence helped lay the foundations of education for diverse student populations (Fraenkel 1992).

The activities I developed also relied on Jerome Bruner's spiral curriculum, which was based on his cognitive theory that all concepts can be taught to students at any age. Even the most complex material, if properly structured and presented, can be understood by very young children. Key features in this curriculum are that the students revisit a topic several times during their schooling, and the complexity of the topic increases with each revisit. The students understand that the new learning has a relationship with the old learning and apply it to new situations (Johnston 2012).

Each curriculum writer partnered with an expert consultant who would review our conceptual framework, guide us, and advise us. I collaborated with Doyle Casteel from the Center for Latin American Studies and Social Studies Education at the University of Florida, Gainesville. One of his areas of expertise was cross-cultural inquiry, the sharing of various cultures and perspectives which became an important component of the curriculum design.

As the writer for the social science strand from New Mexico, I was able to include content and activities that would reflect students' lives in rural New Mexico. As an example, I wrote a story about Jerry Apodaca, governor of New Mexico at the time, describing his life as a young boy and his success as governor.

After working in Miami for three years, I received a call from Rosita, and she asked me if I was ready to come back to New Mexico. I was. Far from my extended family, I wanted to be an advocate for the children of New Mexico the way my colleagues were advocates for the Cuban children of Florida. Rosita mentioned that Henry Pascual had a vacancy for a specialist in his unit. She recommended me to him, I applied for the position, and I was hired. I left Miami in 1975 and went to work in Santa Fe for the Title VI Office of Civil Rights project. The next year, I began working in the Bilingual Teacher Training Unit, also under the direction of Henry Pascual. I remained in contact with SCDC, which continued to develop and publish materials for grades K–12, including special education. In 1978, I helped to pilot-test special education materials in Las Cruces. The process required contacting the Special Education Department of the Las Cruces Schools and requesting a meeting with Spanish-speaking special education teachers in the district. I discovered that there were very few bilingual special education teachers, a situation that created overrepresentation of English-language learners in special education in New Mexico and nationally. Because of this situation, very few teachers were available to pilot-test the materials.

When the SCDC closed in the late 1980s, the ALM materials were bought and distributed by the Crane Publishing Company until the early 1990s; because of the closing of SCDC, there was no process in place to encourage and support their use. The loss of the SCDC-developed materials was unfortunate. However, one positive contribution of the use of SCDC materials was the reinforcement of teachers' Spanish language skills. In 1975, Pascual wrote about a survey of "136 teachers and bilingual aides, many with university training, who were given a simple third grade reading and writing test in Spanish (Bilingual Teacher Training Unit, New Mexico State Department of Education, Placement Test, 1975)." He went on to note that "about ten percent of them were able to function at this level on the test. None could handle the fourth grade level. This situation is not unique to New Mexico" (Pascual 1979, 21) Thanks to the SCDC materials, which they used daily, the Spanish-language skills of the teachers were strengthened.

As the number of bilingual education programs increased in New Mexico under Title VII and state bilingual funding, I conducted program assessments. I also surveyed the teachers' and aides' writing skills, using dictation, Cloze exercises, and the reading of passages of different levels. Most of the difficulties encountered by teachers in this testing were fundamentally interference from English, the language they already knew how to write. They were not familiar with Spanish graphemes (a letter that represents a sound). In Spanish, different sounds were represented by letters such as "h," "v," "b," c," "s," "z," "and "q." Comprehension was not an issue for them. Subsequently, I developed a series of lessons focusing on these linguistic differences and traveled the state providing in-service training for teachers and aides in bilingual education programs. This experience and other information gathered by Pascual and his team stressed the need for teachers and aides to be prepared in Spanish at the university level. Teachers had to graduate from colleges and universities with the ability to read and write in Spanish.

The work being done in the late 1960s and 1970s in Florida by the SCDC was by no means the only bilingual education instructional materials effort being pursued in the country. Around the same time that the SCDC was developing, Dolores Gonzales, a native New Mexican, former school teacher, and University of New Mexico professor, found herself increasingly concerned with the lack of instructional materials designed to meet the needs of Hispanic children in New Mexico. In 1969, she wrote a grant and was funded for three years under the Education Professions Development Act (EPDA) of 1967 to develop bilingual instructional materials.[2] Her goal was to create an institute in New Mexico to train curriculum specialists to develop bilingual instructional materials for Spanish-speaking New Mexico children. Gonzales's concept foresaw the groundbreaking New Mexico bilingual education law that was passed in 1969 (see Blum Martínez, chapter 6 this volume).

The institute served two purposes: to train participants in the understanding of bilingual education philosophy and principles; and to prepare participants in the development of Spanish literacy materials relevant to Chicano children. The participants were recruited for the doctoral program at the University of New Mexico from New Mexico and Southern Colorado to write materials for reading, social studies, and science under Gonzales's direction. The work of the institute was an enormous undertaking and was not fully completed; the most significant outcome was the creation of the Tierra de Encanto reading series. To develop the series, institute participants conducted an extensive review of children's material in Spanish used in bilingual education programs. The review revealed an absence of instructional materials that dealt with the lives and experiences of Chicano children. As researchers Ortiz and Chavez noted in 1981, "Perhaps the most important learning that can be gained from such a study involves the understanding that textbooks and other forms of materials are vehicles for value transmission. As value carriers, textbooks have the power to transmit important messages, either explicit or implicit, which influence a child's view of himself and his world" (Ortiz and Chavez 1981, 110).

Locally developed materials with culturally relevant perspectives would serve as a starting point for children, with the ultimate goal of helping them explore other worlds and other universal concepts. They would begin with their own language and culture and then expand their horizons. Work on the reading series continued until Gonzales's death in 1975.

To learn more about the Tierra de Encanto reading series, I conducted a telephone interview with Leroy L. Ortiz, a retired University of New Mexico professor who participated in the first year of the institute. Ortiz described the contents of the Tierra de Encanto reading series. Six levels were developed. For each level, there was a reader, a teacher's manual, and a workbook that included a list of new words for each reader. For example, the level 1 reader, *Días de Sol*, had thirty additional new words in eleven stories. The workbook was titled *Rayitos de Sol* and included those thirty words. These words would prepare students to master new vocabulary and successfully read the stories.

Because the primary goal was to create relevant materials for Chicano children in the state, the story titles and topics for each level were carefully chosen to exemplify cultural events and linguistic examples set in New Mexico. Eleven stories were included in *Días de Sol*:

1. "Vamos a tu casa" (finding a house for a bird)
2. "Al paseo de los animales" (a reference to the "pet parade" during the Santa Fe Fiestas)

3. "El cumpleaños de Antonio" (Antonio is given *un presente*—a pair of *zancos* [stilts])

4. "El rancho de abuelito" (they look for an adobe *casa de rancho*)

5. ¡Al piñón!" (Jose looks for pinon)

6. "El presente de Alicia" (a birthday present)

7. "El gallinero de adobe" (men and children making adobes for a chicken coop)

8. "El Día de Mamá" (children in school making a present *un ojo de dios* for Mother's Day)

9. "Ramón y la ardillita" (a ranch, a tree house for the squirrel)

10. "El paseo de Tita" (mother works and grandmother cooks)

11. "Colita de rana" (a children's rhyme typical of Hispanic culture)

The stories are illustrated with rural scenes, adobe homes, and New Mexico furniture and rugs. The girls have braids, boys fish in the *acequia*, and men make adobes. As noted above, the themes and vocabulary are those of New Mexico language and culture.

Unlike the SCDC materials, the Tierra de Encanto reading series did not include a teacher's guide or other supplementary materials to accompany the readers. There was a list of new vocabulary words and questions for comprehension at the end of each reader. It is believed that Dolores Gonzales's untimely death precluded the completion of the series, which she had had envisioned as including additional materials to be used in other content areas such as social studies.

The materials were field tested in Albuquerque, Las Cruces, Santa Fe, and Grants. The curriculum writers conducted workshops for teachers in the various school districts, and materials were also pilot-tested by the demonstration teacher training center in Las Vegas, under the direction of Leger in the early 1970s.

While the Tierra de Encanto series lacked the depth and breadth of the SCDC materials, it filled an important gap in curriculum materials related to the language and culture of New Mexican Hispanic students. During his interview, Ortiz shared his experiences and knowledge gained while he participated in the project. He stated that Dolores Gonzales was instrumental in instilling in project participants a sense of pride in their language and culture. She was aware that these participants had attended mainstream schools that had a traditional white Anglo-Saxon Protestant curriculum focus. In a sense, they had to "unlearn" the Anglo cultural concepts and refocus on the Hispanic cultural concepts.

The project took place during the ongoing Chicano civil and human rights movement that began in the late 1960s and early 1970s. At that time, universities were one of the focal points of protest. As part of the institute, participants met on a regular basis under Dolores Gonzales's guidance to discuss issues related to awareness, consciousness, and self-identity, issues of income inequality and gender roles, and issues related to the New Mexico vernacular and the need to recognize the vernacular as a valid linguistic form of instruction in the schools. They were to rethink the early education they themselves had received.

Ortiz described Dolores Gonzales as a soft-spoken Chicana from Pecos, New Mexico. She was a traditionalist in her view of language and culture from northern New Mexico and at the same time a futurist who recognized the evolution of culture. She would forcefully tell the participants to be strong and not to apologize for being outspoken about their feelings about racism and discrimination. As an example, during the Viet Nam War, a protest by Albuquerque High School students led to violence at a nearby park. Although Gonzales did not condone violence, she acknowledged that violence is a response to oppression.

She and Henry Pascual had their differences. Pascual advocated for the use of materials that represented Hispanic world cultures. He believed that we needed to accept and use the vernacular in the classroom but that we also needed to expand the students' horizons by exposing them to literature in Spanish from other countries so they could navigate in the world outside of New Mexico. Since schools teach the standard version of English via a local vernacular, he felt the same should be true for Spanish. Pascual believed in the use of the vernacular in the classroom as a "conceptual bridge" to access concepts in the content areas. Gonzales, on the other hand, was a firm believer in the use of the vernacular for instruction, that it should be represented in the textbooks as a reflection of the rich language and culture of the people of the state and that the use of New Mexico Spanish vernacular and culture for the context of instruction was crucial.[3]

There were valid issues on both sides of this debate. Some people viewed Pascual's ideas as elitist. Others supported his philosophy and advocacy for Spanish world literature. Gonzales's supporters believed in the value of locally developed materials. But both camps had the same goal: to help children succeed in our educational system.[4]

Mary Jean Habermann López, a bilingual teacher in the Bernalillo Public Schools in the mid-1970s, also believed in the value of the Tierra de Encanto series. She recollected vividly how often her students in the Title VII bilingual education program would gravitate to the readers in the series. She was using the SCDC materials for Spanish language arts and Spanish as a second language instruction in the program. She used the criterion-referenced tests to place students in the correct instructional level of the materials and also to determine what students had learned. She reported that she had a rich library of children's literature in Spanish, including Dolores Gonzales's Tierra de Encanto readers. The students were able to relate the stories in the materials to their own community experiences, and they very much enjoyed reading the books.

Interviews with teachers across the state who had used both the SCDC and the Tierra de Encanto series provided insight. Several districts had received intensive training from Mela Leger on how to use the SCDC materials when they were first pilot-tested. Some parts of the state, especially in the north, preferred the Tierra de Encanto series because these materials aligned more closely with the culture and language used in local villages and communities.[5]

Because of limited state bilingual education funds and a lack of teacher training and local districts' preferences, implementation of the materials across New Mexico was uneven and varied. This situation improved as more funds became available from Title VII after 1968.

I was grateful to have had the opportunity to learn more about the Tierra de Encanto reading series. Though I wasn't directly involved in the work, my passion for bilingual education and the children of New Mexico pushed me to learn and document the history of the efforts people have made to educate children in this state.

In my career and my understanding of bilingual education, Henry Pascual was *el maestro*. He was an expert and leader in bilingual education at the state and national levels and was instrumental in the passage of federal and state bilingual laws. From him I learned the importance of always keeping in mind the children. Everything we did was for the children. Because Pascual always kept up with the research literature and new developments, I also learned a lot about bilingual education theory and practice from him.

After I spent three years working in the State Department of Education and became more knowledgeable in the field, Pascual recommended me to Atilano Valencia at New Mexico State University to receive a Title VII fellowship for doctoral study in bilingual education. I had decided that if I were to make a difference, it would be in the preparation of bilingual teachers. At that time, teachers whose last names were Hispanic would be placed in bilingual program classrooms with little preparation. The same situation existed at the university level. These instructors had no bilingual classroom training, though they were passionate about helping students. In time, another doctoral student who came directly from the classroom, Armida Hernandez, and I found ourselves teaching the pedagogy of bilingual education.

As I went on to develop my dissertation topic, which dealt with reading skills of bilingual children, I connected again with Rosita Apodaca, who at the time was the director of bilingual education in the El Paso Independent School Districts. I went to see her, shared my dissertation proposal, and asked if I could conduct my study in El Paso. She presented my proposal to the evaluation department, and it was approved. I had access to eight schools.

I completed my doctorate in 1981, the first person in my family to receive a doctorate. My aunt Margarita Lopez de Mestas hosted a reception for my guests and my family at the Holiday Inn in Las Cruces (I would say that more family members attended my graduation than attended my wedding). Family members came from Mexico City, Chihuahua, and Parral. That August, I was hired at Eastern New Mexico University as an assistant professor, where I followed my goal of preparing bilingual educators. I created the bilingual education teacher-preparation program and wrote many proposals for Title VII funding for scholarships and program support.

I come from a long line of strong women, one of whom was my mother, María de Jesús Vega de López. It was my mother who made it possible for me to follow my professional career. My mother helped raise my own children, Julia Rosa and Alejandro, while I dedicated myself to my career. Because of her, my children grew up bilingual. She spoke and understood English but insisted that they speak Spanish to her. She was always willing to travel and move to different places—Albuquerque, Miami, Santa Fe, and Colombia. Thank you, Madre!

In closing, I can only add that I have been blessed with the people and the opportunities that supported my journey in the education of bilingual children. I will never forget what these friends, colleagues, and family meant to me. I cherish them for showing me the value and importance of my own bilingual skills that gave birth to my passion for bilingual education.

NOTES

1. Rosita Apodoca, phone interview by Julia Rosa López-Emslie, July 15, 2017.

2. United States Department of Education, Education Professions Development Act, 1970. Dias de Sol (HEW-OEG-0-70-2086-(725).

3. Henry W. Pascual, interview by Rebecca Blum Martínez, Mary Jean Habermann López, and Julia Rosa López-Emslie, August 11–12, 2001, at Pascual's home. DVD and partial transcript in the personal collection of Mary Jean Habermann López.

4. Leroy Ortiz, phone interview by Julia Rosa López-Emslie, June 13, 2017.

5. Doreen Burbank, Melinda Gonzalez, Dorothy Gurule, Lupe Castillo, Dru Orona, Roberta Marquez, and Leonila Serna, phone interview by Mary Jean Habermann López, July 3–10, 2019.

REFERENCES

Ada, Alma Flor. 1975. Editorial. *National Association for Bilingual Education Journal* 1, no. 1: 11–12.

Banks, James A. 1977. *Teaching Strategies for the Social Studies: Inquiry, Valuing, and Decision Making.* 2nd. ed. Reading, MA: Addison-Wesley.

Fernandez, Margaret, and Luisa Martinez. 1978. *Dolores Gonzales: Pioneer of Bilingual Education.* University of New Mexico Cultural Awareness Program. Longfellow Elementary School. Special Collections Library (3–9075–04212318–9).

Fraenkel, Jack. R. 1992. "Hilda Taba's Contributions to Social Studies Education. *Social Education* 56, no. 3: 172–78.

Hartner, Eneida. 1977. "How We Develop Bilingual Instructional Materials." *Educational Leadership* 35, no. 1: 42–46.

Johnston, Howard. 2012 "The Spiral Curriculum. Research into Practice." ERIC. https://eric.ed.gov/?id=ED538282.

Ortiz, Leroy, and Luisa Chavez. 1981. "The Development of Culturally Relevant Spanish Literacy Materials." ERIC. https://eric.ed.gov/?id=ED212140.

Pascual, Henry W. 1979. "Clients and Teachers in Bilingual Education Programs." *Bilingual Education Paper Series* 3, no 5. National Dissemination and Assessment Center. https://eric.ed.gov/?id=ED212455.

Pellerano, Cristina, Sandra H. Fradd, and Lourdes Rovira. 1998. "Coral Way Elementary: A Success Story in Bilingualism." *Discover*, 3 (February). Bethesda, MD: National Clearinghouse for Bilingual Education. http://www.ncela.gwu.edu/files/rcd/BE020899/Coral_Way_Elementary_School.pdf.

Rodriguez, Roberto. 1996. "The Origins and History of the Chicano Movement." JSRI Occasional Paper 7. Julian Samora Research Institute. Michigan State University, East Lansing, MI.

University of New Mexico College of Education, Centennial Celebration. "What's in a Name?" Dolores Gonzales Elementary School, Albuquerque Public Schools. University of New Mexico Center for Southwest Research.

[12] The State Bilingual Advisory Committee

When the State Bilingual Advisory Committee (SBAC) was formed in 1970, its members were as new to their advisory roles as their programs were to the newly emerging field of bilingual education. With time, experimentation and emerging research in program delivery helped define content and strategies used in bilingual education classrooms across the state. It also spearheaded trailblazers who, by serving on the SBAC, translated local issues into statewide policy. Mela Leger set the leadership stage for future SBAC chairpersons when she brought an important certification issue to the state superintendent of instruction that directly impacted bilingual education teachers. The synergetic relationship that grew between the New Mexico State Department of Education (SDE) and the committee itself spurred mutual confidence and trust in the work that needed to be done.

Little did the New Mexico State Board of Education (SBE) realize when it created SBAC in 1970 that the committee would become a powerful action agent for practitioner-based policy development in bilingual education.[1] The first SBE policy statement on bilingual education in the nation (see Blum Martínez, chapter 6 this volume) set the framework for an ambitious agenda for the committee. By 1973, many schools across New Mexico had been carrying out bilingual education programs for eight years under state and federal funds and through private foundation grants.[2] It was time for the state to set some guiding principles, both for teacher preparation and for the program itself.

The first major task given to the SBAC was to develop criteria for the licensure of teachers in bilingual education. Working in conjunction with Henry Pascual of the SDE's Bilingual Education Unit, SBE Regulation 73-741—"Prescribing

Program Requirements for Approved Teacher Education Programs in Bilingual Education"—was approved on January 24, 1974. The document described what a bilingual education teacher preparation program would look like (see Hannum and Salazar, chapter 10 this volume). At that time, existing local programs were teaching some content in the native language, all had a native language arts component, and most included cultural activities within the social studies.[3]

Working directly with Henry Pascual, the committee again helped develop guiding principles for the program, which were approved by the SBE on December 5, 1975. The "Guidelines for Implementing Bilingual Multicultural Education Programs" (SBE Regulation No. 75–19) provided a definition of bilingual multicultural education and directed programs to set objectives for "literacy skills to provide proficiency in two languages, one of which is English; and progressive understanding and study of the history and cultures of New Mexico by including these in the curriculum."[4] The instructional program was to consist of daily language arts in the home language, English language development within the English language arts, content areas taught through two languages focusing on "social, cultural and economic values and history of the cultures of the students," and finally, a fine arts component taught in two languages. It also required parent advisory committees to assist and advise in the implementation and evaluation of the program; teachers who were certified in bilingual education; and an annual evaluation "commensurate with local objectives and needs" that should include "student's achievement through English as well as the home language" (SBE Regulation No. 75–19).

Beginning in 1975, the SDE began the process of defining actual university course requirements for prospective Spanish and Native American languages teachers seeking a bilingual education endorsement. Both the SBAC and the Native American Bilingual Education Steering Committee worked on this task for their respective language groups.

SPANISH–ENGLISH BILINGUAL MULTICULTURAL EDUCATION CERTIFICATION REQUIREMENTS

From 1975 to 1979, the SBAC, working in cooperation with Henry Pascual of the SDE, developed the final version of SBE Regulation No. 79–10, New Mexico certification requirements for Spanish/English bilingual/bicultural endorsement.[5] The work was arduous and demanding as the committee and the SDE, working with numerous stakeholders, helped create two other SBE-approved regulations during that time period.[6] Difficulties arose in defining coursework and requirements for the endorsement because university education departments lacked teaching staff who could teach in Spanish. The final regulation (SBE regulation No. 79–10) required teachers to have literacy skills in Spanish and take twelve of twenty-four semester hours taught in Spanish. This regulation remained in existence until 1989.

NATIVE AMERICAN BILINGUAL EDUCATION CERTIFICATION REQUIREMENTS

The Native American Bilingual Education Steering Committee was charged with defining course requirements in February, 1977. The core committee was composed of members approved by tribal councils, tribal chairmen, or education agencies. Mescalero, Jicarilla, Navajo, and Pueblo representatives agreed upon eight necessary content areas courses on August 29, 1980.[7]

According to the minutes, the committee would then develop course descriptions for approval by tribal councils. The New Mexico Educational Standards Commission reviewed final recommendations on January 25, 1982, and tabled its decision on the matter.

In an interview on October 5, 2018, former chair Donna Pino stated that early involvement by the tribes in the 1970s served as a powerful catalyst for future actions in certifying Native language teachers.[8] In those days, there was no one who could teach the courses at the universities, and the only way to certify proficiency was through the tribes. Later, memoranda of agreement between each pueblo and the state set up tribal processes and procedures that lead to the 520 alternative certificate approved for Native language teachers in the schools (see Sims, chapter 3 this volume).

The SBAC and the Bilingual Education Unit at the SDE built a healthy and trusting partnership that consistently linked actual practice with policy. Comprised of Hispanic and Native American practitioners from bilingual education programs across New Mexico, committee members spoke the language being used in their respective program as well as English. In the early years of the committee's history, members served multiple terms, and as their local expertise grew over time, so did their aptitude to pinpoint needed statewide policy adjustments. In many cases, committee members actually did the work necessary to create crucial statewide actions for students and teachers in bilingual education programs.

The SBAC also helped raise awareness and resolve general policy decisions that would be harmful to the education of Hispanic and Native American students in the state. One early example stands out. In a November 29, 1982, letter to then state superintendent of public instruction Leonard J. De Layo, SBAC chairperson Mela Leger wrote about the new SBE policy that would change a teacher's certification to "nonstandard" for any teacher on waiver, and this would threaten their tenure status. Many bilingual education teachers across New Mexico were on waiver while they completed coursework for the endorsement. She wrote:

> It appears to us that it would be grossly unfair for teachers to lose or postpone their tenure because of the lack of the additional endorsement required for bilingual education. . . . Many teachers who are eligible for waivers will not want the district to request a waiver if it will endanger their tenure status. We can appreciate your desire to have fully qualified teachers for bilingual education as well as in every area of instruction. However, we are very concerned that districts will either eliminate bilingual programs or that teachers will be penalized for implementing programs that are sorely needed for proper instruction of Hispanic and Indian children.[9]

Leger asked that the SBAC be placed on the agenda of the next SBE meeting to discuss the issue. Superintendent De Layo responded on December 15, 1982: "I am conducting a series of internal discussions within the State Department of Education relative to the questions you have raised as well as the broader questions regarding substandard certificates and tenure issues," indicating that the SBE might need to review the policy as well.[10]

The SDE recognized the SBAC's commitment and expertise under Leger. A February 7, 1984, letter from then assistant superintendent Alan Morgan to Mela Leger states: "As you may be aware, the State Department of Education has a number of many advisory committees. Few committees conduct their activities with such thoroughness and energy as the Bilingual Education Advisory Committee."[11]

Moreover, the SBAC collaborated directly with other SDE offices, such as special education, assessment and evaluation, instructional materials, and teacher licensure, when necessary. In some cases, the SBAC's findings and conclusions actually helped create new legislation, such as the development of the Prueba exam (see Hannum and Salazar, chapter 10 this volume). This chapter attempts to tell the story of some of the SBAC's significant actions since its inception in 1973.

CREATION OF BILINGUAL EDUCATION AND ESL
COMPETENCIES FOR LICENSURE 1989

In 1989, the SBE authorized a new competency-based teacher preparation system for prospective teachers attending the university. Instead of prescribing
the courses required for a teaching license in New Mexico, it now identified
the desired competencies teachers must have. Universities had to create course
content that would enable teacher candidates to acquire the stipulated teaching
competencies.

A subcommittee of the SBAC developed the competencies for teachers of
bilingual education and also for ESL. For bilingual education, they identified
six crucial topic areas: Native languages, culture, English language development,
instructional methodology, community/parental involvement, and assessment.
To become certified, teachers needed to meet all competencies and demonstrate
"at least a minimum eighth grade level of proficiency in the native language in
oral and written language skills where the written form exists and is allowed."
The latter recognized the fact that Pueblo communities used the oral form. The
competencies went into effect on July 1, 1989.[12]

The Prueba exam was created to certify Spanish proficiency to an eighth-
grade level for teachers completing university courses for the endorsement (see
Hannum and Salazar, chapter 10 this volume). Other than the 1977–1982 work
of the Native American Bilingual Education Steering Committee, nothing was
in place to certify proficiency for Pueblo language teachers who would seek a
bilingual endorsement to their teaching license under the new regulation.

A process used in the 1970s set the stage (see Sims, chapter 10 this volume) for
implementing the 1989 competency requirements for Pueblo languages. While
no university programs were available that could offer the required courses for
the Pueblo endorsement, the Native language proficiency requirement presented
an even more difficult challenge.[13] Nevertheless, a subcommittee of the State
Bilingual Advisory in cooperation with the Indian Education unit at the SDE
took on this work in 1990. It was no simple task. There were myriad complex,
extensive issues the group identified and studied such as how to actually assess
the existing language varieties within each of the of five non-written languages
among the pueblos; how to identify relevant language development issues for
teachers who would be considered for endorsement among each of the tribes;
and how to involve the tribes in designing and planning their process.

The result was the SDE's Indian Education Unit recommendation that each pueblo oversee and drive the tribe's development process to determine Pueblo language proficiency.[14]

The SBAC often testified before the SBE and legislative committees through the years in support of bilingual education.[15] Testimony by SBAC member Carlos Chavez and his students before the SBE in 1999 merits discussion.

Chavez became a member of the committee in the early 1990s. Having received the nationally prestigious Milkin Educator Award for his groundbreaking work in bilingual secondary education, Chavez and his work in bilingual education programs at the secondary level was well known in the Albuquerque area as well as by committee members and the Bilingual Education Unit at the SDE. A graduate of Miguel Encinias's University of Albuquerque bilingual education teacher preparation program (see chapter 9 this volume), Chavez began teaching US history in Spanish in the Title VII ESEA Bilingual Education program at Albuquerque High School in the early 1980s. This program was unique not only because it was at the secondary level, but also because teachers proficient in Spanish taught content courses in the language to immigrant and New Mexican Hispanic students. Since there were no US history textbooks available, Chavez translated the English version into Spanish and added material that told the history of Spanish and Native American people in New Mexico. The Chavez translation was used at Rio Grande High School (RGHS) when he later coordinated a Title VII bilingual education grant there. He was an excellent and sorely needed candidate for the SBAC, especially after Representative Taylor's secondary-level bilingual education legislation was fully implemented in 1991 (see Hannum and Salazar, chapter 10 this volume)

Chavez set about a course of action at RGHS that resulted in the first gold seal placed on the diplomas of students who were proficient in two languages, a goal of the school's Title VII federal grant. His zeal, passion, and belief in his students' language capabilities to attain the seal inspired the bilingual program's teachers who taught US and world history and mathematics in Spanish, advanced placement Spanish, and English as a second language.

In 1998, RGHS graduated its first class of students with the prized gold seal on their diplomas. State Bilingual Advisory Committee member Carlos Chavez presented this stellar accomplishment to the SBE at its October 1999 meeting.

Records from the meeting show what a few of the bilingual seal graduates had to say:

> I respect Rio Grande High School for encouraging, respecting and honoring bilingualism. I would like to graduate from law school and become a lawyer so I can help my community, especially those who cannot speak English and have legal problems. I want to give back to my community what they have given me. (Yahira Olivas)

> It is not simply speaking the language, it is appreciating the culture. My career plans will benefit from my bilingual abilities. I want to be an agent for the FBI. Azucena Sánchez, translated from Spanish.[16]

2004 REVISION OF THE BILINGUAL MULTICULTURAL EDUCATION ACT AND REGULATION

In 2004, Navajo legislator senator Leonard Tsosie was concerned about the lack of accountability in local bilingual education programs within his voting district. He saw inconsistency in program delivery, the severe lack of instructional materials in Native American languages, and the fact that district administrators had limited understanding about the program. To Senator Tsosie, local programs were being implemented in an instructional and administrative vacuum.

The collaboration of the SBAC, the New Mexico Public Education Department (PED) Bilingual Education Unit under the direction of Gladys Herrera Gurule, and proactive engagement by state legislators resulted in an amendment to the Bilingual Multicultural Education Act.[17] The amendment set new expectations for professional development and parent involvement and required districts to conduct an annual bilingual program evaluation analyzing student achievement and proficiency data from state mandated assessment results. It also required the PED "to annually compile and report this data to the appropriate interim legislative committee" (NMSA 1978, 22.23.5).[18]

State Bilingual Advisory Committee members spent an entire year getting feedback on local needs as it worked cooperatively with the Bilingual Multicultural Education Bureau to craft a regulation that would respond to the amendments. The new "Guidelines for Implementing Bilingual Education" (NMAC 6.32.2, 2005) set an explicit goal for bilingualism and biliteracy for written languages for all students in bilingual education programs.[19] Designed to clarify essential elements in approved state programs of bilingual education—program and student eligibility, program instruction, professional development, assessment, evaluation and program renewal—the regulation also set its sights on how to build knowledge, understanding, and a consistent implementation of the approved program. Specifically, the regulation:

1. Authorized bilingual multicultural education programs and new "language revitalization education programs," opening up bilingual education to students suffering language loss in Spanish and indigenous communities;

2. Authorized five program models: dual language, enrichment, Indigenous languages, maintenance, and transitional;

3. Added requirements for assessment and evaluation, application approval, and criteria to renew and continue funding under the act in response to Senator Tsosie's accountability concerns; and

4. Required districts to submit a professional development plan for "teachers, teacher assistants, principals, bilingual directors or coordinators, associate superintendents, superintendents, and financial officers."[20]

Since 1973, honest and mutually respectful dialogue between the SBAC and the SDE/ PED built trustworthy collaboration whenever bilingual education arose. This professional relationship empowered SBAC members because they came to understand state policy development. Likewise, it offered state officials genuine access to stakeholders. When the PED disbanded the SBAC in 2011 under the new Martinez administration, former committee members came together to question the state's rationale for the action and raise statewide concern. After much protest and a good deal of interaction with the new PED administration, the committee was reinstated.

ELD PRACTICES FOR PED'S NEW MEXICO TEACH TEACHER OBSERVATION PROTOCOL

In the fall of 2013, the SBAC voiced its concerns to the PED about the new Mexico TEACH statewide teacher observation protocol, which had been developed as part of the new teacher evaluation system being implemented across New Mexico's school districts under the Martinez administration. The protocol gave principals practice doing classroom observations in its goal to ensure that all principals could look at a given teacher's instruction anywhere in New Mexico through the same lens. It also provided a way to rate teachers' instructional performance across a scale ranging from highly effective to ineffective.

As the SBAC reviewed and discussed the new policy, it was clear that the protocol had not accounted for instructional practices for English learners (ELs), culturally and linguistically diverse students (CLDs), and students in bilingual education classrooms. It did not include any accommodation for instruction in a language other than English, which in many respects nullified the premises of bilingual education. Also, the protocol didn't include any processes for observing either English as a second language (ESL) or English language development (ELD) practices. It was as if the only practices to be observed were those researched as successful for English speakers.

The committee noted that the best classroom practices for monolingual English speakers were not necessarily the same practices used for ELs and CLDs. However, the kinds of classroom practices recommended for ELs and CLDs were actually good teaching practices for all children (see Echeverria, Vogt, and Short 2008; Herrera and Murry 2011).[21] Since all schools in New Mexico serve both populations, the SBAC advanced the idea that *all* teachers should use effective practices for *all* populations they encounter when teaching in English.

Working for three months, the committee crafted a linguistically and culturally sensitive ELD crosswalk observation instrument for use with the New Mexico TEACH observation tool in classrooms throughout the state, consulting, adapting, and integrating a wide range rubrics, evaluation tools, standards, and strategies from educational institutions across the county.[22] The crosswalk aligned best practices for sheltered instruction with the elements and domains listed in the actual New Mexico TEACH protocol and offered evidence and indicators that principals could look for in classrooms where effective sheltered instruction was occurring. Any teacher of English learners would need to modify and scaffold English instruction to ensure equity and comprehension of and access to the New Mexico Common Core standards. He or she would also need to incorporate the student's home language into instruction. A teacher who can skillfully and intentionally shelter content instruction with ELLs would indeed need to demonstrate a highly effective or exemplary level of performance. Teachers who did not use any of these indicators would be classified as ineffective for such students.

The PED recommended that the crosswalk become an actual part of the New Mexico TEACH protocol instead of a supplement. It hired the Center for the Study and Education of Diverse Populations (CESDP) of New Mexico Highlands University and Dual Language Education of New Mexico to use the crosswalk, SIOP, and other sheltered strategies and embed these into the protocol. The working draft was shared with groups across the state and at state conferences, and teachers, professors, and administrators were invited to give feedback. The CESDP also proposed a rollout for statewide training; however, New Mexico's Bilingual Multicultural Education Bureau (BMEB) decided to offer the training instead. While the items were embedded into the New Mexico TEACH protocol, the training has not been provided thus far.[23]

The SBAC continues to be active in decisions affecting state and local policy for bilingual education. In addition to the items described in this chapter, the body has addressed many issues over the years, including the following:

- Licensure in bilingual education instead of an endorsement to a license
- Short- and long-term policy options for bilingual education
- Representing bilingual education needs on SDE 3-Tier License Council
- Shortage of licensed bilingual education and ESL teachers
- Input on Spanish Immersion Institutes
- Development of the BMEB Technical Assistance Manual on Bilingual Education and its Heritage Language program guide
- Implications of the No Child Left Behind (ESEA) for bilingual education
- Networking on behalf of bilingual education

REFLECTION

I was fortunate in my career to understand the power of the SBAC from two vital perspectives: from the work of Henry Pascual in his capacity as SDE bilingual education director; and from my own work and as cochair of the SBAC after my retirement.

In the many SBAC meetings I attended as a bilingual specialist working for Henry Pascual, I saw that advisory committee members felt safe raising real issues to the state director, and vice versa. Pascual respected the concerns, vision, and growth of all the members of the committee, as well as the perspectives of districts and individual schools. Together, the group was able to transform local barriers in implementing the program to statewide policy solutions. Later, as the PED bilingual education director, I experienced how this relationship—one of mutual respect and trust with honest dialogue—rendered powerful results for students in bilingual education programs.

As the SBAC cochair with Michael Chavez in 2013, I knew that the inclusion of English learners made the member-developed crosswalk for English language development a compelling addition to the New Mexico TEACH protocol. The presence of diversity renders a one-size-fits-all education policy useless; keen adjustments are crucial to ensure that all students succeed. Thus, it becomes imperative that bilingual education professionals help transform general "education for all" into relevant, suitable instruction for English learners based in current research in this field.

In closing, I must mention the importance of the leadership of SBAC chairs. As culturally and linguistically diverse educators who lived through an English-only education, these leaders could clearly articulate essential and necessary policy changes. Many—such as Mela Leger, whose contributions have been described in several chapters in this book—had a wide base of experience. Ida Carillo, who began her career as an ESL teacher at Santo Domingo Elementary School long before bilingual education, merits mention. As chair in the 1990s, Carillo valiantly "went right to the top" to directly inform the state superintendent of instruction when statewide issues arose. She had worked across so many platforms by the time she became chair—from the classroom to the university to the Lau Service Centers—and her expertise was so widely known, that she was rarely questioned.

Most importantly, each chair, as a former classroom teacher, could recognize gaps in "standard" teacher preparation, in the "standard" curriculum, and in generic evaluation and assessment practices when applied to bilingual students. They were fearless in their action-based advocacy, and they were committed to lead on behalf of the children. Bilingual education in New Mexico honors their work.

NOTES

1. The New Mexico State Board of Education comprised elected and appointed members who were responsible for setting all education policies, standards, and governing regulations for New Mexico's public schools. The board was charged with appointing a state superintendent of public instruction to administer education in New Mexico through the State Department of Education. On September 23, 2003, Section 6 of Article XII ("Education") of the New Mexico Constitution was amended (by popular vote) to create a Public Education Department led by a secretary of education appointed by and accountable to the governor (the amendment also created a public education commission). The secretary was given administrative and regulatory powers and duties and "all functions relating to the distribution of school funds and financial accounting for the public schools to be performed and provided by law."

2. Between 1963 and 1970, federal dollars and foundation grants funded thirteen experimental programs in bilingual education in New Mexico. With the advent of state funding in 1971, ten additional programs were added. By 1973, thirty-eight programs in twenty-one districts across New Mexico operated Spanish and Navajo bilingual education programs.

3. SB 155 evaluation report and 1972–1973 state and federal program objectives, January 21, 1972, in Habermann López personal collection.

4. SBE Regulation No. 75–19 (December 5, 1975), "Guidelines for Implementing Bilingual Multicultural Education Programs."

5. SBE Regulation No. 79–10 (June 19, 1979), "New Mexico Certification Requirements for Spanish/English Bilingual/Bicultural Endorsement."

6. Both SBE Regulation No 76–26 (issued December 7, 1976) and SBE Regulation No. 79–7 (issued May 3, 1979) set forth courses and Spanish language requirements for the endorsement.

7. Core committee members were Donna Pino, (Pueblo Santa Ana), Carl Naranjo (Pueblo Santa Clara), Gus Keene Wilma Phone (Jicarilla-Dulce), Joe Villa (Mescalero), Judi Martin, Gloria Emerson, and Glen Ellison (Navajo),

8. Donna Pino interview by Mary Jean Habermann Lopez, October 5, 2018, at The Range Café in Bernalillo, NM.

9. Mela Leger, correspondence to Superintendent Leonard De Layo, November 29, 1982, in personal collection of Mary Jean Habermann López.

10. Superintendent Leonard De Layo, correspondence to Mela Leger, December 15, 1982 in personal collection of Mary Jean Habermann López.

11. Assistant superintendent Alan Morgan, correspondence to Mela Leger, February 7, 1984, in personal collection of Mary Jean Habermann López.

12. SBE Regulation 6.64.10.9. (July 1, 1989), "Competencies for Teachers of Bilingual Education."

13. An interview conducted with Chris Sims on October 17, 2017, revealed that the only Pueblo bilingual teacher preparation program ever in existence was the 1973 College of Santa Fe Title VII program. Pueblo teachers received a bilingual endorsement under SBE regulation No. 74–1, "Prescribing Program Requirements for Approved Teacher Education Programs in Bilingual Education," January 24, 1974.

14. "Assessment Procedure for Pueblo Language Communities: A summary and Chronology of Activities," 1992, 1–3. Unpublished SDE document prepared by and in possession of Mary Jean Habermann López.

15. A few examples include testimony for the Prueba exam in 1993 for expansion of the statute to the twelfth grade and testimony concerning new PED changes to the regulation in the spring of 2016.

16. Mary Jean Habermann López, presentation to State Board of Education, October 28, 1999, in personal collection of Mary Jean Habermann López.

17. The legislature also passed a House joint memorial that called for audits of local programs (HJM 3) and one to study the "feasibility of testing students in the home languages" (HJM 18).

18. The PED has published its annual bilingual multicultural education annual report with this data. It is available at https://webnew.ped.state.nm.us/bureaus/language andculture/bilingual-multicultural-education-programs-bmeps/resources/.

19. NMAC 6.32.2 (2005), "Guidelines for Implementing Bilingual Education."

20. NMAC 6.32.2.12 (2005), "Program Element: Professional Development."

21. Minutes, SBAC meeting, October 9, 2003, in Mary Jean Habermann López personal collection.

22. Among the many sources used by the committee were the Charlotte Danielson rubric, which incorporated the sheltered instruction observation protocol (SIOP), a rubric that was popular across states that were implementing similar teacher observation requirements (https://danielsongroup.org/framework/framework-teaching); the Woodburn, Oregon, school teacher evaluation tool (http://www.woodburnsd.org /wp-content/uploads/2016/04/WSD-EVALUATION-PROCESS.pdf); the ELD standards and Can Do Descriptors of WIDA, a multi-state consortium focused on academic language development and academic achievement for pre-K–12 English language learners (https://wida.wisc.edu/); Dearborn Public Schools bilingual and compensatory education resource team pamphlet defining SIOP exemplars for use by schools in the district; chapter eight, "The Sheltered Method of Instruction," in Herrera and Murray, *Mastering ESL and Bilingual Methods*; and Echevarria, Vogt, and Short, *Making Content Comprehensible for English Language Learners*.

23. Patricia Latham, CESDP director, telephone interview by Mary Jean Habermann López, September 21, 2018 in personal collection of Mary Jean Habermann López.

REFERENCES

Echeverria, Jana, Mary Ellen Vogt, and Deborah J. Short. 2008. *Making Content Comprehensible for English Language Learners: The SIOP Model*. Boston: Pearson.

Herrera, Socorro, and Kevin G. Murry. 2011. *Mastering ESL and Bilingual Methods: Differentiated Instruction for Culturally and Linguistically Diverse (CLD) Students*. Boston: Pearson.

New Mexico Public Education Department. 2016. Bilingual Multicultural Education Report, 2015–2016. https://webnew.ped.state.nm.us/bureaus/languageandculture /bilingual-multicultural-education-programs-bmeps/resources.

MARÍA LUISA GONZÁLEZ, BEVERLEY ARGUS-CALVO,
AND REBECCA BLUM MARTÍNEZ

[13] Spanish-Speaking and Indigenous Leaders in New Mexico Who Made Successful Innovations in Bilingual Education *A Chapter in Two Parts*

I: SPANISH-SPEAKING INNOVATORS

María Luisa González and Beverley Argus-Calvo

The success of any kind of social epidemic is heavily dependent on the involvement of people with a particular and rare set of social gifts.
MALCOM GLADWELL [*The Tipping Point*, 2002, 24]

The following chapter covers the work of six heroic figures who were key to the success of bilingual education in the state of New Mexico: Henry W. Pascual, John Paul Taylor, María Spencer, Cecilio Orozco, Mela Leger, and Miguel Encinias. These men and women were the architects of innovations that took place in New Mexico from the 1960s to late 1970s, a period during which New Mexico was a trendsetter in education in the United States. The success of these innovative programs—the "social epidemic" that they energized—can be attributed in no small measure the remarkable skills and expertise—the "rare set of social gifts"—of each of these leaders.

The main catalyst in this movement was Henry W. Pascual, director of the New Mexico State Department of Education (SDE) from 1962–1986. Pascual and the other heroes of bilingual education encountered educational practices in New Mexico that were detrimental to Spanish-speaking and Indigenous children. Given this situation, Pascual became an ardent advocate for teaching and learning in the native language of children and the community, exemplifying a commitment to educational excellence and dignity owed to all children—of all backgrounds and ethnicities—attending schools in New Mexico. Pascual was a man who truly practiced what he preached, and his immediate interventions have become part of his legacy.

The following incident is only one example of what was practiced in schools before bilingual education began its innovative successes. In this example, we see Pascual as the strong advocate confronting adults, but at the same time, we find a touching display of his kindness and caring for children. Such incidents propelled not only Pascual but the other heroes described here to move into promoting creative practices and equitable policies for the children of New Mexico. Recalling a visit to schools in the town of Mora, Pascual described an incident in a fifth-grade classroom in which he "saw a little girl and [he] began talking to her in Spanish. All of a sudden, she began crying." He later found out that there was a punitive policy in the school that did not allow children to speak Spanish. Needless to say, he went directly to speak with the principal and superintendent. He explained the ethical and legal ramifications of what they were doing to make sure their subtractive schooling policy did not continue.[1]

The term "innovation," though commonly heard, has different meanings in different contexts and situations. In education, as Fullan points out (2002), an innovative leader can be characterized as one who knows the difference between being an expert in a given content innovation and being an expert in managing the process of change, creating the conditions for change to occur. Henry Pascual was able to continue as the leading bilingual education expert while managing and promoting those innovations. He ensured that the changes (innovations) would flourish in the multicultural context of New Mexico by choosing gifted individuals who would create needed changes and manage those changes. He was able to promote bilingual education projects and programs throughout the state together with his cadre of distinguished leaders, all of whom worked tirelessly to insure the success of each innovation. Pascual's strength lay in part in his ability to identify and promote individuals who were strong advocates of bilingual education without feeling threatened himself. He intentionally looked for individuals who were the best and the brightest and who shared his beliefs in bilingual education.

Pascual played a key role in bringing an innovation to fruition, from conceptualizing an innovation, to seeking funding, to insuring its proper implementation by identifying the right leader for each effort. Those he chose enjoyed the support and knowledge of a true expert. This made him not only a catalyst but also a vested leader in all bilingual education innovations throughout the state.[2]

There are hundreds of studies conducted on leadership that identify certain characteristics and qualities (Fullan 2002; Glasser 1990; Greer and Short 2002; Moolenar, Daly, and Sleegers 2010). However, few if any studies explore commitment at the state level that involves the transfer of the four characteristics described below (Berman and McLaughlin, 1976; Takanishi and Le Menestrel 2017). We will provide evidence that points to the demonstrable talents and qualities exhibited by these leaders.

Though the innovators in this chapter all had distinct personalities and backgrounds, they all shared a set of defining characteristics. They were believers—with an unflinching belief that bilingual education was the best way to educate children and that language and culture should be maintained in both English and Spanish to continue enriching their lives so that they could succeed academically. They were warriors—with a steadfast commitment to fighting for this cause that went beyond themselves no matter the cost; these warriors came with an uncompromising sense of integrity according to which any other means but the right way to do things would be unacceptable. They were scholars—animated by an unsurpassed expertise that was built on a knowledge base of understanding language and culture through research, policy, and legal parameters, along with teaching and learning. And they were leaders of leaders—with a keen ability to identify other leaders, who themselves could later identify potential leaders so that innovations could be spread and maintained throughout the state.

Another point to consider is that one needs to see leaders in bilingual education differently when one looks at innovations or reform (Feinberg 1999; Schwabsky 2013). Bilingual education, a research-proven means of providing the best education, stands against a history of misinformation, segregation, and isolation (Altis and Tan 1999; Labaree 1997; Nieto and Bode, 2012). Many times, misinformation has been used against the best interests of those who are culturally and linguistically diverse. Leaders in bilingual education thus deal with a highly controversial educational effort that carries major sociopolitical implications reaching far beyond the public school classroom. Fortunately, during the two decades during which these innovations took place, such leaders did emerge, and a very talented group of committed individuals became the warriors, the scholars, the advocates, and the change agents that led the charge for bilingual education.

Henry W. Pascual: Leadership at the State Department

At the center of the bilingual education innovation was the direction from SDE provided by Henry W. Pascual, who served as director of several units within the department—foreign language instruction, the civil rights program, and bilingual education. Under his leadership, innovations took place throughout the state and across educational settings.

Pascual was born and educated in Puerto Rico in a Spanish-speaking home. He attended the University of Wisconsin Army Air Corps training, where he became a communications specialist and an air traffic controller. He graduated in 1943 in the top three of a class of five hundred. He served in the Air Corps until the end of World War II, after which he went to work for the Civil Aeronautics Administration as an air traffic controller and was sent to the Panama Canal Zone. That job later brought him to Santa Fe, New Mexico. While in New Mexico from 1954 to 1958, he did undergraduate and graduate work at the University of New Mexico in Spanish, French, English, and pedagogy. From 1954 to 1966, he did graduate work at the University of Colorado and in Mexico at the Universidad Autónoma de Guadalajara. From 1959 to 1962, he served the Albuquerque Public Schools as a French, English, and Spanish teacher. After several years, Pascual was recognized by the Modern Language Association of America as one of the top thirty-six foreign-language teachers in the country.

In 1962, Pascual moved from the public-school classroom to serve the SDE. During his tenure with the SDE, he received multiple recognitions at the national and international levels. In the United States, he was invited to offer his expertise at many prestigious events, among them the National Commission on the English Language, the Office of Bilingual Education, and the White House Conference for Leaders of Bilingual Education. Several countries also sought his expertise by inviting him to travel abroad on numerous occasions, where he met major dignitaries from countries such as France and Spain. Mexico awarded him an honorary doctorate from the University of Coahuila, and the government invited him many times to visit Mexico in several capacities (Pioneers n.d., 35).

His self-proclaimed war against the educational injustices practiced in schools is fully exemplified by this quote: "The one element which, beginning in 1963, was insulting to me and ego-damaging to the children, was the fact that they were forbidden to speak their home language. The penalty for speaking Spanish was one 'whack' with a ruler for each word spoken."[3] Thus, he began his quest to improve educational opportunities for the children in New Mexico and across the country.

Pascual had a gift to attract and prepare the best individuals to ensure that educational innovations grew wings. The foundations of the innovations entailed strong professional development focused on language and culture; he believed that this led to building self-esteem in individuals. He was at the center of a group of individuals who believed, as he did, in the supreme importance of culture and language and that the success of bilingual education depended on the preparation of fully bilingual bicultural teachers who were knowledgeable and proud of their heritage. There is ample evidence that Pascual was dedicated to ensuring full fluency and biculturalism in the Indigenous languages and that these were just as important as the Spanish language and culture (Indigenous education leaders are discussed in the second part of this chapter).

THE BELIEVER AND WARRIOR FOR THE STATE Numerous situations, incidents, and efforts are detailed throughout this book as evidence of the deep respect that Henry Pascual held for the people, history, and cultural heritage of New Mexicans. He was a fierce advocate and adamant believer that bilingualism was an asset that must be valued throughout one's life. He described how New Mexico's "people were [many times] ignorant of their history and culture," thus creating "an inferiority complex about themselves."[4]

Documents reference the times he and his staff observed teachers displaying racist and reductionist views in the classroom. Most of the time, Pascual took matters into his own hands: "When you begin something like this, first you have to experiment, and that is what we did with the Pecos project and see if success can be attained, and then you carry your proof with you so that you can convince people."[5] He specifically recounted incidents during school visits across the state that compelled him to "not only support bilingual education and the return of language and culture that belong to the people but also (to promote) the right education for teachers about culture."

Pascual reported that during observations, an incident occurred in the rural community of Hatch, New Mexico, during which a teacher told him, "Oh, these Mexicans don't know anything." Wanting to prove her wrong, he asked if he might teach the children himself. He easily moved into the role of teacher and "taught them how to tell time in English to prove that children could readily learn if taught properly." He commented that her reaction was one of "surprised silence." However, the story did not end there. In true Pascual fashion, he wanted to ensure that something would be done to stop this type of emotional damage to children. He recounted, "I went to the principal's office and told him I was going to write a report to the superintendent regarding the comment that 'these Mexicans don't know anything,' and that her teaching had to change."[6]

THE SCHOLAR Leaders who are truly committed to bilingual education are often multicultural, with fluency in several languages. Pascual himself had a very strong background in English, as well as in French and Spanish history and literature (Habermann López 1991). He also had a depth and understanding of the history and literature of New Mexico and could hold his own with published academics in those fields. His use of both English and Spanish in the different communicative domains was unmatched. He was able to use his strong writing and editing skills to motivate districts in seeking external funds through grant writing.

One of his own internal departmental innovations was described by Pascual in 1991 in a document he prepared for the National Association for Bilingual Education Conference in Albuquerque, NM. He explained how he "established a system for assisting local districts to write proposals for the newly established Title VII Bilingual Education Act. He immediately announced the availability of funds and set up a conference to discuss the rules and regulations. He developed a tight formula for developing objectives and activities based on identified needs."[7] As a perfectionist with the editing and reediting of proposals that went out to the different government agencies, he taught many educational administrators and teachers to write grants, allowing them as much time as needed to complete as close-to-perfect a grant as possible.[8] In fact, he was very proud of his grant record, stating that all but two of his many grant requests were funded.

While always a staunch advocate for standard Spanish, Pascual recognized the vernacular spoken in New Mexico as a strong foundation and powerful tool for teaching and learning, as well as for self-concept. However, during his years at the SDE, there were those who felt that Pascual did not honor the vernacular. They often believed that he disrespected the language from the home because he was from Puerto Rico and did not understand the northern New Mexico ways. Yet as is evident by his curriculum vitae, Pascual had lived in New Mexico since 1946 and had taught English, French, and Spanish for many years while working in the public schools. In addition, he had lived, studied, and traveled to other Spanish-speaking countries. Another criticism stemmed from Pascual's strict adherence to following what was delineated in the grants that paid for the children's programs. Some saw this as professionalism and dedication to the children and teachers in New Mexico. Others, not understanding the ethics and moral responsibility of accepting grant monies earmarked for certain learning activities, felt that he was too stringent and rigid.

Pascual was continually involved in providing teacher professional development, including international experiences that taught teachers how to develop their Spanish language skills and pedagogy in Spanish. He also helped support the development of undergraduate and graduate university programs where courses were taught in Spanish. All of these activities were very innovative at the time and were implemented with great success (See Calvo, Habermann López, and Blum Martínez, chapter 9 this volume). Those in opposition felt that one needed to speak the language only as it was spoken in the home, that by "educating" their Spanish—with its many *anglicismos* (anglicisms) and *arcaísmos* (archaisms)—and their culture, they were dishonoring their New Mexican heritage. Yet Pascual and the leaders featured in this chapter believed wholeheartedly that building on what is learned at home by learning more about our language and culture positively impacted teachers' and children's self-esteem. Pascual explained this issue in the following manner: "Bilingualism is a tool, which can be used by a country to advance its foreign policy." He continued by saying that "this country needs to not be so intellectually provincial when it comes to bilingual and multicultural education."[9]

As part of his commitment to set an example for those whom he served, Pascual kept current by being a voracious reader. His vast knowledge of bilingualism, biculturalism, and history is hinted at in his description of how the policy statement he presented to the New Mexico State Board of Education was "unanimously adopted":

> In order to be able to do these things, you have to acquire credibility. I traveled
> throughout the state. I did workshops in contrastive analysis Spanish and
> English, phonology, status of education in the public schools, the state of
> Spanish, English language arts, many, many things, on culture. I was surprised
> that New Mexicans knew so little on Spain, Mexico . . . nonexistent . . . so I used
> to talk about Goya, Velázquez, El Greco.[10]

He was also a scholar in teaching and learning. He could move easily from topics dealing with Piagetian or Vygotskian theories to details about research on the psychology of bilingualism by Lambert or bilingualism from the sociolinguist Fishman. The individuals interviewed for this chapter all expressed how much they had learned from Pascual, who served as mentor, teacher, and ultimate authority in issues of language, culture, and history, as well as teaching and learning. His philosophy on teaching is captured by this statement from an interview conducted with him in 2002:

> Proper teaching of English and good teaching of English begins with a good background for teachers on materials, philosophies and background of the language so they know why children are making mistakes. . . . These concepts have to be taught specifically to teachers . . . also the importance of oral language production and interaction.[11]

A LEADER OF LEADERS This next section provides background and professionalism of some of Pascual's staff and how as a group, they had a process for district and school visits that were unmatched at the state level. Pascual and his staff annually monitored Title VII programs in schools across the state, looking at both funding accountability and especially the quality of implementation.

Henry Pascual's preparation led him to conduct his own research as he visited schools. He saw that the teaching-learning process involved teachers first as learners, with sound preparation and continuous professional development, who in turn would be able to provide sound teaching and learning experiences that would optimize children's academic development. Another major outcome would result in teachers' and students' heightened self-identity and increased self-concept. Often during these school visits, Pascual would demonstrate for teachers by taking over the teaching of children himself.

Pascual trusted that leaders across the state held the same high expectations for themselves that he held for himself. He was able to identify the best and the strongest bilingual educators to work with him internally, within the state department, as well as externally, in public school systems. Within the SDE, Pascual hired well-prepared bilingual educators to work with him, one of whom was Julia Rosa López-Emslie, who had been working in Miami, Florida. Pascual describes how he "acquired" the unit to which López-Emslie was assigned and described her work responsibilities:

> In 1976, I received a visitor from the Office for Civil Rights in Dallas. Within a week, I had prepared a proposal to establish a unit with the Office of Civil Rights [with] funding [that] staffed three specialists, two secretaries, and me as director. This was our infamous Cross Cultural Education Unit. I hired two Hispanics and one Navajo specialist, and we began working directly with teachers providing much information on Native American history and cultures as well that of the Hispanics. The first two years went well, but soon the

complaints came in, and finally, the department gave me notice to stay out of the districts. By this time, the personnel had left, but a super individual, Dr. Julia Rosa López-Emslie, who had been working with Ralph Robinett in Miami, came to work with me. She did excellent teacher training work. When she left, I had to abandon OCR work."[12]

Ralph Robinett, a friend of Pascual's and another highly respected bilingual education pioneer, served as the executive director for the Bilingual Education Program in the Miami Dade County Public Schools from 1963 to his retirement in 2002. He was involved in the development of other materials to develop Spanish skills, known as the Spanish Curricula Development Center (SCDC).[13] López-Emslie had worked with Robinett on the development and field testing of the SCDC materials (see Lopez-Emslie, chapter 11 this volume). Her previous experience in Miami complemented the responsibilities of the workshops she designed for teacher training with the SDE Cross-Cultural Education Unit. After leaving the SDE to work on her doctorate, she continued dedicating her life to preparing hundreds of bilingual teachers through innovative programs and grants at Eastern New Mexico University, eventually becoming the first Hispanic woman in New Mexico to be named dean of Eastern New Mexico University's College of Education in Portales.

Another linchpin of the work at the state level in bilingual education was Mary Jean Habermann López, who continued serving the state after Henry Pascual retired. Habermann López had been a teacher in New Mexico who had also taught in Guadalajara, Mexico, and had participated in Cecilio Orozco's Title VII graduate program at New Mexico Highlands University (see Calvo, Habermann López, and Blum Martínez, this volume). As the director of Title VII and later state-funded bilingual education programs, she continued the Pascual tradition of holding the same high expectations for districts to follow. She became a state leader by motivating districts to seek external funding, offering grant writing support, and providing state oversight. She worked tirelessly to offer the best of bilingual and bicultural education to the children in the state. She also continued to provide professional development for teachers and teacher assistants when other state programs did not offer any of this assistance.

With Pascual's support and friendship, all the educators featured, bound by their shared vision, contagious enthusiasm for change, and passion to demonstrate that bilingual education was in the best interest of the children in this chapter, were able to take advantage of opportunities when they became available.

The strong bonds between these individuals and Pascual are evident as he played an integral role in the establishment and/or development of each innovation. In the late 1960s, Pascual helped John Paul Taylor write the research grant that resulted in one of the first dual-language programs in the country in the Las Cruces schools. In the early 1970s, Pascual wrote a proposal that established a training center for northern New Mexico directed by Mela Leger in West Las Vegas. Given the success of this center, another was established in Silver City, this one directed by María Spencer (see Calvo, Blum Martínez, Habermann Lopez, Chapter 9, this edition. Pascual worked with Cecilio Orozco to design and offer a summer experience for bilingual teachers, affording them the opportunity to develop their pedagogical skills and provide linguistic enrichment in the Spanish language; Orozco also led another innovation at the time in the first a bilingual education graduate program in New Mexico, which he directed at the New Mexico Highlands University. Miguel Encinias worked with Pascual in his bilingual unit and developed a highly innovative undergraduate program in bilingual education for educational assistants. In fact, Encinias went so far as to recognize Pascual in his dissertation (Encinias 1976).

John Paul Taylor: Educational Leader and Innovator in the Las Cruces Public Schools

Dual-language immersion programs are widely mentioned in literature and are widespread in practice throughout the US.[14] For educators, it is surprising to find that one of the forerunners of these programs began nearly forty years ago in the Las Cruces Public Schools. In 1967, as a result of a Title III NDEA research grant funded by the US Office of Modern and Classical languages, a sophisticated two-way bilingual program was established that attended to the needs of children, parents, and the community. In turn, the teaching staff was offered preparation to provide an education in two languages that to this day is lauded by educators and students. Pascual stated, "I followed this program through the twelfth grade and saw how Anglo and Hispanic students studied biology in Spanish very easily."[15] The leader who directed this prototype of modern dual language programs was John Paul Taylor.

At the time of this writing, John Paul Taylor is in his nineties and the only living person among the featured leaders of innovations in this chapter. He continues to speak of the dual language program from the late 1960s with great regard. Taylor was born of a farming and dairy family in the small, poor, rural area of Chamberino and La Union a few miles from Las Cruces. Taylor grew up in a hardworking and bilingual bicultural environment in his home, school, and community. His father was born in Gainesville, Texas, but had relocated to El Paso and was very interested in politics. His mother was a Romero, a historic and well-respected New Mexico Hispanic family. Taylor's mother was always helping others; Taylor recalls her always having food to share with those transients going through the rural roads during the Depression (Pacheco 2012). The youngest of seven children and many years younger than his siblings, he was raised as though he were an only child.

Taylor attended the public schools in those rural areas—Chamberino Elementary, where one of his sisters was a teacher, and Valley High School, where he met First Lady Eleanor Roosevelt. After high school, he enrolled in the New Mexico College of Agriculture and Mechanic Arts, from which he graduated in 1942 with a major in history and a minor in English. He also had enough education credits to teach. In July 1942, he enlisted in the Navy, where he served in naval intelligence during World War II. According to Pacheco (2002), Taylor's having previously worked in the college's registrar's office prepared him for this position, since he could type well, take shorthand, and follow office procedures. He was stationed in El Paso, Texas, as a liaison to the US Cable and Postal Censorship Office.

After military service, Taylor married and moved to Las Cruces. From there, the Taylors relocated into the same home that is now given the distinction of a historic landmark. He left his work at the university to join the teaching ranks of the Las Cruces Public Schools. He then moved into administration, where he served in several positions, including school principal, director of federal programs, and ultimately associate superintendent of the Las Cruces Public Schools. With Henry Pascual's guidance, he established the nationally recognized two-way bilingual education program (see Calvo, Blum Martínez, and Habermann López, chapter 9 this volume).

Taylor was elected as a state representative in 1986, and as a legislator, he continued to advocate for quality education based on using two languages as the medium of instruction. His legislative contributions made it possible for students in grades K–12 to participate in bilingual education. He stated that "the history and culture of the students must be an integral part of the instructional programs."[16] Taylor also sponsored the legislation that supported the development of La Prueba, and the summer Spanish Immersion Institutes for all state universities (see Hannum and Salazar, chapter 10 this volume).

During his eighteen-year tenure as a legislator, Taylor was known for his support of programs to help indigent and disabled New Mexicans and as an advocate for arts and culture. He has been called "the conscience of the New Mexico legislature."[17]

Mela Leger: Educational Leader and Innovator in West Las Vegas

Pascual explained the establishment of the demonstration center in West Las Vegas and subsequent centers in the following way:

> In 1971, I wrote a proposal to establish a training center for northern New Mexico with funds from the [New Mexico] Department of Public School Finance, carried out in NABE pioneer Ray Leger's district under the direction of Mela Leger. Because of the success of the center, the following year, a center was established at Silver City with NABE pioneer Maria Spencer as director, and another was established at Roswell, New Mexico.[18]

Leger held such strong beliefs about the rights of children to receive a bilingual education that she served at district, state, and national levels in different capacities to promote programs and materials that were sound and in the best interest of children's development.

There is a state historical road marker located on the Highway 84 between Santa Rosa and Las Vegas, New Mexico, dedicated to Mela Leger that explains how she was raised by her grandparents and at a very early age learned to read the newspaper in Spanish to her grandfather, who was blind. The marker also includes the fact that Leger was considered a pioneer in bilingual education by establishing one of the first bilingual-multicultural schools to safeguard children's right to speak and learn Spanish as guaranteed by the state Constitution.[19]

As with our other heroic bilingual education warriors, Leger was also a scholar. She graduated from Loretto Heights College in Denver with a degree in sociology and business. She married Ray Leger, another leader in New Mexico's development of bilingual education programs, who served as superintendent of the West Las Vegas School District and in the state legislature. He engaged in many battles in support of bilingual education.

Mela Leger went on to receive a master's degree from New Mexico Highlands University. She continued with coursework to "improve her Spanish" by completing the requisites for bilingual certification.[20] She also served on the State Bilingual Advisory Committee to the State Board of Education; as chair of this body for four years, she was also involved in developing the Guidelines for

Implementing Bilingual Education in 1975 (SBE No. 75–19). She was also the principal of the elementary school that offered the 1965 early Title I bilingual multicultural education program after the Pecos project (see Habermann López, chapter 5 this volume).

Leger became involved in several curriculum pilot projects. The first was with the Miami linguistics readers. Designed as a new approach, these materials assisted teachers in the teaching of reading (see Habermann López, chapter 5 this volume). She piloted material and curriculum, and at Pascual's insistence, offered in-service workshops to teachers throughout the state and then nationally. She was also charged with piloting the SCDC materials from Miami, Florida. These materials were important to New Mexico. At that time, the only materials available in Spanish were from Spain and Latin America and were not always relevant to New Mexico's children (see López-Emslie, chapter 11 this volume). Leger's critical role lay in ensuring that the materials were distributed, used, and evaluated by teachers. She continued to work with the materials even when the curriculum was passed to another publishing company.[21] She continued her dedication to bilingual education and served in major landmark judicial efforts. For example, she was invited to be part of the State Department of Education's monitoring team in Portales, New Mexico, before the Serna family sued the Portales school district. Leger explained that "the children were being ignored. . . . Their needs were definitely not being met. The teaching strategies were definitely at fault. Part of that report that I participated in went into that court case of Serna vs. Portales Board of Education" (see Sosa-Provencio and Sánchez, chapter 7 this volume).[22]

Leger also worked with the Southwest New Mexico Teacher Training Center, helping several districts serve Spanish-speaking children following the landmark Supreme Court case *Lau v. Nichols*. When the *Lau* remedies were put into effect, there was a crucial need to prepare bilingual teachers and teacher assistants. Leger worked at the University of New Mexico and later as a consultant traveling to the state of Washington to offer teacher development. She also served with the Albuquerque Public Schools and taught courses at the University of New Mexico, during which she traveled to Latin American countries to train teachers.

Mela Leger received multiple awards and was recognized as a leader of leaders throughout her lifetime. She was one of the valiant women featured in the Hispanic Women's Council book *Mujeres Valerosas*, which celebrates the "extraordinary women serving on the Hispanic Women's Council" (Samora, Cárdenas, and Martínez 2006).

María Spencer: Leader and Innovator in Silver City

The teacher training demonstration center was led by María Spencer, who tirelessly fought for the rights of Hispanic children and established a nationally recognized English as a second language (ESL) teacher-training center in Silver City, New Mexico.

Spencer is commemorated as "one of the state's boldest natives by the State of NM. She was one of the first teachers of Spanish for native speakers, now called Spanish for heritage speakers in the state of New Mexico, or really throughout the country." Her daughter, Laura Gutierrez-Spencer said, "It was revolutionary in the 1950s."[23] A historical marker was placed in her hometown of Las Cruces, on the New Mexico State University campus, honoring her "legacy as a pioneer of bilingual and bicultural education and advocate of the indo-Hispanic experience."[24] Emma Armendariz fondly described Spencer as "always looking for the most positive things that we could accomplish for students but at the same time not bowing down to philosophies that did not make sense."[25]

María Spencer was born in Las Cruces in 1920 and raised speaking primarily Spanish. Her father was a community leader and entrepreneur who came from a goat-herding family. Her mother came from a well-to-do family from Chihuahua, Mexico, where Spencer spent summers during her childhood. At home, she spoke only Spanish, and when she entered the private girl's school in first grade, the teacher, not knowing what to do with her, sent her to the principal's office for not speaking English. Her initial struggles in school did not last long, as she quickly acquired the English language and continued her education in the public schools. Spencer's daughter relates that during the year, she was tutored by a priest who boarded with the Gutierrez family sometime between 1925 and 1929, when Catholics were persecuted by the Mexican governmental during its anticlerical movement Much to her chagrin, instead of graduating in first place as valedictorian, Spencer ended up as salutatorian. She had taken the more challenging courses of physics and chemistry to follow her dream of becoming a medical doctor. Her rival was her close childhood friend, who took the "easier" typing and home economics courses.[26]

At a time when young women rarely attended universities—much less left town—María tricked her father into permitting her to leave the state so she could attend the University of California at Berkeley. Her father, wanting to protect his daughter but also understanding how important it was to attend an out-of-state institution, consulted with a well-respected Hispanic professor, Fabian Garcia, for advice. Based on the academic's recommendation, María attended a small junior college in California for one year, and because she succeeded there, she went on to the University of California at Berkeley, where she completed her bachelor's degree. During World War II, she began her graduate studies and was the only graduate assistant hired by both the Latin American History Department and Latin American Political Science Department. She continued her graduate work in linguistics at the University of Michigan and Columbia University. At one point during her stay in New York City, a governmental agency tried to recruit her as a spy, which she turned down. She completed a master's degree in Spanish at New Mexico State University (Charland 2015).

By the time María had become a licensed teacher, she had already had teaching experience, having taught in Mexico City and at the university during her teaching assistantships. Knowing the difference that a teacher can make in the life of a child, she made it her life-long mission to prepare bilingual teachers who respected their own language and culture and recognized the strengths of their students and their families and communities. She began teaching bilingual education in the Las Cruces schools and then moved to Silver City when her husband was offered a position at Western New Mexico State University, where she also taught as adjunct faculty. Tom Orona, a recognized master bilingual education teacher first met Spencer when he served as her student teacher and then went on to receive his master's degree because of her mentorship, fondly and respectfully recalled how she was "*una fuente de información*—she was a well of information." He also attested to her tireless efforts by stating, "You could never stop that lady."[27]

Spencer understood firsthand the struggles of second language English learners and fought to build the value of children's heritage language. She focused "on re-teaching" teachers that punishing children for speaking their heritage language was wrong and could not be tolerated. It is interesting to note that Spencer was raised by a father who, although not an educator himself, was dedicated to Hispanic students, acting as an informal mentor to the few Hispanic and a Mexican students who entered New Mexico State University Parents and students went to him when they needed advice on how to handle different situations.[28]

When the Silver City School Board could not accept Spencer's innovations, they shut her program down (Charland 2015). New Mexico's governor moved her program to Deming and converted it to a teacher training program. Dru Orona, a teacher with the program, recalled "how she heard on the radio that

Mrs. Spencer and her staff had been fired."[29] The irony of it all was that at the same time that she was being fired by the school board, she was being honored by national organizations for her innovative approach to teaching children whose primary language was not English. One of her numerous awards was the Wonder Woman Award, which she received on stage in New York alongside the famous civil rights activist Rosa Parks.

Henry Pascual recognized and highly respected María Spencer's work and philosophy. In fact, given her continuous contact with Mexico both as a child and a professional, she was the perfect person to assist him. In 1972, he asked her to direct the third Guadalajara Institute, the Experienced Teacher Fellowship Program in Bilingual Education.

From 1973–1978, María Spencer continued to influence teachers through the teacher training program she had developed. Lessons at the demonstration site were videotaped and evaluated, providing lab experiences to teachers in the field. Over the course of her experience, she conducted over a hundred bilingual teacher-training workshops in sixteen states and in Canada, Mexico, and Ecuador. After retiring from the profession, she volunteered as a social activist in Silver City until her death in 1992. "What's really remarkable," her daughter recalled, "is that her mother did all that while surviving breast cancer for fifty years. That may have been her greatest achievement" (Charland 2015).

Cecilio Orozco: Educational Leader and Innovator at Highlands University for the Bilingual Education University Professional Development Innovations

Another key educator in providing highly innovative professional development for teachers in New Mexico was Cecilio Orozco. Although born in the United States, where he remained for three years while his parents were working before they returned to Mexico, Orozco attended Mexican schools until the age of thirteen, when he and his family returned to the US. Having arrived in the US with almost no facility in English, he quickly acquired the language and graduated with his class in 1948.[30]

Orozco continued into higher education, obtaining his bachelor's and master's degrees from Arizona State College, now Northern Arizona University. He served the Tuba City Public Schools on the Navajo Reservation. Once he completed his master's degree, he became principal of the Tuba City High School. From the public schools, he went to teach at the Cochise College, where he became head of the Spanish Department during the birth of the Chicano movement.

Realizing that he needed his doctorate, Orozco enrolled at University of New Mexico. During his doctoral studies, he worked with Henry Pascual at the New Mexico State Department of Education in developing teacher training institutes and a master's degree program.[31] He assisted Pascual during the first two summers of the Guadalajara Institutes, which offered bilingual education teachers in New Mexico needed professional development in Spanish.

When Orozco received his doctorate in 1971, he was hired by New Mexico Highlands University, where he taught courses in bilingual education and initiated the first master's-level bilingual education teacher preparation program in New Mexico. Once instituted, he wrote a Title VII grant for an institute for bilingual education for teachers delivering bilingual education programs across New Mexico. Master's candidates in the program went to the Universidad Autónoma de Guadalajara, where they received coursework in Spanish and worked with Mexican teachers in elementary schools.

In 1973, Orozco was one of five New Mexico experts who testified before the Senate Subcommittee on Education as Congress considered improvements to the national Bilingual Education Act. Orozco's recorded comments (see Blum Martínez and Habermann López, chapter 8 this volume) echoed his philosophy about the deep preparation that bilingual teachers needed and that he put into practice in the master's program and the Institute at New Mexico Highlands University as discussed above.

In 1975, Orozco was hired by California State University, becoming one of the only Mexican Americans to be hired in a faculty position and the first in the university's College of Education. He also taught in Chicano studies. Fresno State University president John D. Welty stated in his eulogy for Orozco, "Dr. Orozco was a pillar of our Fresno State community whose accomplishments extended far beyond the campus. He was a pioneer in bilingual education, which has helped open educational and career opportunities to millions of young people."[32]

Berta González, associate vice president emerita of continuing and global education and professor emerita of education, knew Orozco as a colleague for more than thirty-five years. She described him as "a tireless and committed educator [who] made an impact on many." She said his mentorship and guidance on bilingual education and diversity issues are "his legacy for thousands of Latino students as well as faculty and media. He was sought after as a speaker statewide, nationally and internationally."[33]

In addition to his impact in bilingual education, Orozco also became a well-respected scholar, alongside his counterpart and mentor, Alfonso Rivas Salmón from the Universidad Autónoma de Guadalajara, on the ancient roots of the Mexicas and Aztec civilizations. He was the first author to claim that the pictographs in Utah were irrefutably linked to those in the Sun Stone (Orozco 1992). He became a world-famous pre-Columbian historian, upsetting many scholars but gaining the respect of others. He received numerous awards in the United States and Mexico, among which was the prestigious National Association of Bilingual Education's Pioneer in Bilingual Education Medal.[34]

As a committed academic, Orozco helped establish several organizations to support both faculty and students. He was a steadfast mentor, and many online testimonies speak to his dedication in his role as an outstanding professor and his support and promotion of individuals at both pre-K–12 and higher education levels.[35]

Miguel Encinias: Educational Leader and Innovator at the University of Albuquerque

Miguel Encinias was born in Las Vegas, New Mexico, the youngest of sixteen children. He joined the Air Force at sixteen, and flew more than forty missions during World War II. He was shot down and spent a year in a prisoner of war camp in Germany. After returning to the United States, he earned his bachelor's and master's degrees. He also studied at the Institut Politique d'Etudes de Paris, achieving full fluency in French.[36] Encinias went on to serve in another two wars—Korea and Vietnam.

In 1971, Encinias retired from a military career having been awarded three Distinguished Flying Crosses, fourteen Air Medals, and two Purple Hearts, making him one of New Mexico's most highly decorated veterans.[37]

After his military retirement, Encinias was hired by Henry Pascual to work in his unit at the State Department of Education. During this time, Encinias's beliefs and experiences were further validated and extended. In his doctoral dissertation for the University of New Mexico on the preparation of bilingual teachers, he described his educational philosophy: "I became more and more convinced that the best way to educate Hispanic children was to allow them to learn through Spanish about the many different Hispanic cultures and literatures" (Encinias 1976).

From 1974 to 1979, Encinias directed the University of Albuquerque's Bilingual Multicultural Teacher Preparation Program, which was renowned for its innovative format. During this same time, he served as a member of the New Mexico Bilingual Advisory Committee, which helped develop teacher certification standards for bilingual education (Habermann López 1991).

As a life-long leader, Miguel Encinias continued his dedication to biculturalism and bilingualism. His words and actions opened many doors to new knowledge and new career paths for many. Finally, Encinias went on to found La Compañía de Teatro de Albuquerque. Encinias modeled the spirit of a true leader's work simply never ending, as Rebecca Blum Martínez reminded us:

> He was one of the founders of the Hispanic Cultural Center, and of the Zarzuela de Albuquerque. He taught New Mexico History, and he co-authored an Annotated Spanish/English edition of Gaspar Villagrá's epic poem: Historia de la Nueva México. Later, he envisioned a textbook that would highlight the significant contributions of the Spanish people in the United States. Four sections would chronicle Spain's role in the formation of what is now Florida, Texas, New Mexico and California. He wanted to make this history come alive for students by producing accompanying videos on major historical figures discussed in the text. He wrote the text in Spanish basing it on much of the research he had done in the archives in Sevilla. Mary Jean Habermann López, the former Director of Bilingual Education for the State of New Mexico, and a pioneer in her own right, collaborated with him on this project, providing the English translation. Unfortunately, that work was never completed.[38]

Among his other accomplishments after retirement was a request by President Bill Clinton to serve on the World War II Memorial Advisory Board to assist with the development of the World War II Memorial in Washington, DC. When the memorial was inaugurated, Encinias spoke on behalf of a whole generation. Blum Martínez's eulogy for Encinias challenges us to follow in his footsteps: "Our task is to ensure that his legacy lives on."

Closing Thoughts

This section reviewed the indefatigable work of Henry Pascual and his colleagues. It demonstrated how one individual could attract others of like mind, dedication, and energy to offer New Mexican children and their teachers sound bilingual education programs. These leaders were exemplary literate and cultured individuals; each grew up speaking, reading, and writing in Spanish, and each would become fluent in two languages (some of them were fully trilingual). Part of their camaraderie may have come from the similarities of their childhood and youth. Although Pascual was raised in Puerto Rico and four of the six heroes were brought up in New Mexico, both regions shared common historical experiences, as Lozano has explained:

> Both [New Mexico and Puerto Rico] had prolonged territorial periods during which the federal "government proffered U. S. citizenship status to residents. . . . This status separated New Mexicans and Puerto Ricans from the vast majority of Spanish-speaking immigrants who were not US citizens. Inadequate funding and their dependence on the US government prevented both territories from advancing their educational systems during their early territorial periods. Each territory expressed dissatisfaction over what they deemed their second-class status because the president appointed high-ranking officials. Each retained Spanish in all aspects of life during their first forty years as US territories. New Mexico and Puerto Rico educators each advocated for the role of Spanish language; it stood second to English in New Mexico, but Puerto Rican educators deemed it their primary concern. (Lozano 2013, 277)

While it is difficult to ascertain to what degree one is affected by the past, one can look for clues at the sociopolitical settings within which our bilingual education leaders lived and worked. New Mexico struggled with the role of Spanish throughout its history, both as a territory and as a state. During statehood, legislators assured a place for Spanish by including it in the state Constitution but had to acquiesce by giving English a more central role (See Gonzalez, chapter 4 this volume. In more progressive times, educators had to advocate for its presence in schools. Despite this history, Miguel Encinias, María Spencer, John Paul Taylor, Cecilio Orozco, and Mela Leger were able to maintain and further develop their heritage language. Cecilio Orozco was the only one of the leaders with immigrant status having come to California from Mexico at age thirteen. However, he did spend considerable time in New Mexico as he pursued his graduate studies dedicated to maintaining Spanish as one of two principal languages in the preparation of teachers and in the teaching-learning processes in their classrooms. On the other hand, Puerto Rico remained a territory that even today struggles to maintain the Spanish language in teaching and learning. During Pascual's formative years, while the US government was "forcing English instruction" on Puerto Rico, its educators deemed the role of Spanish in instruction to be of primary concern. Spanish was the language of the people. Then, from 1937 to 1942, a period that would have included the years of his secondary education, Spanish was kept as the "means of instruction in the first two grades and both languages were used in various experiments with the goal of transition to English by the eighth grade" (Schmidt 2014, 56).

While there are differences between Pascual's upbringing and that of his New Mexican counterparts covered in this chapter (Taylor, Leger, Spencer, Orozco and Encinias), there would have been similarities. In some areas in New Mexico, Spanish was the language of the home, and families were proud of maintaining language and culture; our research suggests that none was forced by his or her family to speak English. All six leaders spoke Spanish as their first language, and their unifying theme was that Spanish should be taught as an important part of the learning process. In one way or another, their upbringings led them to believe that Spanish was a language on par with English and that it was important to maintain and improve Spanish-language facility throughout one's life.

All were lifelong learners who fought for bilingual education with intense passion. They never expected others to do what they themselves were not willing to do. Several of us involved in the development of this book—contributing authors as well as its editors—remember one or all of them well. We were impressed with their personae, each of which was unique. We remember when we first met them, and we felt their importance. Their presence changed our lives, but we never realized how much they had done.

They all lived their lives beyond reproach. Each embodied social justice for our teachers and students in bilingual education. They did not settle for less, nor did they make excuses. They offered the best educational experiences for their own participants, whether they were students or teachers.

Countless examples abound about their work with staff or the participants in their programs. In terms of equity, one thing we can attest to is certain: they never disrespected or made any of their staff members or the teachers feel uncomfortable. None of the men featured here ever made his female colleagues, coworkers, or staff—we included—feel in any way exploited. On the contrary, each held women in high regard, and while many administrators would prefer to hire men, these educational leaders preferred simply to hire the best prepared individuals they could find, whether that person was male or female. Many women were hired, and they were assured the best treatment as professionals. They were never made to feel underappreciated or disrespected—that would never have been tolerated. They set the example by creating safe spaces for all their staff members, as well as anyone else with whom they came into contact.

Such success did not come without a price; all the individuals featured here spent their lives fighting to keep bilingual education programs and projects thriving. Henry Pascual, along with this group of groundbreakers, brought a presence, respect, and commitment to bilingual education that, in our opinion, has not been felt at any other time, before or since.

▢ ▢ ▢

II. INDIGENOUS INNOVATORS
Rebecca Blum Martínez

The previous section of this two-part chapter outlines some of the characteristics that Spanish/English bilingual leaders embodied as believers, warriors, scholars, and leaders of leaders. In this section, we focus on the Navajo and Pueblo innovators who embodied these same characteristics. They too were believers, warriors, scholars and leaders of leaders within their own cultures and speaking their own distinct languages. Their work was informed by their unique cultural, historical and educational perspectives that distinguished them as Navajo or Pueblo leaders. As has been shown in previous chapters (Werito, chapter 2) and Sims (Chapter 3) bilingual education developed differently in these two distinct groups reflecting the specific world views and needs of their peoples. To preserve and honor these distinctions we present them in two subsections, one discussing Navajo innovators and the other, Pueblo innovators.

Navajo Innovators

As described in Vincent Werito's chapter (chapter 2), the history of the Navajo people in becoming bilingual in Navajo and English is a complex one, tied primarily to the interactions between English-speaking missionaries, US federal agents, US federal educational policies, and the Navajo people themselves. The impetus behind all the efforts by these various English-speaking groups and institutions was the eradication of the Navajo language and religion and the imposition of English, a project that was challenged by the life-style of the Navajo people, who have traditionally lived in small family compounds in isolated areas.

In the 1930s, William Morgan, a Navajo, and Robert Young, an Anglo who later became a professor of linguistics at the University of New Mexico, both

working under the direction of John Collier, worked to develop the first comprehensive orthography of the Navajo language, an early version of which they
published in 1937. Their collaboration continued through the 1980s, culminating in publication in 1987 of *The Navajo Language: A Grammar and Colloquial
Dictionary*. The linguistic work that they and others undertook served as an
important support for the bilingual education innovations that Anita Pfeiffer,
Agnes Dodge Holm, Wayne Holm, and Rena Henry initiated. The idea that the
Navajo language could be studied and written allowed these educational leaders
to imagine how their language could be used in a school setting.

Pfeiffer, Agnes Dodge Holm, and Rena Henry all grew up in traditional
Navajo-speaking homes and began learning English at school. Anita Pfeiffer
and Agnes Dodge Holm first attended Bureau of Indian Affairs schools close to
their homes and later enrolled in boarding schools, where they met Indigenous
students from other tribes.

ANITA BRADLEY PFEIFFER   Anita Pfeiffer first attended Hastings College in
Nebraska, spending a year abroad studying in Madras, India. After returning
from India, she transferred to Arizona State University, where she received
her bachelor of arts degree and her master's degree in education. Pfeiffer's first
teaching job was at Brichta School in Tucson, Arizona, where she received
tenure before being recruited to teach at Rough Rock Demonstration School.[39]
At Rough Rock, Pfeiffer's initial responsibility was to teach young children in
Navajo. According to Holm, "There had been scattered precedents for add-on
literacy in Navajo with older students. But Anita was one of the first to teach
basic, initial literacy in Navajo."[40] Later, Pfeiffer became the principal of the
school, coordinating the efforts of the community with the school. She trained
the teachers—both English-speaking and Navajo-speaking—how to work in
such a school while remaining true to the community's wishes. As Holm comments, "Anita must have been the first woman and the first Navajo principal
in Navajoland. . . . I'm sure Anita would say that she was just one of the many
people working toward common goals. But as the principal of a truly community
school, she was truly at the heart of it."[41]

During her time at Rough Rock, Pfeiffer was an important member of the
group that established the Diné Bi'ólta (Navajo Education) Association, which
was instrumental in the preparation of Navajo teachers, Navajo literacy materials,
and the standardization of the Navajo orthography.[42]

In recognition of her pioneering work, Anita Pfeiffer was invited to study at Harvard University. During her studies, she was recruited to teach at the University of New Mexico, where she and her colleagues developed an onsite teacher-education program for potential teachers at Rough Rock Demonstration School. Students graduated with an associate of arts degree from that program, and many of them went on to receive their bachelor's and master's degrees. The second project developed by Pfeiffer at the University of New Mexico was an expansion of Rough Rock to several other Navajo and Apache communities assisting prospective teachers in getting their associate of arts degrees so that they could have an easier time later studying for their bachelor's degrees.

In 1991, Anita was appointed director of the Division of Diné Education by the Navajo Nation's president Peterson Zah. In this capacity, Pfeiffer developed a consortium in which the University of Colorado, Diné College, Ft. Lewis College, the University of New Mexico, and Northern Arizona University participated in educating Navajo elementary teachers. An important aspect of this program was the inclusion and integration of Navajo language and culture so that teachers would be prepared to work with Diné children. By 2006, 60 percent of teachers on the Navajo reservation were Diné, thanks in great part to the efforts of Anita Pfeiffer. Later, Pfeiffer and her colleagues founded the Navajo Preparatory School, dedicated to gifted and talented Navajo students.

Anita Pfeiffer embodies all the characteristics of a great innovator and leader in bilingual education. First and foremost, she has always believed that her language and culture were sources of strength, beauty, and an intellectual tradition that needed to be the basis for the education of Navajo children. She and her colleagues conceived and developed a vision for education that until that time had been unimaginable, and they went on to build the necessary infrastructure to sustain that vision: culturally and linguistically competent teachers, Navajo language literacy materials, and future leaders. She worked tirelessly, never wavering in her beliefs, always inviting others to fight alongside her. She was an activist scholar who ensured that the Navajo intellectual and spiritual worldview and knowledge was at the heart of the many educational projects that she initiated. Pfeiffer was awarded an honorary doctorate from the University of New Mexico in 2016 in recognition of her contributions and lifetime achievements on behalf of the Navajo Nation.

AGNES AND WAYNE HOLM Wayne Holm received his PhD in 1972, focusing on Navajo orthography. He moved to the Navajo reservation in the early 1950s to teach English to Navajo-speaking children. There he met Agnes Dodge. As a young adult, Agnes Dodge studied at the University of New Mexico for both her bachelor of arts and master's degree in education. When Agnes and Wayne married in 1960, they moved to Tsénítsaadeez'áhí, Rock Point, Arizona, where they remained for twenty-five years. They adopted a novel approach to the teaching of English by pairing an English-speaking ESL teacher with a Navajo-speaking Navajo teacher in each room of the elementary grades. The teachers were located at opposite ends of the classroom, with the English-speaking teacher conducting activities in English on one side and the Navajo teacher using Navajo on the other side working with another small group of children (Holm 1971).

> People were shocked when we suggested using Navajo. Nobody had ever
> suggested using Navajo in the school to learn, so how can you do that? School
> is to learn English. But at Rock Point you could do that, and convince them.
> (McCarty and Watahomigie 1999, 84).

Their work also included helping the local chapter's education committee become a school board and later helping transition the BIA school into a community-controlled contract school. The staff at the school came mainly from the community, and the Holms worked with the staff to develop their teaching skills. In 1971, Rock Point School received a Title VII grant, which helped the Holms and the community develop a K–12 coordinate bilingual program with a strong cultural component (see Werito, chapter 2 this volume). Agnes Holm later became the director of the Navajo school-accreditation program, and Wayne Holm helped create the voluntary Navajo immersion program at Tséhootsooí, Fort Defiance, Arizona.

Both Agnes and Wayne worked closely with Bernard Spolsky, a linguist at the University of New Mexico, with whom they coauthored several reports on the Navajo language development of young children. The Holms worked together for over fifty years and also raised four children. Their last publication together is titled "Rock Point, A Navajo Way to Go to School: A Valediction," published in 1990 in the *Annals of the American Academy of Political and Social Science* (508, no. 1: 170–84). Wayne Holm retired in 2002. Anita Holm passed away in 2004.

As in Anita Pfeiffer's case, both Agnes and Wayne Holm took the current understandings of second-language development and bilingualism and applied them to their particular cultural and linguistic context in novel ways that worked for the particular community. They believed in the abilities of Navajo people to develop a strong and rigorous educational program and worked alongside the community members to develop teachers and leaders who supported the community's desires for a bilingual population. Their studies and publications attest to their scholarly abilities. Those publications remain important historical and pioneering testaments of a particular period in Navajo history and have served as models for later Navajo scholars.[43]

RENA HENRY Rena Henry was born and raised in Arizona and moved to Naschitti, New Mexico, when she and her husband married. Her first experiences working in schools was as an educational assistant at Naschitti Elementary in the Central Consolidated School District. As Title VII funding became available, Henry enrolled in a teacher preparation program, first to obtain her associate degree and later for a bachelor of arts degree in education. After work, she would drive to her classes in Gallup (about a forty-five-minute drive each way) and then return to her home late in the evenings. When she received her teaching license, Henry worked as a teacher at Naschitti and soon became lead teacher (there was no official principal). In this capacity, she was responsible for developing and managing the newly established bilingual program, which relied heavily on educational assistants, helping the children to better understand their English texts.

In the early 1980s, Henry joined the board of the Linguistic Institute for Native Americans and the New Mexico Association for Bilingual Education. She was active in both organizations for many years, serving on their boards and garnering an award for her dedication to Navajo bilingual education. In 1982, she wrote a Navajo reader for young students titled *Hastiin Nímazí dóó Asdzáá Nímazí* (The Round Man and the Round Woman). She received her master's degree in education and an administrative license and became the bilingual director of the Central Consolidated Schools. In 2003, during the time she was the bilingual director, she received her doctorate from the Fielding Graduate Institute; her graduate studies focused on the attitudes of young Navajo students toward their languages and literacy. Henry was known for her cheerful outlook and her indefatigable quest for learning. Her remarkable achievement as a PhD after starting out as an educational assistant served as a model for many other Indigenous educators over the years, and she was always happy to guide and mentor those who came after her.

Pueblo Innovators

The context of Pueblo bilingual education is somewhat different from that of the Navajo. The Pueblo people were heavily impacted by the Spanish presence in

New Mexico beginning in the late 1600s until the arrival of the Americans. As agriculturists living in villages, the Pueblo people were easier for the Spanish to control and to impose both the Catholic religion and the encomienda system. The Pueblo people, however, resisted this oppression, first by organizing the Pueblo Revolt (the first American Revolution), driving the Spanish out of New Mexico in 1680, and later after the Spanish returned by concealing their ceremonial life from Spanish eyes. Because language was such an integral part of sacred ceremony, the Pueblo people also sought to protect their languages. These practices became more important with the arrival and impositions of the Americans, their educational system, and their attempts to stamp out Indigenous religions.

Given this history and the fact that there were multiple Pueblo languages, there were no early attempts to study Pueblo languages or to transcribe them. Protestant missionaries and those affiliated with the Wycliff Bible translators began efforts to write and study Pueblo languages in the early 1960s, hoping that with their translations, they would be able to convert new believers.[44] Field linguists affiliated with the Summer Institute of Linguistics (SIL), an affiliation of the Wycliff Bible translators, also worked in several pueblos with tribal members to develop orthographies for their languages, and in the process, introduced them to the tools of linguistic work. Pueblo innovators utilized the newly acquired linguistic knowledge they often acquired from the SIL's linguists primarily for their own purposes and in ways that reflected Pueblo beliefs about language and culture, as Christine Sims describes in chapter 3.

Having been raised in traditional families and communities, the individuals described below followed in the footsteps of their ancestors. Conscious of the sacrifices made by previous generations, Pueblo language innovators of the 1970s and 80s who were steeped in their cultures sought to maintain community language use and to establish appropriate public spaces for their languages.

ESTHER MARTINEZ Esther Martinez, a native Tewa speaker from Okhay Owingeh (formerly San Juan Pueblo), was born in 1912, the year that New Mexico was granted statehood. Her early years were spent working alongside her parents as migrant workers in the fields of Ute Country in Colorado. After a visit from her grandmother, Esther returned to Okhay Owingeh, where she would live for the rest of her life. Martinez attended the Santa Fe Indian School, and she later graduated from the Albuquerque Indian School in 1930. For many years after her graduation, she held a series of service jobs in northern New Mexico.

In the early 1960s, Esther Martinez met John Speirs, an SIL linguist, while she was working as a janitor at the John F. Kennedy School in San Juan Pueblo.

Speirs requested her assistance in documenting the Tewa language. After taking several linguistics classes from the SIL linguists, Martinez became a Tewa
language instructor and the director of bilingual education for her community.[45]
She went on to publish a San Juan Pueblo Tewa dictionary and language curriculum guides and consulted with other communities that were interested in
documenting their languages, many of whom are mentioned in chapter 3. She
also served as an instructor for the Summer Institute of Linguistics for Native
Americans helping to introduce other Native American language teachers to
phonetics classes and bilingual materials development. In 2004, she received her
bachelor of arts degree in early childhood development from Northern New
Mexico College.

As one of the first Indigenous persons to document her own language,
Martinez was recognized by many awards and honors for her work, including
the National Association for Bilingual Education, Pioneer Award (1992), the
Living Treasure Award from the State of New Mexico (1996), and the Indian
Education Award for Teacher of the Year from the National Council of American
Indians, Woman of the Year Award (1997). Martinez died in 2006 after returning
from Washington, DC, where she had received a National Heritage Fellowship
from the National Endowment for the Arts at a banquet in the Great Hall of
the Library of Congress. The Esther Martinez Native American Languages Act
was first passed by the US Senate in 2006, named in her honor and later reau-
thorized in 2019. Esther Martinez led the way for Pueblo and other indigenous
people to follow.[46]

WILFRED ERIACHO Wilfred Eriacho was born into a traditional family that
played a critical role in the ceremonial life of the Zuni people. As a child, he lived
with his parents and extended family, with whom he learned to herd sheep and
cows. He first encountered English when he was enrolled in the Zuni BIA day
school. Zuni was prohibited in that school, as it was in so many other BIA and
public schools. Wilfred and his friends spoke Zuni to each other on the playground, out of the hearing of his teachers and principal, but like so many other
Indigenous children, when they were caught, they experienced the "board of
education."[47] He remained at that school through ninth grade and then attended
the Santa Fe Indian School for high school. There he had the great fortune to
meet Joe Sando, who was his dorm counselor and who provided important
support and advice. As a recognized and beloved leader, Sando mentored many
other young Pueblo people and became a well-known historian for Pueblo

people, publishing important manuscripts representing the Pueblo perspective. Eriacho and Sando would remain close until Sando's passing in 2011.

After high school, Eriacho returned to Zuni and worked several odd jobs, but he soon realized that if he were to have a dependable financial future, he would need a college education. He enrolled at the University of New Mexico, and after completing his general requirements, he decided to study education, based in part on the influence of several teachers, including Sando. At the University of New Mexico, he also had contact with Edmund Ladd, the first Zuni to become an archeologist. Ladd was working with Stanley Newman to develop a preliminary orthography of the Zuni language; this encounter introduced Eriacho to the possibility of writing in his native language.

After graduating from the University of New Mexico as a teacher of art and world history, Eriacho was hired by the Gallup McKinley County Schools as a seventh-grade art teacher. In 1970, he and three Navajo teachers, one of whom was John Pinto (who would later serve in the New Mexico legislature), were asked to move to Central Office and work on a project made possible by a Title VII grant that the district had received. Eriacho's responsibilities included helping the kindergarten teachers at Zuni incorporate Zuni culture and language into their curricula. Each year, the school added a grade until all the elementary grades adopted the language and culture into their regular curricula. During one of the first summers in this new position, Eriacho and his colleagues were sent to Northern Arizona University for intensive work in linguistics and curriculum development.[48]

As Eriacho worked with the teachers, it became evident that more work would be needed on the orthography of the Zuni language. He invited Kirby Gchachu (see below) to work with him and soon hired several other Zuni people to help develop the orthography and the needed materials for the district. During this period, Curtis Cook, a Wycliff Bible translator, came to Zuni and worked with those Zunis who had adopted Protestantism. Eriacho often reviewed their work to ensure that their orthographic interpretations appropriately reflected the Zuni language.

Eriacho established positive working relationships with the New Mexico Department of Education. The state bilingual director, Ezequiel Benavides, visited their program several times, and word spread about the materials that he and his Zuni staff were developing at Central Office. Deganawidah-Quetzalcoatl University, a two-year tribal community college in Davis, California, contacted Eriacho about the possibility of partnering with Gallup McKinley County

Schools on a materials development grant. With approval from the Zuni Tribal Council, the funds from this partnership allowed further development of Zuni language readers and other booklets that supported the reading and writing of Zuni children in their own language.

In 1980, the Zuni people were able to establish their own school district as a result of visionary Zuni leaders, such as Hayes Lewis. Eriacho was asked to be the principal of one of the elementary schools. Soon, he would direct both elementary schools. Given his administrative abilities, Eriacho was asked to direct the support services department of the new district, which included transportation, facilities management, food services, and teacher housing. He remained in that position for ten years.

In 1990, Eriacho became the director of the Zuni Public School District's bilingual program—a program that in essence he had created twenty years earlier. He joined the New Mexico State Bilingual Advisory Committee and was a part of the development of the Pueblo bilingual endorsement and the 520 alternative certificate (see Sims, chapter 3, this volume).

Throughout his long career, Eriacho was always mindful of the sacrifices his ancestors had made throughout time to maintain their language and their Zuni beliefs. Throughout the Spanish incursion and attempts to stamp out Zuni religious convictions and the subsequent arrival of the American government and its oppression of the Zuni language and religion, the Zuni people had remained steadfast in their way of life. "Our ancestors remained strong, and that's what I wanted for myself and for the young people."[49]

KIRBY GCHACHU Kirby Gchachu was born into the Turkey clan and is a child of the Badger clan in Zuni Pueblo. After serving in the US Army in Vietnam, Kirby returned to Zuni to work at the small pueblo airstrip as a mechanic. He was recruited to work in the Zuni elementary school by Wilfred Eriacho to produce Zuni language materials, and it was through Eriacho's leadership that Gchachu was introduced to the Zuni orthography that was being refined.[50] As a part of his responsibilities, he and Eric Bobelu attended the summer institutes offered by SIL in partnership with the University of Albuquerque, and it was there that he met Christine Sims and other Pueblo people new to linguistics. In 1974, the Zuni Tribal Council approved the writing of the language, and Kirby, Eric, Belinda Tsebatsye, Odell Jaramillo, and Edward Wemytewa all worked on developing Zuni language materials for the growing bilingual program. As they developed the materials, they taught the Zuni teachers to read their language, and the teachers then taught the children. In 1976, Gchachu became the director of the Zuni Language Education Program and served in that capacity for two years.[51]

In 1977, Hayes Lewis, a visionary Zuni educator and leader, invited Gchachu to assist him in the research establishment of their own school district. Kirby served as the director of finance for five years. During this time, he and his wife enrolled in a master's program in which Gchachu began to experiment with the incorporation of Zuni cultural concepts into the science curriculum. This work would later become the focus of his work.

Before retiring, Gchachu served as a consultant to NASA and the National Science Teachers Association as their cultural resource for five years. Presently, he is developing curricula related to Indigenous astronomy of the Southwest, and with archaeoastronomer Ana Sofaer, he serves as a resource for the Solstice Project of Santa Fe. He is also mentoring a Zuni doctoral student who is reinterpreting the Zuni language work of the eminent twentieth-century anthropologist Ruth Bunzel.

GUS KEENE   Navajo and Acoma, Gus Keene was born at Acoma Pueblo and lived with his extended family, speaking his native Keres, herding sheep, and growing crops. When his father went to work for Rare Metals Uranium mill in Tuba City, Gus moved with him and attended school there.[52]

After serving in the US Navy in Vietnam and receiving a Bronze Star, Keene returned to Acoma and worked as an educational assistant at the Acoma Day School. During this time, he became interested in the possibility of writing Acoma Keres, especially after attending the SIL institutes at the University of Albuquerque. Upon graduation, he moved to Mescalero to teach and then returned to Acoma, where he became the Title VII director for Sky City School. While there he, continued his studies and received a master's degree in education from the University of New Mexico.[53]

With his characteristic Navajo brim hat, Gus Keene was immediately recognizable at every bilingual meeting or school where he was needed. Keene worked at the Zuni Public Schools as the federal projects and bilingual education director for many years. This experience, coupled with his upbringing in Acoma Pueblo and his love for language and culture, supported him in his many leadership positions in Indigenous bilingual education. Keene served as the president of the New Mexico Association for Bilingual Education and as a member of the New Mexico Bilingual Advisory Committee, on which he, Christine Sims, Donna Pino, and others developed the competencies and processes by which

Pueblo teachers could obtain their bilingual endorsement (see Sims, chapter 3 this volume). Understanding that as sovereign nations, the Pueblo governments had ultimate authority on their languages and cultures, Keene and Sims engaged the Pueblo governments in the process of certifying Pueblo teachers' language competency.

Keene later became superintendent of Cuba Public Schools, worked for the Bureau of Indian Education at Pine Hill, and was principal at St. Anthony school in Zuni. In his later years, Keene worked for the Zuni tribe's Department of Education before his passing in May of 2019.[54]

CHRISTINE SIMS Christine Sims was raised at Acoma Pueblo in a bilingual home, hearing both English and Keres. Keres and its maintenance would become the focus of her work for her community, and for the many Indigenous communities she has worked with for over forty years. Sims attended elementary Catholic schools near her reservation and a Catholic boarding school in Waterflow, New Mexico. As she recounts in chapter 3 in this volume, many fellow Acomas were severely punished in government day schools for speaking their language. For this reason, her parents chose to send her to parochial schools affiliated with the Ursuline Sisters, a Catholic religious order originally based in Kentucky that had established several schools in New Mexico, including the elementary school that Sims attended near the Acoma reservation. Later, she and an Acoma classmate attended the Ursuline's Mount St. Joseph Academy in Kentucky, an all-girls' high school, for two years. Sims completed her last two years of high school in Phoenix, Arizona, graduating from Xavier Preparatory High School in 1969.

Christine Sims attended the University of Albuquerque and received her bachelor of arts degree in secondary education in 1974. After graduation, she worked at the University of Albuquerque as the University's Indian Student Coordinator. While there, she attended some of the first workshops provided by the Summer Institute of Linguistics and became acquainted with several of the SIL linguists and Native language teachers from various backgrounds. Her introduction to linguistics and her subsequent work with Acoma bilingual educators and other field linguists would be instrumental in the later development of an Acoma-Keres orthography suitable for use in the Acoma bilingual program. In 1977, she was hired by the Grants Cibola County School District to develop a Keres language program for Laguna-Acoma High School. She worked with two Keres speakers, one from Laguna Pueblo and the other from Acoma

Pueblo, to plan Keres language instruction for the two dialects. Together, this team of three Keres speakers established the first Keres language classes offered to Laguna-Acoma High School students for course credit. These classes continued for several years after Sims left the program to work for the All Indian Pueblo Council on behalf of Acoma Pueblo.[55]

Between 1976 and 1979, SIL linguists partnered with the BIA to conduct linguistic workshops for Native American teachers. These were held at the University of Albuquerque, and Sims was hired as the coordinator of the program to carry out the logistics and schedules of the project. It was during this time that she met other future leaders in this field, including Esther Martinez and Kirby Gchachu, and became reacquainted with Gus Keene.[56]

The project between SIL and the BIA had no long-term plan for continuing the training of Indigenous teachers and speakers. Because Sims and her colleagues could see the benefit of this training, they decided to form their own organization, which would seek funding and collaborating institutional partners. With their help, this new organization could provide linguistic and bilingual instructors, materials and curriculum development trainings, and lodging support for participants. In 1981, the Linguist Institute for Native Americans (LINA) was established and sponsored by the Summer Institutes of Linguistics for Native Americans (SLINA) for over twenty-five years. Sims served as the chairperson for the LINA board for most of those years. As described in chapter 3, the work of SILNA was instrumental in providing training and support for Indigenous teachers involved in language teaching, not only in New Mexico, but in other states as well.

Sims directed the New Mexico Office of the National Indian Bilingual Center in the late 1970s and later served as the Acoma bilingual program director for her pueblo. She served as a member of the New Mexico Bilingual Advisory Committee for the New Mexico Public Education Department's Bilingual Multicultural Education Bureau. Her work on the endorsement of Pueblo bilingual teachers and the 520 alternative certification of Indigenous language teachers, described in chapter 5, has opened the doors for those tribes who wish to have their languages taught in schools.

During the years that Sims led LINA, she completed her master's degree in education at New Mexico State University. She began her doctoral studies at the University of California, Berkeley, in 1996, and by 1999 was hired as a part-time lecturer in the Department of Linguistics and the College of Education's Department of Language, Literacy, and Sociocultural Studies at the University of

New Mexico. She completed her doctorate in 2004 and subsequently transferred out of the Department of Linguistics into the College of Education as an assistant professor. In 2008, she established the American Indian Language Policy Research and Teacher Training Institute at the University of New Mexico, which is an outgrowth of the early work she and others undertook as a part of LINA.

Sims has received state and national recognition for her work in Native language preservation. She was selected by the National Association for Bilingual Education as the 2002 recipient of the Ramon L. Santiago President's Award for research and advocacy on language rights issues for Native American communities; received the 2002 New Mexico Association for Bilingual Education Award for contributions to Native American Bilingual Education in New Mexico; was recognized by the New Mexico State Senate for her contributions to Native language and culture in 2004; and received the 2013 Senator Joseph M. Montoya Award from the New Mexico Association for Bilingual Education for state and national contributions to Native Language issues.[57]

DONNA PINO Donna Pino was born in the Pueblo of Tamaya (formerly Santa Ana Pueblo) and lived there with her extended family until her mother married a man from Isleta Pueblo and they moved to Isleta. Because her new friends and neighbors all spoke Tiwa, Donna was able to learn that language in addition to her native Keres and the English that was used at school. When she was a freshman, she moved back to Tamaya and lived there with her grandfather, who spoke to her in Keres.[58]

Pino attended New Mexico Highlands University and later completed her bachelor's degree in education at the University of New Mexico. Her undergraduate degree was funded by the Head Start program in Santa Ana, where Pino was working. Even before her introduction to more formal aspects of bilingual education, Pino incorporated traditional songs and storytelling in the preschool program where she was teaching. At the University of New Mexico, she was provided a foundation in multicultural and bilingual education. When she completed her bachelor of arts degree, she was offered a position by Dan Honani to research multicultural materials for Indigenous groups. Part of her responsibilities included providing multicultural materials development workshops to Apache teachers in Dulce, New Mexico. This employment also allowed her to study for her master's degree in education, an important component of which were linguistics courses that gave her the background necessary to study her language more formally.[59]

In 1976, Miguel Encinias offered Pino a position as an instructor at the University of Albuquerque, whose Title VII program for educational assistants (EAs) included a cohort of Native Americans. Pino worked with Amy Zaharlick and the EAs who were mostly from Santo Domingo, San Felipe, and Santa Ana. She remained in this position until the university closed in 1986, teaching Keres-speaking students how to write their language.

Pino moved from there to Albuquerque Public Schools, where she directed the American Indian bilingual program. In this position, she identified the eight schools with significant populations of Native American students. Educational assistants were hired to help the Indigenous students and their teachers, with Pino providing the training they needed. She wrote multiple Title VII grants to fund the program and its materials. Pino remained in this position for ten years until Title VII funding was discontinued.

Pino worked briefly with the Early Childhood Migrant program at Albuquerque Public Schools, and in 1993, she was asked to establish and direct the first Tamaya Department of Education. In this position, she was able to create the Tamaya Language and Culture program and hire a program director, as well as Keres language teachers who would teach their language in the Bernalillo Public Schools (BPS). Pino and her colleagues struggled to establish their community's language classes at BPS because for several years, BPS would not approve of Santa Ana Keres classes. In characteristic fashion, Pino persisted until the BPS Board of Education gave their approval.

Pino served as director of the Tamaya Department of Education for seventeen years. When the tribe chose to hire a former principal of Algodones Elementary School as director, Pino stepped down from the position to become director of the Language and Culture program, a position she chose to remain in for only a year, feeling that the new director had set out to destroy all that she had worked so hard to achieve..

In her retirement, Pino continues to participate in the Language and Culture program as a board member.

The six Pueblo innovators described above all worked directly with language teaching and with the study of their different languages. They were the first to write their languages, some to study their languages more deeply, others to establish language programs in the schools, as in the case of Zuni. The long-term commitment required to study a language and develop an orthography demonstrates not only a scholarly commitment, but more importantly, a deep commitment to one's own community and to Indigenous education more broadly. Esther Martinez and Christine Sims learned about linguistics and applied this new knowledge to their own and other Indigenous languages, assisting others to develop the skills needed to study and teach their languages. Wilfred Eriacho, Kirby Gchachu, Gus Keene, and Donna Pino began studying their languages and writing them, and then moved on to critical positions that have fostered a new school district, new bilingual programs, new curricula, and a new department of education. Each one of them has paved the way for new leaders and mentored younger people who can take up this important work.

The last two innovators described in this section supported many of the efforts described above. Although they themselves did not work directly writing or teaching language, their positions as directors and administrators provided critical financial and policy support that allowed the innovators to continue their work.

PENNY BIRD   Penny Bird, from Kewa Pueblo (formerly Santo Domingo Pueblo), was raised in an extended family where multilingualism was valued and practiced. Bird's grandfather in particular stressed the need for his grandchildren to receive a solid Western education to complement the education provided at home. After first studying at the University of New Mexico, Bird went on to complete her degree in education, with a minor in sociology, at the University of Colorado, Boulder. She then worked as a field representative in northern New Mexico for the All Indian Pueblo Council ensuring that the Johnson O'Malley funds they administered were being utilized correctly. In this capacity, she met and provided funding for Esther Martinez's work mentoring younger Indigenous people and Wilma Martinez's work at the Santa Clara Head Start program. In addition, she set aside funding so that Indigenous people in northern New Mexico could attend the SIL institutes.

Bird later worked at the New Mexico State Department of Education (SDE) as the Indian education director monitoring schools that served indigenous children, including those on the Navajo reservation. She left the SDE to study for her master's in education at the University of New Mexico, during which time she worked at Southwestern Indian Polytechnic Institute conducting a survey of Indigenous nations and Native American studies programs.

After finishing her master's degree, Bird returned to the SDE, where she met Hayes Lewis and Kirby Gchachu, who encouraged her to move to Zuni to direct the Curriculum and Instruction Department, and later, the bilingual education program after Wilfred Eriacho's retirement. After eleven years at Zuni, Bird was named assistant secretary of Indian education by Governor Bill Richardson. In that capacity, she was instrumental in developing the framework for the Indian Education Act and for facilitating the adoption of the 520 alternative certificate for Indigenous language teachers. It was her deep understanding of and respect for tribal leadership and consultation that brought the tribes together with educators and lawmakers to adopt these two critical policies.

Bird completed her doctorate in educational leadership at the University of New Mexico in 2007 and participated in the first Indigenous-led team to study and develop recommendations for the education of New Mexican Indigenous students, sponsored by the New Mexico Public Education Department; the study was later published as Indian Education in New Mexico 2025.[60]

In 2008, Bird was hired to assist Christine Sims in the work of the American Indian Policy Research and Teacher Training Center. Her work with Sims has included many workshops and institutes to assist Indigenous language teachers.

REGIS PECOS Regis Pecos was born and raised in the Pueblo de Cochiti. He served on the Cochiti Tribal Council for twenty-eight years and was named lieutenant governor and governor of the pueblo several times. Pecos attended the Bernalillo Public Schools and then attended Princeton University, where he received his undergraduate degree.

In the early 1970s, he worked as a staff member at the American Indian Bilingual Education Center (AIBEC) at the University of New Mexico. His work at AIBEC established an important source of support and technical assistance for New Mexico tribes and local schools engaged in Native American bilingual program implementation. The center was an important collaborative partner with LINA in bringing SILNA to the University of New Mexico campus during AIBEC's existence.[61]

In the early 1980s, Pecos directed the New Mexico satellite office of the Bilingual Education Service Center (which was based out of Arizona State University). He was instrumental in securing training and technical assistance for Title VII programs serving Native American students in the four corner states.[62]

Pecos went on to serve as the director of the New Mexico Office of Indian Affairs (NMIAD), where he remained for over sixteen years. While there, he directed funding and support for tribal-based language revitalization initiatives as well as the training and mentoring of New Mexico Native language teachers in collaboration with LINA. He also supported the SILNA programs that LINA was conducting. The New Mexico Office of Indian Affairs worked collabora-tively with LINA to provide financial support for paid mentorships of Pueblo language speakers preparing to teach their languages using language immersion approaches. This support during the mid-1990s made it possible for various Pueblo tribes to start community-based language initiatives for the first time.[63]

By 2001, when some of Pueblo community-based language initiatives began to move into school settings, issues of school accountability emerged as a result of No Child Left Behind legislation. This had a major influence on NMPED administrators and legislators, who were intent on assuring that their schools complied with federal regulations tied to No Child Left Behind. This also in-fluenced the department's initial move to establish requirements for certifying Native language instructors in public schools.

At this time, Pecos was working for Representative Ben Luján, speaker of the New Mexico House of Representatives. Because of his prior experience both at NMIAD and his working knowledge of legislators and state agencies, Pecos was especially helpful in assisting those involved in working with Native language programs, including some of those individuals described above, through various contentious issues related to Native speakers teaching their languages in New Mexico public schools. He was a key liaison and guide, assisting them in formulating and articulating proposed plans in response to the NMPED's initial move to establish its own statewide accountability processes. In particular, Pecos was instrumental in helping tribal language programs and Native language advocates to clarify issues on which they needed to take a stand, including how language speakers would be certified by their respective tribes rather than by the Department of Public Education; how memoranda of understanding could be used as a mechanism between tribes and the NMPED to articulate and verify that tribes would maintain ownership of this process; how the NMPED would interface with the larger issue of tribal consultation, especially as it related to language instruction as an integral part of Indian education; that tribes, being the only entities capable of verifying teacher's language proficiency, would certify and select language teachers; and how the language programs would reflect and respond to each tribe's particular view of a language program.

The 520 alternative certification for Native language speakers teaching in New Mexico public schools was the outcome of over a year of deliberations beginning in 2002, with many meetings taking place between Native language teachers, tribes, the NMPED administrators, and later, Penny Bird as the first assistant secretary for Indian education.[64] Pecos was key in bringing together these different groups to help resolve these issues and develop processes that are still in place today.

As can be seen by these brief descriptions of Penny Bird and Regis Pecos, their work and participation as administrators, policy makers, and financial sponsors has been critical in supporting those directly involved in the teaching, teacher training, and materials development of Indigenous languages. Without their active collaboration and backing, much of the work that was accomplished would not have been possible.

NOTES

1. Henry W. Pascual, interview by Rebecca Blum Martínez, Mary Jean Habermann López, and Julia Rosa López-Emslie, August 11–12, 2001, at Pascual's home. DVD and partial transcript in the personal collection of Mary Jean Habermann López.

2. We understand that there were many bilingual educators who are not featured in this chapter. The individuals selected were connected with innovations that were groundbreaking, and they shared the same vision for the full infusion of heritage languages and cultures in public schools as well as in higher education.

3. Pascual interview.

4. Mary Jean Habermann López, interview by Maria Luisa Gonzalez, August 1, 2017, Albuquerque, NM.

5. Pascual, interview.

6. Ibid.

7. Henry W. Pascual, "Bilingual Education Recollections," talk prepared for the National Association for Bilingual Education Conference in Albuquerque, January 21, 1991, unpublished transcript in possession of Mary Jean Habermann López.

8. Habermann López interview.

9. Pascual interview

10. Ibid.

11. Ibid.

12. Ibid.

13. *Miami Herald*, October 21, 2012. Information about Robinette's work can be found in chapter 11, this volume.

14. See the Center for Applied Linguistics for more information about these programs, http://www.cal.org.

15. Pascual interview.

16. John Paul Taylor, personal communication, December 8, 2016.

17. Friends of the Taylor Family Monument, "J. Paul Taylor and Family," http://www.ftfm-mesilla-nm.org/jpaultaylor.html.

18. Pascual, interview.

19. See http://www.waymarking.com/waymarks/WM9DHC_MELA_LEGER
_BILINGUAL_EDUCATION_PIONEER.

20. Mela Leger interview by Mary Jean Habermann López on July 26, 2017.

21. Mela Leger interview by Mary Jean Habermann López, January 31, 2006, at
Leger's home.

22. Pascual interview.

23. "Silver City Teacher's Contributions Recognized in Las Cruces," *Silver City Sun
News*, September 7, 2015, https://www.scsun-news.com/story/news/local/2015/09/07
/pioneer-teacher-honored-with-historical-sign/72294738/.

24. Jocelyn Apodaca, "Historical Narker at NMS to Honor María Gutierrez
Spencer," New Mexico State University New Center, June 5, 2015, https://newscenter
.nmsu.edu/Articles/view/11190/historical-marker-at-nmsu-to-honor-María-gutierrez
-spencer.

25. Emma Armendariz interview by Maria Luisa Gonzalez, July 26, 2017.

26. Laura Gutierrez Spencer interview by Maria Luisa Gonzalez on September 13,
2018.

27. Tom Orona interview by Maria Luisa Gonzalez on February 10, 2017.

28. Gutierrez Spencer interview.

29. Tom Orona interview by Maria Luisa González on February 10, 2017.

30. Tom Uribes, "Dr. Orozco Praised as Bilingual Education Icon," *Fresno State
News*, September 13, 2012, www.fresnostatenews.com/2012/09/13/dr-orozco-oroz-
co-praised-as-bilingual-education-icon.

31. Ibid.

32. Ibid.

33. Alfredo Cuellar, "Cecilio Orozco His Life in Fresno (from 1975–2012)," El
Concilio de Fresno, September 10, 2012, http://elconciliodefresno.org/Memorials
/Dr.CecilioOrozcoLifeInFresno.html.

34. Ibid.

35. Ibid.; Uribes, "Dr. Orozco Praised."

36. Rebecca Blum Martínez, eulogy for Miguel Encinias, Delivered February 25,
2016, Albuquerque, New Mexico, Albuquerque, NM. In private collection of Rebecca
Blum Martínez.

37. *Albuquerque Journal*, Miguel Encinias obituary, February 23, 2016, http://www
.legacy.com/obituaries/abqjournal/obituary.aspx?pid=177816611.

38. Blum Martínez, eulogy for Miguel Encinias.

39. Anita Pfeiffer, personal communication, May 27, 2014.

40. Wayne Holm, correspondence with President Frank, May 14, 2014. Lois, M.
Meyer private collection.

41. Ibid.

42. Teresa McCarty, letter to President Frank. May 24, 2014. Lois M. Meyer private collection.

43. Interview with Agnes Holm, Albuquerque, NM, December 4, 1979. Kathy Harvey, interviewer. Downloadable archival material, University of New Mexico Main Campus Libraries.

44. Christine Sims, personal communication, September 5, 2019.

45. See http://newmexicohistory.org/people/esther-martinez-the-san-juan -storyteller for more information.

46. See "Esther Martinez: The San Juan Storyteller," New Mexico History (web-site), http://newmexicohistory.org/2013/11/08/esther-martinez-the-san-juan -storyteller; and Wikipedia, s.v. "Esther Martinez," https://en.wikipedia.org/wiki /Esther_Martinez.

47. Wilfred Eriacho phone interview by Rebecca Blum Martínez, September 1, 2019.

48. Ibid.

49. Ibid.

50. Kirby Gchachu personal communication, August 30, 2019.

51. Albuquerque Journal, February 16, 1976-p-48.

52. M. Thompson, personal communication, August 23, 2019.

53. Carol Keene, personal communication, August 25, 2019.

54. Ibid.

55. Christine Sims, personal communication, September 5, 2019.

56. Ibid.

57. "Christine Sims, Ph.D.," National Clearing House for English Language Acquisition, Office of English Language Acquisition 2017 Project Directors Meeting, https://ncela.ed.gov/files/uploads/2017/Christine_Sims.pdf.

58. Donna Pino, personal communication, August 28, 2019.

59. Ibid.

60. "Indian Education in New Mexico" (2025), a study contracted by New Mexico Public Education Department, Indian Education Division. Conducted by eight Northern Indian Pueblos Council, Indigenous Education Study Group (June 2010).

61. Christine Sims, personal communication with author, September 5, 2019.

62. Ibid.

63. Ibid.

64. The New Mexico State Department of Education was renamed the New Mexico Public Education Department in 2003 as a result of a constitutional amend-ment during the Richardson administration (2003–2011).

REFERENCES

Alatis, James E., and Ai Hui Tan, eds. 1999. *Language in Our Time: Bilingual Education and Official English, Ebonics and Standard English, Immigration and Unz Initiative.* Washington, DC: Georgetown University Press.

Berman, Paul, and Milbrey Wallin McLaughlin. 1976. "Implementation of Educational Innovation." *Educational Forum* 40, no. 3: 345–370. https://doi.org/10.1080 /00131727609336469.

Charland, B. "Silver City Teacher's Contributions Recognized in Las Cruces," Silver City Sun News, September 7, 2015, https://www.scsun-news.com/story/news/local /2015/09/07/pioneer-teacher-honored-with-historical-sign/72294738/.

Creswell, John W. 2013. *Qualitative Inquiry and Research Design: Choosing among Five Approaches.* 3rd ed. Thousand Oaks, CA: Sage.

Encinias, Miguel. 1976. *Hispanic Bilingual-Bicultural Education in New Mexico: A Study Of Teacher Preparation.* PhD diss., University of New Mexico, Albuquerque, NM.

Feinberg, Rosa C. 1999. "Administration of Two-Way Bilingual Elementary Schools: Building on Strength," *Bilingual Research Journal* 23, no. 1: 47–68. https://doi.org /10.1080/15235882.1999.10162734.

Fullan, Michael. 2002. "The Change Leader." *Beyond Instructional Leadership* 59, no. 8: 16–21. http://www.ascd.org/publications/educational leadership/may02/vol59 /num08/The-Change-Leader.aspx.

Gladwell, Malcom. 2000. The Tipping Point: How Little Things Can Make a Big Difference. Boston: Little, Brown.

Glasser, William. 1990. *The Quality School: Managing Students without Coercion.* New York: Harper and Row.

Greer, John T., and Paula M. Short. 2002. *Leadership in Empowered Schools: Themes from Innovative Efforts.* 2nd ed. New York: Pearson.

Habermann López, Mary Jean, 1991. "Pioneers, Summary of NM Pioneers in Bilingual Education." Prepared for the National Association for Bilingual Education National conference in Albuquerque, NM. Non published paper. Copy in possession of Mary Jean Habermann López.

Holm, Wayne. 1971. "Bilagaana Bizaad (the English Language): ESL/EFL in a Navajo Bilingual Setting." https://eric.ed.gov/contentdelivery/servlet/ERICServlet?accno =ED053613.

Labaree, David. 1997. "Public Goods, Private Goods: The American Struggle over Educational Goals." *American Educational Research Journal* 34, no. 1: 39–81. https:// doi.org/10.3102/00028312034001039.

Logan, Joseph Lee. 1967. "Coral Way: A Bilingual School." *TESOL Quarterly* 1, no. 2 (June): 55.

Lozano, Rosina A. 2013. "Managing the 'Priceless Gift': Debating Spanish Language Instruction in New Mexico and Puerto Rico, 1930–1950." *Western Historical Quarterly* 44: 271–93.

McCarty, Teresa, and Lucille Watahomigie. 1999. "Indigenous Community-Based Language Education in the USA." In *Indigenous Community-Based Education*, edited by Stephen May. Clevedon: Multilingual Matters.

Moolenaar, Nienke M., Alan. J. Daly, and Peter C. Sleeters. 2010. "Occupying the Principal Position: Examining Relationships Between Transformational Leadership, Social Network Position, and Schools' Innovative Climate." *Educational Administration Quarterly* 46, no. 5: 623–70.

Nieto, Sonia, and Patty Bode. 2012. *Affirming Diversity: The Sociopolitical Context of Multicultural Education*. 6th ed. New York: Pearson.

Orozco, Cecilio. 1992. The Book of the Sun, Tonatiuh. 2nd ed. Fresno CA: California State University Press.

Pacheco, Ana. 2012. *Paul Taylor: The Man from Mesilla*. Santa Fe: Museum of New Mexico Press.

Samora, Vangue, Theresa Cárdenas, and Raquel I. Martínez, eds. 2006. *Mujeres Valerosas . . . Meet the Extraordinary Women of the New Mexico Hispanic Women's Council*, vol. 2, issue 1. Albuquerque: Hispanic Women's Council.

Schmidt, Jorge R. 2014. *The Politics of English in Puerto Rico's Public Schools*. Boulder, CO: First Forum Press.

Schwabsky, Barry. 2013. *Words for Art: Criticism, History, Theory, Practice*. Sternberg Press, Berlin.

Takanishi, Ruby, and Suzanne Le Menestrel. 2017. *Promoting the Educational Success of Children and Youth Learning English: Promising Futures*. Washington, DC: National Academies Press.

Young, Robert W. 1972. *Written Navajo: A Brief History*. Albuquerque: Navajo Reading Study, University of New Mexico.

Timeline *Early Experimentation in ESL and Bilingual Education to the Richardson Administration*

1930s

The first early attempts at a bicultural/bilingual approach to educating Navajo and other American Indian students was being designed and implemented by the Bureau of Indian Affairs (BIA).

Early bilingual readers, titled *Indian Life Readers*, were developed and used by members of the US Indian Office/Service.

1941

State Senator Joseph Montoya introduces a bill requiring the teaching of Spanish in grades five through eight in New Mexico schools.

1943

Senate Bill 129 establishes a supervisor of Spanish at the New Mexico State Department of Education (SDE) to improve instruction in Spanish and ensure retainment and development of the Spanish language in the state.

1946

The BIA creates the Special Navajo Education program (SNEP) as a response to the overwhelming number of Navajo children who had never been to school. The educational program was designed to educate over-school-age Navajo children by emphasizing a child-centered approach as well as Navajo/English instruction to help children learn about white culture and English in a five-year specialized program.

1958–1961

Leroy Condie of the SDE directs experimentation of English as a second Language (ESL) programs in Gallup, Magdalena, Cuba, BIA schools, and in Bernalillo at Santo Domingo Elementary School.

1963

The SDE receives a Ford Foundation grant to "explore effective and innovative programs of instruction." The experimental program taught language arts and social studies in Spanish to students in the small village of Pecos. After three years, a film was made and presented at the October 30–31, 1966, New Voices of the Southwest Symposium ("The Spanish-speaking Child in the Schools of the Southwest") held in Tucson, later referred to as the Tucson Symposium. United States senator Montoya, seeing the film at the conference, asked the New Mexico Department of Education to help the federal government draft the national Bilingual Education Act.

1963–1968

The SDE focuses efforts on teaching English as a second language by field testing the Miami linguistics experimental materials at ESL programs in Albuquerque, Gallup, Grants, Española, and West Las Vegas, with demonstration sites at West Las Vegas and Albuquerque.

1965

The West Las Vegas Public Schools receives a Title I grant to begin a full program of bilingual education.

As part of President Lyndon B. Johnson's War on Poverty, the Office of Economic Opportunity (OEO) is created. The BIA was no longer the exclusive funding source for Indian programs. The Office of Economic Opportunity was responsible for funding basic and far-reaching innovations in Navajo education—first, the Lukachukai Demonstration School, and a year later in 1966, the Rough Rock Demonstration School. In 1968, the OEO funded the Navajo Community College (now Diné College). The Navajo Nation began to develop its own programs designed to help solve the problems it identified.

1966

DINE Incorporated, the nonprofit entity that received funds and operated schools, evolves out of grassroots efforts to create the first Indigenous community-controlled school and programs in Arizona that led to the creation of the Rough Rock Demonstration School.

1967

The Las Cruces Public Schools begins a "sustained K–3" bilingual education program through funding from Title III of the National Defense Student Act. Approximately 85–90 percent of the participating students were Spanish speakers, and 10–15 percent were English speakers. The program followed the students through the twelfth grade. A follow-up study of the students by the district showed there were no dropouts.

1968

The New Mexico State Board of Education (SBE) issues the first-ever state policy in New Mexico and the United States in support of bilingual education.

1969

Bilingual Education Statute, House Bill 270. The New Mexico Legislature approves the first Spanish-English bilingual education bill in the nation to maintain the language and culture of the children of the state and to add richness to the curriculum. Senator Roberto Modragón sponsors the bill without an appropriation. It "provides an opportunity for any public school in the state to offer bilingual programs for Mexican-Americans and Native American children."

The SBE approves the first-ever certification criteria for teachers of English as a second language in New Mexico and in the US, Regulation No. 69-5.

1970

The SBE creates an ad hoc State Bilingual Advisory Committee after the 1969 state law is passed.

1970–1973

The Guadalajara Institutes. The SDE receives a $300,000 grant from the Office of Language Research in the US Department of Health, Education and Welfare to conduct a training institute for bilingual education teachers in Guadalajara, Mexico. Henry Pascual directed the institute and Cecilio Orozco of the University of New Mexico was the assistant director. Sixty teachers participate each year in a rigorous course of study and travel. In its third year, the institute is moved to New Mexico Highlands University (NMHU) and is directed by María Gutiérrez Spencer.

1971

New Mexico Highlands University begins a master's program in bilingual education, directed by Cecilio Orozco. In 1973, Title VII funds the MA Bilingual Education Program Institute for elementary teachers. It includes coursework at NMHU, intensive studies at the Universidad Autónoma de Guadalajara, teaching experience in Mexico, and student teaching in the West Las Vegas bilingual education program.

Senate Bill 155, sponsored by Senator Jack Eastham, is the second bill for bilingual education in New Mexico. The $100,000 appropriation provides for the special needs of children of limited English ability and prioritizes services in grades one through three. The goal is to develop greater competence in English and greater proficiency in the use of two languages.

The Serna family sues the Portales Public Schools for segregation of their children. This results in the *Serna v. Portales* decision, one of the court cases that served as a basis for the US Supreme Court decision *Lau v. Nichols*.

1971–1976

The Bilingual Demonstration Teacher Training Network. Title III, ESEA funds at the New Mexico SDE sponsors the Bilingual Teacher Training Network. This network establishes demonstration centers in bilingual education at Armijo Elementary (West Las Vegas Schools), Sixth Street Elementary (Silver City Schools), and in Roswell schools. In 1972–73, 109 teachers and aides statewide received professional development through these centers.

1972

The New Mexico Indian Education Act is passed by the New Mexico State Legislature.

1973

The New Mexico Bilingual Multicultural Education Act, Senate Bill 421. The legislature passes the third and final bill for bilingual education, sponsored by Senator Matías Chacón of Española, with an appropriation of $700,000 to establish programs in grades one through six. The law opens up bilingual education for all students in the state and encourages cognitive and affective development by using students' language and culture in the curriculum.

Henry Pascual of the New Mexico SDE, Maria Spencer of the Silver City Schools, and Cecilio Orozco of NMHU testify in US Senate Committee hearings for the re-authorization of Bilingual Education Act, Title VII of the Elementary and Secondary Education Act.

The first proposal to establish a Pueblo bilingual endorsement is presented to the state bilingual office by a task force comprised of Pueblo bilingual educators. The process is piloted by Pueblo Keres-speaking Pueblo teachers through the Multicultural Education Program at the College of Santa Fe under Henry Shonerd's directorship.

1974

Certification for Bilingual Education. The SBE approves regulation no. 74-1, the first program requirements for university teacher education programs in bilingual education in New Mexico and in the United States. By 1979, Regulation No. 79-10 finalizes New Mexico Certification Requirements for a Spanish/English Bilingual/Bicultural Endorsement.

Miguel Encinias directs the University of Albuquerque teacher preparation program in bilingual education under Title VII ESEA funds, which continues until 1979.

1975

The Indian Self-Determination and Education Assistance Act (Public Law 93-638) is authorized by the secretary of the interior, the secretary of health, education, and welfare, and several other US governmental agencies.

The SBE approves endorsement criteria for teaching English as a second language (ESL) and is first in the nation to do so.

1978

The SBE approves endorsement criteria for bilingual multicultural education.

First Summer Institute of Linguistics for Native American (SILNA) bilingual teachers is offered at the University of Albuquerque campus.

1980

The New Mexico SDE oversees the development of the Four Skills Examination in Spanish for prospective teachers seeking an endorsement to their teaching license in bilingual education. Guadalupe Valdés of New Mexico State University, Thomasina Pagán Hannum, and Sam Guyler of the University of New Mexico develop the exam, which is field tested on teachers of bilingual education throughout the state.

1982

The Linguistic Institute for Native Americans (LINA) is established by New Mexico Native American bilingual educators to continue summer training institutes for Native bilingual teachers.

1986

The New Mexico SDE's Policy Statement on Indian Education was established (and later revised in 1994). This policy became the foundation for the 2003 Indian Education Act.

1987

The legislature amends the New Mexico Bilingual Multicultural Education Act to serve students through the twelfth grade, with a phase-in from 1988 to 1991. Representative J. Paul Taylor of Las Cruces sponsored the bill.

1989

The New Mexico legislature adopts House Joint Memorial 16, "English Plus Declaration in New Mexico." This resolution made New Mexico the first state in the nation to adopt "English Plus." In part it states, "Proficiency in English plus other languages should be encouraged throughout the State" (http://www.languagepolicy.net /archives/nm.htm).

1990

The SDE establishes a process to verify Pueblo language proficiency for the bilingual endorsement via the tribes.

1990–1995

International partnerships in education with Spain and Mexico are developed over a five-year period in response to the North American Free Trade Agreement and Spain's preparation for its five-hundredth anniversary of Columbus's voyage to the "new" world. Memoranda of understanding between the education agencies of New Mexico, Spain, and the Mexican states of Nuevo Leon and Guanajuato delineate joint education endeavors in Spanish, such as teacher exchanges, professional development, the creation of a Spanish resource center, and employment of Spanish and Mexican teachers for bilingual education programs. Many of these activities continue today under continuing memoranda of understanding.

1994

House Bill 224, introduced by Representative J. Paul Taylor, appropriates $89,250 to the New Mexico SDE for the purpose of creating a new position in the department, developing a new Spanish proficiency exam, and funding three part-time coordinators for university immersion institutes.

1995

The Navajo Nation, under President Albert Hale's administration, passes an executive order to make Navajo the medium of instruction in all Navajo Head Start programs.

1997

The SDE pilots two-way dual language immersion programs in five public schools: two in Albuquerque, two in Las Cruces, and one in Gadsden.

1999

The New Mexico state legislature appropriates funding for ten pilot schools to implement dual language immersion programs.

2002

The 520 alternative certificate creates an alternative pathway for certifying Pueblo Native language teachers. It authorizes essential personnel with the fluency and necessary language skills to teach Pueblo language classes in the schools.

2004

The New Mexico State Legislature passes

Senate Bill 471a, amending the Bilingual Multicultural Education Act of 1973

House Bill 2. The General Appropriations Act of 2004, which requires PED to evaluate the effectiveness and use of funds in bilingual multicultural education programs

House Memorial 3, which requires an audit of bilingual multicultural education programs

House Joint Memorial 18, which requires a study of the feasibility of testing students in the home languages

2005

The New Mexico State Legislature appropriates $100,000 to the New Mexico Public Education Department (NMPED) to develop three new forms for Prueba de Español Para la Certificación Bilingüe (a Spanish-language proficiency test for teachers seeking an endorsement in bilingual multicultural education).

The SDE revises the Bilingual Multicultural Education Regulation, NMAC 6.32.2, 2005. The new "Guidelines for Implementing Bilingual Education" set an explicit goal for bilingualism and biliteracy for written languages for all students in bilingual education programs.

The 20th Navajo Nation Council passes the Navajo Nation Sovereignty in Education Act (an amendment of Title X and II). The purpose of the act is to establish a Navajo Board of Education, Department of Diné Education, and confirm the commitment of the Nation to the education of its people. The act also establishes the Navajo Nation Diné Language Act to ensure the preservation and education of the Diné language.

2006

Governor Bill Richardson issues an official proclamation declaring New Mexico a multicultural state.

2008

The Navajo Language Assessment Advisory Committee pilots a Navajo language proficiency assessment in six school districts.

The American Indian Language Policy Research and Teacher Training Center is established in the College of Education at the University of New Mexico by Christine Sims. The center provides training to all the Native Pueblo language teachers and supports early childhood immersion programs.

Contributors

BEVERLEY ARGUS-CALVO, PhD, is associate dean for graduate programs and research of the College of Education at the University of Texas at El Paso and associate professor in the department of educational psychology and special services. Beverley earned her PhD in bilingual special education from New Mexico State University. She is a member of an international, interdisciplinary research team that investigates how schools address the educational needs of students living in vulnerable settings along the US-Mexico Border. Her most recent research has focused on the mental health and academic-related issues that influence children and youth in schools.

REBECCA BLUM MARTÍNEZ, PhD, is professor of bilingual education in the Department of Language Literacy and Sociocultural Studies at the University of New Mexico, where she specializes in bilingualism, second language learning, language maintenance, and revitalization in language minority communities, particularly Spanish-speaking and American Indian populations. Her research and scholarly interests have long centered on the study of language development in bilinguals and second language development across varied learning contexts. Blum Martínez has also served as the director of Latin American Program in Education that serves as a liaison between the University of New Mexico College of Education and Latin American educational institutions. Her recent publications include a coauthored piece with Preston Sanchez titled "A Watershed Moment in the Education of American Indian Students: A Judicial Strategy to Mandate the State of New Mexico to Meet the Unique Cultural and Linguistic Needs of American Indian Students in New Mexico Public Schools," in *Journal of Gender, Social Policy & the Law*; "Preparing Teachers of Bilingual Students," in the *Education, Immigrant Students, Refugee Students, and English Learners*; and with M. E. Romero, "In Retrospect, Revitalizing the Cochiti language—A Proposal for Community Re-engagement in Collective Spirit and Mutual Respect," in *The Journal of American Indian Education*.

PHILLIP B. (FELIPE) GONZALES, PhD, is professor emeritus of sociology at the University of New Mexico, where he was director of the School of Public Administration, senior associate dean of faculty in the College of Arts and Sciences, chair of the Sociology Department, and director of the Southwest Hispanic Research Institute. He authored *Política: Nuevomexicanos and American Political Incorporation, 1821–1910* (University of Nebraska Press, 2016); *Forced Sacrifice: The Hispano Cause in New Mexico and the Racial Attitude Confrontation of 1933* (Peter Lang, 2001); coauthored, with Louise Lamphere, *Sunbelt Working Mothers: Reconciling Family and Factory* (Cornell University Press, 1993); and edited *Expressing New Mexico: Nuevomexicano Creativity, Ritual and Remembrance* (University of Arizona Press, 2007).

MARÍA LUISA GONZÁLEZ, PhD, worked as a bilingual teacher, teacher leader, curriculum writer, and instructional specialist throughout Texas and New Mexico. After receiving her doctorate, she joined the Research and Development Unit in the Dallas Independent School District, where she conducted district-wide testing, research, and evaluation. In her twenty-year tenure at New Mexico State University, where she is now a professor emerita, she also established a center to support rural and border schools serving Hispanic and Indigenous children. González subsequently served the University of Texas at El Paso's College of Education as associate dean and Patricia Daw-Yetter endowed professor. Her publications include a book on the education of Latino children, chapters in edited books, and articles in national journals on school leadership and Latinos in the borderlands. She continues her commitment to study the educational heroes who go beyond borders to serve these children.

MARY JEAN HABERMANN LÓPEZ has been active in bilingual multicultural education throughout her fifty-year professional career at local, state, national, and international levels. She has taught students and teachers K–8 in English and Spanish in New Mexico and Mexico and offered professional development to teachers and administrators in the field. As state director for bilingual education at the New Mexico Public Education Department, she oversaw local program approval and implementation, established binational agreements for teacher exchanges and professional institutes, and helped launch the Spanish Resource Center. Of her many recognitions, she is most proud of the Ben Luján Lifetime Achievement Award that she received from the New Mexico Association for Bilingual Education in 2017. She received her BA in Spanish, graduating cum laude, and her MA in bilingual education from New Mexico Highlands University in 1971.

JULIA ROSA LÓPEZ-EMSLIE, PhD, was born in Mexico and migrated to New Mexico to pursue her studies and a career as a teacher. She received her degrees from the University of Albuquerque, Florida International University, and New Mexico State University. As a professor of bilingual education at Eastern New Mexico University, she developed and implemented the bilingual/ESL teacher preparation program. She retired as faculty emerita from that university. López-Emslie currently serves as an educational consultant translating educational documents for the states of New Mexico and Texas and is a member of the Coalition for the Majority, a board member of the Hispanic Advisory Council, Somos un Pueblo Unido, and Mentoring Kids Works New Mexico.

THOMASINA PAGÁN HANNUM, a graduate of SUNY Albany and the University of New Mexico, is a retired Spanish teacher with thirty years' experience in public schools and at the University of New Mexico, and has taught in the Spanish immersion program at New Mexico Highlands University. She has coauthored textbooks and other materials for Spanish-English bilingual high school students, contributed to other texts for heritage language learners at the secondary and university levels, and coauthored the Four Skills Exam for Bilingual Teacher endorsement. She has served as a consultant on language testing with the Bilingual Unit of the New Mexico Public Education Department.

REGIS PECOS was born and raised in the Pueblo of Cochiti and is a fluent speaker of his native Keres language. He attended the Bernalillo Public Schools and received his undergraduate degree at Princeton University. Pecos served as the chief executive of the New Mexico Office of Indian Affairs for sixteen years, and the chief of staff of the Office of the Speaker of the New Mexico House of Representatives for twelve years. He later became chief of staff of the Majority Floor Leader in the New Mexico House of Representatives. Currently, he serves as the senior policy advisor in the Majority Office in the House of Representatives. Pecos is also the cofounder and codirector of the New Mexico Leadership Institute (affiliated with Princeton University's Woodrow Wilson School of Public and International Affairs), which prepares young Indigenous leaders. Pecos has served multiple times as lieutenant governor and governor of his tribe and was a member of the Cochiti Tribal Council for over thirty years.

LORETTA C. SALAZAR, PhD, emeritus associate professor of education, New Mexico Highlands University, provided technical assistance with the University of New Mexico/United States Agency for International Development in El Salvador and taught bilingual education, Spanish, and English as a second language. She directed the New Mexico Highlands University Bilingual Education/TESOL programs, a Career Ladder grant, and the Spanish Immersion Institutes for that university. She has also taught in Granada, Spain, and in Veracruz and Oaxaca, Mexico. Salazar, former president of the New Mexico Association for Bilingual Education, was honored with the Bilingual Professor of the Year award by the New Mexico Bilingual Education Association and the Matías Chacón award.

REBECCA SÁNCHEZ, PhD, is an associate professor in the Department of Teacher Education, Educational Leadership, and Policy at the University of New Mexico. She teaches courses in social studies education, social justice education, and curriculum development. She seeks to expose students and teachers to both the place-based social studies of New Mexico and the history that is overlooked in the national narrative of American history. Dr. Sánchez is involved in research focusing on historical topics, teacher activism in a high-stakes environment, translating research to the arts, and meaningful arts integration for language learning and social justice.

CHRISTINE SIMS, PhD, is an associate professor in the Department of Language, Literacy, and Sociocultural Studies in the College of Education at the University of New Mexico. She specializes in Indigenous language revitalization and maintenance issues, providing technical assistance to tribes in Native language planning, and trains Native language teachers through the American Indian Language Policy Research and Teacher Training Center. She is a member of Acoma Pueblo and resides on the Acoma Pueblo Indian reservation.

MÍA ANGÉLICA SOSA-PROVENCIO, PhD, is an assistant professor of secondary education in the Department of Teacher Education, Educational Leadership, and Policy at the University of New Mexico. Previous to earning her doctorate in curriculum and instruction from New Mexico State University, Mía taught ninth through twelfth grade language arts for seven years at Rio Grande High School in Albuquerque's South Valley. Her research focuses on framing education as a means for social justice. Her work focuses on partnering with youth and educators alike to build academically rigorous, culturally fortifying schooling that fosters young people—especially diverse youth of color—in their rich communicational competencies and multiple identities.

VINCENT WERITO (Diné), PhD, is an associate professor in the College of Education at the University of New Mexico in the Department of Language, Literacy, and

Socio-cultural Studies. He is originally from Na'neelzhiin (Torreon, New Mexico), a Navajo community southwest of Cuba, New Mexico. He is Taneeszahnii (Tangle Clan), born for Naakai Dine'e (Travelers Band clan). His primary research interests are in teacher education, Indigenous pedagogy, Diné (Navajo) education, and Navajo language and cultural revitalization. Werito teaches graduate and undergraduate courses in bilingual education, Indigenous education, and educational thought and sociocultural studies.

Index